2ND EDITION

Federal Jobs in Law Enforcement

Australia • Canada • Mexico • Singapore • Spain • United Kingdom • United States

An ARCO Book

ARCO is a registered trademark of Thomson Learning, Inc., and is used herein under license by Peterson's.

About Peterson's

Founded in 1966, Peterson's, a division of Thomson Learning, is the nation's largest and most respected provider of lifelong learning resources, both in print and online. The Education Supersite^{SM} at www.petersons.com—the Internet's most heavily traveled education resource—has searchable databases and interactive tools for contacting U.S.-accredited institutions and programs. In addition, Peterson's delivers unmatched financial aid resources and test-preparation tools. Peterson's serves more than 100 million education consumers annually.

Peterson's is a division of Thomson Learning, one of the world's largest providers of lifelong learning. Thomson Learning serves the needs of individuals, learning institutions, and corporations with products and services for both traditional and distributed learning. Headquartered in Stamford, Connecticut, with offices worldwide, Thomson Learning is a division of The Thomson Corporation (www.thomson.com), one of the world's leading e-information and solutions companies in the business, professional, and education marketplaces. For more information, visit www.thomsonlearning.com.

For more information, contact Peterson's, 2000 Lenox Drive, Lawrenceville, NJ 08648; 800-338-3282; or find us on the World Wide Web at: www.petersons.com/about

ISBN 0-7689-0614-8

Printed in the United States of America

10 9 8 7 6 5 4 3 2 1   03 02 01

DEDICATION

This book is dedicated to
Tracey and John
and to
D'Andrea, Eddie, Catherine,
David, and Timothy,
with love.

CONTENTS

PART FOUR: OFFICES OF INSPECTORS GENERAL

PART FIVE: CIVIL SERVICE CAREER INFORMATION RESOURCES

ABOUT THE AUTHORS

Retired as an Assistant Director of the U.S. Secret Service, Jack Warner serves as a consultant to law enforcement executives on media relations.

For fifteen years he supervised the public affairs program of the Secret Service while also serving as a member of their management team. Before assuming his headquarters position, Jack worked as a criminal investigator and served on the Presidential Protective Division.

Born in Albany, New York, he has a bachelor's degree from Colgate University and a masters degree from the American University.

Among his many professional and civic activities are life membership in the International Association of Chiefs of Police and membership on the National Law Enforcement Exploring Committee, Boy Scouts of America.

Beverly Sweatman spent twenty-one years in the law enforcement/public affairs field, first as a writer/editor with the U.S. Secret Service. She later served as Public Affairs Officer for the INTERPOL-U.S. National Central Bureau in Washington, D.C., as well as Chief Media Spokesperson for the agency.

Originally from Charleston, South Carolina, Ms. Sweatman studied journalism at the American University in Washington, D.C., and magazine editing at George Washington University. She served on the board of the National Association of Government Communicators. Aftering retiring, she was a consultant to Logicon-Syscon Services, Inc., doing work for the International Criminal Investigative Training Assistance Program (ICITAP), a U.S. Department of Justice agency.

Together, they wrote and produced the *Law Enforcement Media Relations Handbook, a Guide to Effective Media Relations.*

ACKNOWLEDGMENTS

We wish to thank wholeheartedly the countless persons representing the various agencies of the federal law enforcement community who provided us the material for this work. Their invaluable contribution, counsel, and support are deeply appreciated.

The United States Government Manual, 2000-01, published by the Office of the Federal Register, National Archives and Records Administration, also served us well.

FOREWORD

The need for a comprehensive portrayal of the federal law enforcement community had been on my mind for a long time.

During my career, first as a Special Agent with the U.S. Secret Service and then as a law enforcement consultant, I noticed that most printed material, books, newspapers, and government publications seemed to cover only the larger and more well-known organizations. Very little, if anything, was available to the public about the smaller, lesser-known organizations.

Furthermore, there was often confusion among the public and even within the police community as to who is responsible for certain federal violations. This confusion could be critical to the effective process of reporting, investigating, and solving a violation of federal law.

Based on these observations, I decided to develop a comprehensive book that provides information on all known federal law enforcement agencies, both civilian and military.

In addition, this book is intended as a reference tool for high school and college students, especially administration of justice majors; a reference for public libraries and news media organizations; a guide for government administrators; a reference and guide for local, county, state, and federal police agencies and their training academies; a reference and guide for foreign police organizations; a resource guide for people interested in a career in law enforcement; and lastly, a book for those countless people who simply enjoy reading about police work.

So, for all these reasons, this book has been prepared with the invaluable and appreciated assistance of my co-author, Beverly Sweatman, and representatives of the more than 100 agencies and organizations included herein.

Federal Jobs in Law Enforcement will provide the reader with unique insight into the responsibilities of the many federal law enforcement organizations who are serving our nation by preventing and detecting violations of our national laws.

Jack Warner
Assistant Director (Ret.)
U.S. Secret Service

WHAT THIS BOOK WILL DO FOR YOU

HOW DO I USE THIS BOOK?

If you don't know what type of law enforcement job you'd like to apply for, this book will help you. You will find information here about various types of careers, and perhaps it will narrow down your choices. This book offers you an overview of the world of civil service; a brief introduction to federal, state, and city employers and their hiring requirements; and in-depth descriptions of a particular agency's history, initiatives, and work requirements.

PART ONE

There are five parts to this book. Part One covers the major employment sectors: federal, state, municipal (city), and private industry careers. There's more than enough for everyone here. Each sector has its own requirements and tests. However, as you will see, there are certain types of questions that will appear on most of these exams, regardless of the type of test you will take.

Also in this section is important information on test-taking techniques that will be useful if you decide to take a law enforcement exam. This will give you guidelines to help you prepare for the actual test. Feeling anxious before you take a test is a normal reaction. We provide you with tips on feeling relaxed and comfortable with your exam so you can get a great test score.

PART TWO

Part Two is an overview of the various types of careers available with the federal government. If you haven't already been in the field, you will be surprised by the number of different job opportunities there are as well as the varied jobs within an area. For example, did you know that there are almost 2,000 different job titles just within the United States Postal Service? This is just *one* federal agency.

If you are beginning your career or job shopping at this time, you should read this section carefully. It will help introduce you to the different jobs and the many opportunities that await you. We hope you will be inspired and excited and will be motivated to apply for, study for, and land one of those jobs. If this section helps you narrow your area of interest, you can then concentrate on the exams that will help you prepare for the job you want. If you are still wide open, give equal attention to each exam.

PART THREE

That leads us into Part Three of this book. In this section, we detail law enforcement careers with independent agencies. Here you can find out the job descriptions and requirements of agencies such as the Securities and Exchange Commission, the U.S. Postal Service, and the Central Intelligence Agency. There is also a wealth of information on employment opportunities within the Legislative and Judicial branches.

PART FOUR

Part Four introduces you to the Offices of Inspectors General, comprising fifty-seven statutory Inspectors General branch departments, agencies, quasi-official agencies, one legislative branch, and one Commission. Here you will discover the inner-workings of the Department of Treasury, the Department of State, the Social Security Administration, the FBI, and more. This section will help you understand auditing and investigative initiatives of designated federal entities. Each Office of Inspectors General is fully described, permitting you to see how each office functions and the important roles it plays. Application procedures for these offices are also provided.

PART FIVE

Finally, Part Five contains civil service career information resources. Here you will find out how to go about looking for available jobs, as well as important addresses, phone numbers, and Internet Web sites that will help you pursue your career in civil service.

The most important thing is to *use* this book. By going through all of the sections and reading them, you will be using what you learned here to the best of your ability to succeed in your intended career path.

PART ONE

So You Want to Work for The Government

Government service is one of the nation's largest sources of employment. About one in every six employed persons in the United States is in some form of civilian government service. Of those government employees, five out of six workers are employed by state or local governments, and the remainder work for the federal government.

As you can see, government employees represent a significant portion of the nation's work force. They work in large cities, small towns, and remote and isolated places such as lighthouses and forest ranger stations, and a small number of federal employees work overseas. In this chapter, we will outline the various types of careers that are available in the federal, state, and local governments.

WHERE THE JOBS ARE: FEDERAL CIVILIAN EMPLOYMENT

The federal government is the nation's largest employer. It employs almost 3 million civilian workers in the United States and an additional 130,000 civilian workers—half of them U.S. citizens—in U.S. territories and foreign countries. The headquarters of most government departments and agencies are in the Washington, D.C., area, but only one out of eight federal employees works there.

Federal employees work in occupations that represent nearly every kind of job in private employment as well as some unique to the federal government such as regulatory inspectors, foreign service officers, and Internal Revenue agents. Most federal employees work for the executive branch of the government.

The executive branch includes the Office of the President, the cabinet departments, and about 100 independent agencies, commissions, and boards. This branch is responsible for activities such as administering federal laws, handling international relations, conserving natural resources, treating and rehabilitating disabled veterans, delivering the mail, conducting scientific research, maintaining the flow of supplies to the armed forces, and administering other programs to promote the health and welfare of the people of the United States.

The Department of Defense, which includes the Departments of the Army, Navy, and Air Force, is the largest department. It employs about one million civilian workers. The Departments of Agriculture, Health and Human Services, and the Treasury are also big employers. The two largest independent agencies are the U.S. Postal Service and the Veterans Administration.

There is also federal civilian employment available in the legislative branch, which includes Congress, the Government Printing Office, the General Accounting Office, and the Library of Congress. The judicial branch, the smallest employer, hires people for work within the court system.

WHITE-COLLAR OCCUPATIONS

Because of its wide range of responsibilities, the federal government employs white-collar workers in a great many occupational fields. About one of four of these are administrative and clerical workers.

General clerical workers are employed in all federal departments and agencies. These include office machine operators, secretaries, stenographers, clerk-typists, mail- and file-clerks, telephone operators, and workers in computer and related occupations. In addition, there are the half million postal clerks and mail carriers.

Many government workers are employed in engineering and related fields. The engineers represent virtually every branch and specialty of engineering. There are large numbers of technicians in areas such as engineering, electronics, surveying, and drafting. Nearly two-thirds of all engineers are in the Department of Defense.

Of the more than 120,000 workers employed in accounting and budgeting work, 35,000 are professional accountants or Internal Revenue officers. Among technician and administrative occupations are accounting technicians, tax accounting technicians, and budget administrators. There are also large numbers of clerks in specialized accounting work. Accounting workers are employed throughout the government, particularly in the Departments of Defense and the Treasury and in the General Accounting Office.

Many federal employees work in hospitals or in medical, dental, and public health activities. Three out of five are either professional nurses or nursing assistants. Other professional occupations in this field include physicians, dieticians, technologists, and physical therapists. Technician and aide jobs include medical technicians, medical laboratory aides, and dental assistants. Employees in this field work primarily for the Veterans Administration; others work for the Departments of Defense and Health and Human Services.

Other government workers are engaged in administrative work related to private business and industry. They arrange and monitor contracts with the private sector and purchase goods and services needed by the federal government. Administrative occupations include contract and procurement specialists, production control specialists, and Internal Revenue officers. Two out of three of these workers are employed by the Departments of Defense and Treasury.

Another large group works in jobs concerned with the purchase, cataloging, storage, and distribution of supplies for the federal government. This field includes many managerial and administrative positions such as supply management officers, purchasing officers, and inventory management specialists, as well as large numbers of specialized clerical positions. Most of these jobs are in the Department of Defense.

Throughout the federal government, many people are employed in the field of law. They fill professional positions, such as attorneys or law clerks, and administrative positions, such as passport and visa examiners or tax law specialists. There also are many clerical positions that involve examining claims.

The social sciences also employ many government employees. Economists are employed throughout the government; psychologists and social workers work primarily for the Veterans Administration; and foreign affairs and international relations specialists, for the Department of State. One third of the workers in this field are social insurance administrators employed largely in the Department of Health and Human Services.

About 50,000 biological and agricultural science workers are employed by the federal government, mostly in the Departments of Agriculture and Interior. Many of these work in forestry and soil conservation activities. Others administer farm assistance programs. The largest number are employed as biologists, forest and range fire controllers, soil conservationists, and forestry technicians.

The federal government employs another 50,000 people in investigative and inspection work. Large numbers of these are engaged in criminal investigation and health regulatory inspections, mostly in the Departments of Treasury, Justice, and Agriculture.

Physical sciences is another area of government employment. Three out of four workers in the physical sciences are employed by the Departments of Defense, Interior, and Commerce. Professional workers include chemists, physicists, meteorologists, cartographers, and geologists. Aides and technicians include physical science technicians, meteorological technicians, and cartography technicians.

And in the mathematics field are professional mathematicians and statisticians and mathematics technicians and statistical clerks. They are employed primarily by the Departments of Defense, Agriculture, Commerce, and Health and Human Services.

Entrance requirements for white-collar jobs vary widely. A college degree in a specified field or equivalent work experience is usually required for professional occupations such as physicists and engineers.

Entrants into administrative and managerial occupations usually are not required to have knowledge of a specialized field, but must instead indicate a potential for future development by having a degree from a 4-year college or responsible job experience. They usually begin as trainees and learn their duties on the job. Typical jobs in this group are budget analysts, claims examiners, purchasing specialists, administrative assistants, and personnel specialists.

Technician, clerical, and aide-assistant jobs have entry-level positions for people with a high school education or the equivalent. For many of these positions, no previous experience or training is required. The entry level position is usually that of trainee. Persons who have junior college or technical school training or those who have specialized skills may enter these occupations at higher levels. Typical jobs are engineering technicians, supply clerks, clerk-typists, and nursing assistants.

BLUE-COLLAR OCCUPATIONS

Blue-collar occupations—craft, operative, laborer, and some service jobs—provide full-time employment for more than half a million federal workers. The Department of Defense employs about three fourths of these workers in establishments such as naval shipyards, arsenals, and the Air or Army depots as well as on construction, harbor, flood control, irrigation, or reclamation projects. Others work for the Veterans Administration, U.S. Postal Service, General Services Administration, Department of the Interior, and Tennessee Valley Authority.

The largest single blue-collar group consists of manual laborers. Large numbers also are employed in machine tool and metal work, motor vehicle operation, warehousing, and food preparation and serving. The federal government employs a wide variety of individuals in maintenance and repair work, such as electrical and electronic equipment installation and repair, and in vehicle and industrial equipment maintenance and repair. All these fields require a range of skill levels and include a variety of occupations comparable to the private sector.

Although the federal government employs blue-collar workers in many different fields, about half are concentrated in a small number of occupations. The largest group, the skilled mechanics, works as air-conditioning, aircraft, automobile, truck, electronics, sheet-metal, and general maintenance mechanics. Another large number of craft workers is employed as painters, pipefitters, carpenters, electricians, and machinists. A similar number serves as warehouse workers, truck drivers, and general laborers. An additional group of workers is employed as janitors and food service workers.

ENTRANCE REQUIREMENTS

Persons with previous training in a skilled trade may apply for a position with the federal government at the journey level. Those with no previous training may apply for appointment to one of several apprenticeship programs. Apprenticeship programs generally last four years; trainees receive both classroom and on-the-job training. After completing this training, a person is eligible for a position at the journey level. There are also a number of positions which require little or no prior training or experience, including janitors, maintenance workers, messengers, and many others.

THE MERIT SYSTEM

More than nine out of ten jobs in the federal government are under a merit system. The Civil Service Act, administered by the U.S. Office of Personnel Management, covers six out of ten federal titles. This act was passed by Congress to ensure that federal employees are hired on the basis of individual merit and fitness. It provides for competitive examinations and the selection of new employees from among the most qualified applicants.

Some federal jobs are exempt from civil service requirements either by law or by action of the Office of Personnel Management. However, most of these positions are covered by separate merit systems of other agencies such as the Foreign Service of the Department of State, the Federal Bureau of Investigation, the Nuclear Regulatory Commission, and the Tennessee Valley Authority.

EARNINGS, ADVANCEMENT, AND WORKING CONDITIONS

Most federal civilian employees are paid according to one of three major pay systems: the **General Pay Schedule,** the **Wage System**, or the **Postal Service Schedule.**

GENERAL PAY SCHEDULE

More than half of all federal workers are paid under the General Schedule (GS), a pay scale for workers in professional, administrative, technical, and clerical jobs, and for workers such as guards and messengers. General Schedule jobs are classified by the U.S. Office of Personnel Management in one of fifteen grades, according to the difficulty of duties and responsibilities and the knowledge, experience, and skills required of the workers. GS pay rates are set by Congress and apply to government workers nationwide. They are reviewed annually to see whether they are comparable with salaries in private industry. They are generally subject to upwards adjustment for very high-cost-of-living regions. In low-cost areas, the GS pay scale may exceed that of most private-sector workers.

Most employees receive within-grade pay increases at one-, two-, or three-year intervals if their work is acceptable. Within-grade increases may also be given in recognition of high-quality service. Some managers and supervisors receive increases based on their job performance rather than on time in grade.

High school graduates who have no related work experience usually start in GS-2 jobs, but some who have special skills begin at grade GS-3. Graduates of 2-year colleges and technical schools often can begin at the GS-4 level. Most people with bachelor's degrees appointed to professional and administrative jobs such as statisticians, economists, writers and editors, budget analysts, accountants, and physicists, can enter at grades GS-5 or GS-7, depending on experience and academic record. Those who have a master's degree or Ph.D. or the equivalent education or experience may enter at the GS-9 or GS-11 level. Advancement to higher grades generally depends upon ability, work performance, and openings in jobs at higher grade levels.

FEDERAL WAGE SYSTEM

About one quarter of federal civilian workers are paid according to the Federal Wage System. Under this system, craft, service, and manual workers are paid hourly rates established on the basis of "prevailing" rates paid by private employers for similar work in the same locations. As a result, the federal government wage rate for an occupation varies by locality. This commitment to meeting the local wage scale allows the federal wage earner to bring home a weekly paycheck comparable to that which he or she would earn in the private sector and to enjoy the benefits and security of a government job at the same time. The federal wage earner has the best of all possible worlds in this regard.

Federal government employees work a standard 40-hour week. Employees who are required to work overtime may receive premium rates for the additional time or compensatory time off at a later date. Most employees work eight hours a day, five days a week, Monday through Friday, but in some cases, the nature of the work requires a different workweek. Annual earnings for most full-time federal workers are not affected by seasonal factors.

Federal employees earn 13 days of annual (vacation) leave each year during their first three years of service; 20 days each year until the end of 15 years; after 15 years, 26 days each year. Workers who are members of military reserve organizations also are granted up to 15 days of paid military leave a year for training purposes. A federal worker who is laid off, though federal layoffs are uncommon, is entitled to unemployment compensation similar to that provided for employees in private industry.

Other benefits available to most federal employees include: a contributory retirement system, optional participation in low-cost group life and health insurance programs which are partly supported by the government (as the employer), and training programs to develop maximum job proficiency and help workers achieve their highest potential. These training programs may be conducted in government facilities or in private educational facilities at government expense.

GENERAL SCHEDULE
(Range of Salaries)

Effective as of January 1, 2001

GS Rating	Low	High
1	$14,244	$17,819
2	16,015	20,156
3	17,474	22,712
4	19,616	25,502
5	21,957	28,535
6	24,463	31,798
7	27,185	35,339
8	30,107	39,143
9	33,254	43,226
10	36,621	47,610
11	40,236	52,305
12	48,223	62,686
13	57,345	74,553
14	67,765	88,096
15	79,710	103,623

WHERE THE JOBS ARE: STATE AND LOCAL GOVERNMENTS

State and local governments provide a very large and expanding source of job opportunities in a wide variety of occupational fields. About fifteen million people work for state and local government agencies; nearly three fourths of these work in units of local government such as counties, municipalities, towns, and school districts. The job distribution varies greatly from that in federal government service. Defense, international relations and commerce, immigration, and mail delivery are virtually non-existent in state and local governments. On the other hand, there is great emphasis on education, health, social services, transportation, construction, and sanitation.

EDUCATIONAL SERVICES

About one half of all jobs in state and local government are in educational services. Educational employees work in public schools, colleges, and various extension services. About half of all education workers are instructional personnel. School systems, colleges, and universities also employ administrative personnel, librarians, guidance counselors, nurses, dieticians, clerks, and maintenance workers.

HEALTH SERVICES

The next largest field of state and local government employment is health services. Those employed in health and hospital work include physicians, nurses, medical laboratory technicians, dieticians, kitchen and laundry workers, and hospital attendants. Social services make up another aspect of health and welfare. Unfortunately, the need for welfare and human services has been increasing greatly. As the need grows, the opportunities for social workers and their affiliated administrative and support staff also grows.

GOVERNMENT CONTROL/FINANCIAL ACTIVITIES

Another million workers work in the areas of general governmental control and financial activities. These include chief executives and their staffs, legislative representatives, and persons employed in the administration of justice, tax enforcement and other financial work, and general administration. These functions require the services of individuals such as lawyers, judges and other court officers, city managers, property assessors, budget analysts, stenographers, and clerks.

STREETS AND HIGHWAYS

The movement of people is of great concern to both state and local governments. Street and highway construction and maintenance are of major importance. Highway workers include civil engineers, surveyors, operators of construction machinery and equipment, truck drivers, concrete finishers, carpenters, construction laborers, and, where appropriate, snow removers. Toll collectors are relatively few in number, but they too are state or county employees or employees of independent authorities of the states or counties. Mass transportation within municipalities and between the cities and their outlying suburbs is also the province of local government. Maintaining vehicles, roadbeds and signaling systems, and staffing the vehicles themselves, requires a large and varied work force.

POLICE AND FIRE PROTECTION SERVICES

Police and fire protection is another large field of employment. Along with uniformed officers, these services include extensive administrative, clerical, maintenance, and custodial personnel.

MISCELLANEOUS STATE AND LOCAL OCCUPATIONS

Other state and local government employees work in a wide variety of activities, including local utilities (water in most areas, electricity in some); natural resources; parks and recreation; sanitation; corrections; local libraries; sewage disposal; and housing and urban renewal. These activities require workers in diverse occupations such as economists, electrical engineers, electricians, pipefitters, clerks, foresters, and bus drivers.

CLERICAL, ADMINISTRATIVE, MAINTENANCE, AND CUSTODIAL WORKERS

A large percentage of employment in most government agencies is made up of clerical, administrative, maintenance, and custodial workers. Among the workers involved in these activities are word processors, secretaries, data processors, computer specialists, office managers, fiscal and budget administrators, bookkeepers, accountants, carpenters, painters, plumbers, guards, and janitors. The list is endless.

Most positions in state and local governments are filled by residents of the state or locality. Many localities have residency requirements. Exceptions are generally made for persons with skills that are in special demand.

EARNINGS

Job conditions and earnings of state and local government employees vary widely, depending upon occupation and locality. Salary differences from state to state and even within some states tend to reflect differences in the general wage level and cost of living in the various localities.

As with the federal government, a majority of state and local government positions are filled through some type of formal civil service test; that is, personnel are hired and promoted on the basis of merit. State and local government workers have the same protections as federal government workers: they cannot be refused employment because of their race; they cannot be denied promotion because someone else made a greater political contribution; and they cannot be fired because the boss's son needs a job. Jobs tend to be classified according to job description and pegged to a salary schedule that is based upon the job classifications. Periodic performance reviews also are standard expectations. Nearly every group of employees has some sort of union or organization, but the functions and powers of these units vary greatly.

Since states and local entities are independent, the benefits packages they offer their employees can be quite different. Most state and local government employees are covered by retirement systems or by the federal social security program. Most have some sort of health coverage. They usually work a standard week of 40 hours or less with overtime pay or compensatory time benefits for additional hours of work.

PREPARING YOURSELF FOR THE CIVIL SERVICE EXAMINATION

Most federal, state, and municipal units have recruitment procedures for filling civil service positions. They have developed a number of methods to make job opportunities known. Places where such information may be obtained include:

1. The offices of the State Employment Services. There are almost two thousand throughout the country. These offices are administered by the state in which they are located, with the financial assistance of the federal government. You will find the address of the one nearest you in your telephone book.

2. Your state Civil Service Commission. Address your inquiry to the capital city of your state.

3. Your city Civil Service Commission. It is sometimes called by another name, such as the Department of Personnel, but you will be able to identify it in your telephone directory under the listing of city departments.

4. Your municipal building and your local library.

5. Complete listings are carried by such newspapers as *The Chief-Leader* (published in New York City), as well as by other city and state-wide publications devoted to civil service employees. Many local newspapers run a section on regional civil service news.

6. State and local agencies looking for competent employees will contact schools, professional societies, veterans organizations, unions, and trade associations.

7. School boards and boards of education, which employ the greatest proportion of all state and local personnel, should be asked directly for information about job openings.

You will find more in-depth information at the end of this book.

THE FORMAT OF THE JOB ANNOUNCEMENT

When a position is open and a civil service examination is to be given for it, a job announcement is drawn up. This generally contains everything an applicant has to know about the job.

The announcement begins with the job title and salary. A typical announcement then describes the work, the location of the position, the education and experience requirements, the kind of examination to be given, and the system of rating. It may also have something to say about veteran preference and the age limit. It tells which application form is to be filled out, where to get the form, and where and when to file it.

Study the job announcement carefully. It will answer many of your questions and help you decide whether you like the position and are qualified for it. We have included sample job announcements in a later chapter.

There is no point in applying for a position and taking the examination if you do not want to work where the job is. The job may be in your community or hundreds of miles away at the other end of the state. If you are not willing to work where the job is, study other announcements that will give you an opportunity to work in a place of your choice. A civil service job close to your home has an additional advantage since local residents usually receive preference in appointments.

The words **Optional Fields**—sometimes just the word **Options**—may appear on the front page of the announcement. You then have a choice to apply for that particular position in which you are especially interested. This is because the duties of various positions are quite different even though they bear the same broad title. A public relations clerk, for example, does different work from a payroll clerk, although they are considered broadly in the same general area.

Not every announcement has options. But whether or not it has them, the precise duties are described in detail, usually under the heading, **Description of Work.** Make sure that these duties come within the range of your experience and ability.

Most job requirements give a **deadline for filing** an application. Others bear the words **No Closing Date** at the top of the first page; this means that applications will be accepted until the needs of the agency are met. In some cases a public notice is issued when a certain number of applications has been received. No application mailed past the deadline date will be considered.

Every announcement has a detailed section on **education and experience requirements** for the particular job and for the optional fields. Make sure that in both education and experience you meet the minimum qualifications. If you do not meet the given standards for one job, there may be others open where you stand a better chance of making the grade.

If the job announcement does not mention **veteran preference,** it would be wise to inquire if there is such a provision in your state or municipality. There may be none or it may be limited to disabled veterans. In some jurisdictions, surviving spouses of disabled veterans are given preference. All such information can be obtained through the agency that issues the job announcement.

Applicants may be denied examinations and eligible candidates may be denied appointments for any of the following reasons:

- intentional false statements

- deception or fraud in examination or appointment

- use of intoxicating beverages to the extent that ability to perform the duties of the position is impaired

- criminal, infamous, dishonest, immoral, or notoriously disgraceful conduct

The announcement describes the **kind of test** given for the particular position. Please pay special attention to this section. It tells what areas are to be covered in the written test and lists the specific subjects on which questions will be asked. Sometimes sample questions are given.

Usually the announcement states whether the examination is to be **assembled** or **unassembled.** In an assembled examination applicants assemble in the same place at the same time to take a written or performance test. The unassembled examination is one where an applicant does not take a test; instead, he or she is rated on his or her education and experience and whatever records of past achievement the applicant is asked to provide.

In the competitive examination all applicants for a position compete with each other; the better the mark, the better the chance of being appointed. Also, competitive examinations are given to determine desirability for promotion among employees.

Civil service written tests are rated on a scale of 100, with 70 usually as the passing mark.

FILLING OUT THE APPLICATION FORM

Having studied the job announcement and having decided that you want the position and are qualified for it, your next step is to get an application form. The job announcement tells you where to send for it.

On the whole, civil service application forms differ little from state to state and locality to locality. The questions that have been worked out after years of experimentation are simple and direct, designed to elicit a maximal amount of information about you.

Many prospective civil service employees have failed to get a job because of slipshod, erroneous, incomplete, misleading, or untruthful answers. Give the application serious attention, for it is the first important step toward getting the job you want.

Here, along with some helpful comments, are the questions usually asked on the average application form, although not necessarily in this order.

- **Name of examination or kind of position applied for.** This information appears in large type on the first page of the job announcement.

- **Optional job** (if mentioned in the announcement). If you wish to apply for an option, simply copy the title from the announcement. If you are not interested in an option, write *None*.

- **Primary place of employment applied for.** The location of the position was probably contained in the announcement. You must consider whether you want to work there. The announcement may list more than one location where the job is open. If you would accept employment in any of the places, list them all; otherwise list the specific place or places where you would be willing to work.

- **Name and address.** Give in full, including your middle name if you have one, and your maiden name as well if you are a married woman.

- **Home and office phones.** If none, write *None*.

- **Legal or voting residence.** The state in which you vote is the one you list here.

- **Height without shoes, weight, sex.** Answer accurately.

- **Date of birth.** Give the exact day, month, and year.

- **Lowest grade or pay you will accept.** Although the salary is clearly stated in the job announcement, there may be a quicker opening in the same occupation but carrying less responsibility and thus a lower basic entrance salary. You will not be considered for a job paying less than the amount you give in answer to this question.

- **Will you accept temporary employment if offered you for (a) one month or less, (b) one to four months, (c) four to twelve months?** Temporary positions come up frequently and it is important to know whether you are available.

- **Will you accept less than full-time employment?** Part-time work comes up now and then. Consider whether you want to accept such a position while waiting for a full-time appointment.

- **Were you in active military service in the Armed Forces of the United States?** Veterans' preference, if given, is usually limited to active service during the following periods: 12/7/41–12/31/46; 6/27/50–1/31/55; 6/1/63–5/7/75; 6/1/83–12/1/87; 10/23/83–11/21/83; 12/20/89–1/3/90; 8/2/90 to end of Persian Gulf hostilities.

■ **Do you claim disabled veterans credit?** If you do, you have to show proof of a war-incurred disability compensable by at least 10 percent. This is done through certification by the Veterans Administration.

■ **Special qualifications and skills.** Even though not directly related to the position for which you are applying, information about licenses and certificates obtained for teacher, pilot, registered nurse, and so on, is requested. List your experience in the use of machines and equipment and whatever other skills you have acquired. Also list published writings, public speaking experience, membership in professional societies, and honors and fellowships received.

■ **Education.** List your entire educational history, including all diplomas, degrees, and special courses taken in any accredited or armed forces school. Also give your credits toward a college or a graduate degree.

■ **References.** The names of people who can give information about you, with their occupations and business and home address, are often requested.

■ **Your health.** Questions are asked concerning your medical record. You are expected to have the physical and psychological capacity to perform the job for which you are applying. Standards vary, of course, depending on the requirements of the position. A physical handicap usually will not bar an applicant from a job he can perform adequately unless the safety of the public is involved.

■ **Work history.** Considerable space is allotted on the form for the applicant to tell about all his past employment. Examiners check all such answers closely. Do not embellish or falsify your record. If you were ever fired, say so. It is better for you to state this openly than for the examiners to find out the truth from your former employer.

On the following pages are samples of a New York City Application for Examination and a state application from Louisiana.

WHY PEOPLE CHOOSE GOVERNMENT SERVICE

There are many similarities between work in the private sector and work for the government. Within each occupation, the similarities of the daily duties far outweigh the differences in employers. Regardless of the nature of the employer—government, private business, nonprofit organization—typists type; doctors heal; teachers teach; electricians install wiring.

As was mentioned at the beginning of this chapter, one in six of employed persons in the United States is in government service. The five in six persons who are employed by nongovernmental employers all hope for just compensation for their work, for promotions when merited, and for fair and equal treatment with reference to their coworkers. They all hope that they will not be discriminated against for any non-job-related reasons, that they will not be fired capriciously, and that their opinions and suggestions will be taken seriously. In the great majority of cases, these expectations will be met.

But, in the private sector, there are no guarantees of employment practices. In government service these guarantees are a matter of policy and law. Each governmental jurisdiction has its own body of rules and procedures. In other words, not all government service is alike. The Federal Civil Service does serve as a model for all other governmental units.

NEW YORK CITY APPLICATION FOR EXAMINATION

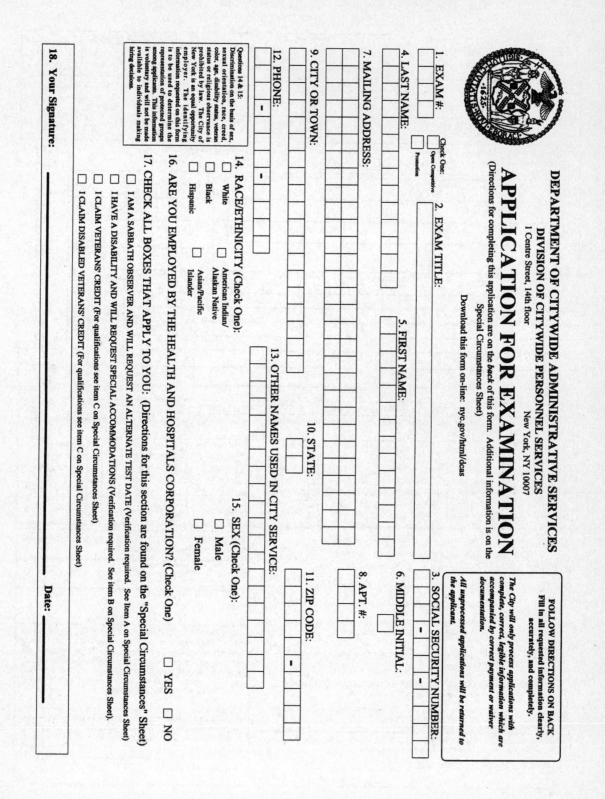

STATE OF LOUISIANA APPLICATION—page 1

SF10
(Page 1)
REV. 1/97

STATE PRE-EMPLOYMENT APPLICATION

STATE OF LOUISIANA
DEPARTMENT OF CIVIL SERVICE
P.O. Box 94111, Capitol Station
Baton Rouge, Louisiana 70804-9111

AN EQUAL OPPORTUNITY EMPLOYER

FOR OFFICE USE
Special ____
Promo ____
Action(s) ____
Session ____
Data Entry Completed ____

1. TEST LOCATION-Check only one.

Baton Rouge (3) (Weekday) ☐	New Orleans (6) (Weekday) ☐	Lafayette (4) (Sat. only) ☐	Shreveport (7) (Sat. only) ☐
	New Orleans (12) (Saturday) ☐	Lake Charles (5) (Sat. only) ☐	West Monroe (8) (Sat. only) ☐

2.Enter Name and Complete Address below.

3. Parish of Residence

4. Are you 18 or older? ☐ Yes ☐ No

5. Other names ever used on SF-10

NAME - First Middle Last

Mailing Address

City State Zip Code

6. Social Security Number
(For identification purpose)

Work Telephone No.

Home Telephone No.

→ PRINT NAME → LAST FIRST MIDDLE

7. REGISTER TITLE(S) APPLIED FOR	FOR OFFICE USE SER	CD	REJ	GRD	TR	ADDITIONAL TITLES	FOR OFFICE USE SER	CD	REJ	GRD	TR

JS No.
V.P.
S.R.

ALL TITLES LISTED ABOVE MUST HAVE THE SAME SERIES NO.

8. JOB LOCATION AVAILABILITY - IMPORTANT: Read Item 9 on the Instruction Page before completing this item. Mark at least one (1), but no more than twenty (20) parishes.

☐ 01 Acadia	☐ 09 Caddo	☐ 17 E. Baton Rouge	☐ 25 Jackson	☐ 33 Madison	☐ 41 Red River	☐ 49 St. Landry	☐ 57 Vermillion
☐ 02 Allen	☐ 10 Calcasieu	☐ 18 E. Carroll	☐ 26 Jefferson	☐ 34 Morehouse	☐ 42 Richland	☐ 50 St. Martin	☐ 58 Vernon
☐ 03 Ascension	☐ 11 Caldwell	☐ 19 E. Feliciana	☐ 27 Jeff Davis	☐ 35 Natchitoches	☐ 43 Sabine	☐ 51 St. Mary	☐ 59 Washington
☐ 04	☐ 12 Cameron	☐ 20 Evangeline	☐ 28 Lafayette	☐ 36 Orleans	☐ 44 St. Bernard	☐ 52 St. Tammany	☐ 60 Webster
☐ 05 Avoyelles	☐ 13 Catahoula	☐ 21 Franklin	☐ 29 Lafourche	☐ 37 Ouachita	☐ 45 St. Charles	☐ 53 Tangipahoa	☐ 61 W. Baton Rouge
☐ 06 Beauregard	☐ 14 Claiborne	☐ 22 Grant	☐ 30 LaSalle	☐ 38 Plaquemines	☐ 46 St. Helena	☐ 54 Tensas	☐ 62 W. Carroll
☐ 07 Bienville	☐ 15 Concordia	☐ 23 Iberia	☐ 31 Lincoln	☐ 39 Pte. Coupee	☐ 47 St. James	☐ 55 Terrebonne	☐ 63 W. Feliciana
☐ 08 Bossier	☐ 16 DeSoto	☐ 24 Iberville	☐ 32 Livingston	☐ 40 Rapides	☐ 48 St. John	☐ 56 Union	☐ 64 Winn

9. ☐ Permanent ☐ Temporary—Type of employment you will accept
NOTE: Most Temporary Appointments are 3 - 12 months

10. ☐ YES ☐ NO Do you possess a valid driver's license?

11. ☐ YES ☐ NO Do you possess a valid commercial driver's license?

12. ☐ YES ☐ NO Are you currently holding or running for an elective public office?

13. ☐ YES ☐ NO Have you ever been on probation or sentenced to jail/prison as a result of a felony conviction or guilty plea?

14. ☐ YES ☐ NO Have you ever been fired from a job or resigned to avoid dismissal?

NOTE: If answers to Items 13 and/or 14 are "YES", you MUST complete Item 24 on Page 2 of this application

15. ☐ YES ☐ NO Are you claiming Veteran's Preference points on this application? (If "YES", see Item 20 on Page 2.)

The following information is collected to complete Equal Opportunity Reports required by law. You ARE NOT LEGALLY OBLIGATED to provide this information.

16. RACIAL/ETHNIC GROUP ____ **16A.** DATE OF BIRTH ____ **17.** SEX ☐ Male ☐ Female

I HAVE READ THE FOLLOWING STATEMENTS CAREFULLY BEFORE SIGNING THIS APPLICATION:

18. Date | Social Security No. (for verification)

19. Signature of Applicant

AUTHORITY TO RELEASE INFORMATION: I consent to the release of information concerning my capacity and/or all aspects of prior job performance by employers, educational institutions, law enforcement agencies, and other individuals and agencies to duly accredited investigators, personnel technicians, and other authorized employees of the state government for the purpose of determining my eligibility and suitability for employment.

I certify that all statements made on this application and any attached papers are true and complete to the best of my knowledge. I understand that information on this application may be subject to investigation and verification and that any misrepresentation or material omission may cause my application to be rejected, my name to be removed from the eligible register and/or subject me to dismissal from state service.

STATE OF LOUISIANA APPLICATION—page 2

20. ACTIVE MILITARY SERVICE/VETERAN'S PREFERENCE
See Item 10 on the Instruction Page to determine your eligibility for Veteran's Preference. If you are a first-time applicant or if you are claiming Veteran's Preference for the first time, required PROOF MUST BE ATTACHED to this application to have preference points added to your score.

List the dates (month and year) and branch for all ACTIVE DUTY military service. Was this service performed on an active, full-time basis with full pay and allowances? (Check YES or NO for each period of service.)

FROM	TO	BRANCH OF SERVICE	YES	NO

List all GRADES held and dates of each grade. Begin with the highest grade. IMPORTANT: Use E-, O-, or WO-grade.

FROM	TO	GRADE HELD	FROM	TO	GRADE HELD

21. TRAINING AND EDUCATION

Have you received a high school diploma or equivalency certificate? ☐ YES Date received _____ ☐ NO Highest grade completed

A. LIST BUSINESS OR TECHNICAL COLLEGES ATTENDED	NAME/LOCATION OF SCHOOL	Dates Attended (Month & Year) FROM / TO	Did You Graduate? YES / NO	TITLE OF PROGRAM	CLOCK HOURS PER WEEK

List any accounting practice sets completed: _____

B. LIST COLLEGES OR UNIVERSITIES ATTENDED (Include graduate or professional schools)	NAME OF COLLEGE OR UNIVERSITY/ CITY AND STATE	Dates Attended (Month & Year) FROM / TO	Total Credit Hours Earned Semester / Quarter	Type of Degree Earned	Major Field of Study	Date Degree Received (Month & Yr.)

C. MAJOR SUBJECTS	CHIEF UNDERGRADUATE SUBJECTS (Show Major on Line 1.)	Total Credit Hours Earned Semester / Quarter	CHIEF GRADUATE SUBJECTS (Show Major on Line 1.)	Total Credit Hours Earned Semester or Qtr.
1				
2				
3				

22. LICENSES AND CERTIFICATION / **23. TYPING SPEED**

List any job-related licenses or certificates that you have (CPA, lawyer, registered nurse, etc.)

TYPE OF LICENSE OR CERTIFICATE (Specify Which One)	DATE ORIGINALLY LICENSED/ CERTIFIED	EXPIRATION DATE	NAME AND ADDRESS OF LICENSING OR CERTIFYING AGENCY	
1				WPM
2				DICTATION SPEED / WPM

24. Explain a "YES" answer to Items 13 and/or 14 here. A "YES" ANSWER WILL NOT NECESSARILY BAR YOU FROM STATE EMPLOYMENT. WE WILL CONSIDER THE DATE, FACTS, AND CIRCUMSTANCES OF EACH INDIVIDUAL CASE. For Item 13, give the law enforcement authority (city police, sherrif, FBI, etc.), the offense, date of offense, place, and disposition of case.

_____

_____

Name _____

STATE OF LOUISIANA APPLICATION—page 3

Name _____

25.	WORK EXPERIENCE — <u>IMPORTANT</u>: Read Item 11 of Instruction Page carefully before completing these items. List all jobs and activities including military service, part-time employment, self-employment, and volunteer work. BEGIN with your FIRST job in Block A; END with your MOST RECENT or PRESENT job.

A | EMPLOYER/COMPANY NAME | KIND OF BUSINESS

STREET ADDRESS | YOUR OFFICIAL JOB TITLE

CITY AND STATE | BEGINNING SALARY | ENDING SALARY

DATES OF EMPLOYMENT (MO/DA/YR) | AVERAGE HOURS WORKED PER WEEK | REASON FOR LEAVING | NO. OF EMPLOYEES YOU DIRECTLY SUPERVISED

FROM | TO

NAME/TITLE OF YOUR SUPERVISOR) | LIST JOB TITLES OF EMPLOYEES YOU DIRECTLY SUPERVISED

NAME/TITLE OF PERSON WHO CAN VERIFY THIS EMPLOYMENT (IF OTHER THAN SUPERVISOR)

DUTIES: List the major duties involved with job and give an approximate percentage of time spent on each duty.

% OF TIME	MAJOR DUTIES
100%	

B | EMPLOYER/COMPANY NAME | KIND OF BUSINESS

STREET ADDRESS | YOUR OFFICIAL JOB TITLE

CITY AND STATE | BEGINNING SALARY | ENDING SALARY

DATES OF EMPLOYMENT (MO/DA/YR) | AVERAGE HOURS WORKED PER WEEK | REASON FOR LEAVING | NO. OF EMPLOYEES YOU DIRECTLY SUPERVISED

FROM | TO

NAME/TITLE OF YOUR SUPERVISOR) | LIST JOB TITLES OF EMPLOYEES YOU DIRECTLY SUPERVISED

NAME/TITLE OF PERSON WHO CAN VERIFY THIS EMPLOYMENT (IF OTHER THAN SUPERVISOR)

DUTIES: List the major duties involved with job and give an approximate percentage of time spent on each duty.

% OF TIME	MAJOR DUTIES

STATE OF LOUISIANA APPLICATION—page 4

100%

USE REVERSE SIDE OF THIS PAGE IF ADDITIONAL SPACE REQUIRED FOR WORK EXPERIENCE

Name _____

25. WORK EXPERIENCE (Continued)

C

EMPLOYER/COMPANY NAME	KIND OF BUSINESS	
STREET ADDRESS	YOUR OFFICIAL JOB TITLE	
CITY AND STATE	BEGINNING SALARY	ENDING SALARY
DATES OF EMPLOYMENT (MO/DA/YR) / AVERAGE HOURS WORKED PER WEEK / FROM / TO	REASON FOR LEAVING	NO. OF EMPLOYEES YOU DIRECTLY SUPERVISED
NAME/TITLE OF YOUR SUPERVISOR	LIST JOB TITLES OF EMPLOYEES YOU DIRECTLY SUPERVISED	
NAME/TITLE OF PERSON WHO CAN VERIFY THIS EMPLOYMENT (IF OTHER THAN SUPERVISOR)		

DUTIES: List the major duties involved with job and give an approximate percentage of time spent on each duty.

% OF TIME	MAJOR DUTIES

100%

D

EMPLOYER/COMPANY NAME	KIND OF BUSINESS	
STREET ADDRESS	YOUR OFFICIAL JOB TITLE	
CITY AND STATE	BEGINNING SALARY	ENDING SALARY
DATES OF EMPLOYMENT (MO/DA/YR) / AVERAGE HOURS WORKED PER WEEK / FROM / TO	REASON FOR LEAVING	NO. OF EMPLOYEES YOU DIRECTLY SUPERVISED
NAME/TITLE OF YOUR SUPERVISOR)	LIST JOB TITLES OF EMPLOYEES YOU DIRECTLY SUPERVISED	
NAME/TITLE OF PERSON WHO CAN VERIFY THIS EMPLOYMENT (IF OTHER THAN SUPERVISOR)		

DUTIES: List the major duties involved with job and give an approximate percentage of time spent on each duty.

% OF TIME	MAJOR DUTIES

TEST-TAKING TECHNIQUES

Many factors enter into a test score. The most important factor should be ability to answer the questions, which in turn indicates the ability to learn and perform the duties of the job. Assuming that you have this ability, knowing what to expect on the exam and familiarity with techniques of effective test taking should give you the confidence you need to do your best on the exam.

There is no quick substitute for long-term study and development of your skills and abilities to prepare you for doing well on tests. However, there are some steps you can take to help you do the very best that you are prepared to do. Some of these steps are done before the test, and some are followed when you are taking the test. Knowing these steps is often called being "test-wise." Following these steps may help you feel more confident as you take the actual test.

"Test-wiseness" is a general term which simply means being familiar with some good procedures to follow when getting ready for and taking a test. The procedures fall into four major areas: (1) being prepared, (2) avoiding careless errors, (3) managing your time, and (4) guessing.

BE PREPARED

Don't make the test harder than it has to be by not preparing yourself. You are taking a very important step in preparation by reading this book and taking the sample tests which are included. This will help you to become familiar with the tests and the kinds of questions you will have to answer.

As you use this book, read the sample questions and directions for taking the test carefully. Then, when you take the sample tests, time yourself as you will be timed in the real test.

As you are working on the sample questions, don't look at the correct answers before you try to answer them on your own. This can fool you into thinking you understand a question when you really don't. Try it on your own first, then compare your answer with the one given. Remember, in a sample test, you are your own grader; you don't gain anything by pretending to understand something you really don't.

On the examination day assigned to you, allow the test itself to be the main attraction of the day. Do not squeeze it in between other activities. Be sure to bring admission card, identification, and pencils, as instructed. Prepare these the night before so that you are not flustered by a last-minute search. Arrive rested, relaxed, and on time. In fact, plan to arrive a little bit early. Leave plenty of time for traffic tie-ups or other complications that might upset you and interfere with your test performance.

In the test room, the examiner will hand out forms for you to fill out. He or she will give you the instructions that you must follow in taking the examination. The examiner will tell you how to fill in the grids on the forms. Time limits and timing signals will be explained. If you do not understand any of the examiner's instructions, ASK QUESTIONS. It would be ridiculous to score less than your best because of poor communication.

At the examination, you must follow instructions exactly. Fill in the grids on the forms carefully and accurately. Misgridding may lead to loss of veteran's credits to which you may be entitled or misaddressing of your test results. Do not begin until you are told to begin. Stop as soon as the examiner tells you to stop. Do not turn pages until you are told to do so. Do not go back to parts you have already completed. Any infraction of the rules is considered cheating. If you cheat, your test paper will not be scored, and you will not be eligible for appointment.

The answer sheet for most multiple-choice exams is machine scored. You cannot give any explanations to the machine, so you must fill out the answer sheet clearly and correctly.

HOW TO MARK YOUR ANSWER SHEET

1. Blacken your answer space firmly and completely. ● is the only correct way to mark the answer sheet. ◖, ⊗, ⊘, and ⊘ are all unacceptable. The machine might not read them at all.

2. Mark only one answer for each question. If you mark more than one answer, you will be considered wrong, even if one of the answers is correct.

3. If you change your mind, you must erase your mark. Attempting to cross out an incorrect answer like this ✖ will not work. You must erase any incorrect answer completely. An incomplete erasure might be read as a second answer.

4. All of your answering should be in the form of blackened spaces. The machine cannot read English. Do not write any notes in the margins.

5. MOST IMPORTANT: Answer each question in the right place. Question 1 must be answered in space 1; question 52 in space 52. If you should skip an answer space and mark a series of answers in the wrong places, you must erase all those answers and do the questions over, marking your answers in the proper places. You cannot afford to use the limited time in this way. Therefore, as you answer each question, look at its number and check that you are marking your answer in the space with the same number.

6. For the typing tests, type steadily and carefully. Just don't rush, since that's when the errors occur. Keep in mind that each error subtracts 1 wpm from your final score.

AVOID CARELESS ERRORS

Don't reduce your score by making careless mistakes. Always read the instructions for each test section carefully, even when you think you already know what the directions are. It's why we stress throughout this book that it's important to fully understand the directions for these different question-types before you go into the actual exam. It will not only reduce errors, but it will save you time—time you will need for the questions.

What if you don't understand the directions? You will have risked getting the answers wrong for a whole test section. As an example, vocabulary questions can sometimes test synonyms (words which have similar meanings), and sometimes test antonyms (words with opposite meanings). You can easily see how a mistake in understanding in this case could make a whole set of answers incorrect.

If you have time, reread any complicated instructions after you do the first few questions to check that you really do understand them. Of course, whenever you are allowed to, ask the examiner to clarify anything you don't understand.

Other careless mistakes affect only the response to particular questions. This often happens with arithmetic questions, but can happen with other questions as well. This type of error, called a "response error," usually stems from a momentary lapse of concentration.

Example

The question reads: "The capital of Massachusetts is ...." The answer is (D) Boston, and you mark (B) because "B" is the first letter of the word "Boston."

Example

The question reads: "8 - 5 = ..." The answer is (A) 3, but you mark (C) thinking "third letter."

A common error in reading comprehension questions is bringing your own information into the subject. For example, you may encounter a passage that discusses a subject you know something about. While this can make the passage easier to read, it can also tempt you to rely on your own knowledge about the subject. You must rely on information within the passage for your answers—in fact, sometimes the "wrong answer" for the questions are based on true information about the subject not given in the passage. Since the test-makers are testing your reading ability, rather than your general knowledge of the subject, an answer based on information not contained in the passage is considered incorrect.

MANAGE YOUR TIME

Before you begin, take a moment to plan your progress through the test. Although you are usually not expected to finish all of the questions given on a test, you should at least get an idea of how much time you should spend on each question in order to answer them all. For example, if there are 60 questions to answer and you have 30 minutes, you will have about one-half minute to spend on each question.

Keep track of the time on your watch or the room clock, but do not fixate on the time remaining. Your task is to answer questions. Do not spend too much time on any one question. If you find yourself stuck, do not take the puzzler as a personal challenge. Either guess and mark the question in the question booklet or skip the question entirely, marking the question as a skip and taking care to skip the answer space on the answer sheet. If there is time at the end of the exam or exam part, you can return and give marked questions another try.

MULTIPLE-CHOICE QUESTIONS

Almost all of the tests given on civil service exams are multiple-choice format. This means that you normally have four or five answer choices. But it's not something that should be overwhelming. There is a basic technique to answering these types of questions. Once you've understood this technique, it will make your test-taking far less stressful.

First, there should only be one correct answer. Since these tests have been given time and again, and the test-developers have a sense of which questions work and which questions don't work, it will be rare that your choices will be ambiguous. They may be complex, and somewhat confusing, but there will still be only one right answer.

The first step is to look at the question, without looking at the answer choices. Now select the correct answer. That may sound somewhat simplistic, but it's usually the case that your first choice is the correct one. If you go back and change it, redo it again and again, it's more likely that you'll end up with the wrong answer. Thus, follow your instinct. Once you have come up with the answer, look at the answer choices. If your answer is one of the choices, you're probably correct. It's not 100 percent infallible, but it's a strong possibility that you've selected the right answer.

With math questions you should first solve the problem. If your answer is among the choices, you're probably correct. Don't ignore things like the proper function signs (adding, subtracting, multiplying, and dividing), negative and positive numbers, and so on.

But suppose you don't know the correct answer. You then use the "process of elimination." It's a time-honored technique for test-takers. There is always one correct answer. There is usually one answer choice that is totally incorrect—a "distracter." If you look at that choice and it seems highly unlikely, then eliminate it. Depending on the number of choices (four or five), you've just cut down the number of choices to make. Now weigh the other choices. They may seem incorrect or they may be correct. If they seem incorrect, eliminate them. You've now increased your odds at getting the correct answer.

In the end, you may be left with only two choices. At that point, it's just a matter of guessing. But with only two choices left, you now have a 50 percent chance of getting it right. With four choices, you only have a 25 percent chance, and with five choices, only a 20 percent chance at guessing correctly. That's why the process of elimination is important.

SHOULD YOU GUESS?

You may be wondering whether or not it is wise to guess when you are not sure of an answer (even if you've reduced the odds to 50 percent) or whether it is better to skip the question when you are not certain. The wisdom of guessing depends on the scoring method for the particular examination part. If the scoring is "rights only," that is, one point for each correct answer and no subtraction for wrong answers, then by all means you should guess. Read the question and all of the answer choices carefully. Eliminate those answer choices that you are certain are wrong. Then guess from among the remaining choices. You cannot gain a point if you leave the answer space blank; you may gain a point with an educated guess or even with a lucky guess. In fact, it is foolish to leave any spaces blank on a test that counts "rights only." If it appears that you are about to run out of time before completing such an exam, mark all the remaining blanks with the same letter. According to the law of averages, you should get some portion of those questions right.

If the scoring method is *rights minus wrongs*, such as the address checking test found on Postal Clerk Exam 470, DO NOT GUESS. A wrong answer counts heavily against you. On this type of test, do not rush to fill answer spaces randomly at the end. Work as quickly as possible while concentrating on accuracy. Keep working carefully until time is called. Then stop and leave the remaining answer spaces blank.

In guessing the answers to multiple-choice questions, take a second to eliminate those answers that are obviously wrong, then quickly consider and guess from the remaining choices. The fewer choices from which you guess, the better the odds of guessing correctly. Once you have decided to make a guess, be it an educated guess or a wild stab, do it right away and move on; don't keep thinking about it and wasting time. You should always mark the test questions at which you guess so that you can return later.

For those questions that are scored by subtracting a fraction of a point for each wrong answer, the decision as to whether or not to guess is really up to you.

A correct answer gives you one point; a skipped space gives you nothing at all, but costs you nothing except the chance of getting the answer right; a wrong answer costs you 1/4 point. If you are really uncomfortable with guessing, you may skip a question, BUT you must then remember to skip its answer space as well. The risk of losing your place if you skip questions is so great that we advise you to guess even if you are not sure of the answer. Our suggestion is that you answer every question in order, even if you have to guess. It is better to lose a few 1/4 points for wrong guesses than to lose valuable seconds figuring where you started marking answers in the wrong place, erasing, and re-marking answers. On the other hand, do not mark random answers at the end. Work steadily until time is up.

One of the questions you should ask in the testing room is what scoring method will be used on your particular exam. You can then guide your guessing procedure accordingly.

SCORING

If your exam is a short-answer exam such as those often used by companies in the private sector, your answers will be graded by a personnel officer trained in grading test questions. If you blackened spaces on the separate answer sheet accompanying a multiple-choice exam, your answer sheet will be machine scanned or will be hand scored using a punched card stencil. Then a raw score will be calculated using the scoring formula that applies to that test or test portion— rights only, rights minus wrongs, or rights minus a fraction of wrongs. Raw scores on test parts are then added together for a total raw score.

A raw score is not a final score. The raw score is not the score that finds its way onto an eligibility list. The civil service testing authority, Postal Service, or other testing body converts raw scores to a scaled score according to an unpublicized formula of its own. The scaling formula allows for slight differences in difficulty of questions from one form of the exam to another and allows for equating the scores of all candidates. Regardless of the number of questions and possible different weights of different parts of the exam, most civil service clerical test scores are reported on a scale of 1 to 10. The entire process of conversion from raw to scaled score is confidential information. The score you receive is not your number right, is not your raw score, and, despite being on a scale of 1 to 100, is not a percentage. It is a scaled score. If you are entitled to veterans' service points, these are added to your passing scaled score to boost your rank on the eligibility list. Veterans' points are added only to passing scores. A failing score cannot be brought to passing level by adding veterans' points. The score earned plus veterans' service points, if any, is the score that finds its place on the rank order eligibility list. Highest scores go to the top of the list.

Test-Taking Tips

1.   Get to the test center early. Make sure you give yourself plenty of extra time to get there, park your car, if necessary, and even grab a cup of coffee before the test.

2.   Listen to the test monitors and follow their instructions carefully.

3.   Read every word of the instructions. Read every word of every question.

4.   Mark your answers by completely darkening the answer space of your choice. Do not use the test paper to work out your answers.

5.   Mark only ONE answer for each question, even if you think that more than one answer is correct. You must choose only one. If you mark more than one answer, the scoring machine will consider you wrong.

6.   If you change your mind, erase completely. Leave no doubt as to which answer you mean.

7.   If your exam permits you to use scratch paper or the margins of the test booklet for figuring, don't forget to mark the answer on the answer sheet. Only the answer sheet is scored.

8.   Check often to be sure that the question number matches the answer space, that you have not skipped a space by mistake.

9.   Guess according to the guessing suggestions we have made.

10.   Stay alert. Be careful not to mark a wrong answer just because you were not concentrating.

11.   Do not panic. If you cannot finish any part before time is up, do not worry. If you are accurate, you can do well even without finishing. It is even possible to earn a scaled score of 100 without entirely finishing an exam part if you are very accurate. At any rate, do not let your performance on any one part affect your performance on any other part.

12.   Check and recheck, time permitting. If you finish any part before time is up, use the remaining time to check that each question is answered in the right space and that there is only one answer for each question. Return to the difficult questions and rethink them.

PART TWO

Federal Government Law Enforcement Careers

EXECUTIVE OFFICE OF THE PRESIDENT

OFFICE OF NATIONAL DRUG CONTROL POLICY

MISSION

The Office of National Drug Control Policy (ONDCP) coordinates federal, state, and local efforts to control illegal drug abuse and devises national strategies to effectively carry out anti-drug activities. The ONDCP mission includes:

- the coordination of programs to motivate America's youth to reject illegal drug and substance abuses;

- increasing the safety of American citizens by substantially reducing drug-related crime and violence;

- the reduction of health, welfare and crime costs resulting from illegal drug use;

- shielding of America's air, land, and sea frontiers from the drug threat; and

- the breaking of foreign and domestic drug sources of supply.

HISTORICAL REVIEW

The Office of National Drug Control Policy was established by the National Narcotics Leadership Act of 1988 (21 U.S.C. 1501 *et seq.*), effective January 29, 1989, as amended by the Violent Crime Control and Law Enforcement Act of 1994 (21 U.S.C. 1502, 1506, 1508).

The Director of National Drug Control Policy is appointed by the President with the advice and consent of the Senate. The Director is assisted by a Deputy Director, a Deputy Director for Demand Reduction, and a Deputy Director for State and Local Affairs.

FUNCTIONS AND ACTIVITIES

The Director of National Drug Control Policy is responsible for establishing policies, objectives, priorities, and performance measurement for the national drug control program, and for annually promulgating a national drug control strategy and supporting annual reports to be submitted to the Congress by the President. The Director advises the President regarding necessary changes in the organization, management, budgeting, and personnel allocation of federal agencies involved in drug enforcement activities and is also responsible for notifying federal agencies if their policies are not in compliance with their responsibilities under the national drug control strategy.

Sources of Information

Employment:

Inquiries regarding employment should be directed to the Personnel Section, Office of National Drug Control Policy (telephone: 202-395-6695) or the Office of the Chief of Staff (telephone: 202-305-6732.

Publications:

To receive publications about drugs and crime, to get specific drug-related data, to obtain customized bibliographic searches, and to find out about data availability and other information resources that may meet your needs, contact the Drugs and Crime Clearinghouse; telephone: 800-666-3332; fax: 301-251-5212; Web site: http://www.whitehousedrugpolicy.gov.

For further information, contact:

Office of National Drug Control Policy

Executive Office of the President

Washington, D.C. 20503

Telephone: 202-395-6700

E-mail, askncjrs@aspensys.com

or call the Office of Public Affairs at (202) 395-6618

EXECUTIVE BRANCH DEPARTMENTS

DEPARTMENT OF AGRICULTURE

U.S. FOREST SERVICE

MISSION

The U.S. Forest Service is responsible for the management of the National Forests, "America's Great Outdoors," a task encompassing 175 National Forests and National Grasslands, covering an area about the size of California, Oregon, and Washington combined, and stretching from Alaska to Puerto Rico.

Within the forests, there are 133,000 miles of trails and 10,000 recreation sites, where people can hike, fish, camp, ski, or just relax and enjoy the surroundings.

The objective of the Law Enforcement and Investigations program is to serve people and protect natural resources and property within the authority and jurisdiction of the Forest Service.

Forest Service Law Enforcement Officers and Special Agents are responsible for the protection of the natural resources, detecting crimes, and arresting persons who violate the laws and regulations relating to the National Forests. Arson, timber theft, vandalism, camping and hunting violations, and theft and damage to archaeological sites are just a few of the criminal activities they investigate. The work of suppressing illegal drug activities such as methamphetamine production, growing of marijuana, and smuggling across both international borders on the National Forest System Lands has become an increasing workload for law enforcement personnel.

Early Forest Service Rangers. (Photo courtesy of the USDA Forest Service, Department of Agriculture.)

HISTORICAL REVIEW

Congress established the Forest Service as an agency of the Department of Agriculture in 1905 and authorized Forest Service employees to make arrests for violations occurring in the National Forests. In those days, most of the arrests were for wild game law violations and livestock violations, and much of this enforcement was conducted by legendary Forest Rangers who worked their varied assignments alone in the vast wilderness.

An increase in arson in the forests brought about the hiring of the first criminal investigators in the 1950s. In the following years, with the advent of the production of marijuana plants and an increase in recreational use in the forest, the number of law enforcement personnel grew. Today, there are about 150 special agents and approximately 450 uniformed law enforcement officers.

AUTHORITY AND DESIGNATIONS

The Chief of the Forest Service, acting under delegated authority from the Secretary of Agriculture, has designated special agents and law enforcement officers to carry out the Forest Service's law enforcement responsibilities.

Law Enforcement Officer, or LEO, is the working title for those employees assigned to full-time uniformed law enforcement duties. Special Agent is the criminal investigator's working title. These officers have been authorized to:

"Perform all duties conferred upon such officers under all laws and regulations administered by the Forest Service, including the authority to conduct investigations; to execute and serve search warrants and arrest warrants, to serve orders, subpoenas or other judicial processes as directed; and to carry firearms, make arrests and perform other duties as directed in connection with the enforcement or administration of all laws, rules and regulations in which the Department of Agriculture (USDA), Forest Service is or may be a party of interest."

Forest employees who are assigned regulatory compliance duties in addition to their normal duties supplement the special agents and the law enforcement officers. These Forest Protection Officers generally issue citations for violations of regulations relating to the administration of the National Forest system. They receive training commensurate with their law enforcement duties.

NEW AUTHORITY

The hallmark for Forest Service law enforcement is its ability to work well with other enforcement agencies at every level of government.

In 1971, Congress authorized the Secretary of Agriculture to work with state and local governments in the enforcement of state and local laws, rules, and regulations within the National Forest system. The Public Law stipulates:

> "Be it enacted by the Senate and House of Representatives of the United States of America in Congress assembled, that the Secretary of Agriculture, in connection with the administration and regulation of the use and occupancy of the National Forests and National Grasslands, is authorized to cooperate with any state or political subdivision thereof, on lands which are within or part of any unit of the National Forest system, in the enforcement or supervision of the laws or ordinances of a state or subdivision thereof. Such cooperation may include the reimbursement of a state or its subdivision for expenditures incurred in connection with activities on National Forest System lands. This Act shall not deprive any state or political subdivision thereof of its right to exercise civil and criminal jurisdiction, within or on lands which are a part of the National Forest system."

In 1988, Forest Service law enforcement personnel were cross-designated with the authority of Drug Enforcement Administration agents for the purpose of investigating and suppressing illegal drug activities in the forest. With enactment of the "1988 Omnibus Drug Bill," the number of agents and officers that could be authorized to enforce drug laws increased from 500 to 1,000. In addition, the Forest Service received authority to expand its drug investigations outside of the boundaries of the National Forest system and to cooperate with the Attorney General in asset seizure and forfeiture actions. The Drug Bill also authorized the Secretary of Agriculture to cross-designate law enforcement officers from other federal agencies to have Forest Service authority when assisting the Forest Service on drug and general law enforcement activities.

For the purpose of improving the government's ability to limit drug production and trafficking on public lands, a Memorandum of Agreement between the Department of Agriculture and the Department of the Interior in 1990 further enhanced the law enforcement efforts of the Forest Service by providing for the cross-designation of law enforcement powers between officers of the two departments. Law Enforcement personnel from the Interior Department's National Park Service, Fish and Wildlife Service, Bureau of Indian Affairs, and Bureau of Land Management were given the power and authority of the Forest Service to perform the law enforcement function in the National Forests. In turn, Forest Service law officers were provided with the power and authority of the enforcement arms of the Interior Department.

For the Forest Service, this cooperative agreement has also improved its ability to provide for security at both emergency and planned incidents, and enhanced its ability to conduct other joint investigations.

In 1994, Congress mandated that Forest Service Law Enforcement should be a 'separate reporting structure' within the Forest Service. As a result of this mandate, law enforcement officers report upward through a supervisory system consisting of Law Enforcement personnel to the Director of Law Enforcement and Investigations who, in turn, reports to the Chief of the Forest Service. Prior to 1994 the law enforcement officers reported directly to the District Rangers and Forest Supervisors and not other law enforcement personnel.

FUNCTIONS AND ACTIVITIES

Halting Marijuana Cultivation

The cultivation of marijuana (also known as cannabis) within the 191 million acres of National Forests continues to be a major problem. Growers use the forest because the environment is ideal for their covert methods of growing marijuana, and if discovered, they don't risk losing their own property under "asset forfeiture laws."

Marijuana growers pose a threat to the environment and to the millions of people who use the forest for recreational purposes. They pollute the natural environment with their potent fertilizers and kill wildlife with poisons used to protect their crops. The use of armed guards, dogs, and booby traps to guard against theft of their plants is of major concern to the Forest Service. Such measures are a potential danger to unsuspecting campers who inadvertently get too close to one of the illegal gardens.

The National Forest System Drug Control Act of 1986 made growing and distributing marijuana in the National Forests a federal felony and provided stiffer penalties for those who place booby traps at and around drug cultivation sites.

As marijuana cultivation becomes more organized, there are brokers in some areas who control the cultivation activity of several growers. They handle the distribution of the marijuana through organized networks on a nationwide basis. Brokers hire growers to cultivate plants so that the broker is less exposed to arrest and prosecution. Cultivation sites are becoming more scattered and located in places where the plants blend into natural vegetation to avoid detection.

The increase in detection, eradication, and arrests by Forest Service law enforcement officers and investigators, has made the National Forests safer for the recreational visitor.

Clandestine Laboratories

Concurrent with the problem of growing marijuana on National Forest land is the increase in production of chemical drugs in clandestine laboratories. For example, labs for producing Methamphetamine can be set up very cheaply and can produce profits into the millions of dollars. These illegal labs can be located anywhere on National Forest lands and are becoming more common in campgrounds and near roads. The dumping of the chemicals left after manufacture of the drugs has become a major cleanup problem for the Forest Service and other agencies. The chemicals used to produce methamphetamine are very toxic and flammable and are classified as major chemical spills. Forest Service law enforcement personnel investigate, arrest, and prosecute the people who manufacture these drugs, and dump the residue on federal land.

Arson

Fire is an enormous threat to the National Forests, and when it happens, investigators must find the origin of the fire, determine the cause, and pursue the arsonists. In conducting these investigations, the Forest Service relies on reward programs, matching prior cases with current investigations, and cooperation with other federal, state and local law enforcement agencies.

Today wildland fires are sometimes deliberately set to retaliate against the federal government for their crackdown on drugs in the forest and in protest of other federal policies.

Unauthorized Mining Claims

Among the thousands of mining claims in the federal forest, few actually are productive. Some people use these claims as an excuse to squat on federal land without the right to do so. Forest Service law enforcement personnel investigate unauthorized use of mining claims and often find that these sites are also being used as a cover for growing marijuana or other illegal activities.

Timber Theft

Timber theft is a major area of concern to the Forest Service. Timber valued in the millions of dollars has been stolen from National Forest lands. Despite log accountability controls, theft has occurred in all facets of the timber sale program. In many areas of the country, timber theft investigations are a major focus of Forest Service law enforcement personnel.

Archaeological Crime

The Archaeological Resources Protection Act (ARPA) makes it a federal crime to excavate, remove, damage, or sell items from any archaeological sites on public lands. Looting these sites and theft of artifacts are continuing problems. Forest Service law enforcement personnel conduct investigations involving monitoring and surveillance of these sites and arrests of offenders.

Radical Environmentalists

Radical environmentalist groups seek attention for their cause by public demonstrations and 'direct action' activities. Forest Service offices and other facilities throughout the country are often targeted for demonstrations. Most demonstrations are peaceful; however, some result in vandalism and destruction of government and public property.

Search and Rescue

The Forest Service supports and assists local and state law enforcement personnel in protecting the lives of those who visit the National Forests, including search and rescue missions. If the responsible authority is not immediately available in an emergency situation, the Forest Service takes a temporary lead role in order to reduce suffering and save lives.

Law Enforcement K-9 Teams

The Forest Service utilizes K-9 teams on National Forest lands to help patrol recreation areas, surveil marijuana plots, track wanted persons, protect law enforcement officers and locate lost persons. The dogs are trained in basic obedience, handler protection, building searches, tracking, and drug detection.

TRAINING

Each special agent and law enforcement officer attends a basic eleven week law enforcement or criminal investigator course specially designed for land management agencies at the Federal Law Enforcement Training Center in Glynco, Georgia. Law Enforcement officers and Criminal Investigators also attend other specialized courses in photography, emergency medicine, wildland fire cause determination, drug enforcement investigations, archeological resource protection, rescue and survival training and firearms instruction. All employees assigned law enforcement duties are also required to attend annual refresher training courses.

QUALIFICATIONS

Selection for Special Agent and Law Enforcement Officer positions are generally based on experience, training, and educational qualifications. An oral interview may be conducted at the regional level. Hiring levels differ and are based on the individual's qualifications with hiring at the GS-5 through GS-11 grades. The journeyman level for special agents is at the GS-12 level and GS-9 for the Law Enforcement Officer position.

For specific information about qualifications or further information, visit the Forest Service online at http://www.fs.fed.us or contact:

USDA Forest Service
Law Enforcement and Investigations
LEI National Academy
FLETC, Townhouse 378A
Glynco, Georgia 31524
Telephone: 912-267-3501

DEPARTMENT OF COMMERCE

OFFICE OF EXPORT ENFORCEMENT

BUREAU OF EXPORT ADMINISTRATION

MISSION

The Office of Export Enforcement within the Bureau of Export Administration, U.S. Department of Commerce, is responsible for the security of America's technology by preventing the illegal diversion of strategically-sensitive products and technology to potential adversaries. Export Enforcement investigates breaches of the export control laws and analyzes export intelligence to assess diversion risks.

Commerce agents have, for example, uncovered diversion schemes and networks designed to avoid Western export laws. These diversion networks often employ intermediaries who illegally buy and ship high-tech goods, many of which could enhance the military capabilities of foreign adversaries. Preventing these diversions to unfriendly nations is done in the interest of national and free-world security. In addition, Export Enforcement administers and enforces the anti-boycott provisions of the Export Administration Act.

HISTORICAL REVIEW

In 1774, the first Continental Congress convened in Philadelphia and declared the importation of British goods to be illegal. A year later, Congress outlawed the exportation of goods to Great Britain, thereby establishing the first American export controls.

Over the years Congress enacted other export control acts, and during World War II added specific penalties under the Neutrality Act of 1940. This Act authorized the President to prohibit or curtail the export of "any articles, technical data, materials or supplies" which might have military application. Violations of this Act at that time were investigated by the Federal Bureau of Investigation.

Legislation for export control of goods in short supply was initiated by Congress in 1948. The result of this Congressional action was the Export Control Act of 1949. This Act gave the Department of Commerce primary responsibility for administering and enforcing export controls.

Specific purposes for controlling exports were defined in the Export Administration Act (EAA) of 1969. This act authorized the control of exports for three purposes: national security, foreign policy, and short supply.

The Export Administration Act of 1989 divided the enforcement of export control between the Department of Commerce and the U.S. Customs Service of the Treasury Department. Today, exporting from the United States is a multi-billion dollar business.

The Bureau

The Bureau of Export Administration (BXA) was established by the Commerce Department in 1987 as a central agency for high-level direction of national export control policy. The Bureau's purpose is to improve the federal government's management of export controls, strengthen enforcement of export laws, reduce administrative burdens on exporters, and enhance America's export competitiveness.

The Commerce Department's Export Enforcement Office has fostered a relationship with the private sector which encourages extensive business community cooperation in identifying and preventing illegal export transactions. Many enforcement cases are now developed as a result of leads given to Commerce by business executives. (Photo courtesy of Export Enforcement Office, Department of Commerce.)

The Office

Since 1980, preventing the illegal flow of strategically sensitive products and technology to potential adversaries has been a high priority within the federal government. The Office of Export Enforcement was created in 1982 to address this need, and throughout the 1980s, the Commerce Department provided the resources needed to develop a forceful and effective enforcement program.

The Export Administration Amendments Act of 1985 granted export enforcement special agents the authority to execute search warrants, make arrests, and carry firearms. In addition, the agents were given authority to seize goods or technology in the process of being exported illegally.

The amended Act also established new criminal violations. It added "attempts to violate" in addition to "conspiracy to violate" the Act. The Act also made it a crime for persons to possess goods or technology with the intent to export those items in violation of any national security or foreign policy export control imposed under the Act.

FUNCTIONS AND ACTIVITIES

The Office of Export Enforcement (OEE) and the Office of Enforcement Analysis (OEA) conduct programs to prevent and investigate dual-use export control violations and thereby protect important national security and foreign policy interests safeguarded by the Export Administration Act (EAA) and Export Administration Regulations (EAR). Additionally, Export Enforcement's Office of Antiboycott Compliance continues to administer and implement the antiboycott policy and program.

BXA's Export Enforcement arm has trained professionals, including special agents, who enforce the EAA and the EAR, the Fastener Quality Act, and the Chemical Weapons Convention Implementation Act. Export Enforcement educates exporters, interdicts illegal exports, and prosecutes violators. Working closely with BXA's licensing officers and policy staff, BXA's export law enforcement officers apply their special skills and understanding of the export control system to minimize exports of potentially damaging dual-use items to unreliable users.

EXPORT ENFORCEMENT INITIATIVES

Chemical Weapons Convention

Under the Chemical Weapons Convention (CWC) Implementation Act of 1998, certain commercial chemical production and processing facilities are required to submit data declarations and to permit international inspections. In preparation for fulfilling its responsibilities under this legislation, OEE participated in host team training for CWC inspections, as well as a mock inspection exercise with BXA's Export Administration and the Office of Chief Counsel for Export Administration at a chemical production and processing facility. OEE worked with the State Department and other government agencies to clarify OEE's enforcement roles under the CWC implementing legislation and regulations.

National Defense Authorization Act of 1998

The National Defense Authorization Act (NDAA), enacted on November 18, 1997, contains provisions requiring regulation and careful scrutiny of sales of high-performance computers (HPCs) to certain countries of concern. The NDAA requires those who wish to export high-performance computers to these countries to notify the Department at least ten days prior to export. During the ten-day period, relevant government agencies review the pre-export notification. If any agency has an objection, a license is required. The NDAA also requires the exporters to submit a post-shipment report to the Department, and requires that the Department conduct post-shipment verifications (PSVs) on-site at the end user's location to verify the installation and the end use of each HPC. OEE maintains a high-performance computer division in OEA to coordinate and supervise all enforcement responsibilities under the NDAA.

Project Outreach

As part of its public education efforts, OEE special agents participated in numerous seminars and trade shows across the country. They also developed contacts with private sector firms through Project Outreach, a program which provides firms with specific export guidance, gives OEE a better understanding of the private sector's needs, and provides valuable investigative leads.

Safeguards Verification Program

OEE's Safeguards Verification Program was developed in 1990 to ensure the legitimate use of strategic U.S. goods and technology by the newly emerging democracies of Central Europe, traditional points of diversion to the former Soviet Union. OEE's Safeguards Verification Program has expanded worldwide to conduct on-site pre-license and post-shipment checks using Export Enforcement personnel instead of officers from Commerce's U.S. and Foreign Commercial Service. The Safeguards Verification Teams travel overseas to determine the disposition of licensed or otherwise controlled U.S.-origin commodities, particularly those of proliferation concern. These Safeguards Verification Teams also assess the suitability of foreign firms to receive U.S.-origin licensed goods and technology and conduct educational visits to foreign firms, often in cooperation with host government officials.

International Law Enforcement Cooperation

Export Enforcement (EE) expanded its international cooperative efforts. EE's export control attaché at the U.S. Embassy in Beijing conducted numerous post-shipment visits in the People's Republic of China. EE conducted these visits under the End-Use Visit Arrangement, which it successfully negotiated with its counterparts at China's Ministry of Foreign Trade and Economic Cooperation. In addition, EE helped organize the first-ever U.S.-China export control seminar designed for businesses from those two countries.

Antiboycott Laws

The Office of Antiboycott Compliance administers and enforces the antiboycott provisions of the EAA. The EAA applies to all "U.S. persons" defined by the rules to include individuals and companies located in the United States and their foreign affiliates. These persons are subject to the law when their activities relate to the sale, purchase, or transfer of goods or services between the United States and a foreign country.

This covers U.S. exports and imports, financing, forwarding and shipping, and certain other transactions that may take place wholly offshore.

The antiboycott laws, promulgated in 1976 and 1977, were adopted to encourage or require U.S. firms to refuse to participate in foreign boycotts not sanctioned by the United States. The laws have the effect of preventing U.S. firms from being used to implement foreign policies of other nations which run counter to U.S. policy.

Case Illustrations

Bayer Corporation Penalized $200,000 to Settle Charges for Unlicensed Exports

The Commerce Department imposed a $200,000 civil penalty on Bayer Corporation of Tarrytown, New York, to settle allegations that the company's Diagnostics Division exported glucose and other reagents of U.S. origin to various destinations. The Department alleged that on 57 occasions Bayer Corporation exported glucose and other reagents from the United States to Hong Kong, Malaysia, Mexico, Singapore, South Africa, South Korea, and Taiwan without obtaining the required export licenses. The Department also alleged that Bayer made false or misleading representations of material fact on an export control document. The U.S. government controls glucose and other reagents because of concerns that they may be used for chemical or biological weapons.

Guilty Plea for Illegal Exports to Libya and Sudan

International High Tech Marketing (IHTM), a Miami-based computer exporting company, pled guilty in the U.S. District Court, Southern District of Florida, Miami Division, to a criminal information charging the firm with export violations. The charges related to the illegal export of U.S.-origin computer equipment to Libya and Sudan, and making unlawful misrepresentations on export documents. The Court ordered the firm to pay a $250,000 criminal fine. The criminal information charged IHTM, a wholly-owned subsidiary of CHS Electronics, Inc., with two felony counts for illegally exporting computers and related items to Libya and Sudan, and three felony counts charging that the firm under-declared the value of export shipments, thereby evading reporting requirements to the U.S. government.

Joint Commerce-Customs Cases

McDonnell Douglas, China National Aero Technology Import and Export Corporation and others Indicted on Federal Charges for Making False and Misleading Statements in Connection with the Export of Machining Equipment to the People's Republic of China.

A Federal grand jury in the District of Columbia returned a 16-count indictment against McDonnell Douglas Corporation and the China National Aero Technology Import and Export Corporation (CATIC), a People's Republic of China government-formed corporation in Beijing, China, for making false and misleading statements and material omissions in connection with McDonnell Douglas' export to CATIC of machining equipment used to build aircraft parts.

Abdulamir Mahdi Sentenced for Illegal Exports to Iran and Iraq

A U.S. District Court judge in Orlando, Florida, sentenced Abdulamir Mahdi, a Canadian businessman, to imprisonment for 51 months, supervised release for three years and a $7,500 criminal fine for violating U.S. export controls restricting trade with Iran and Iraq. Mahdi, an Iraqi national, pled guilty to an indictment charging him with conspiracy to violate export controls. Mahdi used two Toronto companies, OTS Refining Equipment Corporation and Tech-Link Development Corporation, to buy U.S.-origin oil-field and industrial equipment for diversion to Iran and Iraq.

TRAINING

In addition to the basic training program for federal agents at the Federal Law Enforcement Training Center in Glynco, GA, special agents receive specialized and refresher training in a number of areas.

One of the most recent training programs is in nuclear, biological, and chemical warfare (NBC). This course is designed to teach the export enforcement agents a variety of subjects including basic chemistry and biology, NBC technology and treaty obligations, missile technology, and diversion techniques. It covers safety procedures for handling chemicals and identification procedures for those chemicals that should be controlled.

This training is conducted by personnel from the U.S. Army Chemical Research and Engineering Development Center, the Environmental Protection Agency, the Commerce Department's Office of Export Licensing, and intelligence agents.

For qualifications and further information, visit the Office of Export Enforcement online at http://www.bxa.doc.gov/Enforcement or contact:

Office of Export Enforcement
Department of Commerce
14th and Constitution Ave., NW
Washington, D.C. 20230
Telephone: (202) 482-1561
or the Office of Public Affairs at (202) 482-2721

OFFICE OF LAW ENFORCEMENT STANDARDS

NATIONAL INSTITUTE OF STANDARDS AND TECHNOLOGY

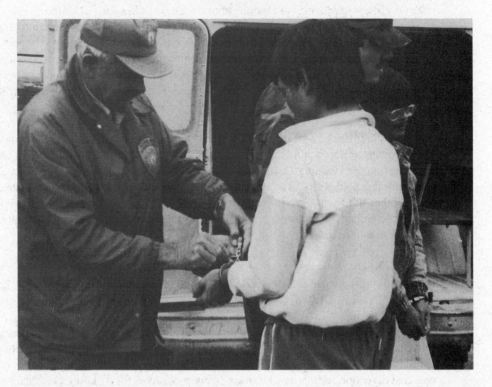

OLES Enforcement Officer makes an arrest for illegal fishing. (Photo courtesy of NOAA Fisheries, Department of Commerce.)

MISSION

The Office of Law Enforcement Standards (OLES) of the National Institute of Standards and Technology (NIST) helps law enforcement and criminal justice agencies ensure that the equipment they purchase and the technologies they use are safe, dependable, and effective.

OLES conducts research on protective clothing, communication systems, emergency equipment, investigative aids, protective equipment, security systems, vehicles, weapons, and analytical techniques and standard reference materials used by the forensic science community. Other research areas include vehicle speed measuring devices (radar, lidar, photoradar), surveillance systems (video, Integrated Services Digital Network/Digital Intercept System (ISDN/DIS), dialed number recorders, and batteries.

To help law enforcement and criminal justice agencies acquire the high-quality resources that they need to do their jobs, OLES:

- develops methods for testing equipment performance and for examining evidentiary materials

- develops standards for equipment and operating procedures

- develops standard reference materials

- performs other scientific and engineering research as required by the National Institute of Justice (NIJ)

Activities sponsored by the National Institute of Justice are performed by OLES as part of an overall Law Enforcement and Corrections Standards and Testing Program that includes the development of standards and test protocols, the testing of equipment, and the publication of test results. For example, the Communications Systems Program resulted in the development of standards for communication systems items such as portable transceivers, base stations, mobile digital equipment, and surveillance devices. The Weapons and Protective Equipment Program developed standards for revolvers and semi-automatic pistols, shotguns, body armor, protective helmets, and handcuffs.

HISTORICAL REVIEW

Since 1971, OLES has applied science and technology to the needs of the criminal justice community, including law enforcement, corrections, and forensic science, as well as the fire service. The Office focuses on the development of minimum performance standards, which are promulgated by the NIJ as voluntary national standards. OLES also conducts studies that result in the publication of technical reports and user guidelines.

NIJ is the primary sponsor of OLES projects. Projects also are occasionally supported by the National Highway Traffic Safety Administration (NHTSA), the Federal Bureau of Investigation (FBI), and the Office of Management and Budget (OMB).

OLES has published, mostly through NIJ, more than 200 standards, guides, and technical reports over its 28 years. Early studies and standards centered on emergency vehicle warning systems, police clothing, components of intrusion alarm systems, physical security of door and window assemblies, metal and explosive vapor detectors, arson accelerant detectors, and narcotic test kits. OLES also developed standard reference materials for glass comparison and reference collections of automobile paints and synthetic fibers for use by forensic laboratories.

Accomplishments

OLE has made significant contributions to the criminal justice system through its major sponsor, NIJ:

■ Since NIJ developed body armor for routine full-time wear by police officers, many officers have been spared serious injury or death. The fact that armor has performed so well in the field is due in large part to the availability and use of the NIJ body armor standard developed by OLES.

■ OLES developed standards for the physical security of doors and windows, the first organization to do so. These standards were subsequently adopted by the American Society for Testing and Materials (ASTM) and are used in building codes.

■ The NIST Building and Fire Research Laboratory Office developed the Fire Safety Evaluation System to enable corrections facilities to select from options in the National Fire Protection Association (NFPA) code to comply with its requirements in the most cost-effective manner possible.

■ When DNA genetic profiles were first introduced into trial evidence, OLES, at NIJ's request, recognized the ultimate need for standardization of the analytical procedures. The NIST Chemical Science and Technology Laboratory developed two standard reference materials (SRMs); inter-aboratory tests using these SRMs have demonstrated excellent agreement between laboratories.

For further information, visit the OLES Web site at http://www.nlectc.org. You may also write to:

Office of Law enforcement Standards
National Institute of Standards and Technology
100 Bureau Drive, Stop 8102
Technology Building 225, Room A323
E-mail: oles@nist.gov.
Gaithersburg, Maryland 20899-8102
Telephone: (301) 975-2757
Fax: (301) 948-0978

OFFICE FOR LAW ENFORCEMENT

NATIONAL OCEANIC AND ATMOSPHERIC ADMINISTRATION (NOAA)

The National Oceanic and Atmospheric Administration (NOAA) warns of dangerous weather, charts the seas and skies, guides the use and protection of ocean resources, and endeavors to enrich mankind's understanding of the oceans, atmosphere, space, and sun. The NOAA Fisheries is a component of the NOAA within the U.S. Department of Commerce. The NOAA Fisheries, Office for Law Enforcement (OLE) employs Special Agents to enforce the provisions of federal laws aimed at protecting the nation's maritime resources.

MISSION

The mission of the Office for Law Enforcement is to enforce federal statutes and regulations under the jurisdiction of NOAA in order to conserve and protect living marine resources of the United States. The most significant of the federal laws and regulations enforced by the OLE are the Magnuson Fishery Conservation and Management Act (MFCMA or Magnuson Act), the Endangered Species Act (ESA) of 1973, the Marine Mammal Protection Act (MMPA) of 1972, the Lacey Act Amendments of 1981, and the Marine Mammal Protection, Research, and Sanctuaries Act (MSA).

The Office for Law Enforcement also investigates criminal and civil violations of all federal laws within NOAA's environmental responsibilities and jurisdiction. This includes participating with the U.S. Coast Guard, U.S. Customs Service, state fish and wildlife departments, and various other federal, state and tribal enforcement agencies to patrol, inspect and investigate any activities related to the protection of our marine resources.

HISTORICAL REVIEW

In 1871, Congress passed a joint resolution authorizing the President to appoint a Commissioner of Fish and Fisheries, whose duties were:

> "To prosecute investigations on the subject (of the diminution of valuable fishes) with the view of ascertaining whether any and what diminution in the number of food-fishes of the coast and the lakes of the United States has taken place; and, if so, to what causes the same is due; and also whether any and what protection, prohibitory or precautionary measures should be adopted in the premises, and to report upon the same to Congress."

Specific authority to study the methods and statistics of the fisheries was granted in 1879 and has been regularly carried on since that time. The biological and economic inquiries provided for in the original Act have also continued without interruption and have greatly increased in scope and magnitude.

By Act of Congress approved February 14, 1903, the Fish Commission became a bureau of the new Department of Commerce and Labor, and its independent existence was subsequently terminated.

In the early 1970s, Congress passed two laws which provided protection to living marine resources. These laws are the Marine Mammal Protection Act of 1972 (MMPA) and the Endangered Species Act of 1973 (ESA). The MMPA prohibits, among other things, the killing, harming, or harassing of any marine mammal, including whales, dolphins, seals, sea lions, walruses, manatees, dugongs, polar bears, and sea otters. Also prohibited is the importation into the United States of any marine mammal or any part or product of a marine mammal. Under the ESA, NOAA Fisheries has jurisdiction over most marine animals which have been declared endangered or threatened with extinction, including all the great whales and most species of sea turtles. The ESA prohibits virtually the same activities as does the MMPA with respect to any endangered or threatened species and regulates any potential adverse affects on the habitat of these threatened species. ESA also prohibits the interstate sale or transportation of endangered species, their parts, or products.

Under the MMPA and ESA, case investigations involve unlawful importation or interstate commerce in products made from these animals, such as sperm whale teeth carvings, cosmetic and pharmaceutical products with whale oil, seal skins, and sea turtle jewelry. Many cases are also made each year against persons who kill or harass animals protected by these two laws.

In 1976, the Magnuson Act became law and extended U. S. jurisdiction over its fisheries resources within the Exclusive Economic Zone (EEZ), a protected fishery management and conservation zone extending from 3 miles to 200 miles offshore from the United States. Prior to enactment of the Magnuson Act, the United States had little control over foreign fleets fishing off the U.S. coast. Particularly troublesome were fishing fleets from the former Soviet Union, Poland, then-East Germany, Japan, and South Korea, which had severely depleted certain fish stock. Under the Magnuson Act, the United States gained complete control over foreign fishing within the 200-mile Fishery Conservation Zone. Foreign vessels are required to obtain permits to fish within the zone. The permits specify when and where they may fish, as well as what species of fish and how much of each they may take. In addition, each foreign vessel must carry on board a U.S. observer who collects statistical and scientific data and monitors the vessel's compliance with U.S. regulations.

By enacting the Lacey Act Amendments of 1981, Congress revamped and strengthened some of the nation's oldest federal legislation aimed at protecting wildlife. The Lacey Act now makes it unlawful for any person to ship, sell, receive, or transport across state lines or into the United States, any fish or wildlife taken or possessed in violation of any federal, state, foreign,or Indian tribal law. The Lacey Act also helps to augment the enforcement of state laws whose penalties, in many cases, are too weak to effectively deter violations.

FUNCTIONS AND ACTIVITIES

NOAA Fisheries Enforcement Initiatives:

- A large-scale southeastern Massachusetts seafood corporation was charged monetary penalties of $5.8 million for 300 violations involving massive illegal landings and fraudulent reporting schemes designed to circumvent fishery regulations and fishery management measures. The corporation illegally netted over 396,000 pounds of seafood worth $2.4 million.

- Sea Rich Seafood agreed to pay more than $1 million and had its fishing permit permanently revoked for not reporting and misreporting purchases of illegally retained fish.

- An individual was sentenced to 30 days in jail for shooting a stellar sea lion, which is protected under the Endangered Species Act. This was the first time in Alaska that an individual served jail time for violation of the ESA.

- Working closely with the Mexican authorities, OLE agents seized 45,000 pounds of undersized spiny lobster being shipped illegally (contrary to Mexican law) from Mexico to the U.S.

- Working closely with the U.S. Coast Guard, U.S. Navy, and foreign enforcement officials, OLE seized the Foreign Fishing Vessel (FFV) Cao Yu 6025 (Chinese) for illegal driftnet fishing on the high seas.

- The FFV Arctic Wind (Honduran registry with Russian crew) was seized by the U.S. Coast Guard off the Alaskan coast for violation of the High Seas Driftnet Act. Three tons of salmon were removed and donated to the Anchorage Food Bank.

- Off the coast of Alaska, the FFV Ming Chang (Chinese) was seized for trawling in the U.S. EEZ without a permit. The Chinese owner posted a $1.5 million bond and the vessel was released.

Case Illustration

The IRISH ROVER

The Alaska State Troopers Department of Fish and Wildlife Protection, Criminal Investigation Division, in Yakutat, Alaska, received information from an ex-crew member of the fishing vessel IRISH ROVER regarding commercial fish violations. The former crew member stated he had witnessed halibut being processed, packed, and stored in the hold. He estimated there to be approximately 1,500 pounds of halibut fillet packed in 5 pound shrimp boxes aboard the vessel. The IRISH ROVER was not licensed to fish halibut and the halibut season for the year had closed; therefore, fishing for halibut would be in violation of both state and federal law. In addition, the IRISH ROVER was a trawler and International Pacific Halibut Commission (IPHC) regulations did not allow for the taking of halibut by the use of a trawler net nor the possession of halibut aboard a vessel which had other than longline gear aboard, as the IRISH ROVER did.

NOAA Fisheries and Wildlife Protection officers located the IRISH ROVER in Pelican, Alaska, and the vessel was searched. Although no processed halibut was found, seven whole halibut and three boxes containing halibut parts were found concealed under a set of binboards. In addition, a total of approximately 208 pounds of unprocessed halibut was found aboard the vessel. All halibut was seized and the captain was cited by the NOAA Fisheries for violating IPHC regulations.

Subsequently, an Alaska NOAA Fisheries agent learned from a U.S. Coast Guard special agent that he had uncovered more incriminating information regarding the IRISH ROVER. According to the USCG Special Agent, he was informed about certain illegal activities including insurance fraud, illegal fishing, and income tax evasion.

NOAA Fisheries obtained records related to the activities of the IRISH ROVER, from which it became evident that the vessel was involved in at least one interstate shipment of unlawfully taken halibut and, on approximately three occasions, had fished for shrimp in a closed area and had transported and sold in interstate commerce at least a portion of the shrimp caught. In addition, records of dock moorings, check purchases and payments, fuel pier receipts, hotel bills, airline tickets and invoices, statements of crew members, and other records played a major part in documenting approximately $70,846 worth of shrimp which had been caught and sold unlawfully. The NOAA Fisheries ultimately charged the owner of the IRISH ROVER with multiple federal and state violations.

TRAINING

OLE special agents attend the ten-week Criminal Investigation Course, while OLE Enforcement Officers attend the newly-created sixteen-week Natural Resource Police Training program that has replaced the eleven-week Land Management Training Program. The special agents' course is designed to provide traditional investigative law enforcement skills with further expertise in criminal human behavior, modern technology, law, and other interdisciplinary approaches to effective law enforcement. The enforcement officers' course is designed for natural resource management agencies with emphasis on the patrol functions of enforcement in a natural resource environment. The enforcement officers receive training in patrol techniques including interviewing, suspect control, arrest techniques, driving skills, law, firearms, narcotics, and communications. These courses are taught at the Federal Law Enforcement Training Center (FLETC) in Glynco, Georgia. Both special agents and enforcement officers also attend other advanced and specialized courses in photography, Spanish language, emergency medical response, computer forensics, witness and suspect interviewing, marine vessel operation, firearms qualification, and survival training. All employees assigned law enforcement duties are also required to attend annual refresher training courses.

QUALIFICATIONS

Potential candidates for criminal investigator or enforcement officer positions must meet certain qualification and physical standards as defined in the Office of Personnel Management Qualification Standards for General Schedule Positions. Interested and qualified individuals can view vacancy announcements at the OPM website (www.usajobs.opm.gov) or call 912-757-3100. Information about NOAA Fisheries OLE positions can also be viewed directly at The Commerce Opportunities Online (COOL) Web site at http://www.jobs.doc.gov.

> For further information, contact:
> National Oceanic and Atmospheric Administration
> Office for Law Enforcement
> 8484 Georgia Avenue, Suite 415
> Silver Spring, Maryland 20910
> Telephone: (301) 427-2300

DEPARTMENT OF DEFENSE

DEFENSE CRIMINAL INVESTIGATIVE SERVICE

MISSION

The Defense Criminal Investigative Service (DCIS), established by the Secretary of Defense in 1981, is the investigative arm of the Office of Inspector General (OIG), Department of Defense (DoD). The DCIS is the investigative organization within the Office of the Secretary of Defense that detects, investigates, and prevents fraud, waste, and abuse and other improper acts through the continual development of DCIS personnel and effective use of all applicable resources.

HISTORICAL REVIEW

The Secretary of Defense established the Defense Criminal Investigative Service on April 20, 1981, as a worldwide civilian federal law enforcement agency to investigate suspected criminal activity involving DoD components and contractors.

In 1982, the Inspector General Act of 1978 was amended by Congress to establish a statutory IG in the DoD, charged with the responsibility for matters relating to the prevention and detection of fraud, waste, and abuse in the programs and operations of the DoD. The IG, DoD, appointed an Assistant Inspector General for Investigations, who is also the Director of DCIS.

FUNCTIONS AND ACTIVITIES

The DCIS investigates allegations of criminal, civil, and administrative violations and promotes economy, efficiency, and effective operations within the Department of Defense (DoD). The introduction of counterfeit material and other forms of unauthorized product substitution into the procurement system has historically been and continues to be DCIS' highest priority for deterrence, investigation, and prosecution. Product substitution investigations have always comprised a major part of the DCIS case inventory.

DCIS investigations of contract accounting fraud in DoD contracts, and, in particular, cost mischarging and defective pricing cases, are labor intensive, long-term and among the most complex types of fraud investigations. With the advent of electronic commerce and electronic data interchange, new cases involving fraud are evolving in the electronic area.

The Defense draw down and base closure and realignment process has resulted in increased disposal and transfer of excess military equipment. Most of the equipment has significant resale value, and the volume and value of the equipment creates a potential for corruption. DCIS aggressively pursues all information related to the unlawful disposal of Defense-related supplies and equipment. These investigations involve numerous offenses, including major theft, public corruption, kickbacks, U.S. Customs violations, antitrust, and false statements by recipients of the equipment.

DCIS has the responsibility for national health-care fraud investigations involving programs administered by the Assistant Secretary of Defense (Health Affairs). The programs provide health care to active-duty dependents, retired military personnel and their dependents, and survivors of military personnel through a health insurance program formerly known as the Civilian Health and Medical Program of the Uniformed Services (CHAMPUS), now known as TRICARE.

The Environmental Protection Agency (EPA) has primary jurisdiction for matters involving hazardous waste spills or other hazardous situations and environmental crimes. DCIS is responsible for investigating fraud in the DoD environmental programs, including contract fraud with regard to the removal, transport, and disposal of hazardous material from DoD installations.

TRAINING

DCIS special agents must complete the nine-week Basic Agent Training Course at the Federal Law enforcement Training Center (FLETC) at Glynco, Georgia. Basic training is followed by four weeks of specialized training at the Inspector General Academy located at the FLETC facility.

QUALIFICATIONS

DCIS special agents are classified in the GS-1811 (criminal investigator) job series. To considered for a DCIS special agent position, an individual must:

- be a U.S. citizen,

- be between the ages of 21 and 35

- pass the complete applicant screening process, which includes the special agent applicant examination, interview battery, drug screening, medical examination, and a physical fitness test

- pass an extensive background investigation

- be in excellent physical condition

- have good communication skills

- complete the nine-week Basic Agent Training Course at FLETC and the four-week specialized training at the IG Academy

Entry pay level is GS-5 or GS-7, depending upon applicant's education and/or experience. DCIS special agents may advance to GS-9, GS-11 and GS-12 in one-year increments. Once an agent has demonstrated the ability to investigate complex cases, he or she is then eligible for promotion to GS-13, after one year in grade as a GS-12.

Visit the DCIS Web site at http://www.dodig.osd.mil/dcis or for additional information regarding a career with the DCIS, contact:

Department of Defense
Office of the Inspector General
Defense Criminal Investigative Service
400 Army Navy Drive, Room 901E
Arlington, Virginia 22202
Telephone: (703) 604-8600
Fax: (703) 602-0607

DEFENSE INTELLIGENCE AGENCY

MISSION

The mission of the Defense Intelligence Agency (DIA) is to satisfy the intelligence requirements of the Department of Defense. Through its Director, DIA serves as the primary intelligence advisor to the Secretary of Defense and other senior decision makers. The Agency's Director is also the intelligence staff officer for the Joint Chiefs of Staff, responsible for providing intelligence support for both planning and military operations.

HISTORICAL REVIEW

On February 8, 1961, Secretary of Defense Robert S. McNamara advised the Joint Chiefs of Staff (JCS) of his decision to establish a Defense Intelligence Agency and assigned them the task of developing a plan that would integrate the military intelligence efforts of all DoD elements. The agency became effective October 1, 1961. Its mission was the continuous task of collecting, processing, evaluating, analyzing, integrating, producing, and disseminating military intelligence for the DoD.

There was a major reorganization in July 1970 and on November 3, 1971, the post of Assistant Secretary of Defense (Intelligence) was established. The Congressional appropriation funded a new building in fiscal years 1981 and 1982 and the Defense Intelligence Analysis Center became operational in 1984.

FUNCTIONS AND ACTIVITIES

To fulfill its mission, DIA maintains an extensive intelligence database capable of providing accurate, timely information on ground, naval, air, and missile and space forces around the world. The Agency also manages and evaluates the intelligence production of other Department of Defense components and closely cooperates with other organizations within the intelligence community, such as the Central Intelligence Agency (CIA) and the National Security Agency (NSA).

Employees participate in a worldwide intelligence program covering military and paramilitary ground, naval, air, and missile forces. Other responsibilities involve the collection and evaluation of information on a wide range of subjects. These could include topics such as economic, social, cultural, physical, geographic, scientific, and military conditions, trends, and forces in foreign areas.

In addition to intelligence professionals, DIA also employs a large support staff. These employees take care of all the services needed to back up the intelligence gathering and production of others. Their responsibilities include human resources, information systems, purchasing, contracting, and logistics.

Positions are primarily in the Washington, D.C., metropolitan area with other positions in Frederick, Maryland, and Huntsville, Alabama.

QUALIFICATIONS

All candidates and their immediate family members must be U.S. citizens and are subject to a thorough background inquiry and drug testing.

Candidates should have backgrounds in international affairs, regional studies, political science, (foreign language in conjunction with these majors is highly desired), history, geography, international economics, information technology, engineering (aerospace, chemical, communications, computer, electrical, electronic, missile, nuclear, and systems), and science (biology, chemistry, microbiology, pharmacology, physics, and toxicology). Competitive candidates also possess an overall grade point average of 3.0 or above on a 4.0 scale.

In addition, highly competitive candidates possess a combination of the following:

- The research skills to identify, collect, and evaluate research data; to absorb and synthesize large amounts of information; and to draw logical interpretive conclusions

- The ability to develop logical thoughts into well-written documents, such as studies reports, instruction, guides, etc.

- The ability to convey ideas fully and accurately through discussions, briefings, and similar presentations

- General knowledge and familiarity with contemporary affairs

- Candidates meeting the above qualifications are invited to submit a resume via email to: dia@alexus.com or visit DIA's Web site at http://www.dia.mil or call 202-231-8228 for additional information about careers with DIA.

DEFENSE PROTECTIVE SERVICE

MISSION

The Defense Protective Service (DPS) is responsible for providing law enforcement and security services to the Pentagon and other Department of Defense facilities in the National Capitol Region (NCR).

HISTORICAL REVIEW

The DPS was established on October 1, 1987, as an organizational element of the Washington Headquarters Service, Office of the Secretary of Defense. The DPS was created to meet the specific needs of the DoD community that could not be met by a conventional Police Department. Along with enforcing federal, state, and local laws, DPS officers are tasked with such things as access control, security of classified material and executive protection. To meet the constantly changing needs inherent in security and law enforcement, the DPS has continued to grow since its creation and has become a self-sufficient entity with a K-9 Unit, Emergency Response Team, and Physical and Technical Security divisions.

Defense Protective Service (DPS) Security Officer controls access to the Pentagon. (Photo courtesy of the Defense Protective Service, Department of Defense.)

FUNCTIONS AND ACTIVITIES

The DPS is composed of several branches that work together to accomplish the DPS mission. The backbone of these is the Operations Services Branch (OPS). The OPS Branch is responsible for conducting the majority of police and security duties on the Pentagon reservation, one of the world's largest office buildings and the nerve center of the Department of Defense. Security officers maintain a high profile at all times, providing security for visiting dignitaries, such as the President of the United States, or conducting antiterrorist patrols as a member of the Emergency Response Team.

The Security Services Branch is responsible for the physical and technical security of the Pentagon and surrounding DoD leased facilities in the NCR. These duties include installation and maintenance of alarm systems, destruction of classified materials, and issuance of credentials. Security services is responsible for a customer base of nearly 30,000 people and for providing the means to ensure that no information or persons exit the Pentagon unless authorized.

The Support Services Branch (SSB) provides the support needed to complete the mission of the DPS. The Records and Communication Section (RCC) of the SSB maintains the communications network that dispatches patrols and emergency services, as well as all incident reports. SSB also ensures that each officer is properly equipped and trained.

TRAINING

New police appointees must successfully complete an intensive eight-week program at the Federal Law Enforcement Training Center in Glynco, Georgia. Training includes police procedures, first aid, criminal law, search and seizure, human relations, firearms, and self-defense techniques. Annual in-service training is provided in Washington, D.C.

Defense Protective Service (DPS) Security Officers provide security for the Joint Chiefs of Staff. (Photo courtesy of the Defense Protective Service, Department of Defense.

QUALIFICATIONS

Applicants must:

- be a U.S. citizen

- have a high school diploma or equivalent

- possess a valid automobile drivers license

- successfully complete a background investigation

- successfully complete a basic training program

- undergo a physical exam to comply with DoD regulations

- have 20/100 vision correctable to 20/20

- have weight in proportion to height

For additional information, visit the DPS online at http://www.dtic.mil/ref/Security/Security.htm or call 703-693-3685. To Apply online, go to: http://www.hsrc.osd.mil or submit an SF-171 for federal employment to:

Human Resources Center
5001 Eisenhower Avenue
Room 2E22
Alexandria, Virginia 22333-0001

DEFENSE SECURITY SERVICE

MISSION

As a Department of Defense (DoD) agency, the Defense Security Service (DSS), formerly known as the Defense Investigative Service, conducts personnel security investigations, provides security products and services to other members of the national security community, and offers comprehensive security education and training to DoD and other government entities. Although no longer chartered as a law enforcement agency, the DSS offers the advantage of integrating counterintelligence into its core security disciplines through training programs, policy development, and operational support to field elements to complement its three primary missions: The Personnel Security Investigations Program (PSI); the Industrial Security Program (ISP); and the Security Education, Training, and Awareness Program.

The mission of DSS is realized through the efforts of approximately 2,500 employees located throughout the U.S. and Puerto Rico. Almost one-half of the DSS work force is comprised of special agents who accomplish approximately 400,000 personnel security investigations each year. Another 220 DSS Industrial Security Representatives oversee, advise, and assist more than 11,000 contractor facilities involved with classified contracts and research/development efforts.

HISTORICAL REVIEW

Until the early 1970s, Department of Defense personnel security investigations were conducted by the Army Intelligence Command, the Naval Investigative Service, and the Air Force Office of Special Investigations on civilian and industrial employees as well as on military personnel. As a result of studies completed in the early 1970s by a Blue Ribbon Defense Panel and the Office of Management and Budget, it was concluded that the military services were duplicating office locations, geographical coverage, communications, administration and training. It was further determined that personnel security investigations were a noncombatant function in which consolidation could lead to savings. Shortly thereafter, President Richard M. Nixon approved creation of an Office of Defense Investigation.

Recommendations were made to the Secretary of Defense to establish the Defense Investigative Service, effective January 1, 1972, and to assign the new agency responsibility for the Department of Defense personnel security investigative program within the United States. With this action, the Secretary clearly separated the personnel security investigative function from the intelligence function within the Department of Defense. The military investigative agencies retained the personnel security investigative mission overseas along with the funds and personnel to accomplish that mission. On October 2, 1972, the Defense Investigative Service became fully operational, forming its field organization from portions of the existing military service investigative agencies.

Over the ensuing years, the functional mission of the Defense Investigative Service underwent several major changes. In October 1977, at the direction of the Secretary of Defense, a Special Investigative Unit was established within DIS to supervise the conduct of criminal investigations and fraud prevention surveys. The Special Investigations Unit became the Defense Criminal Investigative Service in 1981. The largest functional change occurred on October 1, 1980, when, at the direction of the Deputy Secretary of Defense, administration of the Defense Industrial Security Program, the Key Asset Protection Program, and the Arms, Ammunition, and Explosives Security Program were transferred from the Defense Logistics Agency to the Defense Investigative Service. Like the personnel security investigative mission, the industrial security programs had previously been accomplished by the three military departments or, as in the case of the Key Asset Protection Program, the Department of the Army.

Today, the Defense Security Service is no longer chartered as a law enforcement agency. However, as a separate agency of the Department of Defense under the direction, authority, and control of the Deputy Under Secretary of Defense for Security Policy, the DSS is chartered as a national security, personnel security investigative, and industrial security agency.

FUNCTIONS AND ACTIVITIES

Personnel Security Investigations Program

DSS administers one of the most comprehensive and enduring Personnel Security Investigations (PSI) programs offered in the defense industry. The background investigations conducted by special agents on DoD military, civilian, and contractor personnel are used to determine an individual's suitability to enter the armed forces, access classified information, or hold a sensitive position within DoD.

Industrial Security Program

DSS administers three industrial security programs, of which the National Industrial Security Program (NISP) is the largest. Under the NISP, DSS Industrial Security Representatives oversee cleared contractor facilities and assist the organizations' management staff and Facility Security Officers in formulating their security programs. The remaining two DSS Industrial Security programs, the Arms, Ammunition and Explosives (AA&E) Program and the Critical Assets Assurance Program (CAAP), provide protection for arms, ammunition and explosives and DoD Critical Assets and Infrastructure, respectively.

Security Education, Training, and Awareness Program

The Security Education, Training, and Awareness Program is administered by the DSS Academy (DSSA), which provides security education, training, and awareness courses to over 4,500 students within the DoD and Defense Industry each year. Through formal classroom training, computer-based training, correspondence/distance learning, and tele-training, the Academy offers a curriculum focusing on the core security disciplines while integrating counterintelligence and information systems security.

The Department of Defense Polygraph Institute

The Department of Defense Polygraph Institute (DoDPI), integrated into the DSS organizational structure in 1997, provides education forensic psychophysiology for all federal agencies with polygraph programs. Additionally, the Institute facilitates the continuing education needs of all federally certified polygraphers to further their expertise in the fields of security, law enforcement and intelligence. DSS special agents also receive training in some of the courses offered by DoDPI. In addition to its commitment to education, DoDPI has a research mission that focuses on the field of credibility assessment and future psychophysiological detection of deception (PDD) methodologies. The DoDPI also oversees the federal government's quality control program for PDD through a detailed inspection process conducted by the Quality Assurance Program, which is also responsible for establishing PDD examination standards and inspection criteria.

Visit the Defense Security Web site at http://www.dss.mil to learn more about the organization or write to:

Office of Congressional and Public Affairs
Defense Security Service
1340 Braddock Place
Alexandria, Virginia 22314
Telephone: 703-325-9471

NATIONAL SECURITY AGENCY/CENTRAL SECURITY SERVICE (NSA/CSS)

MISSION

The National Security Agency/Central Security Service is the Nation's cryptologic organization. Its two-fold mission is to protect U.S. information systems and to produce foreign signals intelligence information.

The signals intelligence (SIGINT) side of the mission is to intercept and analyze foreign adversaries' communications signals, many of which are protected by codes and other complex countermeasures. The Agency collects, processes, and disseminates intelligence information from foreign signals for national foreign intelligence and counterintelligence purposes and in support of military operations. The information systems security side of the mission is to prevent foreign adversaries from gaining access to classified U.S. national security information. It does this by providing solutions, products and services, and by conducting defensive information operations to achieve information assurance for infrastructures critical to U.S. national security interests.

The NSA/CSS exists to protect the nation. Specifically, it provides intelligence products and services to the White House; executive agencies, such as the Central Intelligence Agency and State Department; the Chairman of the Joint Chiefs of Staff (JCS); military Commanders-in-Chief (CINCs) and component commands; military departments; multinational forces; and our allies. In addition, it provides information assurance products and services to our government customers and to government contractors.

Although the NSA/CSS is not a law enforcement agency, its mission does include providing signals intelligence on such matters as international terrorism and international drug trafficking, and it also contributes to the efforts of the federal intelligence and law enforcement communities through its communications and information assurance programs.

HISTORICAL REVIEW

President Truman and the National Security Council issued a revised version of the National Security Council Intelligence Directive (NSCID) No. 9 on 24 October 1952, which resulted in the formation of the NSA on 4 November 1952. The Central Security Service (CSS) was established by Presidential Directive in 1972 to promote full partnership between the NSA and the cryptologic elements of the Armed Forces. Combining the NSA and CSS provided a more unified Department of Defense cryptologic effort.

FUNCTIONS AND ACTIVITIES

NSA/CSS conducts one of the U.S. government's leading research and development programs in the field of specialized communications equipment. Some of these R & D projects have significantly advanced the state of the art in the scientific and business worlds. An early interest in cryptanalytic research led to the first large-scale computers and the first solid-state computer, predecessors to the modern computer. NSA also pioneered efforts in flexible storage capabilities, which led to the development of the tape cassette and made groundbreaking developments in semiconductor technology.

QUALIFICATIONS

NSA/CSS is particularly interested in applicants from the areas of computer science, mathematics, language, and engineering. Because of the nature of the work, the application process is lengthy, consisting of physical, psychological, and polygraph exams, interviews, and background checks for a security clearance. At a minimum, applicants should be U.S. citizens. Several disciplines at NSA/CSS have intern programs and the Agency has a number of student programs.

For further information, visit the NSA Web site: http://www.nsa.gov or call the Office of Public and Media Affairs at 301-688-6524.

DEPARTMENT OF THE AIR FORCE

AIR FORCE OFFICE OF SPECIAL INVESTIGATIONS

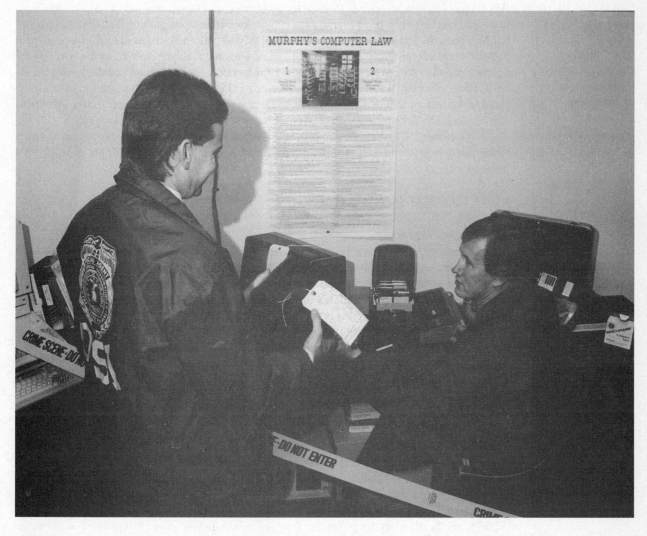

AFOSI Special Agents examine evidence. (Photo courtesy of the Air Force Office of Special Investigations, Department of the Navy.)

MISSION

The Air Force Office of Special Investigations (AFOSI), with headquarters at Andrews Air Force Base (AFB), Maryland, is a field operating agency which has been the Air Force's major investigative service since August 1, 1948. The agency reports to the Inspector General, Office of the Secretary of the Air Force.

AFOSI makes investigative services available to commanders of all Air Force activities. AFOSI seeks to identify, investigate and neutralize espionage, terrorism, fraud and other major criminal activities that may threaten Air Force and Department of Defense resources. The command focuses on four priorities:

- ■ to exploit counterintelligence activities for force protection

- ■ to resolve violent crime impacting the Air Force

- ■ to combat threats to Air Force information systems and technologies

- ■ to defeat and deter acquisition fraud

HISTORICAL REVIEW

AFOSI was founded on Aug. 1, 1948, at the suggestion of a Congressional oversight committee to establish a centrally directed agency to conduct Air Force investigations. The first secretary of the Air Force, W. Stuart Symington, created AFOSI and patterned it after the FBI. He appointed Special Agent Joseph Carroll, an assistant to FBI Director J. Edgar Hoover, as the first AFOSI commander and charged him with providing independent, unbiased and centrally directed investigations of criminal activity in the Air Force. AFOSI evolved with the addition of criminal, fraud, and counterintelligence missions overseas and worldwide personnel protective antiterrorism services. On December 31, 1971, AFOSI became a separate operating agency.

In October 1972, the stateside personnel security investigations mission was turned over to the newly organized Defense Investigative Service. Overseas, AFOSI still performs personnel security investigations.

FUNCTIONS AND ACTIVITIES

Counterintelligence

The counterintelligence mission counters the threat to Air Force security posed by hostile intelligence services and terrorist groups. AFOSI manages offensive and defensive activities to detect, counter, and destroy the effectiveness of hostile intelligence services and terrorist groups that target the Air Force for espionage. This includes investigating the crimes of espionage, terrorism, technology transfer, and computer infiltration. The counterintelligence mission also includes providing personal protection to senior Air Force officers and other officials, as well as supervising an extensive antiterrorism program in geographic areas of heightened terrorist activity.

Criminal Investigations

The vast majority of AFOSI's investigative activities involve felony crimes, including robbery, rape, assault, major burglaries, drug trafficking, and others.

Fraud Investigations

A significant amount of AFOSI investigative resources are assigned to fraud investigations, such as violations of the public trust involving Air Force contracting matters, appropriated and non-appropriated funds activities, computer systems, pay and allowance matters, environmental matters, acquiring and disposing of Air Force property, and major administrative irregularities. AFOSI uses fraud surveys to determine the existence, location, and extent of fraud in Air Force operations or programs and provides briefings to base and command-level resource managers to help identify and prevent fraud involving Air Force or DoD resources.

Information Operations

The Air Force is now countering a global security threat to its information systems. The role in support of Information Operations recognizes that future threats to the Air Force, and the response to these threats, will occur in cyberspace. AFOSI's support to Information Operations comes in many facets. AFOSI's computer-crime investigators provide rapid worldwide response to intrusions into Air Force systems. In addition, AFOSI is the administrator of the Air Force Technical Surveillance Countermeasures Program.

Technology Protection

The desires of potential adversaries to acquire or mimic the technological advances of the U.S. Air Force have heightened the need to protect critical Air Force technologies and collateral data. The AFOSI Research and Technology Protection Program provides focused, comprehensive counterintelligence and core mission investigative services to safeguard Air Force technologies, programs, critical program information, personnel and facilities.

Specialized Services

AFOSI has numerous specialists who are invaluable in the successful resolution of investigations. They include technical specialists, polygraphers, behavioral scientists, computer experts, and forensic advisers.

Computer Forensics

AFOSI is the DoD's executive agent for both the Defense Computer Forensics Laboratory and the Defense Computer Investigations Training Program. The lab provides processing, analysis, and diagnosis of counterintelligence, criminal, and fraud computer evidence. The training program provides computer investigation and computer forensics training to DoD investigators and examiners.

Antiterrorism

To meet the increasing challenges presented by worldwide terrorism, AFOSI's Antiterrorism Specialty Team complements the Air Force's force protection team. Operating out of Lackland AFB, Texas, this highly trained and specialized unit stands ready on a moment's notice to deploy globally to provide antiterrorism, counterintelligence information collection, and investigative services to Air Force personnel and units.

TRAINING

To perform its investigative mission, AFOSI recruits, selects, and trains its own agents. Officer, enlisted, and civilian candidates attend a mandatory, eleven-week Special Investigator Course at the U.S. Air Force Special Investigations Academy at Andrews. The basic investigator course includes instruction in law, investigative theory, report writing, forensics, interview techniques, and other subjects to prepare special agents for the challenges of investigative duty. Upon graduation, new AFOSI special agents spend a twelve-month probationary period in the field. Upon successful completion of the probationary period, the agents may return to Andrews for further specialized training. Selected special agents attend twelve weeks of technical training to acquire electronic, photographic, and other skills required to perform technical surveillance countermeasures. Experienced agents selected for polygraph duties attend a fourteen-week DoD course.

Beginning in 2002, the basic investigations training for AFOSI recruits will be conducted at the Federal Law Enforcement Training Center, located in Glynco, Georgia.

QUALIFICATIONS

AFOSI special agents are Air Force officers, enlisted members, or civilians. Different entrance rules apply to each category. Those interested may visit the OSI Web site at http://www.dtic.mil/afosi or contact the nearest OSI unit. You may also call the OSI Public Affairs Directorate at 240-857-0989, or write to:

HQAFOSI/PA
1535 Command Drive, Suite C-309
Andrews AFB, Maryland 20762

AIR FORCE SECURITY FORCES

MISSION

The primary mission of security forces units is to provide security to help ensure operational readiness and to protect war fighting resources. This mission is accomplished through a system of base and area entry control points, vehicle patrols, foot patrols, and sensor detection equipment. In addition, the security forces units at 102 locations worldwide are assigned to seven major commands and provide base law enforcement services similar to those provided to communities by civilian police agencies. Their responsibilities include traffic control, crime prevention, and investigations. Another key mission is the protection of classified and sensitive information. This mission is done through several security programs such as information, industrial, personnel, and physical security, as well as systems security engineering management.

HISTORICAL REVIEW

The position of Air Provost Marshal came into being in March 1943 at the direction of General H.H. 'Hap' Arnold, Commander of the Army-Air Forces. When the Air Force became a separate entity in January 1948, its military police became air police. The Air Provost Marshal came under the Air Force Inspector General. The organization title became Director of Security and Law Enforcement in 1960. The term air police became security police in 1967. Then, in 1997, it was changed to security forces.

The security police function left the inspector general umbrella in 1975 and began reporting directly to the Air Force Chief of Staff. The title of Chief of Security Police then replaced the title Director. In 1978, the security police headquarters moved from Washington, D.C., to Kirtland AFB, New Mexico, and became the Air Force Office of Security Police (AFOSP), a separate operating agency, again under the Inspector General. In 1991, as part of an Air Staff reorganization, the Chief of Security Police was aligned directly under the Air Force Chief of Staff with the policy and plans portion of the staff, moving to the Pentagon, Washington, D.C.

A little over half of the AF Security Police staff remained at Kirtland AFB as a field operating agency, the Air Force Security Police Agency (AFSPA). AFSPA reported directly to the Air Force Chief of Security Police. AFSPA was comprised of four directorates: security, law enforcement and training, resources, and corrections.

As a result of the Khobar Towers bombing in Saudi Arabia, AFSPA was reorganized in 1997 and moved to Lackland AFB, Texas. The new organization, designated the Air Force Security Forces Center, consists of three units: the Headquarters, the AF Force Protection Battlelab, and the 820th Security Forces Group.

FUNCTIONS AND ACTIVITIES

The Headquarters Air Force Security Forces Center (HQ AFSFC) is commanded by the dual-hatted Air Force Director of Security Forces. HQ AFSFC is an extension of the Pentagon staff, conducting staff studies dealing with a wide range of topics, including nuclear security, force protection, base defense, police services, combat arms and security forces training, equipment management, and military working dogs. The Headquarters consists of four divisions: Force Protection, Operations, Corrections, and Training and Combat Arms. The Headquarters also includes three geographically separated units conducting confinement operations at Miramar, California; Fort Leavenworth, Kansas; and Charleston, South Carolina.

The Force Protection Battlelab's commander reports to the HQ AFSFC commander. The Force Protection Battlelab's mission is to rapidly identify and prove the worth of innovative force protection ideas which improve the ability of the Air Force to execute it's core competencies and joint warfighting. The Battlelab rapidly measures the worth of new ideas involving changes to the way the Air Force currently organizes, trains, equips, executes, plans, and commands. Subsequently, the innovations are presented to the Air Force senior leadership for consideration and implementation.

The 820th Security Forces Group provides a highly trained, rapidly deployable "first-in" force protection capability to any operating location in support of the USAF Global Engagement mission. The 820th gives the Air Force a totally dedicated composite unit for force protection, drawing from many disciplines, not just security forces. The unit is composed of personnel from security forces, the Office of Special Investigations, civil engineering, logistics and supply, communications, intelligence, administration, personnel, and medical career fields, providing the capability to assess each threat and act accordingly.   In 2001, the 820th moved from Lackland AFB to Moody AFB Georgia.

TRAINING

When Security Forces (SF) was formed in 1997, the dynamics of world events necessitated change in order to defeat a known enemy and emerging threats. The edict was to merge separate career paths (security and law enforcement), each with differing missions that did not intersect, into a singular fighting force. The ability to develop core skill sets designed to produce an expeditionary airman able to perform in garrison, as well as deploy and protect national assets supporting a variety of worldwide taskings was essential. A typical three-skill-level airman graduates from a fifty-one-day tech school having learned basic security, police services, and ground combat skills. Airmen arrive at their first base responsible for knowing and implementing over 187 diverse core tasks comprised of hundreds of sub-tasks and line items. SF specialists will spend hundreds of hours in recurring and proficiency training throughout their first year, honing core task knowledge and expeditionary war fighting skills. They receive one formal quality evaluation annually for each major task certification (such as installation controller, security response team member, etc.) as well as dozens of informal performance reviews by supervisors, flight chiefs, team and squad leaders, and members in the chain of command.

The 341st Training Squadron, at Lackland AFB Texas, trains military working dogs and handlers for all branches of the services as well as the Federal Aviation Administration.

The 342nd Training Squadron, Lackland AFB Texas, provides initial skills training for SF officers and SF personnel retraining into the combat arms shred. The 342nd also conducts a variety of other advanced and specialized courses. These include advanced officer and enlisted ground combat skills courses, various weapons courses, traffic management, accident investigation, the enlisted craftsman course, and an electronic security sensor course.

The 343rd Training Squadron (Security Forces Academy), Lackland AFB Texas, provides initial skills training to all security forces enlisted personnel in the areas of ground combat skills, police services, and installation security. The 343rd also provides oversight of the Naval Corrections Courses.

For further information, write to:
SAF/PAM
1690 Air Force Pentagon
Room 5C879
Washington, D.C. 20330-1690
Telephone: 800-423-USAF or 703-697-6061

DEPARTMENT OF THE ARMY

CRIMINAL INVESTIGATION COMMAND

CID agents, during the Gulf War, stand beside Humvee loaded with Stinger missiles. (Photo courtesy of the Army Criminal Investigation Command, Department of the Army.)

MISSION

The mission of the U.S. Army Criminal Investigation Command is to investigate felony crime of Army interest. Serious crimes are defined as felonies punishable under the Uniform Code of Military Justice. The U.S. Army Criminal Investigation Command (USACIDC or CID) also provides worldwide criminal investigative support to all U.S. Army elements; deploys on short notice in support of contingency operations worldwide; conducts other sensitive or special interest investigations as required or directed; conducts protective service operations for the Department of Defense, Joint Chiefs of Staff, and the Department of the Army; provides forensic laboratory support for Department of Defense investigative agencies; and maintains the repository for Army crime records.

In addition to the basic mission, CID provides felony crime investigative support to field commanders, which includes: general crimes (against persons or property), economic crime, and counter-drug operations.

Besides peacetime functions, CID's contingency operations and battlefield missions include logistics security; criminal intelligence; criminal investigations, expanded to include war crimes; antiterrorism; protective service operations, and force protection operations. Force protection protects soldiers, civilian employees, family members, facilities, and equipment in garrison and deployed scenarios.

HISTORICAL REVIEW

Prior to World War I, the Army relied on private agencies, such as the Pinkerton Detective Agency, to investigate serious military crime. In 1917, the Military Police Corps was established to function as a uniformed police force serving the American Expeditionary Forces in France. But as the crimes encountered by the Expeditionary Forces mounted, the need for a detective element became apparent. In 1918, General John J. Pershing, commanding the Army Expeditionary Forces, directed his provost marshal to organize a criminal investigation division. This action is the first recorded instance of an Army criminal investigation capability. It is also the origin of the Criminal Investigation Division (CID).

During the years between World War I and World War II, the Army returned to its former policy of relying on local civilian law enforcement officials for investigating crime in the Army. When America entered the second World War, the CID was reconstructed and provided investigative support to local area commanders. In January 1944, a Criminal Investigation Division of the Provost Marshal General's Office was established to provide staff supervision over criminal investigations as well as to coordinate investigations between commands and set standards for investigations.

A 1964 study called "Project Security Shield" pinpointed the need to centralize the Army's investigative efforts and in 1965 an attempt was made to organize CID groups corresponding to specific Army areas in the United States. Later this concept was expanded to include Europe and Korea. CID was reorganized in 1969 and became the U.S. Army CID Agency.

In 1971, Secretary of Defense Melvin R. Laird directed that centralization of Army CID be completed and a criminal investigation command be restructured to have control over all CID activities worldwide. With this order, the U.S. Army Criminal Investigation Command, designated as USACIDC, was established as a major Army command. The "D" was retained in the acronym for historical reasons and also to avoid confusion with the old Counter Intelligence Corps, known as the CIC.

Today, USACIDC is organized with a headquarters and six subordinate operating elements: four regions, a separate crime laboratory, and the U.S. Army Crime Records Center.

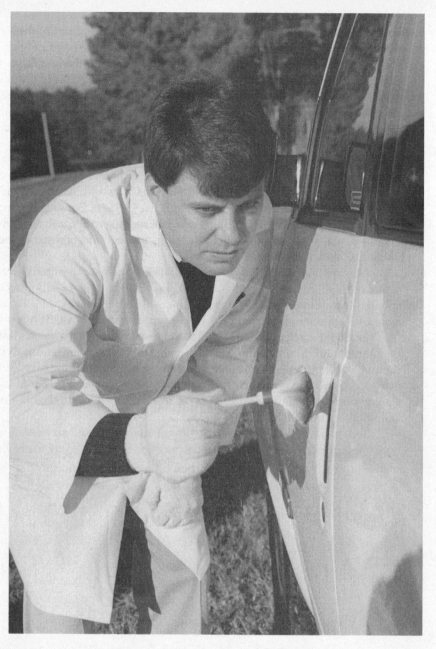

Army Criminal Investigation Command Examiner dusts a car door for fingerprints. (Photo courtesy of the Army Criminal Investigation Command, Department of the Army.)

FUNCTIONS AND ACTIVITIES

3rd Military Police Group (CID)

The 3rd Military Police Group (CID), headquartered in Fort Gillem, Georgia, is responsible for all felony criminal investigation matters with a U.S. Army interest throughout the eastern half of the U.S., the Caribbean, Central and South America (with the exception of Mexico), Puerto Rico, and Southwest Asia. They are also prepared to conduct stability and support operations as directed during contingency operations.

6th Military Police Group (CID)

The 6th Military Police Group (CID), headquartered in Fort Lewis, Washington, is responsible for all felony criminal investigation matters with a U.S. Army interest throughout the 22 states west of the Mississippi River, including Alaska and Hawaii, and throughout the Pacific Rim, focused primarily in South Korea, Japan, and Okinawa. Key Army field elements include the Pacific Command and the 25th Infantry Division (Light), Hawaii; Eighth Army and 2nd Infantry Division, Korea; I Corps, Fort Lewis, Washington; and III Corps, 4th Infantry Division (Mechanized), and the 1st Cavalry Division, Fort Hood, Texas.

701st Military Police Group (CID)

The 701st Military Police Group (CID), headquartered at Fort Belvoir, Virginia, conducts sensitive, classified investigations, major fraud investigations associated with the Army's acquisition programs, and computer intrusion investigations and provides protective services for key DoD, DA, and visiting foreign officials. As part of the 701st MPG CID, the Computer Crime Investigative Unit (CCIU) conducts investigations involving intrusions into Army computer network/ systems. Evolving technology and the genius of intruders constantly challenges highly skilled agents of this unit. Intruders range from nonmalicious hackers to those intent upon disrupting a network or Web site to foreign intelligence probes. CCIU investigations have led to arrests of soldiers, civilians, and foreign nationals throughout the world who were engaged in cybercrime directed at the U.S. Army.

USACIDC special agents conduct an interview in the field during Operation Desert Storm. (Photo courtesy of the Army Criminal Investigation Command, Department of the Army.)

202nd Military Police Group (CID)

The 202nd Military Police Group (CID), located at Stem Kaserne in Seckenheim, Germany, provides command and control over primarily tactical CID units in Europe. Elements of the Second Region provide thorough, timely, and quality criminal investigative support to commanders and military communities of the U.S. Army, Europe, and supports contingency operations throughout the European, African, Middle East, and Southwest Asian areas of responsibility.

Special agents assigned to the 202nd MP Group (CID) operate within more than 30 countries and routinely conduct investigative operations in the Netherlands, Italy, Hungary, Croatia, and Bosnia-Herzegovina.

U.S. Army Criminal Investigation Laboratory

The U.S. Army Criminal Investigation Laboratory (USACIL), located at Fort Gillem, Georgia, provides forensic laboratory services to DoD investigative agencies and other federal law enforcement agencies. The USACIL also operates an Army school to train forensic laboratory examiners and manages the USACIDC criminalistics and visual information programs.

Historically, the USACIL system of three labs included a laboratory in North Africa, then Europe (1943-96), Japan (1948-93), and the United States (1945-Present). With one remaining laboratory, the USACIL now provides worldwide forensics support from its current location since 1983, at Fort Gillem, Georgia.

The USACIL has been accredited by the American Society of Crime Laboratory Directors (ASCLD) since 1985. The laboratory provides state-of-the-art forensic examinations in the following disciplines: drug chemistry, trace evidence, serology/DNA, latent prints, questioned documents, imaging and technical services, and firearms and toolmarks.

Crime Records Center

The U.S. Army Crime Records Center (CRC), is located with the USACIDC headquarters at Fort Belvoir, Virginia. The CRC is a multifunctional center, supporting not only the Army and this command, but also foreign, federal, state, and local law enforcement agencies. Established in 1950, the CRC receives, safeguards, maintains, and disseminates information from Army law enforcement records. The center has accumulated 2.5 million reports. It also serves as the Army's Freedom of Information and Privacy Act authority, and annually responds to approximately 2,000 such requests.

Another major function of the center is to manage the Army law enforcement Polygraph Program. CID polygraphers conduct more than 1,700 criminal specific polygraph examinations a year.

CID Headquarters Building

The CID headquarters building is on Fort Belvoir, Virginia. The headquarters was dedicated June 23, 1995 and honors an American hero, Corporal Daniel D. Schoonover, of the 13th Combat Engineer Battalion, who posthumously received the Medal of Honor for bravery during the Korean War.

TRAINING

After a fifteen-week training course at the U.S. Army Military Police School, agents spend their first year as apprentice agents. They are fully accredited upon successful completion of the apprenticeship. Warrant officers must have at least two years of experience as an enlisted criminal investigator before applying for warrant officer positions.

All agents receive advanced training in specialized investigative disciplines throughout their careers. Selected agents also receive advanced training at the FBI Academy and Scotland Yard. Others hold a master's degree in forensic science from George Washington University and the Armed Forces Institute of Pathology.

QUALIFICATIONS

CID agent applicants must already be in the Army and must meet strict standards of qualification. CID special agents are both enlisted soldiers and warrant officers. They must pass a rigorous physical and mental screening process and meet other qualifications as well.

The minimum qualifications to become a special agent are to be on active duty with a rank of specialist or higher. It normally takes two years of active duty to make the rank of specialist. Agents must also be U.S. citizens, at least 21 years old, have two years or equivalent of college, have a general technical score of at least 110, meet Army physical fitness standards, and have six months police experience.

Civilian special agents are classified as criminal investigators under Office of Personnel Management guidelines. To qualify for a criminal investigator position, an individual must meet specific criteria as established by the Office of Personnel Management in the Handbook for General Schedule Positions.

For further information, visit the Army CID website at http://www.belvoir.army.mil/cidc or write to:

Army Criminal Investigation Command
6010 - 6th Street
Fort Belvoir, Virginia 22060
Telephone: 703-806-0374

MILITARY POLICE CORPS

MISSION
Military Police soldiers serve the United States during times of peace, conflict, and war. They train for and perform the critical functions of combat support, traffic control, law enforcement, criminal investigations, civil disturbance operations, physical security, and corrections.

HISTORICAL REVIEW
Throughout the history of armies, soldiers have been delegated to perform the duties of military police. However, it was not until the War for American Independence, when the United States Army adopted the organization and regulations of the British system, that a provost corps was established in the United States.

From the Revolutionary War until World War II, soldiers from the ranks were detailed to perform police duties or a provost corps was organized for the duration of a specific conflict such as the Civil War. On September 26, 1941, the Military Police Corps became a permanent combat service support branch of the United States Army, and it has maintained an active role in the Army since that time.

During the Vietnam "Tet Offensive," the Military Police Corps merited special recognition, resulting in the Corps being redesignated a combat support arm and branch of the U.S. Army.

In 1983, Military Police soldiers participated in the invasion of Grenada, and they have since been deployed to Panama, Honduras, the Persian Gulf, Somalia, Haiti, Cuba, Bosnia, and Kosovo.

Army Military Police team on maneuvers. (Photo courtesy of U.S. Army Chemical and Military Police Centers, Fort Leonard Wood, Missouri.)

FUNCTIONS AND ACTIVITIES

Military Police (MP) support the combat commander's mission to win the battle. The five MP functions are: Maneuver and Mobility Support Operations, Area Security Operations, Internment and Resettlement Operations, Law and Order Operations, and Police Intelligence Operations.

Maneuver and Mobility Support Operations involve numerous measures and actions necessary to support the commander's freedom of movement in his area of responsibility. The Military Police expedite the forward and lateral movement of combat resources and ensure that commanders get forces, supplies, and equipment when and where they are needed.

The MP function of Area Security Operations is designed to protect the force and enhance the freedom of units to conduct their assigned missions. As part of their Area Security missions, the MP serve as the eyes and ears of the battlefield commander by seeking out the enemy and reporting information obtained by reconnaissance patrols. The MP conduct area and zone reconnaissance, screens, surveillance, and counter-surveillance to gain information to guard against unexpected attack. The Military Police also can serve as the primary response force for the rear area. They are trained and equipped to fight enemies in the rear area that threaten military operations.

Internment and Resettlement Operations include the evacuation, processing, control and release of enemy prisoners of war, civilian internees, and U.S. military prisoners, as well as refugee resettlement.

The Law and Order Operations include law enforcement, criminal investigations, U.S. Customs operations, and law and order training. The MP dedicate assets to conduct law enforcement operations based on the commander's needs. Military Police investigate offenses against U.S. forces and property committed by persons subject to military law. The MP also support the U.S. Customs Service, the U.S. Department of Agriculture, and other federal enforcement agencies.

Police Intelligence Operations support, enhance, and contribute to the commander's protection program and situational awareness by collecting information that may affect the battlefield environment. Police Intelligence involves the analysis of criminal, police, and combat information within an area of responsibility to provide the combat commander with the most accurate picture of the battlefield.

TRAINING

Before receiving Military Police training, soldiers undergo eight weeks of Initial Entry Training, often referred to as "basic training."

The U.S. Army Military Police School, Fort Leonard Wood, Missouri, provides instruction annually to some 14,000 Army, Air Force, Navy, Marine, civilians, and international military students.

The Military Police School also provides commanders with doctrinal and training publications to train MPs in the field and develops operational doctrine and how-to-fight tactics for Military Police employment in any environment.

In addition, the school performs branch and personnel proponent functions for all Military Police officers, warrant officers and enlisted personnel worldwide.

For more information, visit the Web site http://www.wood.army.mil or contact:
Department of the Army
U.S. Army Military Police School
Building 3203, Bandholtz Wing
Fort Leonard Wood, Missouri 65473
(573) 596-0131, Extension 3-7801
or call the Office of Public Affairs at (573) 563-4013.

DEPARTMENT OF THE NAVY

NAVAL CRIMINAL INVESTIGATIVE SERVICE

Naval Criminal Investigative Service (NCIS) agents relax after a successful operation. (Photo courtesy of the Department of the Navy.)

MISSION

The Naval Criminal Investigative Service (NCIS) is a worldwide federal law enforcement organization whose mission is to protect and serve the Navy and Marine Corps. NCIS investigates felony crimes, conducts counterintelligence, and oversees approximately 1,600 employees, 850 of whom are civilian special agents posted at more than 140 locations around the globe, including ships and carriers.

NCIS' mission expanded during the 1980s to include such additional security functions as the operation of the Navy's Antiterrorist Alert Center; management of the Navy's Law Enforcement and Physical Security Program, which includes the Master-at-Arms rating and the Military Working Dog Program; management of the Navy's Information and Personnel Security Program; and the establishment and operation of the Central Adjudication facility.

HISTORICAL REVIEW

NCIS special agents are the successors of the operatives and agents who served as part of the Office of Naval Intelligence (ONI) in World War I. ONI's responsibilities grew in the years that followed World War I, and in 1939, President Franklin Delano Roosevelt directed ONI to investigate Navy cases relating to sabotage, espionage, and subversive activities.

During World War II, ONI's mission continued to expand to include personnel security inquiries, war fraud cases, and other intelligence-related activities. Later, the investigation of other felonious crimes was added to the mission of ONI.

After World War II, a small group of civilian special agents were retained and their jurisdiction was extended by the Secretary of Navy. When the U.S. entered the Korean Conflict in 1950, a major build-up of the civilian Special Agent corps began.

The name Naval Investigative Service (NIS) was adopted on February 4, 1966, to distinguish the Navy's investigative service from the rest of ONI.

As it did in World Wars I and II and Korea, NIS served in Vietnam, and in recent years its special agents have served in Lebanon, the Persian Gulf, and in other parts of the Middle East.

NIS assumed responsibility for the Navy's Law Enforcement and Physical Security Program in 1982, and in early 1984 established the Navy Antiterrorist Alert Center, a 24-hour operational intelligence center providing indications and warning to Department of the Navy assets worldwide.

Following a major espionage case in 1985 involving the arrest of John Walker, the mission of NIS was expanded and elevated to command status with a rear admiral as its commander. Later that year, NISCOM added the Information and Security Department, and in January 1986, initiated the Central Adjudication Facility.

In 1992, the name of the agency was changed to the Naval Criminal Investigative Service and the first civilian director was appointed.

FUNCTIONS AND ACTIVITIES

Criminal Investigations Department

Unlawful acts by or against Department of the Navy personnel (including civilian employees and contractors) which result in property damage, financial loss, or serious personal injury, carry the additional threat of impairing the Navy's ability to effectively carry out its mission.

NCIS special agents investigate felonies such as homicide, rape, arson, robbery, narcotics trafficking, larceny, destruction or theft of government property, and procurement fraud.

At shore installations overseas and around the United States, NCIS special agents are active in antidrug operations. Overseas, teams of NCIS special agents join with local authorities in cooperative drug sweeps prior to U.S. Navy ship visits to foreign ports. In major U.S. cities, they work with other federal and local law enforcement agencies by conducting undercover operations to gather evidence against drug dealers looking for military customers.

NCIS Regional Fraud Units, dedicated to the investigation of major procurement fraud and staffed with special agents trained as fraud specialists, are located in the continental United States near major contracting centers and are supplemented by fraud squads and smaller contingents at other locations where specialized expertise is needed.

NCIS fraud agents continually investigate cases of conflict of interest, antitrust, bank fraud, wire fraud, false statements in contracting, bribery, kickbacks, cost mischarging, product substitution, false quality certification, racketeering, and environmental crime.

Counterintelligence Department

Counterintelligence is the business of protecting Naval information from espionage, Naval personnel against subversion, and Navy installations and equipment from sabotage. In the U.S., NCIS counterintelligence activities are coordinated with the Federal Bureau of Investigation; overseas they are coordinated with the Central Intelligence Agency.

Case Illustration

Some counterintelligence operations involve the use of double agents who pose as traitors in order to surface and apprehend hostile intelligence service agents.

Operation Station Zebra

Operation Station Zebra, conducted jointly by NCIS, the Royal Canadian Mounted Police (RCMP) and the Canadian Security Intelligence Service, occurred in St. John's, Newfoundland, and utilized a woman Navy lieutenant as the double agent.

The double agent walked onboard a Russian scientific research vessel that was visiting St. John's and met with the captain and the chief mate. After portraying herself as a disgruntled naval officer, she left an address where she could be contacted.

Two months later, a man who identified himself as "Michael" contacted her and a series of meetings followed during which she was given money for classified information. In addition, she was given a camera modified for document photography, secret writing materials, a contact address in East Berlin, and instructions to collect sensitive information such as what the United States knew about the acoustics of Russian submarines and U.S. methods of tracking them.

Their final meeting occurred in a room at the Hotel Newfoundland. By this time, "Michael" had been identified as a Canadian-born son of a Hungarian emigre. Unknown to Michael, the room had been outfitted with audio and visual surveillance. As soon as he left the room, he was arrested.

Michael subsequently pleaded guilty to spying for the Russians and was sentenced in Canadian court to two concurrent nine-year prison terms.

Technical Services Department

After an NCIS special agent has completed one year of service, he or she may qualify to apply for the Polygraph Program or the Technical Surveillance Countermeasures (TSCM) Program, which are part of the NCIS Technical Services Department.

Those selected for the Polygraph Institute attend a three-month course at Fort McClellan, Alabama. Upon successful completion of that course, they must complete a six-month internship under the supervision of a senior polygraph examiner before they are certified.

NCIS special agents selected to become Technical Investigative Specialists receive a total of thirty-two weeks of intensive electronics training during their first year. Following that, they receive training in crime scene forensics, fingerprints, photography, arson investigation, forensic pathology, and security systems.

As TSCM agents, they conduct TSCM surveys and provide support to the field in areas such as audio intercepts (body wires), surveillance video, vehicle tracking, sensors and intrusion detection devices, body armor, and weapons.

Protective Operations

Assassination, kidnapping and hostage-taking are hazards faced by American military personnel at some overseas bases and diplomatic posts, and sometimes by foreign visitors to the United States.

NCIS special agents are frequently called upon to help prevent such acts by providing Protective Service Details (PSDs). Overseas, they work closely with security and police forces of the host countries. In the United States, they often work with the Secret Service, the Department of State Bureau of Diplomatic Security, and other military law enforcement agencies to provide protective service support for high-ranking personnel of the Department of Defense, the Department of the Navy, and for foreign dignitaries.

The PSD is a two-phase operation. The first consists of a comprehensive threat assessment to identify potential danger to the "principal," or person being protected. The second is 24-hour protection of the principal by specially trained teams of NCIS special agents.

SPECIAL AGENT AFLOAT

Qualified NCIS special agents serve aboard all aircraft carriers, generally for a one-year tour of duty, and occasionally aboard other major combatant vessels as needed.

As one of only a handful of civilians aboard an aircraft carrier, the NCIS special agent is responsible for all major criminal investigations and counterintelligence matters on the carrier and on all other ships of the accompanying battle group.

NCIS Special Agent identifies himself. (Photo courtesy of the Department of the Navy.)

TRAINING

Prospective agents come to NCIS from a wide variety of backgrounds: law enforcement, law, engineering, the military, and from other sectors of public and private business and industry. All are college graduates and all are required to complete a fourteen-week basic agent course at the Federal Law Enforcement Training Center (FLETC) at Glynco, Georgia.

The agent-trainee receives instruction in practical exercises, physical specialties, and fire-arms. Classroom instruction covers such matters as investigative techniques, criminal law and procedure, and the rules of evidence.

Practical exercises cover surveillance techniques, fingerprinting, raids and apprehensions, courtroom testimony and demeanor, and crime scene examinations.

Physical specialties include conditioning and instruction in unarmed self-defense. Firearms training includes the proficient use of weapons and survival under various tactical conditions.

In the course of their careers, NCIS special agents periodically receive advanced training in a number of specialized areas. Specialty training includes undercover operations, white collar crime, computer fraud, technical surveillance countermeasures, photography, forensics, counte-respionage, counterintelligence, and the polygraph.

NCIS special agents must be:

■ College graduates

■ 21 – 37 years old

■ U.S. citizens

■ willing to serve afloat

■ in excellent physical condition

■ pass an extensive background investigation

For more information, contact:
Naval Criminal Investigative Service Headquarters
Code 0025 AP
716 Sicard Street, SE
Washington Navy Yard
Washington, D.C. 20388-5388
Telephone: (202) 433-9544 (Government and Liaison Public Affairs Office)
Fax: (202) 433-0904

MASTER-AT-ARMS RATING

MISSION

There are about 1,700 members of the Master-at-Arms (MA) rating in the Navy. They are responsible for antiterrorism, force protection, and a variety of law enforcement and security functions.

MAs have a large number of afloat billets as well as ashore assignments in security detachments. They operate afloat brigs, handle military working dogs, conduct investigations, oversee physical security measures, and perform other security and law enforcement related duties.

HISTORICAL REVIEW

The MA rating is by no means a modern innovation. Naval records show that these "sheriffs of the sea" were keeping order as early as the reign of Charles I of England. At that time, they were charged with keeping swords, pistols, carbines, and muskets in good working order as well as ensuring that bandoleers were filled with fresh powder before combat.

Besides being chiefs of police at sea, the sea corporals, as they were called in the British Navy, had to be qualified in close order fighting under arms and be able to train seamen in hand-to-hand combat.

The MAs in the U.S. Navy trace the beginning of the rating to the Union Navy during the Civil War.

MASTER-AT-ARMS TRAINING

Members of the MA rating are highly skilled professionals who must complete the Master-at-Arms "A" School at San Antonio, Texas. The course is eight weeks long and includes training in physical security, law enforcement, antiterrorism, unarmed self-defense, legal jurisdiction, first aid, and basic report writing.

Throughout their careers, MAs receive specialized training. There are currently four areas of specialization to reflect this higher degree of proficiency: Detector Dog Handler, Kennel Master, Military Investigator, and Afloat Corrections Specialist.

BECOMING AN MA

Personnel who have reached the rank of E-4 (third class petty officer) or E-5 (second class petty officer) and have less than eight years service may apply for the MA rating. Navy personnel may also apply directly for the MA rating. A written request must be submitted requesting a change of rate.

COMMISSIONS

MA personnel may apply for Limited Duty Officer (LDO) or Chief Warrant Officer (CWO) status. Those accepted to the LDO program will be designated as Physical Security Officers. Those selected for the CWO program will be designated as Physical Security Technicians.

For more information about the MA program, contact your nearest Navy Recruiter or write to:

The Naval Criminal Investigative Service

Training, Antiterrorism and Security Forces Department

716 Sicard Street, SE

Washington Navy Yard, D.C. 20388-5380

Further information about the Naval Criminal Investigative Service can be found online at http://www.ncis.navy.mil or by writing to:

The Naval Criminal Investigative Service Headquarters

716 Sicard Street, SE, Code 25

Washington Navy Yard, D.C. 20388-5380

Telephone: (202) 433-9544 (Government and Liaison Public Affairs Office)

Fax: (202) 433-0904

MILITARY POLICE/PHYSICAL SECURITY SECTION

THE PROVOST MARSHAL OFFICE—SECURITY AND LAW ENFORCEMENT BRANCH

U. S. MARINE CORPS

BACKGROUND

U.S. Marine Corps commanding officers have the responsibility for the preservation of good order and discipline. Commanding officers exercise this responsibility through the delegation of authority to military police for execution of those missions pertaining to law enforcement and the maintenance of installation security. Accordingly, the Provost Marshal (PM) serves as the installation commander's senior law enforcement representative and as a special staff officer responsible for the operation of the Provost Marshal Office (PMO). The PM is charged with responsibility for, and authority to execute, the following missions:

- conduct law enforcement operations

- conduct criminal and traffic accident investigations

- provide police community services

Other law enforcement functions include patrol; traffic enforcement; military working dogs; critical incident response; flight line security; game warden; customs; installation access control; detention cells; protective services; polygraph; special events; registration for vehicles; pets; and weapons; crime prevention; physical security; police records; lost and found; vehicle impound; animal control; statistical reporting; police/court liaison; special reaction team; and training.

MISSION

Military Police are vested with the authority to perform law enforcement, investigative and police services on behalf of the installation commander. All criminal incidents/complaints which occur aboard the installation will be reported to the provost marshal who will take action to cause an initial investigation of the offense by military police.

The authority of military police to enforce military law, orders, and regulations is derived primarily from the powers granted by Congress and the President.

The Marine Corps Military Police are responsible for battlefield circulation control, area security, enemy prisoner of war (EPW) operations, and law enforcement.

HISTORICAL REVIEW

Prior to 1945, the Marine Corps did not have a specific Military Occupational Specialty (MOS) for Military Police (MP) personnel. In June of 1945 the MOS Manual first listed a specialty for both "military policeman" and for "investigator."

In June of 1970, the designation "military police officer" was added although only for officers in limited duty status (prior enlisted), which meant that they could only serve with the MP field and could not assume command. In 1971, a military occupational specialty was designated for corrections personnel, as well as dog handler, accident investigator, polygraph examiner, and drug investigator. In 1977, the Military Police field was opened to standard, unrestricted officers as a career field. The Military Police field presently consists of approximately 3,500 officers and enlisted personnel.

FUNCTIONS AND ACTIVITIES

There are two basic fields for U.S. Marine Corps Military Police. First, as a combat, combat-support, and combat-service-support resource for commanders of the various-sized Marine Air Ground Task Forces (MAGTF), with four primary missions:

- Battlefield Circulation Control includes traffic control, convoy escorts, traffic enforcement, route reconnaissance, and analysis of traffic data to ensure the expeditious movement of personnel and equipment away from the beach or landing zone.

- Area Security performs offensive and defensive infantry operations against minor enemy elements, including motor patrols and foot patrols to support Air Base ground defense.

- Enemy Prisoner of War (EPW) Operations operates an EPW collection system and provides for the evacuation, processing, temporary internment, and safeguarding of EPWs.

- Law Enforcement enforces laws, orders, and regulations within the area of operations in conjunction with allied forces and host country military/civil police authorities; provides criminal investigations, traffic investigations, and VIP security and counterterrorism support; and operates a temporary detention facility for U.S. military personnel awaiting trial or convicted military prisoners awaiting evacuation.

An evolving criminal threat will have an adverse affect on military operations and will require commanders to take actions that will reduce the negative impacts on forces, resources, and operations. As part of this effort, MP enforce laws and appropriate directives of the commander. This includes maintaining liaison and coordination with other Department of Defense (DoD) police organizations, other military and civilian authorities, and multinational police organizations. A coordinated law enforcement effort removes the conditions and opportunities that promote crime, thereby preventing diversion of military resources and maintaining military discipline.

Regardless of the operational environment, offenses committed against U.S. forces and property degrade military discipline, morale, and operational capabilities. Crimes and offenses must be investigated to support the commander's responsibility to protect personnel, supplies, facilities, readiness, and operational capabilities. Depending on the type and seriousness of the offense under investigation, such investigations may be conducted by Military Police Investigators (MPI) or CID/NCIS, working in coordination with other investigative agencies.

MPs provide the commander a high degree of operational flexibility through the execution of customs operations. Personnel, equipment, and material entering the Customs Territory of the

U.S. must meet customs, postal, immigration, agriculture and other federal agency requirements. During the redeployment of forces, customs-trained MP, working with joint and U.S. federal agencies, help ensure compliance with regulations and applicable provisions of international agreements. They also work with those agencies to detect and investigate violations of those provisions.

Counter-drug operations support federal, state, and local law enforcement agencies in their efforts to disrupt the transfer of illegal drugs into the United States. MAGTF support may include providing intelligence analysts, logistical support personnel, and support to interdiction. An integral part of this effort is the support provided by military working dog teams and customs trained MP.

Such law enforcement/physical security missions are performed by Provost Marshal Offices (PMO) located at each of the Marine Corps installations throughout the world where Marines train for combat.

TRAINING

Marines currently entering the Military Police field after boot camp attend an eight-week basic law enforcement training course at Lackland Air Force Base, Texas. During this period, they receive entry-level classroom and practical application training in all aspects of law enforcement including combat support instruction and small arms training. Marines entering the corrections field attend a six-week corrections course, also at Lackland AFB.

Upon joining an actual Military Police unit, each MP participates in mission-oriented training which is designed to provide the minimum necessary training to maintain a desired level of proficiency. Mission-oriented training includes, but is not limited to, jurisdictional and organizational structure; legal aspects of apprehension/detention of persons, search and seizure; vehicular law enforcement; traffic control; report writing; evidence collection; testimonial evidence; crime prevention; first aid; self-defense; special operations; weapons training; and local policies, orders, directives and standard operating procedures.

At some point after completion of entry-level training, certain Military Police may be selected to attend one of several MOS-specific schools, after which their MOS is changed to identify their occupational specialty.

In addition to the standard training listed above, Marines annually attend other military and civilian schools, including the FBI National Academy, School of Police Command and Staff, Installation Provost Marshal Training, and various technical training and management courses.

For further information, visit the USMC Web site at http://www.usmc.mil or contact:
Division of Public Affairs
Headquarters, U.S. Marine Corps
2 Navy Annex
Washington, D.C. 20380-1775
Telephone: (703) 614-1034 or
(703) 614-1492

DEPARTMENT OF ENERGY

OFFICE OF SAFEGUARDS AND SECURITY

MISSION

The mission of the Office of Safeguards and Security (OSS), U. S. Department of Energy (DOE), is to ensure the continued progress and security of the many energy and weapons programs of the Department of Energy. To accomplish this mission, OSS takes care of codifying badges, training specialized security personnel, and issuing policy and procedural documents. OSS is also responsible for inspections and evaluations to ensure compliance with those policy documents. Other security inspections are conducted by the DOE Office of Security Evaluations.

FUNCTIONS AND ACTIVITIES

To establish and maintain a certain level of security, the objectives or goals of the Department of Energy are to:

- protect against theft or diversion of special nuclear material

- prevent sabotage of government facilities

- prevent loss or compromise of classified information

- prevent damage to government property

- counteract the collection of security-related or sensitive information by foreign agents

For further information, write to:

Department of Energy
19901 Germantown Road
Germantown, Maryland 20874
Telephone: (301) 903-5106
Transportation Safeguards Division

THE TRANSPORTATION SAFEGUARDS DIVISION

MISSION

The Transportation Safeguards Division (TSD) is part of the Albuquerque Operations Office of the U. S. Department of Energy (DOE). The mission of the TSD is the safe and secure shipment of government-owned special nuclear material nationwide in support of the DOE's nuclear research and production programs. Department of Energy couriers guard each rail and highway shipment. They also drive the highway tractors and the escort vehicles and operate all convoy equipment en route. Couriers are federal officers, employees of the Department of Energy who are authorized by the Atomic Energy Act to make arrests and carry firearms in the performance of their duties nationwide.

HISTORICAL REVIEW

Since 1947, the DOE and its predecessor organizations, the Atomic Energy Commission (AEC) and the Energy Research and Development Administration (ERDA) have moved nuclear materials by a variety of commercial and government transportation modes. The more safety and security-sensitive materials, such as nuclear weapons, have always moved in vehicles controlled and guarded by armed federal courier escorts.

In the late 1960s, worldwide terrorism and acts of violence prompted the AEC to review its procedures for safeguarding special nuclear material (SNM) in all forms and amounts. These reviews resulted in immediate and long-range plans for improvements, especially upgrading the domestic transportation of nuclear weapons and SNM used in the weapons programs.

In the early 1970s, AEC started development of its first "Safe-Secure Trailer" for the transport of nuclear weapons and nuclear components. Design and installation of a communications system was also initiated to assure reliable contact between selected shipments and the headquarters of the Albuquerque Operations Office, the AEC office with field responsibility for the nuclear weapons programs. By the end of 1972, ten Safe-Secure Trailers (SSTs) were in operation and the nationwide security communications system was providing reliable communications for these shipments.

In 1974, the Albuquerque Operations Office was directed to expand its transportation system to provide weapons-level protection to all AEC shipments involving strategic quantities of special nuclear materials. As of September 1976, all strategic quantities of SNM were being transported by this safe and secure Transportation Safeguards System (TSS). Today, the system serves approximately 125 shippers/receivers of SNM and other sensitive materials at approximately 100 locations throughout the United States.

FUNCTIONS AND ACTIVITIES

Management and control of this system is centralized in TSD, DOE, Albuquerque Operations Office. Sandia National Laboratories in Albuquerque, a prime contractor of the DOE, provides engineering and other technical support for the system.

The TSS has been carefully designed and is continuously tested to assure a very high level of safety and security protection for nuclear materials. The system is an effective combination of specially designed transportation equipment, armed couriers, and nationwide communications.

Equipment

Special nuclear material is transported two ways: in specially constructed SSTs and in Safe-Secure Railcars (SSRs).

Trailers

The SSTs are modified from shells of standard 40-foot highway trailers into "mobile vaults." The walls contain special deterrent and denial features and insulative material. The trailer is highly resistant to unauthorized entry and attack, and also provides a high degree of cargo protection in the event of serious accident including fire. Reliable tie down equipment assures further safety by holding cargo in place under high stress situations. Head-on crashes at 60 mph have been simulated to test tie down integrity, and petroleum fire tests have been simulated to prove the insulative quality of trailer walls.

The tractors that tow the SSTs are standard production units modified to provide their occupants protection against attack. They are equipped with communications and electronic systems that further enhance security in transit.

Several types of escort vehicles are utilized and are also equipped with communications and electronics equipment.

Railroad Cars

For more than 20 years, AEC, ERDA and the DOE have used all-steel cars with double-locking couplers, wheels equipped with roller bearings, and a superstructure with sloping ends to minimize damage in event of end-on collision. The top-loading cars also have highly reliable tie down features and equipment to hold cargo in place in the event of a serious accident. The SSRs are modified and upgraded to further improve cargo safety and security. The deterrent, denial, and safety systems of the SSR are comparable to the SST.

SSRs move in special train service, with other special safety rules in effect. Escort coaches manned by armed DOE Couriers are part of the special trains. These escort coaches have built-in personnel protective features and are equipped with communications and electronic systems, much the same as the highway vehicles.

Aircraft

DOE aircraft are available for shipments of SNM, but are rarely used due to severe DOE restrictions on air transport of plutonium. While restrictions on uranium shipments are less severe, few such shipments are made by air. SNM shipments by air are accompanied by armed DOE Couriers.

Shipping Containers

Shipping containers used for the transport of SNM meet or exceed requirements set forth in current regulations governing the packaging and transportation of radioactive materials. These requirements are specified in regulations of the Nuclear Regulatory Commission (NRC) and the Department of Transportation, which are incorporated into the DOE regulations.

Law Enforcement Agency Liaison and Response

AEC, ERDA, and the DOE maintain liaison with state law enforcement organizations. When the TSS was expanded, more formal arrangements for emergency assistance were established at the state governors' level and with each state law enforcement organization. Personal briefings were given to some governors' staffs and to the managers and supervisors of state law enforcement organizations. Most of the DOE's liaison effort with law enforcement is directed at the state law enforcement authorities and the FBI.

TSD does not advise any organization of convoy itineraries, routes, or destinations, since publication of such information would increase the exposure of the shipment to possible threats or acts of violence. However, in the event of riots, strikes, civil unrest or adverse weather conditions in a particular area, state law enforcement organizations are contacted to discuss the advisability of moving through that locale.

TRAINING

The courier trainees undergo twelve weeks of basic training during which they must pass tests on tractor/trailer driving, qualify with firearms, meet specific physical standards, operate communications and electronic systems, and become familiar with basic standard operating procedures. All facets of the program must be successfully completed. The courier spends the balance of the first year in on-the-job training. Since the first year is probationary, the couriers must complete it successfully for retention.

Couriers receive firearms training as well as special physical and tactical training. Advanced training includes offensive and defensive tactics, with emphasis on teamwork.

In keeping with DOE policy for maintaining a low profile, the couriers do not wear uniforms. They carry both a photo identification card and shield which certify their federal officer status and their authority to make arrests and carry firearms.

For additional information, visit TSD online at www.doe.gov. For qualifications and additional information, write to:

Director, Transportation Safeguards Division
U.S. Department of Energy
Albuquerque Operations Office
P.O. Box 5400
Albuquerque, New Mexico 87115
Telephone: (505) 846-5214

DEPARTMENT OF HEALTH AND HUMAN SERVICES

OFFICE OF CRIMINAL INVESTIGATIONS

FOOD AND DRUG ADMINISTRATION

MISSION

Office of Criminal Investigations (OCI) special agents employ customary federal law enforcement methods and techniques in the investigation of suspected criminal violations of the Federal Food, Drug, and Cosmetic Act; the Federal Anti-Tampering Act; and other related federal statutes. OCI investigations concentrate on significant violations of these laws, with a priority on conduct that may present a danger to the public health.

OCI's experienced criminal investigators employ a traditional law enforcement approach to the systematic collection of evidence necessary to ensure successful criminal prosecutions. OCI provides its special agents with numerous resources to support investigations. Among these are an experienced staff of investigative analysts, technical equipment specialists, and agent polygraph examiners.

Pursuant to its investigative priorities, OCI maintains liaison and cooperative investigative efforts with various federal, state, local, and international law enforcement agencies.

The Office of Criminal Investigations is dedicated to protecting the health and welfare of the public by investigating criminal allegations falling within the jurisdiction of the U.S. Food and Drug Administration (FDA). OCI Headquarters is located in Rockville, Maryland, and field offices are located throughout the United States.

HISTORICAL REVIEW

The Office of Criminal Investigations was established in 1992 to provide the Food and Drug Administration with a specific office to conduct and coordinate criminal investigations.

The FDA regulates more than $1 trillion dollars worth of products, which account for 25 cents of every dollar spent annually by American consumers. The FDA, one of the nation's legislated protectors of the public health, is responsible for regulating products to ensure their safety and efficacy. These products include:

- foods

- drugs, biological products, medical devices

- cosmetics

- radiation-emitting devices (from microwave ovens to magnetic resonance imagers)

FUNCTIONS AND ACTIVITIES

OCI special agents are charged with investigating suspected criminal violations within FDA's jurisdiction. These violations include:

- frauds and other crimes involving the adulteration/misbranding of FDA regulated products

- manufacture and sale of counterfeit/unapproved drugs

- illegal diversion of pharmaceuticals and other regulated products

- product substitution crimes

- product tampering

- health fraud—schemes involving fraudulent treatments/cures/devices

- new drug application fraud

- crimes affecting the safety/integrity of the nation's blood supply

- crimes related to fraudulent clinical studies

- Prescription Drug Marketing Act (PDMA) violations

- Internet facilitated criminal violations involving FDA regulated products.

TRAINING

Special agents come to OCI as experienced federal law enforcement officers, bringing with them a wide range of experience, expertise, and training in the conduct of criminal investigations. OCI agents attend specialized training at the Federal Law Enforcement Training Center (FLETC) in Glynco, Georgia, as an introduction to the FDA in general and OCI in particular. A food and drug law course is also part of this initial training.

Throughout their career with OCI, special agents continue to receive instruction in areas designed to enhance job performance and promote career development. These areas include interviewing, financial crimes, computer forensics, asset forfeiture, continuing legal education, Internet investigations, and management/leadership training.

For further information, visit the OCI online at http://www.fda.gov or contact:

OCI Headquarters
7500 Standish Place, Suite 250N
Rockville, Maryland 20855
Telephone: (301) 294-4030
Fax: (301) 594-1971

NATIONAL INSTITUTES OF HEALTH

POLICE BRANCH, DIVISION OF PUBLIC SAFETY

MISSION

The Police Branch of the Division of Public Safety is composed of police personnel and support staff assigned to a wide range of activities aimed at insuring the personal safety of all National Institutes of Health (NIH) employees, visitors, contractors, patients and guests.

FUNCTIONS AND ACTIVITIES

Law enforcement responsibilities at the NIH are addressed through two primary organizational entities: the NIH Police Branch and the Crime Prevention Branch. The Police Branch is comprised of a Patrol Unit, Investigations Unit, K-9 Unit, Traffic Squad, Hospital Station, and Training Officer. The Crime Prevention Branch encompasses the Security Section and Locksmith Unit. In addition, the Parking Office and Government Driver's Permit Issuance Officer work under the supervision of the Chief of the Crime Prevention Branch.

THE NIH POLICE BRANCH

The NIH Police Branch, a full-service police agency with exclusive jurisdiction on the NIH enclave, is the largest section in the Division of Public Safety.

The Crime Prevention Branch

The Crime Prevention Branch is responsible for:

- surveys of NIH properties, buildings, offices, and labs to identify security vulnerabilities

- presentation of crime prevention seminars

- publication of crime prevention literature

- investigation of all civil liability claims

- security of classified documents

- liaison with security and equipment vendors

- managing NIH security systems such as the Cardkey Access System

- destruction of controlled and contaminated substances

- supervision of security guard contracts

- preparation of supervisory directives for security guard personnel.

For further information, visit NIH Police Branch online at http://www.nih.gov/od/ors/dps/police or contact:

The Police Branch
National Institutes of Health
31 Center Drive, MSC2012
Building 31, Room B3B17
Bethesda, Maryland 20892-2012
Telephone: (301) 496-2387
Office of Communications and Public Liaison at (301) 496-4461.

DEPARTMENT OF THE INTERIOR

BUREAU OF LAND MANAGEMENT LAW ENFORCEMENT

MISSION

The Bureau of Land Management (BLM) is charged by law to manage and protect the more than 300 million acres of public lands and the vast resources—timber, minerals, livestock forage, historic artifacts, wild horses, and others—associated with them.

BLM has special agents and uniformed rangers to enforce applicable federal laws on the public lands. They work closely with law enforcement officers from federal and state agencies and sheriff's departments to better coordinate law enforcement on the public lands within their jurisdiction.

HISTORICAL REVIEW

1829 - Department of the Interior created

1877 - Secretary of the Interior establishes "special clerks" to investigate timber trespass, gather evidence and seek prosecution

1905 - Congress authorizes special agents for the general protection of public lands

1946 - Bureau of Land Management created

1971 - Wild Horse and Burro Act authorizes designation of law enforcement personnel

1974 - First BLM special agents hired to enforce Wild Horse and Burro Act

1978 - First BLM rangers are hired and delegated law enforcement authority

FUNCTIONS AND ACTIVITIES

Special Agents

The special agents are responsible for enforcing federal laws and regulations relating to the public lands and resources. This includes conducting criminal investigations and the arrest of violators.

Rangers

The ranger force is also a law enforcement arm of BLM. The uniformed rangers, driving marked vehicles, patrol the vast public lands as a deterrent against violators of laws and regulations. Preventing law violations and assisting stranded visitors and other users are the main focus of a ranger's job. However, all rangers are trained in law enforcement procedures and are authorized to arrest or otherwise cite violators when circumstances warrant.

Federal Statutes

A number of federal statutes give BLM the authority to enforce laws and regulations on the public land. Among these are the Federal Land Policy and Management Act of 1976 which, among its many other provisions, called for establishment of a ranger force and authorized the designation of federal personnel to carry out law enforcement responsibilities; the Wild Free-Roaming Horse and Burro Act of 1971, directing the protection of these historically significant animals on the public lands; and the Archeological Resources Protection Act of 1979, making destruction or theft of cultural artifacts a misdemeanor or felony.

Financial gain is a major reason behind the deliberate breaking of laws, since many public land resources have high value, which make them tempting targets of illegal exploitation. For example:

▪ a 16-foot sawlog may bring as much as $500 at a sawmill

▪ a clay pot taken in good condition from an Indian ruin can be worth up to $15,000 to a collector of artifacts

▪ production from a single marijuana plant may be worth $2,000 in the illegal drug market;

▪ cactus plants removed from the public lands find a ready market for distribution throughout the United States

▪ a wild horse can be sold to a pet food processor or a rendering plant for as much as $450

▪ unauthorized grazing of livestock damages forage for the lawful grazer and circumvents the payment of appropriate grazing fees

Archaeological Resources

One of the most destructive and insensitive violations of federal law involves stealing cultural artifacts—pottery, carvings, ornaments and even bones of Indians who once inhabited parts of the West.

Some thefts are by amateur "treasure hunters" who may not know the law or who do not realize that their actions may permanently erase vital cultural records. The most destructive of such violations, however, are by commercial "black market" suppliers who sell stolen artifacts to private museums and collectors throughout the world.

Wild Horses and Burros

Wild horses and burros have no natural enemies on the public lands and their numbers can and do increase rapidly unless controlled. To achieve a necessary balance between horses and burros and their environment—the food and water they need to survive — excess animals are gathered and removed from the public lands. The captured animals are then offered for adoption to individuals or groups with facilities to care for them. The federal government retains title to adopted animals for at least one year.

Treating either free-roaming or adopted wild horses and burros in an inhumane manner, selling them to slaughter houses or rodeos, or otherwise misusing these animals are federal violations and, when reported to BLM, are investigated by special agents.

Marijuana Growers

Cultivation of marijuana on public lands has become a major concern. Illegal growers of marijuana sometimes use intimidation, armed guards, and booby traps to protect their crops. These growers endanger BLM employees as well as individuals who use and enjoy these public lands for hunting, fishing, family recreation, and camping; or thosewho carry out authorized uses such as livestock grazing, mining, or other commercial operations.

BLM works closely with other agencies to combat these illegal actions.

TRAINING

BLM rangers and special agents attend the sixteen-week Police School for Land Management Agencies at the Federal Law Enforcement Training Center in Glynco, Georgia.

Upon completion of this course, and contingent upon successful completion of a full field background investigation, BLM rangers and special agents are delegated law enforcement authority. BLM rangers and special agents must maintain their delegation of law enforcement authority through successful completion of 40 hours of annual law enforcement in-service training and qualifying with their firearm at least twice per year.

QUALIFICATIONS

Applicants may apply for special agent and ranger vacancies as they occur. For further information, check the BLM Web site at http://www.blm.gov/nhp/ or contact:

Bureau of Land Management Law Enforcement
U.S. Department of the Interior
18th and C Streets, NW
Washington, D.C. 20240
Telephone: (202) 452-5118
(202) 452-5125 (Office of Public Affairs)

DIVISION OF LAW ENFORCEMENT

U.S. FISH AND WILDLIFE SERVICE

MISSION

The U.S. Fish and Wildlife Service, U.S. Department of the Interior, conserves, protects, and enhances fish and wildlife and their habitats for the continuing benefit of the American people. As part of this mission, the Service's Division of Law Enforcement is responsible for enforcing U.S. and international laws, regulations, and treaties that protect wildlife resources. The Division's special agents, wildlife inspectors, and forensic scientists contribute to Service efforts to manage ecosystems, save endangered species, conserve migratory birds, preserve wildlife habitat, restore fisheries, combat invasive species, and promote global wildlife conservation.

HISTORICAL REVIEW

Federal wildlife law enforcement dates back to the passage of the Lacey Act in 1900. This first U.S. wildlife protection law prohibited interstate commerce in illegally taken game and banned the importation of injurious species. Migratory game bird hunting was first regulated by the federal government in 1913; even broader protections for migratory birds followed in 1918 with the passage of the Migratory Bird Treaty Act. For some 70 years, Federal wildlife law enforcement functioned primarily as a game protection and management operation, first in the Department of Agriculture and later in the Interior Department.

During the closing decades of the century, however, growing threats to native species and world wildlife resources prompted new legislation and treaties and an expanded focus for Service law enforcement. The 1970s, for example, saw the passage of the endangered Species Act and the Marine Mammal Protection Act; signing of migratory bird treaties with Mexico and the Soviet Union; and creation of the Convention on International Trade in Endangered Species of Wild Fauna and Flora (CITES) and the Service's wildlife inspection program—a program that now keeps track of an annual trade worth more than $1 billion.

Other laws enforced by the Service include the Bald and Golden Eagle Protection Act, Migratory Bird Hunting and Conservation Stamp Act, Airborne Hunting Act, National Wildlife Refuge System Administration Act, Antarctic Conservation Act, Archeological Resources Protection Act, Wild Bird Conservation Act, African Elephant Conservation Act, and Rhinoceros-Tiger Conservation Act.

FUNCTIONS AND ACTIVITIES

Service law enforcement today focuses on potentially devastating threats to wildlife resources—illegal trade, unlawful commercial exploitation, habitat destruction, and environmental contaminants. The Division investigates wildlife crimes, regulates wildlife trade, provides forensic analyses to support wildlife investigations, helps Americans understand and obey wildlife protection laws, and works in partnership with international, state, and tribal counterparts to conserve wildlife resources.

Special Agents

Service special agents enforce federal wildlife protection laws throughout the United States. As plainclothes criminal investigators with full federal law enforcement authority, they work in settings that range from major cities to one-person duty stations that cover some of the few remaining wilderness areas left in this country.

Service special agents investigate wildlife crimes involving the illegal taking, trade, and commercialization of federally protected species. They break up international smuggling rings that target imperiled animals and prevent the unlawful commercial exploitation of U.S. wildlife. They support special recovery and reintroduction efforts, pursue habitat destruction cases, and forge partnerships with industry groups to remove threats to wildlife. Agents enforce federal migratory game bird hunting regulations, work closely with the states to protect other game species and preserve hunting opportunities, and conduct wildlife law enforcement training for state, tribal, and international counterparts.

Wildlife Inspectors

Service wildlife inspectors provide the nation's front-line defense against illegal wildlife trade. These uniformed import/export control officers monitor wildlife shipments to ensure compliance with U.S. and foreign wildlife protection laws. Inspectors are stationed at major U.S. airports, ocean ports, and border crossings, where they uphold trade controls and interdict smuggled wildlife and wildlife products.

Day-to-day monitoring of wildlife imports and exports facilitates legal trade and helps detect and deter illegal trafficking. Wildlife inspectors make sure that required licenses and permits have been obtained, that the contents of shipments match the item declared, and that live animals have been shipped humanely. They also work the passenger terminals at airports, conduct inspections at international mail facilities, participate in special enforcement task forces, and provide training to other federal inspection agencies and to counterparts in other countries.

Case Illustrations

- A multiyear undercover probe of the illegal international reptile trade broke up two major global smuggling operations, producing charges against more than 40 people in the United States, Canada, and Germany.

- A major U.S. caviar company investigated by the Service was fined $10.4 million—the most ever in a wildlife trafficking case—for illegal trade activities that included fraudulently selling eggs from U.S. paddlefish as high-priced Russian roe.

- Two large-scale, multi-state investigations of illegal mussel trafficking exposed poaching and profiteering by the nation's two leading exporters of shell (a product used by the cultured pearl industry) and resulted in the assessment of more than $1.4 million in fines and restitution.

- Service officers exposed one of the largest poaching operations ever encountered in Alaska. Those prosecuted included guides and high-paying clients who illegally killed moose, caribou, Dall sheep, black bears, and grizzly bears on national park land.

■ The investigation of a Georgia chemical company for mercury contamination of coastal waters resulted in prison terms for corporate officials totaling more than 21 years. The case involved water pollution that jeopardized the safety of plant workers, poisoned endangered wildlife, and threatened the health of coastal residents.

■ Service agents played a key role in investigating a major oil spill off the coast of Rhode Island that killed more than 2,400 protected birds. The three companies responsible paid $8.5 million in federal and state fines and restitution.

Wildlife Forensics

The Clark R. Bavin National Fish and Wildlife Forensics Laboratory, which opened in 1988 in Ashland, Oregon, remains the world's first and only full-service crime laboratory devoted exclusively to wildlife law enforcement. Laboratory scientists, who include experts in morphology, serology, chemistry, criminalistics, and pathology analyze thousands of evidence items each year, providing crucial support to Service special agents and wildlife inspectors, state conservation agencies, and enforcement officers around the world.

The primary mission of the laboratory is to make species-specific identifications of wildlife parts and products seized as evidence and to link suspect, victim, and crime scene through the examination and comparison of physical evidence, much like a police crime lab. Laboratory scientists also determine the cause of death of wildlife crime victims.

Because there were few wildlife forensic techniques available to support species-specific identifications and other necessary analyses, research has been an important and essential part of the laboratory's work. Laboratory scientists investigate and develop new identification methods and analytical techniques, and present their results to the scientific community. Examples of key research accomplishments include ways to distinguish ancient and modern ivories, the application of DNA analysis to species identification, and work to pinpoint the contents of traditional Asian medicines, many of which claim to contain endangered species.

TRAINING

New Service special agents complete the nine-week Criminal Investigators School at the Federal Law Enforcement Training Center (FLETC) in Glynco, Georgia, followed by a special nine-week Service-developed training program focused specifically on wildlife law enforcement. After this period of formal instruction, new agents receive their first field assignment, where they complete twelve to eighteen months of on-the-job training. New wildlife inspectors complete a four-week Service-developed Wildlife Inspector Basic School at FLETC and receive on-the-job instruction and guidance. Both agents and inspectors complete annual in-service training programs.

For further information about job opportunity and qualifications, check the Division's website at http://www.le.fws.gov or contact:

U.S. Fish and Wildlife Service
Division of Law Enforcement
4401 N. Fairfax Drive, Room 520
Arlington, Virginia 22203
Telephone: (703) 358-1949

OFFICE OF LAW ENFORCEMENT SERVICES

BUREAU OF INDIAN AFFAIRS

Protective Service Detail for an Indian Admiral. (Photo courtesy of the Department of the Navy.)

MISSION

The Office of Law Enforcement Services (OLES), Bureau of Indian Affairs (BIA), U.S. Department of the Interior, is responsible for the prevention and deterrence of crime, investigation of violations, and enforcement of tribal laws and federal statutes throughout Native American lands. The Office detects and apprehends offenders, maintains and operates places of detention, coordinates cases with the U.S. Attorney, and assists tribal, state, and federal law enforcement officers in criminal justice services.

HISTORICAL REVIEW

The first Indian police officers were appointed in 1869. This was the beginning of the modern day Indian criminal justice system that resembles in many ways rural county sheriff or police programs.

In 1908, the first Chief Special Officer was appointed mainly for the suppression of liquor trafficking on Native American reservations.

Under the Reorganization Act of 1934, Native American tribes were able to reorganize under tribal constitutions, including the establishment of tribal courts with tribal police. Tribal police function as the enforcement arm of the individual tribe, much as the local police function under a traditional police chief, and as an arm of the elected officials of the council.

The BIA function has evolved into the present-day criminal investigation program, which oversees law enforcement operations on the reservations, provides technical assistance, and conducts investigations of major federal crimes.

Native American Indians have served honorably as federal law enforcement officers to the people of the reservtions. This proud tradition continues today with the men and women of the Bureau of Indian Affairs, Office of Law Enforcement Services. As police officers, criminal investigators, correctional officers, and telecommunication equipment operators, BIA employees carry on a tradition of helping American Indian people in communities throughout the United States while showing great reverence to our history, tradition, and culture.

For many, becoming a part of BIA Office of Law Enforcement Services represents the achievement of a life-long dream when they, as children, were taught to serve the community. For others, there is the significance of protecting the delicate balance of life for those who hold the past and the future. Currently, 800 Native American Indians serve their communities nationwide through the Bureau of Indian Affairs, Office of Law Enforcement Services.

FUNCTIONS AND ACTIVITIES

BIA patrol officers perform a critical patrol function throughout the reservations and act as the primary responders to a wide variety of crimes and incidents. They respond to crimes against persons and property. Patrol officers enforce both tribal and federal law in their designated area of jurisdiction. Patrol officers typically start at the GS-4 level with the potential of reaching the GS-9 level.

BIA criminal investigators are assigned to reservations throughout the United States. They are responsible for in-depth and complex investigations of major crimes such as murder, rape, and federal narcotics violations. Criminal investigators work closely with other law enforcement agencies at the federal, state, and tribal level. Entry-level criminal investigators start at the GS-7 level with potential of reaching the GS-13 level.

QUALIFICATIONS

BIA patrol officers must:

- be a U.S. citizen between the ages of 21 and 37
- possess a high school diploma or equivalent
- pass a written exam
- pass a medical examination
- pass a background investigation
- successfully complete a rigorous basic police training academy
- possess a valid drivers license
- be in excellent physical condition

There is no written exam for criminal investigators. Applicants for criminal investigators must possess one of the following:

- at least one year of criminal investigative or comparable experience
- one full year of graduate education, or
- have accomplished superior academic achievement in undergraduate studies.

For further information, visit the Bureau of Indian Affairs' Web site at http://www.bialaw.fedworld.gov or write to:

Bureau of Indian Affairs
P.O. Box 66
Albuquerque, New Mexico 87103
Telephone: (505) 248-7937
Fax: (505) 248-7905

OFFICE OF SURFACE MINING RECLAMATION AND ENFORCEMENT

MISSION

The mission of the Office of Surface Mining (OSM) is to protect people and the environment from the impacts of coal mining, while allowing access to the coal that is vital to the nation.

To accomplish this mission, the Office of Surface Mining performs two major functions: regulation of active surface coal mining operations to assure protection of the environment during mining and reclamation of the land after the coal is extracted; and repairing lands affected by past coal mining operations that were unreclaimed and abandoned before the 1977 Surface Mine Law was enacted.

In carrying out these functions, the Office of Surface Mining works closely with coal-producing states, with industry, and with the public, and provides financial, technical, and enforcement assistance to the states.

HISTORICAL REVIEW

The Office of Surface Mining was established in 1977, at a time when the United States was faced with a host of demands on the protection and use of its natural resources.

By 1977, the nation had endured the worst of the energy crisis and had come to realize that total dependence on foreign sources of fuel was unacceptable. As a result, the country committed itself to substantially increasing coal production, drawing on its massive domestic deposits of coal.

At the same time, the country was deeply concerned about the environment and was committed to its protection. That commitment demanded that a balance be struck, a balance between the protection of the environment and the nation's need for coal.

One result was the Surface Mining Law, signed by the President on August 3, 1977. That law established the Office of Surface Mining in the U.S. Department of the Interior.

In the years following enactment of the law, thousands of acres of mined land were reclaimed and became productive crop lands, pastures, and grazing ranges.

FUNCTIONS AND ACTIVITIES

Surface mining is often the most economical and the safest method of mining coal. In large operations, draglines and power shovels remove the overlying earth, or overburden, to expose a coal seam. In smaller operations, the same work is performed by bulldozers, front-end loaders, and trucks. Properly handled, the overburden can be replaced, the earth's surface re-contoured, and the site made productive once again.

Assuring that this reclamation is properly carried out is a prime goal of the Office of Surface Mining. Federal regulations spell out minimum uniform reclamation standards that must be met to produce coal without permanently affecting the environment. The states then develop their own programs for enforcing those standards on nonfederal lands. State programs are designed to be at least as effective as the federal standards and regulations, but geared to the unique climate and geology of the individual states.

OSM reviews the states' regulatory programs. Those programs that are found consistent with the minimum federal standards are approved and become the basis for state enforcement under primacy. Once a state has achieved primacy, enforcement of the regulations is in the hands of the state. Enforcement actions include review and issuance of permits, bonding, on-site inspection of mine operation, issuance of notices of violations, and assessment and collection of civil penalties. OSM provides federal backup, when needed, to reinforce and strengthen the state regulations and enforcement actions.

For further information, visit OSM online at http://www.osmre.gov or contact:
Office of Communications
Office of Surface Mining
1951 Constitution Avenue NW
Washington, D.C. 20240
Telephone: (202) 208-2565

RANGER ACTIVITIES DIVISION

BRANCH OF RESOURCES AND VISITOR PROTECTION, NATIONAL PARK SERVICE

MISSION

The law enforcement mission of the Ranger Activities Division, Branch of Resources and Visitor Protection, is to protect park resources as well as visitors and personal property, and:

■ protect the resources for which the park was established

■ protect the public and the areas to which it is assigned

■ protect government property located in the areas from physical damage and theft

■ represent the first line of law enforcement within the National Park Service

■ detect violations of criminal laws and regulations that have occurred in their areas

■ apprehend, arrest, or cause the arrest of violators

■ provide visitor and emergency services and resource management

HISTORICAL REVIEW

The National Park Service (NPS) is a bureau of the U.S. Department of the Interior. Since its creation in 1916, it has been preserving, protecting, and managing the natural, cultural, historical, and recreational areas of the National Park System. Presently, the National Park System comprises 384 units and more than 80 million acres of land in forty-nine states, Puerto Rico, Guam, and the Virgin Islands.

Shortly after the National Park Service was created in 1916, park rangers began replacing the U.S. Army Cavalry troops who had been enforcing the laws in the national park system.

During the 1920s, the parks began responding to the increased visitation and increased appearance of motor vehicles. The first rangers at Grand Canyon were hired to handle traffic, fire control, and police work. Many other parks established traffic divisions in which motorcycle-mounted rangers were charged with the responsibilities of traffic law enforcement. Also in the 1920s, rangers found themselves faced with many problems associated with the illegal use, possession, and manufacture of alcohol.

The National Park Service Law Enforcement Manual for the 1950s stated "Law enforcement is now a primary duty in the successful operation of the areas administered by the National Park Service." Also, "It is the duty of law enforcement officers to help preserve a National Park atmosphere that is one of dignity and restraint, and, therefore, one that is in keeping with the public mission of the National Park Service. The rights of visitors must be preserved by preventing prohibited activities on the part of overexuberant, thoughtless, or selfish persons."

FUNCTIONS AND ACTIVITIES

Park rangers perform a wide variety of duties in managing parks, historical sites, and recreational areas. They supervise, manage, and perform work in the conservation and enjoyment of resources in National Parks and other NPS units.

Park rangers carry out various tasks associated with wildland and structural fire control; protection of property; gathering and dissemination of natural, historical, or scientific information; development of interpretative material for the natural, historical, or cultural features of an area; demonstration of folk art and craft; enforcement of laws and regulations; investigation of violations, complaints, trespass encroachment, and accidents; search and rescue; emergency medical services; and management of historical, cultural, and natural resources, such as wildlife, forests, lake shores, seashores, historic buildings, battlefields, archeological properties, and recreation areas. They also operate campgrounds, including such tasks as assigning sites, performing safety inspections, providing information to visitors, and leading guided tours.

Location

Park rangers work in urban, suburban, and rural areas. More than half of the park rangers work in areas east of the Mississippi River. Much of their work is performed outdoors, but often rangers must work in offices, especially as they advance and assume more managerial responsibilities. During their careers, most rangers can expect to be assigned to several different parts of the country.

Rangers work with other federal law enforcement agencies, such as the Federal Bureau of Investigation, the Drug Enforcement Administration, and the Border Patrol, on federal violations in National Park Service areas. They also cooperate with police and sheriffs' departments on investigations of mutual jurisdiction. Rangers are involved in a variety of enforcement activities, from violation of park regulations to felonies such as burglary, assault, homicide, larceny, and drug violations.

TRAINING

The orientation and training a ranger receives on the job is sometimes supplemented with formal training courses. Training for duties which are unique to the Park Service is available at the Horace M. Albright Training Center at Grand Canyon National Park, Arizona, and the Stephen T. Mather Training Center at Harpers Ferry, West Virginia. In addition, law enforcement rangers must successfully complete training at the Federal Law Enforcement Training Center in Glynco, Georgia.

QUALIFICATIONS

For qualifications and further information, visit the National Park Service online at http://www.nps.gov, or call the Office of Personnel at 202-208-5228, or write to:

U.S. Department of the Interior
National Park Service
Ranger Activities Division
1849 C Street, NW
Washington, D.C. 20240
Telephone: (202) 208-6843

HOOVER DAM POLICE DEPARTMENT

BUREAU OF RECLAMATION

On duty at the Hoover Dam. (Photo courtesy of the Bureau of Reclamation, Department of the Interior.)

MISSION

The Hoover Dam Police Department, Bureau of Reclamation, Department of the Interior, provides security and law enforcement services for Hoover Dam and its surrounding security zone. This area of jurisdiction encompasses approximately 22 square miles, including 3.3 miles of U.S. Highway 93.

Hoover Dam Police enforce federal and state laws and regulations in this security zone, which lies within both Arizona and Nevada; assist local and federal enforcement agencies with various assignments, such as handling motor vehicle accidents, traffic violations, public assistance, and the apprehension of wanted persons; protect employees and visitors from physical harm; investigate crimes against people and property; prepare and maintain various reports, records, and logs; respond to any fire or hazardous materials spill within their jurisdiction; check detection alarm devices, identification passes, and buildings; and remain current in managing various potential threats to the dam or its appurtenant structures.

HISTORICAL REVIEW

The Bureau of Reclamation engineers successfully harnessed the Colorado River by designing and constructing one of the most significant engineering achievements of all time—the Hoover Dam. This achievement provides much-needed flood control, water supply, and hydroelectric power for the arid southwestern United States.

Law enforcement authority for Hoover Dam was delegated by the General Services Administration to the Secretary of the Interior on August 2, 1973. Currently, Hoover Dam is the only Bureau of Reclamation facility with law enforcement authority, and The Hoover Dam Police Department has concurrent jurisdiction with Nevada and Arizona. A 1984 Congressional Act also allows Reclamation to enter into agreements for state and local law enforcement on lands under Reclamation jurisdiction.

The Hoover Dam Police Department has a complement of 14 officers and a Chief of Police. All are trained and commissioned per Department of the Interior policy, and all must successfully complete the nine-week mixed basic police training program at the Federal Law Enforcement Training Center at Glynco, Georgia. Officers also are covered under the Federal Law Enforcement Retirement System.

This facility, the Hoover Dam, is protected by the Hoover Dam Police. (Photo courtesy of the Bureau of Reclamation, Department of the Interior.)

FUNCTIONS AND ACTIVITIES

More than a million people take the guided tour of Hoover Dam and Power Plant, and an additional two million-plus people stop at the dam for a photograph or refreshments without taking the tour. In addition, nearly five million vehicles a year cross the dam, and that number is growing annually. Hoover Dam Police officers provide law enforcement, protection, safety, and security service to these visitors, as well as employees and contractors working at the site. Officers also ensure that the facility and all associated buildings and other property are secure, enabling the continued functioning of one of the nation's major water storage and power generation structures and a national civil engineering landmark. Officers also ensure compliance with state laws and the Hoover Dam Rules of Conduct, prevent destruction or theft of government and/or private property, and deal with a variety of law enforcement problems ranging from minor violations to felony crimes.

QUALIFICATIONS

Candidates must have one year of acceptable specialized experience, which includes experience as an active member of a federal, state, county, municipal, or local police force; a military police officer experience; or comparable experience involving responsibility for maintaining order and protecting life and property.

Applicants must be able to be commissioned as law enforcement officers in both Nevada and Arizona. A valid state driver's license is required, along with satisfactory completion of a thorough background security check (security clearance required), physical examination, drug screening, and Physical Efficiency Battery Test.

For additional information visit the Bureau of Reclamation online at http://www.usbr.gov or contact:

Bureau of Reclamation
Lower Colorado Regional Office
Human Resources Office
P.O. Box 61470
Boulder City, Nevada 89006-1470
Telephone: (702) 293-8000

U.S. PARK POLICE

NATIONAL PARK SERVICE

MISSION

The United States Park Police is a law enforcement arm of the Department of the Interior, under the administrative control of the National Capital Region of the National Park Service.

The U.S. Park Police general mission objectives include:

- crime prevention: to minimize the occurrence of crime in park areas by providing essential services to reduce the number of major violent crimes against park visitors, to reduce the number of major crimes against property, and to minimize the number of each of the lesser crimes against persons and property

- crime control: to provide essential services to maximize police knowledge of crime; investigate reported crimes; maximize adherence to constitutional safeguards; present all facts to, and participate in, as required, the judicial process; and to recover and return crime-related and stolen property

- conflict resolution: to provide essential services to minimize disorder, deaths, injuries, property damage and criminal consequences during special events and demonstrations and to minimize deaths, injuries, property damage and criminal consequences brought about by personal stress or disorientation problems.

- services: to provide essential services to maximize the level and quality of police services authorized or required by federal, state and local governments, such as mandated dignitary protection; to minimize the number of motor vehicle accidents, the number and severity of related injuries, and the amount of property damage; to minimize traffic congestion and maximize the availability, effectiveness, and courtesy of police response to park visitors' requests for information and assistance; to maximize the quality of services provided to park area superintendents, such as crime prevention programs, traffic flow analysis, planning for special events, etc.

HISTORICAL REVIEW

From the earliest days of the city's history (1791), the parks of Washington, D.C., have been under federal control. Many present-day parks have belonged to the United States since the days of President George Washington. The control of federal lands has been handed down through a long succession of federal officials and through the hands of many agencies, and, as far as the park system is concerned, rest now in the United States Department of the Interior.

The U.S. Park Police was created in 1791 when a Board of Commissioners, established by President George Washington, appointed Park Watchmen to protect the new parklands and federal buildings in the nation's capital. Park Watchmen have served in these federal parks continuously since their inception, changing their name to the U.S. Park Police in 1919.

By an Act of Congress of August 5, 1882, the U.S. Park Police were given concurrent jurisdiction in all areas of the District of Columbia. Prior to this Act, their arrest authority was limited to the federal park areas within the city.

The expansion of the police authority and responsibility of the U.S. Park Police from local to regional jurisdiction began in 1929 with the assignment to police Mount Vernon Memorial Parkway in nearby Virginia. Now, the U.S. Park Police provide protection and enforce the laws and statutes of the federal government within the geographical confines of the District of Columbia, and in federal parks and various other federally owned reservations in the State of Maryland; Commonwealth of Virginia; the Golden Gate National Recreation Area in San Francisco, California; and the Gateway National Recreation Area in New York and New Jersey.

FUNCTIONS AND ACTIVITIES

The U.S. Park Police is composed of officers whose duties go beyond protection from crime; they must also act as host to millions of visitors to the nation's capital each year.

Protection of visitors in park areas requires the use of several types of patrol. For instance, in the areas of heavy visitation, the U.S. Park Police employ foot, bicycle, cruiser, horse-mounted, motorcycle, motor-scooter, marine, helicopter, and plainclothes patrols.

Since the spring of 1973, the U.S. Park Police have operated Bell Jet Ranger helicopters throughout the Washington metropolitan area to provide aerial observation, photography, and other police services, including rescue and air ambulance services, for numerous outdoor events which attract local, national, and international visitors, such as the National Cherry Blossom Festival, the Independence Day Celebration, and Presidential inaugurations.

Since the White House is surrounded by federal parks for which the Force is responsible, the U.S. Park Police shares responsibility with other agencies for the security of the President of the United States and numerous visiting foreign dignitaries.

TRAINING

The U.S. Park Police training program ranges from the thirty-one weeks of indoctrination training for new officers to professional management and technical police science training throughout an officer's career.

The Federal Law Enforcement Training Center in Glynco, Georgia, provides an eight-week basic training program for the Force that includes such subjects as due process in criminal interrogations, scientific aids to investigation, civil rights, the U.S. Constitution and Bill of Rights, and ethics in law enforcement. During this training, special emphasis is placed on the arts of self-defense, protecting the public, and skilled vehicle operation. The U.S. Park Police incorporates their eleven-week training into the Federal Law Enforcement Training Center's curriculum, to total a nineteen-week training program. This eleven-week course, conducted by the U.S. Park Police staff, consists of patrol techniques; District of Columbia Criminal Code; Code of Federal Regulations; Maryland, Virginia, and District of Columbia traffic regulation; motor vehicle accident investigation; human relations; and other subjects necessary to prepare the new officer to perform police service.

After completing this phase, new officers enter a twelve-week field training program, during which they rotate assignments as partners to Force Field Training Instructors and apply their education to supervised patrol operations. New officers then assume normal patrol duties for the remainder of their probationary year.

QUALIFICATIONS

U.S. Park Police must:

- be U.S. citizens

- be at least 21 years of age and not have reached their 35th birthday before appointment

- have 20/100 vision or better that is correctable to 20/20 with glasses or contact lenses

- possess a valid drivers license (must have good driving record)

- have a high school diploma or equivalent

- have two years of education above the high school level

- have two years of progressively responsible experience that has demonstrated the ability to learn and apply detailed and complex regulations and procedures or have a combination of acceptable experience and education of at least two years. In combining education and experience, and academic year of study (30 semester hours or 45 quarter hours) will be considered equivalent to one year of experience.

The Office of Personnel Management determines the testing sites for the written examination. Interested persons may apply when the test is announced by the Office of Personnel Management. Military personnel may apply to the Office of Personnel Management to take the examination within 120 days prior to or within 120 days after honorable discharge.

For further information, visit the U.S. Park Police online at http://www.doi.gov/usparkpolice, or contact:

U.S. Park Police
Personnel Office, Room 177
1100 Ohio Drive SW
Washington, D.C. 20024
Telephone: (202) 619-7056

DEPARTMENT OF JUSTICE

BUREAU OF PRISONS

MISSION

The mission of the Bureau of Prisons is to protect society by confining offenders in the controlled environments of prisons and community-based facilities that are safe, humane, cost-efficient, and appropriately secure, and that provide work and other self-improvement opportunities to assist offenders in becoming law-abiding citizens.

OVERVIEW

The Federal Bureau of Prisons was established in 1930 to provide more progressive and humane care for federal inmates, to professionalize the prison service, and to ensure consistent and centralized administration of the eleven federal prisons in operation at that time. Today, the Bureau consists of ninety-eight institutions, six regional offices, a central office (headquarters), three staff training centers, and twenty-eight community corrections offices. The regional offices and the central office provide administrative oversight and support to the institutions and community corrections offices. Community corrections offices oversee community corrections centers and home confinement programs.

The Bureau is responsible for the custody and care of approximately 148,000 federal offenders. Approximately 126,000 of these inmates are confined in Bureau-operated correctional institutions or detention centers. The remainder are confined through agreements with state and local governments and through contracts with privately-operated community corrections centers, detention centers, prisons, and juvenile facilities.

The federal prison system is a nationwide system of prisons and detention facilities for the incarceration of inmates who have been sentenced to imprisonment for federal crimes and the detention of individuals awaiting trial in federal court.

FUNCTIONS AND ACTIVITIES

The Bureau protects public safety by ensuring that federal offenders serve their sentences of imprisonment in institutions that are safe, humane, cost-efficient, and appropriately secure. The Bureau helps reduce future criminal activity by encouraging inmates to participate in a range of programs that are proven to help them adopt a crime-free lifestyle upon their return to the community.

The Bureau ensures institution security through a combination of physical features, security technologies, the classification of inmates based on risk factors, and direct staff supervision. The Bureau operates institutions at four security levels (minimum, low, medium, and high) to meet the various security needs of its diverse inmate population, and has one maximum-security prison for the less than 1 percent of the inmates who require that level of security. It also has administrative facilities, such as pretrial detention centers and medical referral centers, that have specialized missions and confine offenders of all security levels.

The Bureau believes that inmates should participate in self-improvement programs that will provide them with the skills they need to conduct themselves as productive, law-abiding citizens upon release. The Bureau provides many self-improvement programs, including work in prison industries and other institution jobs, vocational training, education, substance abuse treatment, religious observance, parenting, anger management, counseling, and other programs that teach essential life skills. Bureau research has shown that industrial work programs, vocational training, education, and drug treatment reduce recidivism and misconduct in prison. Drug treatment programs also decrease offenders' relapse to drug use after release.

Correctional programs and activities also reduce inmate idleness and the stresses associated with living in a prison. Such programs are critical to managing a safe and secure prison. The Bureau also provides other structured activities designed to teach inmates productive ways to use their time.

STAFF ISSUES AND TRAINING

Although architecture and technological innovations help the Bureau maintain the safety and security of its institutions, the most important way to maintain accountability, ensure security, and manage inmate behavior is direct supervision of inmates by staff members. The Bureau has continued to add technological innovations to increase the physical security of institutions. Nonetheless, to facilitate the direct supervision of inmates, the Bureau has eliminated structural barriers (such as bars and grilles) between staff members and inmates wherever possible. In addition, many staff offices are located near the areas where programs and services are delivered.

Regardless of the specific discipline in which a staff member works, all employees are correctional workers first. This means that everyone is responsible for the security and order of the institution. All staff members are expected to be vigilant and attentive to inmate accountability and security issues, to respond to emergencies, and to maintain a proficiency in custodial and security matters and in their particular job specialty.

Bureau staff members are the inmates' primary role models during their incarceration, and the Bureau emphasizes employee ethics, responsibility, and standards of conduct. The Bureau expects its employees to conduct themselves in a manner that creates and maintains respect for the agency, the Department of Justice, the Federal Government, and the law. Bureau employees are expected to avoid situations that involve conflicts of interest with their employment and to uphold and comply with the ethical rules and standards that govern their professions, as well as the laws and regulations that ensure institution security and protect the safety of inmates and the general public.

Staff training is an integral part of Bureau of Prisons staff development. Introductory training is conducted at the Bureau's Staff Training Academy in Glynco, Georgia. Specialized professional training is conducted at the Management and Specialty Training Center in Aurora, Colorado, and at the Staff Training Academy's Specialty Training Center in Artesia, New Mexico.

For further information, visit the Bureau's Web site at http://www.bop.gov, or call 888-317-8455, or contact:

Office of Public Affairs
Federal Bureau of Prisons
320 First Street, NW
Washington, D.C. 20534
Telephone: (202) 307-3198

CRIMINAL DIVISION

MISSION

The Criminal Division develops, enforces, and supervises the application of all federal criminal laws, except those specifically assigned to other divisions.

In addition to its direct litigation responsibilities, the Division formulates and implements criminal enforcement policy and provides advice and assistance. The Division approves or monitors sensitive areas of law enforcement, such as participation in the Witness Security Program and the use of electronic surveillance; advises the Attorney General, Congress, the Office of Management and Budget, and the White House on matters of criminal law; provides legal advice and assistance to federal prosecutors and investigative agencies; and provides leadership for coordinating international, federal, state, and local law enforcement matters.

FUNCTIONS AND ACTIVITIES

Areas of responsibility include:

- asset forfeiture and money laundering, including developing regulatory and legislative initiatives; ensuring the uniform application of forfeiture and money laundering statutes; litigating complex, sensitive, and multidistrict cases; adjudicating petitions for remission or mitigation of forfeited assets; and distributing forfeited funds and properties to appropriate domestic and foreign law enforcement agencies and community groups within the United States

- child exploitation and obscenity, including prosecuting violators of federal criminal statutes relating to child support; sexual exploitation of minors; obscenity; possession, manufacture, and distribution of child pornography; selling, buying, or transporting women and children to engage in sexually explicit conduct; and international parental abduction

- computer crime and intellectual property, including cyber-attacks on critical information systems; improving domestic and international infrastructure to pursue network criminals most effectively; and initiating and participating in international efforts to combat computer crime

- enforcement, including overseeing the use of the most sophisticated investigative tools at the division's disposal; reviewing all federal electronic surveillance requests and requests to apply for court orders permitting the use of video surveillance, authorizing or denying the entry of applicants into the federal Witness Security Program (WSP), coordinating and administering matters relating to all aspects of the WSP among all program components, and approving or denying requests by federal agencies to utilize federal prisoners for investigative purposes; and reviewing requests for witness immunity, transfer of prisoners to and from foreign countries to serve the remainder of their prison sentences, attorney and press subpoenas, applications for S-visa status, and disclosure of grand jury information

- fraud, including investigations and prosecutions of fraud and white-collar crime including business crimes, such as financial institution fraud, Internet fraud, and insurance industry fraud; multidistrict schemes that victimize consumers, such as telemarketing scams and fraudulent bankruptcy mills; and fraud involving government programs and payments, including health care, housing, and government regulatory commodities markets

- internal security, including cases affecting national security, foreign relations, and the export of military and strategic commodities and technology

- narcotics and dangerous drugs, including statutes pertaining to controlled substances; developing and implementing domestic and international narcotics law enforcement policies and programs; and developing and administering other cooperative drug enforcement strategies, initiatives, and projects conducted by the law enforcement and intelligence communities

- organized crime and racketeering efforts against traditional groups and emerging groups from Asia and Europe, such as Chinese triads, the Sicilian mafia, and Russian organized crime

- overseas prosecutorial development, assistance, and training for prosecutors and judicial personnel in other countries to develop and sustain democratic criminal justice institutions

- policy and legislation, including developing legislative proposals, legal memoranda, and congressional testimony; preparing comments on pending legislation affecting the federal criminal justice system; and working closely with the U.S. Sentencing Commission on a variety of sentencing-related issues

- public integrity efforts to combat corruption of elected and appointed public officials at all levels of government

- special investigations of individuals who took part in Nazi-sponsored acts of persecution abroad before and during World War II and who subsequently entered or seek to enter the United States illegally and/or fraudulently, and interagency investigation into assets looted from victims of Nazi persecution

- terrorism and violent crime, involving design, implementation, and support of law enforcement efforts, legislative initiatives, policies, and strategies relating to international and domestic terrorism; immigration enforcement efforts relating to alien terrorists; and prosecution of firearms and explosives violations

For further information, contact:

Office of the Assistant Attorney General
Criminal Division
Department of Justice
Tenth Street and Pennsylvania Avenue, NW
Washington, D.C. 20530
Telephone: (202) 514-2601

DRUG ENFORCEMENT ADMINISTRATION

MISSION

The mission of the Drug Enforcement Administration (DEA) is to enforce the controlled substances laws and regulations of the United States and to bring to the criminal and civil justice system of the U.S., or any other competent jurisdiction, those organizations and individuals involved in growing, manufacturing, and distributing controlled substances appearing in or destined for illicit traffic in the United States and to recommend and support nonenforcement programs aimed at reducing the availability of illicit controlled substances on the domestic and international markets.

The DEA's primary responsibilities include:

- investigation and preparation for prosecution of major violators of controlled substances laws operating at interstate and international levels, in keeping with established drug priority goals

- management of a national narcotics intelligence system in cooperation with other federal, state, local, and foreign officials to collect, analyze, and disseminate strategic and operational intelligence information

- seizure and forfeiture of assets derived from, traceable to, or intended to be used for illicit drug trafficking

- enforcement of the provisions of the Controlled Substances Act as they pertain to the manufacture, distribution, and dispensing of legally produced controlled substances

- coordination and cooperation with other federal, state, and local law enforcement officials on mutual drug enforcement efforts and enhancement of such efforts through exploitation of potential interstate and international investigations beyond local or limited federal jurisdictions and resources

■ coordination and cooperation with other federal, state, and local agencies, and with foreign governments, in programs designed to reduce the availability of illicit abuse-type drugs on the U.S. market through nonenforcement methods such as crop eradication, crop substitution, and training of foreign officials

■ responsibility, under the policy guidance of the Secretary of State and U.S. Ambassadors, for all programs associated with drug-law enforcement counterparts in foreign countries

■ liaison with the United Nations, INTERPOL, the INTERPOL-U.S. National Central Bureau, and other organizations on matters relating to international narcotics control programs

HISTORICAL REVIEW

The earliest federal drug enforcement work can be traced to the Treasury Department's Internal Revenue Service (IRS) in 1915. In 1927, drug law enforcement became a function of the Bureau of Prohibition, Department of Justice, where it remained until 1930 when the responsibilities fell to the newly created Federal Bureau of Narcotics.

In 1968 the Justice Department's Bureau of Narcotics and Dangerous Drugs was formed. The organization then was composed of personnel from the Federal Bureau of Narcotics and the Bureau of Drug Abuse Control (Food and Drug Administration) of the Department of Health, Education and Welfare.

In 1973 the Drug Enforcement Administration was created by merging the Bureau of Narcotics and Dangerous Drugs, the Office for Drug Abuse Law Enforcement, the Office of National Narcotics Intelligence, U.S. Customs Service elements that worked in drug trafficking intelligence and investigations, and the Narcotics Advance Research Management Team. This amalgamation combined all federal drug enforcement under DEA's leadership.

In January 1982 the Attorney General assigned the Federal Bureau of Investigation concurrent jurisdictional powers to conduct drug investigations. The reporting relationship for DEA was changed to give the FBI Director general supervision over drug law enforcement.

FUNCTIONS AND ACTIVITIES

Forensic Science Laboratories

DEA laboratories directly support DEA and FBI drug investigations by performing qualitative and quantitative analyses of purchased and seized drug evidence, providing expert scientific testimony for prosecutive purposes, participating in clandestine laboratory seizures and vacuum sweeps for traces of drugs, and by providing other technical assistance, such as forensic photographic capabilities and examinations for latent fingerprints.

The seven field laboratories provide support to state and local law enforcement agencies through supplemental laboratory analyses of drug evidence, meeting applicable State Speedy Trial Act provisions, and through provision of technical assistance to aid and encourage other state and local agencies in achieving forensic analytical self-sufficiency.

Aircraft Fleet

Using trained special agent-pilot observers, aircraft are employed in searches for hidden airfields used by drug smugglers and to spot marijuana and poppy fields and concealed laboratories. With the aircraft fleet, agents and equipment are moved quickly from one point to another as investigations demand. The aircraft are also used in developing new enforcement techniques and in testing experimental detection equipment.

The DEA's aircraft and pilots work in conjunction with the Armed Forces and other agencies and are occasionally made available to help in rescue operations during floods and other natural catastrophes.

Special Operations

State and Local Task Forces

Task forces bring DEA special agents and state and local police officers together in teams to increase the effectiveness of investigations aimed at the mid-level drug violator, the link between supplier and consumer. Statistics indicate that the overall conviction rate for task force cases ranges up to 95 percent in federal and state courts.

Domestic Marijuana Eradication/Suppression Program

This program supports state and local drives to eradicate domestically cultivated marijuana. Through the program, the DEA promotes the sharing of intelligence information, training, equipment, investigative and aircraft support, and technical assistance with state and local law enforcement agencies. The DEA also coordinates the work of several federal agencies, such as the U.S. Forest Service and the Bureau of Land Management; the Bureau of Alcohol, Tobacco and Firearms; and County Sheriffs' offices in the fight against illegal domestic cultivation of marijuana.

The Financial Investigations Program

DEA has become a world leader in the field of financial investigations including "covert undercover" money laundering operations. DEA agents and task force officers have developed financial expertise through their coordination with other law enforcement and regulatory agencies that specialize in these investigations as well as the compliance divisions maintained by private business. This coordination is accomplished through the sharing of information from the various financial databases available to the investigators. The DEA investigators use their personal expertise and past experience conducting narcotic and conspiracy investigations to assist with the financial probes of these criminal organizations. These covert undercover investigations target the international organizations responsible for flooding the United States and other countries with illegal narcotics. The scope of these investigations enables the DEA to disrupt the flow of narcotic proceeds and cripple the criminal organization.

The El Paso Intelligence Center (EPIC)

The El Paso Intelligence Center is an intelligence clearinghouse for drug enforcement information. Its primary function is exchanging time-sensitive information dealing with drug movements. Staffed by personnel from the DEA; Immigration and Naturalization Service; Coast Guard; Customs; Bureau of Alcohol, Tobacco and Firearms; Federal Aviation Administration; FBI; U.S. Marshals' Service, and the IRS; EPIC supports participating agencies' programs, such as interdicting alien smuggling and weapons trafficking.

Special Field Intelligence Programs (SFIP)

Special Field Intelligence Programs are designed to collect intelligence information not available through conventional means. For example, part of the SFIP's resources are devoted to gathering information from a network of paid informants. Another effort is the heroin signature program through which drug origins are identified and the price and purity of the samples are determined. These facts give an early warning of fluctuations in domestic drug availability.

Organized Crime Drug Enforcement Task Forces (OCDE)

Recognizing the increased involvement of organized crime in drug trafficking, OCDE task forces single out and pursue the highest levels of organized criminal enterprises trafficking in drugs.

Controlled Substances Act and Diversion Control

The purpose of the DEA's Drug Diversion Control Program is to prevent, detect, and investigate the diversion of controlled substances and listed chemicals from legitimate channels, while at the same time ensuring an adequate supply of these substances to meet legitimate need in the United States. The 1970 Controlled Substances Act (CSA) authorizes the DEA to enforce this law as it applies to all handlers of controlled drugs and chemicals, to include manufacturers, distributors, researchers, and dispensers of such controlled substances. Control is maintained by the Diversion Control Program through the registration of these individuals and entities with the DEA.

Central to the Diversion Control Program and enforcement of the CSA are the diversion investigators who conduct all investigations, including criminal, public interest, preregistrant, and CSA-mandated cyclic investigations. The Diversion Control Program also engages in a broad range of activities, including establishment of production quotas, controlled substances scheduling actions, control of drug and chemical imports and exports, development of legislative initiatives and regulations, diplomatic missions and the enforcement of U.S. obligations under international treaties, and the development and furthering of initiatives aimed at fostering voluntary compliance within the regulated community.

Asset Forfeitures

The Asset Forfeiture Program is one of the mechanisms relied heavily upon to deter criminals who make their living selling drugs. Seizing the assets that were used to facilitate and/or gain illegal sale from this multibillion-dollar drug industry is an effective tool in attacking criminal activity.

TRAINING

The DEA's training program provides the agency's employees and law enforcement counterparts with the skills and knowledge necessary to attack international organized crime syndicates and their domestic distribution organizations. The DEA's comprehensive program consists of basic, field agent training, in-service, specialized, and state and local training.

The Basic Agent Training Program provides instruction to new special agents on all facets of drug law enforcement operations. The sixteen-week program, held at the DEA Training Academy, consists of training in the areas of self-defense, use of firearms, practical exercise scenarios, laws, court procedures, criminology, investigative techniques, drug and narcotics identification, and other related topics. FBI instructors provide all basic agent instruction relating to the FBI mission, organization, and jurisdiction. Conversely, the DEA trains FBI agents in the nature and characteristics of drug law enforcement. The DEA Field Agent Training Program provides on-the-job training to new special agents by pairing them with senior agents for a sixteen-week period upon completion of the Basic Agent Training Program.

The Office of Training has developed career-spanning leadership, executive development, and special agent in-service training programs that are ideally suited to the agency's long-term continuing education and career development needs for all employees and the agency. State and local training is provided to commanders of state and local departments through the DEA's Drug Unit Commander Academy.

Due to the potential hazards of clandestine laboratory seizures, special instructions are also provided to DEA personnel and state and local law enforcement officers on techniques for safely seizing and dismantling clandestine laboratories. The DEA offers a comprehensive Train-the-Trainer Program that provides awareness training to state and local first responders. The DEA provides international training through mobile teams that travel throughout the world to provide specialized drug enforcement training to foreign officials.

QUALIFICATIONS

Special agent entry-level salary is at the GS-7 or GS-9 level. Candidates must:

- be U.S. citizens

- be at least 21 years of age and not older than 36 at appointment

- be in excellent physical condition

- have a valid drivers license

- have uncorrected vision of no less than 20/200 (Snellen) in both eyes, corrected 20/20 in one eye and 20/40 in the other

- have a college degree and/or substantive professional or administrative experience

Contact DEA Headquarters Personnel Office at (202) 307-4100 for further information or to obtain the phone number for the local DEA Special Agent Recruiter. All applications are obtained and processed by the DEA Recruiter at the Division level.

To apply, candidates must submit a Standard Form 171, a voluntary Background Survey Questionnaire, OPM Form 1386, and a complete college transcript or Supplemental Qualifications Statement to DEA at the address shown below. Standard Form 171 and OPM Form 1386 may be obtained from any Office of Personnel Management, DEA office, or federal agency with a personnel office. Incomplete application packages cannot be processed. Additional information may be obtained by contacting the DEA headquarters Personnel Office or any DEA Division.

For further information, visit the DEA online at http://www.usdoj.gov/dea or contact:

Drug Enforcement Administration
Personnel Office
700 Army-Navy Drive
Arlington, Virginia 22202
Telephone: (202) 307-4000

FEDERAL BUREAU OF INVESTIGATION

FBI Headquarters in Washington, D.C. (Photo courtesy of the FBI, Department of Justice.)

MISSION

The mission of the Federal Bureau of Investigation (FBI) is to uphold the law through the investigation of violations of federal criminal law; to protect the United States from foreign intelligence and terrorist activities; to provide leadership and law enforcement assistance to federal, state, local, and international agencies; and to perform these responsibilities in a manner that is responsive to the needs of the public and is faithful to the Constitution of the United States.

The FBI is the principal investigative arm of the United States Department of Justice (DOJ). Title 28, United States Code, Section 533, which authorizes the Attorney General to "appoint officials to detect . . . crimes against the United States," and other federal statutes give the FBI the authority and responsibility to investigate specific crimes. At present, the FBI has investigative jurisdiction over violations of more than 200 categories of federal crimes.

The Bureau is also authorized to investigate matters where no prosecution is contemplated. For example, under the authority of several Executive Orders, the FBI conducts background security checks concerning nominees to sensitive government positions. In addition, the FBI has been directed or authorized by Presidential statements or directives to obtain information about activities jeopardizing the security of the nation.

Information obtained through an FBI investigation is presented to the appropriate U.S. Attorney or DOJ official, who decides if prosecution or other action is warranted. Top priority has been assigned to the five areas that affect society the most: counterterrorism, drugs/organized crime, foreign counterintelligence, violent crimes, and white-collar crimes.

The FBI also is authorized to provide other law enforcement agencies with cooperative services, such as fingerprint identification, laboratory examinations, and police training; to publish annual Uniform Crime Reports; and to administer the National Crime Information Center (NCIC).

HISTORICAL REVIEW

The agency now known as the Federal Bureau of Investigation was founded in 1908 when Attorney General Charles J. Bonaparte appointed an unnamed force of special agents to be the investigative force of the DOJ. Prior to that time, the DOJ borrowed agents from the U.S. Secret Service to investigate violations of federal criminal laws within its jurisdiction.

By order of Attorney General George W. Wickersham, the special agent force was named the Bureau of Investigation in 1909. Following a series of changes in name, the Federal Bureau of Investigation officially received its present title in 1935.

During the early period of the FBI's history, its agents investigated violations of some of the comparatively few existing federal criminal violations, such as bankruptcy frauds, antitrust crime, and neutrality violations. The first major expansion of the Bureau's jurisdiction came in 1910 when the Mann Act ("White Slave") was passed. It provided a tool by which the federal government could investigate criminals who evaded state laws but had no other federal violations. During World War I, the Bureau was given responsibility for espionage, sabotage, sedition, and draft violations. Passage of the National Motor Vehicle Theft Act in 1919 further broadened the Bureau's jurisdiction.

The Gangster Era began after passage of Prohibition in 1920. A number of highly visible criminals engaged in kidnapping and bank robbery, which were not federal crimes at that time. This changed in 1932 with the passage of a federal kidnapping statute. In 1934, many additional federal criminal statutes were passed and Congress gave special agents the authority to make arrests and to carry firearms.

The FBI's size and jurisdiction during World War II increased greatly and included intelligence matters in South America. With the end of that war and the advent of the Atomic Age, the FBI began conducting background security investigations for the White House and other government agencies, as well as probes into internal security matters for the Executive Branch.

Civil rights violations and organized crime became major concerns of the FBI in the 1960s, as did counterterrorism, white-collar crime, drugs, and violent crimes during the 1970s and 1980s.

The 1990s brought even more investigative responsibilities to the Bureau, such as computer crimes, health-care fraud, economic espionage, and threats from weapons of mass destruction.

Official seal of the Federal Bureau of Investigation. (Photo courtesy of the FBI, Department of Justice.)

FUNCTIONS AND ACTIVITIES

The FBI has divided its investigations into a number of programs:

Background Investigations

The FBI's Applicant Program manages background investigations on all persons who apply for positions with the Department of Energy, the Nuclear Regulatory Commission, the Department of Justice, and the FBI. The program also oversees background checks for Presidential appointees and U.S. court candidates. Background investigations involve interviewing neighbors and coworkers of applicants and checking criminal and credit records.

Civil Rights

The FBI's Civil Rights Program investigates violations of the Civil Rights Act of 1964 and the Equal Credit Opportunity Act. The program also oversees police brutality and housing discrimination matters. Most recently, the Civil Rights Program was charged with enforcing the Freedom of Access to Clinic Entrances Act, which bars conduct that would obstruct access to reproductive health facilities.

Domestic Terrorism

The FBI is the lead federal law enforcement agency in the fight against terrorism in the U.S. In carrying out this responsibility, the Domestic Terrorism Program investigates threats involving atomic energy, weapons of mass destruction, sabotage, hostage-taking, and civil unrest.

National Foreign Intelligence

The FBI also is the lead counterintelligence agency within the U.S. intelligence community. The National Foreign Intelligence Program is tasked with preventing foreign espionage, economic espionage, and with investigating foreign counterintelligence cases within U.S. borders. The program also is involved in international terrorism threats, weapons of mass destruction threats, and attacks on the nation's critical infrastructures (i.e., communications, banking systems, and transportation systems).

Organized Crime/Drug Cases

Organized crime and drug matters are linked under the Organized Crime/Drug Program (OCDP) because many of the organized crime groups are drawn to the lucrative profits associated with drug trafficking. The OCDP investigates criminal enterprises, illegal drug cases, money laundering matters, and labor racketeering cases, often under the Racketeer Influenced and Corrupt Organizations statute. The OCDP also coordinates national Organized Crime/Drug Enforcement Task Forces.

Violent Crime

The Violent Crimes and Major Offenders Program (VCMOP) investigates threatened or actual injury or loss of life, including cases of kidnapping, sexual exploitation of children, extortion, bank robbery, consumer product tampering, crimes on Indian reservations, and unlawful flight to avoid prosecution. The VCMOP also oversees cases involving threatened or actual assault, and kidnapping or murder involving the president, vice president, or members of Congress.

White-Collar Crimes

The White-Collar Crime Program—the largest of the FBI's criminal programs— targets such criminal activity as money laundering, bank fraud and embezzlement, public corruption, environmental crimes, fraud against the government, health-care fraud, election law violations, and telemarketing fraud.

FBI Laboratory Services

The FBI laboratory is one of the largest and most comprehensive forensic laboratories in the world, and it is the nation's only full-service federal forensic laboratory. The laboratory examines evidence free of charge for federal, state, and local law enforcement agencies. Examiners also provide expert witness testimony in court regarding the results of forensic examinations. The mission of the FBI laboratory is to support the federal, state, local, and international law enforcement agencies.

Criminal Justice Information Services

The Criminal Justice Information Services (CJIS) Division, located in Clarksburg, West Virginia, centralizes criminal justice information and provides accurate and timely information and services to local, state, federal, and international law enforcement agencies; the private sector; academia; and other government agencies.

The CJIS Division serves as the national repository for fingerprint information and criminal record data. The division also manages Law Enforcement Online (LEO), a law enforcement intranet that provides secure communications, distance learning, and information services to the law enforcement community.

On November 30, 1998, the CJIS Division began operating the National Instant Check System (NICS), mandated by the Brady Bill. This national system was created to prevent handguns, rifles, and shotguns from being purchased by convicted felons, wanted persons, illegal immigrants, and the mentally ill.

INVESTIGATIVE ACCOMPLISHMENTS

La Cosa Nostra (LCN)

In the early 1990s, Vincent "Chin" Gigante, the boss of New York's Genovese LCN, was indicted and arrested as a result of the FBI's investigations of LCN infiltration of New York City's construction industry. Gigante was charged with ordering six murders, including that of Gambino LCN Boss John Gotti, and conspiring in three others. He was also charged with labor racketeering and extortion. Feigning mental illness, Gigante had his trial postponed twice, but in June

1997, after being ruled mentally competent, his trial began. Gigante was convicted and sentenced to twelve years in prison. As a result of this investigation, 20 other LCN members were convicted and $4 million in illegally obtained LCN assets were forfeited.

Mir Amal Kasi

In January 1993, Mir Amal Kasi, armed with an AK-47 assault rifle, shot five people as they were stopped in traffic at the entrance to CIA headquarters in Langley, Virginia. Two CIA employees were killed and 3 were seriously wounded. In the confusion of the shootings, Kasi fled the scene. Over the next four years, the FBI, CIA, State Department, and other intelligence and law enforcement agencies conducted a massive worldwide search for Kasi. He was extradited to the U.S. in 1997, tried for murder, convicted, and ultimately sentenced to death.

Oklahoma City Bombing

The bombing of the Alfred P. Murrah Federal Building in Oklahoma City on April 19, 1995, remains the worst terrorist attack ever to occur on American soil, killing 168 and wounding approximately 700. The investigation resulted in the largest single collection of evidence ever submitted to the FBI laboratory (more than 7,000 pounds). The initial investigative effort led to the identification of Timothy McVeigh and Terry Nichols as the perpetrators. McVeigh was convicted for his role in the bombing in June 1997, sentenced to death, and executed. Nichols was convicted for his role in the bombing in December 1997 and was sentenced to life if prison. Michael Fortier, the third person charged in connection with the bombing, was a key witness at both trials. He was sentenced to two years in prison.

Shattered Shield

This undercover operation began in 1993 after a cooperating witness claimed that he was being extorted by two uniformed officers of the New Orleans Police Department. Using an undercover agent (UCA) posing as a drug dealer, several officers were paid protection money to assist the UCA in protecting drug shipments. As a result of the investigation, 12 officers were convicted or pleaded guilty. During the undercover phase of the investigation, one of the officers ordered the murder of a woman who had filed a brutality report on him. He was convicted of civil rights violations and, in the first ever sentence of its kind, received the death penalty.

UNABOM

UNABOM (abbreviated for UNiversity and Airline BOMbing) is the code name for the FBI investigation into sixteen improvised bombs that were mailed or placed during a seventeen-year period beginning on May 25, 1978. The bombings resulted in three deaths and 23 injuries to people throughout the U.S. In February 1996, the FBI received information on the possible involvement of Theodore J. Kaczynski, a former professor of mathematics at the University of California at Berkeley, who was a recluse living in Lincoln, Montana. In April, the FBI and the Bureau of Alcohol, Tobacco and Firearms obtained a search warrant and Kaczynski was subsequently arrested during the search. On June 18, 1996, a ten-count indictment was returned against Kaczynski, charging him with four bombings that killed 2 individuals and injured 2 others. On October 1, 1996, a three-count indictment was returned against Kaczynski charging him with a bombing that killed 1 individual. At the beginning of his trial, Kaczynski agreed to an unconditional plea of guilty to all of the charged acts as well as bombings for which he was not formally charged. He was sentenced on May 15, 1998, to life in prison with no chance for parole.

U.S. Embassy Bombings in Kenya and Tanzania

On August 7, 1998, bombs were exploded near the U.S. embassies in Nairobi, Kenya, and Dar es Salaam, Tanzania. As a result of the explosions, more than 250 people were killed and over 5,000 were injured in Nairobi, and 11 people were killed and 86 injured in Dar es Salaam. In the aftermath of the bombings, the FBI dispatched more than 500 personnel to assist the local authorities with the investigation. As a result of the cooperative efforts of the FBI and Kenyan and Tanzanian law enforcement agencies, a number of suspects were identified and subsequent charges were filed. Arrested and charged shortly after the bombings were Mohamed Sadeek Odeh, Mohamed Rashed Daoud Al-Owhali, and Haroun Fazil. Osama Bin Laden and Muhammed Atef, were indicted in November 1998. Bin Laden is believed to be the head of Al-Qaeda, a worldwide terrorist organization.

World Trade Center Bombing

In February 1993, a massive explosion at the World Trade Center in New York City killed 6 people, injured 1,042, and caused more than $500 million in damage. Two days after the explosion, investigators identified the vehicle that carried the explosive device into the parking garage, a discovery which eventually led to the arrests of four of the perpetrators. In March 1994, a jury in the Southern District of New York convicted Muhammad Amin Salameh, Nidal Ayyad, Mahmud Abouhalima, and Ahmed Ajaj for their roles in the bombing. They were each sentenced to 240 years in prison. Ramzi Yousef, another bombing suspect, was arrested in Pakistan by the FBI and returned to the U.S. He and Eyad Mahmoud Simail Najim were convicted for their roles in the bombing, and each were also sentenced to 240 years in prison.

PENTTBOM

PENTTBOM (Code name for the probe investigating terrorist attacks on the World Trade Center and the Pentagon) Minutes after two hijacked airliners crashed into the twin towers of the World Trade Center on September 11, 2001, the FBI deployed thousands of agents and support personnel to investigate a conspiracy that is believed to have killed more than 6,000 people. Less than an hour after the two passenger jets crashed into the towers of the World Trade Center, another terrorist-seized plane smashed into the Pentagon. The September 11th attack on the U.S. by 19 suicidal hijackers also involved a fourth American commercial airliner aimed at some other target in the U.S. The hijacked airliner crashed in western Pennsylvania. Attorney General John D. Ashcroft called this "the largest single investigation in the history of the U.S." At the time this publication went to press, the investigation was still ongoing; U.S. authorities believed that suspected terrorist Osama Bin Laden was the mastermind behind these attacks. The Saudi-born millionaire is linked to Ramzi Ahmed Yousef, perpetrator of the first World Trade Center bombing in 1993, and has reportedly been associated with related plots to blow up New York City landmarks. Bin Laden remains at the top of the FBI's 10 Most Wanted List.

TRAINING

With the increased hiring of special agents over the past few years, new agents training is a core initiative of the Training Division. The course lasts sixteen weeks and consists of ethics training, academics, physical training and defensive tactics, firearms training, and practical applications. Emphasis is placed on individual integrity and accountability, investigative techniques, interviewing skills, interrogation, and gathering intelligence information.

QUALIFICATIONS

Professional Support Personnel

To qualify for professional support positions, which include jobs classified as professional, administrative, technical, clerical, craft, trade, and maintenance, applicants must be U.S. citizens. A high school diploma or its equivalent is the minimum educational requirement; a bachelor's or advanced degree or technical training is required for some positions. Work experience also may be required.

Professional support positions include job titles such as Budget Analyst, Language Specialist, Intelligence Research Specialist, Writer, Electronics Technician, Computer Programmer, Engineering Technician, Laboratory Technician, Paralegal, Administrative Assistant, Secretary, Typist, Clerk, Electrician, and Carpenter.

Special Agents

To qualify for training as an FBI agent, a candidate must be a U.S. citizen who is between the ages of 23 and 37 when entering on duty and must meet certain physical requirements. All special agent candidates must hold at least a bachelor's degree obtained in an accredited, four-year resident program at a college or university.

All newly appointed special agents must complete sixteen weeks of intensive training at the FBI Academy in Quantico, Virginia. Training consists of 645 classroom hours spread over four major concentrations: academics; firearms; physical training/defensive tactics; and practical exercises. Agent trainees begin with classes on ethics and core law enforcement values; these lessons are reinforced throughout the curriculum, particularly in practical exercises.

SALARY AND CAREER PATHS

Professional Support Personnel

Entry-level positions are generally offered at the GS-4 through GS-9 grade levels on the federal government pay scale. In some specialty areas, exceptions may be made to the normal grade level, depending upon education, work experience, prior government service, and vacancies.

An FBI career can provide a variety of career paths. Employees may apply for training in fields other than those in which they work. Promotional opportunities are consistent with overall qualifications and proficiency.

Special Agents

Special agents enter FBI service in grade GS-10 and can advance to grade GS-13 in field assignments. Promotions to supervisory, management, and executive positions are available in grades GS-14 and GS-15, as well as in the Senior Executive Service (SES). All special agents may qualify for overtime compensation. Special agents are also eligible for an additional 25 percent law enforcement availability pay.

After graduation from the FBI Academy in Quantico, Virginia, a new special agent is assigned to an FBI field office. This assignment is determined by the individual's special skills and needs of the Bureau. As part of their duties, special agents are required to relocate during their careers.

Salaries and Wages

Most FBI white-collar personnel are paid according to the General Schedule (GS) contained in Title 5, U.S. Code, Section 5332(A). Some General Schedule personnel in specialized or competitive job categories are paid at a higher level under a Special Pay Rate System. In addition, special geographic locality rates may apply; therefore, the pay scales used in different parts of the country vary. The highest-ranking FBI personnel are paid under the Senior Executive Service (SES) Schedule or the Executive Schedule.

How to Reach the FBI

The FBI's field offices are located in major cities throughout the United States and in San Juan, Puerto Rico. In addition, resident agencies are maintained in smaller cities and towns across the country.

The first page of most local telephone directories shows the telephone number of the nearest FBI office. All of these offices may be contacted 24-hours-a-day, every day.

For further information, visit the FBI Web site online at http://www.fbi.gov or contact:
Federal Bureau of Investigation
Office of Public and Congressional Affairs
J. Edgar Hoover Building
935 Pennsylvania Avenue, NW
Washington, D.C. 20535-0001
Telephone: (202) 324-3000

POLICE OFFICER—FEDERAL BUREAU OF INVESTIGATION

MISSION

The primary mission of FBI police officers is to maintain law and order and protect life, property, and the civil rights of individuals. Their secondary mission is the protection of government property and national security information from acts of sabotage, espionage, terrorism, trespassing, theft, fire, and accidental and/or willful damage and destruction.

FUNCTIONS AND ACTIVITIES

Police Officers serve at the J. Edgar Hoover Building in Washington, D.C., and have authority to make arrests and carry firearms after completing firearms training and attending lectures on legal matters, rules and regulations, search and seizure, operating procedures, etc. They accompany more experienced personnel on various assignments in order to gain on-the-job experience concerning the structure and contents of the building, protective devices, facilities, methods, and procedures involving the utilization of CCTV alarm terminals, etc.

At stationary posts, they check for proper identification of pedestrian and vehicular traffic prior to admittance through the Security Access Control System. They perform unscheduled periodic perimeter and internal patrols of the building and grounds by checking for unsecured doors and windows, illegal entry, and suspicious persons and vehicles.

QUALIFICATIONS

A Police Officer candidate must:

- be a high school graduate

- be at least 21 years of age at the time of selection for this position

- possess a driver's license and qualify for a U.S. government driver's license

For GS-6/7/8, candidates must have one year of specialized experience equivalent to the next lower grade level in the normal line of progression for the occupation in the organization. Specialized experience is experience that provides knowledge of a body of basic laws and regulations, law enforcement operations, practices and techniques, and involved responsibility for maintaining order and protecting life and property. Creditable specialized experience may have been gained in work on a police force; through service as a military police officer; in work providing visitor protection and law enforcement in parks, forests, or other natural resource or recreational environment; in performing criminal investigative duties; or in other work that provided the required knowledge and skills. If selected for the position, then individuals must successfully complete a comprehensive police training program at the Federal Law Enforcement Training Center in Glynco, Georgia.

Applicants claiming Veteran's Preference who meet minimum qualifications will be contacted and asked to submit a copy of his/her DD-214, Report of Separation from Active Duty, or a statement specifying the type of discharge, dates of service, campaign badges receive. If applicable, an SF-15, Application for 10-point Veteran's Preference, together with the proof required by the form, such as a letter dated within the last year from the Department of Veterans Affairs are also required. Applicants must be U.S. citizens and consent to a complete background investigation, urinalysis, and polygraph. Only those candidates determined to be best qualified will be contacted to proceed in the selection process.

The FBI welcomes and encourages applications from persons with physical and mental disabilities, and will reasonably accommodate the needs of those persons. The decision on granting reasonable accommodation will be on a case-by-case basis. The FBI is firmly committed to satisfying its affirmative obligations under the Rehabilitation Act of 1973 to ensure that persons with disabilities have every opportunity to be hired and advanced on the basis of merit within the FBI.

As with all federal agencies, the FBI is an Equal Opportunity Employer. All qualified applicants receive consideration for Police Officer vacancies. Except where otherwise provided by law, selection is made without regard to, and there will be no discrimination because of race, religion, color, national origin, sex, political affiliations, marital status, nondisqualifying physical or mental disability, age, sexual orientation, membership or nonmembership in an employee organization, or on the basis of personal favoritism or other nonmerit factors.

For further information, visit the FBI Web site at http://www.fbi.gov or contact:

Federal Bureau of Investigation
Office of Public and Congressional Affairs
J. Edgar Hoover Building
935 Pennsylvania Avenue, NW
Washington, D.C. 20535-0001
Telephone: (202) 324-3000

IMMIGRATION AND NATURALIZATION SERVICE

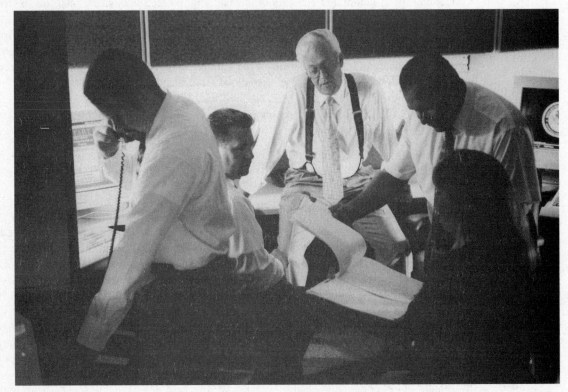

Immigration agents go over flight manifest. (Photo courtesy of the Immigration and Naturalization Service, Department of Justice.)

MISSION

The Immigration and Naturalization Service (INS) enforces the immigration laws of the United States and adjudicates applications for naturalization and other types of benefits available to individuals under the immigration and nationality laws.

The INS faces diverse challenges in support of its two very distinct missions. One mission is to manage and facilitate immigration to this country and provide services and benefits to those seeking legal entry to the United States. The other is to control U.S. borders, deter illegal immigration, ward off drug smugglers and arrest, detain, and remove noncitizens found to be deportable. In carrying out its two missions, the INS touches the lives of millions of people every year.

HISTORICAL REVIEW

Immigration

The first immigration office in the federal government was created in 1864 by a law intended to encourage immigration. Under this law, the President appointed a Commissioner of Immigration within the State Department to regulate the transportation and settlement of "emigrants," but the law had no effect on the commissions, boards, or other officers who were responsible for immigration in each of the states. The commissioner's office was abolished when the law was repealed four years later. Other federal laws were passed in the 1880s to prevent the admission of undesirable aliens and to control contract labor, but authority over immigration, including enforcement of the federal statutes, remained at the state level. At the same time, the number of immigrants coming to America was rising rapidly.

In 1888, Congress established a select committee to investigate problems caused by the divided authority over immigration matters. It recommended consolidating this authority within a single federal agency and drafted legislation that Congress enacted as the Immigration Act of 1891. President Benjamin Harrison signed it into law on March 3, 1891. It established complete and definite federal control over immigration by providing for an office of the Superintendent of Immigration under the Secretary of the Treasury.

As a result of this new law, all the duties previously reserved to the states were transferred by the end of fiscal year 1891 to U.S. Inspection Officers and the first federal immigration organization was established on July 12, 1891, when the Bureau of Immigration began operations in the Treasury Department.

In 1903, the Bureau of Immigration was moved to the newly established Department of Commerce and Labor and given broader responsibilities.

Naturalization

The naturalization side of the INS did not come into being until Congress passed the Naturalization Act of 1906. Before then, naturalization was a function of the courts. The new law created the Bureau of Immigration and Naturalization and made it responsible for administering and enforcing U.S. immigration laws and for supervising the naturalization of aliens and keeping naturalization records.

Restrictive laws made the inspection and admission of immigrants and foreign visitors more complex. As a result, more immigrants tried to sneak in across the border or around the ports of entry. This increase in unlawful entry led Congress to authorize funds in 1924 to establish the Border Patrol within the Bureau of Immigration. Immigration and Naturalization were consolidated again in 1933 by Executive Order to form the Immigration and Naturalization Service, still within the Labor Department.

The INS moved to the Department of Justice in June 1940 as a result of a reorganization plan based on concerns for national security. The transfer was meant to provide more effective control over aliens at a time when international tensions were increasing.

The next major changes in the organization occurred after the passage of the Immigration and Nationality Act of 1952, which increased the INS's responsibilities in processing applicants for immigration benefits. This law also increased the work of the INS in both law enforcement and litigation to deal with problems in interpreting its complex provisions.

Subsequent amendments to the law have required corresponding changes in the INS's organization and function. For example, the Immigration and Nationality Act Amendments of 1965 required improvements in processing and adjudicating applicants for immigration benefits. The Immigration Reform and Control Act of 1986 authorized substantial increases in the Border Patrol and other enforcement activities. It also created new programs for granting legal status to qualified illegal aliens and for educating employers and workers about new requirements for verifying the legal status of job candidates.

FUNCTIONS AND ACTIVITIES

As part of their routine duties and responsibilities in a typical year, the men and women of the INS Officer Corps will:

- protect 8,000 miles of international boundaries in vehicles, aircraft, and boats as well as on horseback and on foot

- dismantle smuggling organizations and conduct investigations into criminal activities originating overseas

- seize approximately one million pounds of marijuana a year from drug smugglers attempting to cross this nation's borders

- protect people seeking asylum, track down people to be deported, and return illegal immigrants to their home country

- apprehend more than 1.5 million illegal aliens along the Southwest border

- return 175,000 illegal immigrants to their home countries

- conduct more than 525 million inspections at U.S. ports of entry

- investigate almost 50,000 criminal alien, work-site, fraud, and smuggling cases

- conduct more than 250,000 immigration interviews, including more than 60,000 asylum cases

- assist legal immigrants in becoming U.S. citizens

CAREER OPPORTUNITIES

The INS offers a number of career opportunities within its Officer Corps for individuals interested in law enforcement. The following describes these occupations.

Border Patrol Agent and canine search for illegal drugs. (Photo courtesy of the Immigration and Naturalization Service, Department of Justice.)

Border Patrol Agent

The Border Patrol is an organization with a history of enforcing immigration and nationality laws along U.S. borders. As the mobile uniformed enforcement arm of the INS, the Border Patrol detects and prevents the smuggling and unlawful entry of undocumented aliens into the United States and acts as the primary drug-interdicting agency along all U.S. land borders. Border Patrol agents arrest more people annually than all other federal agencies combined. Border Patrol agents work alone or as a member of a team in preventing and detecting illegal entry. They also intercept and arrest alien smugglers, drug smugglers, and other criminals.

In their jobs, Border Patrol agents:

- detect illegal aliens by checking farms, ranches, and other areas near the border for signs of illegal entry

- patrol cities or work at Border Patrol checkpoints

- apprehend smugglers of illegal aliens

- identify people suspected of violating immigration laws, question them, and inspect their documents to determine their status

- apprehend violators, transport suspects, prepare reports concerning apprehensions, and arrange for the return of violators to their country of origin

- develop evidence for prosecution and appear as a witness as in court proceedings

Immigration Agent

An Immigration Agent (IA) interviews people to determine their immigration status, works with other law enforcement officers to identify criminal aliens in custody, and helps deport illegal aliens. IAs are the nonuniformed officers who enforce the Immigration and Nationality Act and other related statutes.

In their jobs, IAs:

- identify people who have violated immigration law

- locate and arrest aliens who fail to appear for deportation hearings, fail to leave the United States voluntarily after deportation, or escape from INS custody

- arrest and deport aliens who are in the United States illegally

Criminal Investigator-Special Agent

An INS Special Agent (SA) is a detective who enforces immigration laws within the nation's borders. New agents are responsible for investigating criminal aliens, work-site violations of immigration law, or fraud. As SA careers progress, assignments could include work with the INS Anti-Smuggling Unit, the Violent Gang Task Force, the Joint Terrorism Task Force, the Organized Crime and Drug Enforcement Task Force, or the International Fugitives Task Force. In addition to investigative work, an SA prepares cases for prosecution by collecting evidence and presenting it to the U.S. Attorney.

In their jobs, criminal investigators:

- conduct criminal investigations and participate in field enforcement operations to apprehend, arrest, interrogate, and remove criminal aliens from the United States

- develop cases for prosecution using various sophisticated investigation techniques, including electronic information gathering, consensual monitoring, surveillance, interrogation, undercover operations, cultivation and use of informants, search and arrest warrants, and subpoenas

- conduct investigations into criminal alien activities originating overseas in conjunction with the many federal agencies, including the Department of State, Department of Labor, the Customs Service, Department of the Interior, Drug Enforcement Administration, the Bureau of Alcohol, Tobacco and Firearms, and the FBI

■ assist the U.S. Attorney's Office in preparing cases for presentation to grand juries and for trial

Deportation Officer

A Deportation Officer (DO) is essential to the successful deportation of aliens and for maintaining the United States' relationships with other countries. At the same time, DOs need to ensure the constitutional rights of illegal aliens. DOs are responsible for making sure that illegal aliens are treated with due process from the time they are apprehended until they are either deported or allowed to remain in the United States. DOs work in airports and other locations, concentrating on legal issues and links with other countries.

In their jobs, DOs:

■ review deportation cases to determine whether people apprehended should be released or held in custody

■ conduct legal research to support decisions on deportation and exclusion cases, prepare cases for court, and assist the INS and U.S. attorneys in representing the federal government in court

■ conduct hearings and adjudicate cases involving the benefits, stays and relief, status, parole, and custody of immigrants

■ establish and maintain liaison with enforcement agencies and foreign governments, embassies, and consulates in dealing with deportation issues

■ provide protective custody for immigrants cooperating with U.S. authorities in the prosecution of others

Detention Enforcement Officer escort illegal immigrants. (Photo courtesy of the Immigration and Naturalization Service, Department of Justice.)

Detention Enforcement Special Unit inspects aircraft. (Photo courtesy of the Immigration and Naturalization Service, Department of Justice.)

Detention Enforcement Officer

DEOs perform a variety of tasks in Service Processing Facilities, Districts, and Sectors. DEOs locate, apprehend, arrest, transport, safeguard, supervise, and process aliens being detained or deported for violations of immigration laws. Aliens being detained and escorted represent a wide variety of individuals from countries all around the world who are subject to exclusion and deportation proceedings.

In their jobs, DEOs:

- manage detainee cases

- process detainees— referring them for medical and other services, assigning living quarters, and issuing clothing and other necessities

- review documentation and inform detainees about their rights and obligations

- ensure the safety, well-being, and order of detainees at detention facilities

- assist other officers in locating aliens who are violating the law

- transport detainees to detention facilities and to other countries

Immigration Inspector

Immigration Inspectors (II) are uniformed officers of the INS. They are often the first officials that travelers meet at airports and other ports of entry to the United States. As people cross the border or disembark from their flights or sea voyages, IIs ask questions, examine documents, and determine the intent of those entering the country. Although not a law enforcement position, IIs investigate and verify the immigration status of illegal aliens and, when necessary, detain and remove them. They also perform searches and seizures and, in the process, must make quick judgments. IIs work with the INS' canine force to detect illegal drugs and aliens. Some IIs are intelligence agents who gather information on terrorists and smugglers. Immigration inspectors work closely with the U.S. Department of Agriculture, the Public Health Service, the Customs Service, the Drug Enforcement Administration, and the FBI to enforce immigration laws.

In their jobs, IIs:

- establish professional, friendly contact with people as they enter the United States

- enforce immigration and related laws

- detect and prevent illegal entry into the United States

- assist other professionals in performing duties associated with immigration and customs

QUALIFICATIONS

All candidates for Immigration Agent, Deportation Officer, Criminal Investigator-Special Agent, and Immigration Inspector positions must have either three years of work experience that demonstrates strong analytical, planning, organization, and communication skills;   a bachelor's degree (any major) from an accredited college or university; or a combination of experience and college course work (one year of education equals nine months of experience).

All candidates for Border Patrol Agent position at the GS-5 entry level must have either one year of experience that demonstrates an ability to take charge, make decisions and maintain composure in stressful situations; ability to gather factual information through questioning, observation, and examination of documents and records; and demonstrate a propensity to learn both on the job and through formal instruction; a bachelor's degree in any field from an accredited university or college; or a combination of education and work experience (each year of full-time college equates to three months experience). Candidates may also qualify for the GS-7 entry level for Border Patrol Agent, depending upon having other specialized experience or education.

All candidates for Detention Enforcement Officer positions at the GS-4 entry level must have either one year of progressively responsible clerical, office, or other work experience that indicates ability to acquire the particular knowledge and skills needed to perform the duties of a DEO; or two years of education obtained in an accredited business, secretarial or technical school, junior college, college, or university; or a combination of experience and education (experience and education are converted into a percentage of the total experience and education requirements, the percentages are added together, and equate to at least 100 percent to qualify.) Candidates may also qualify for the GS-5 entry level for DEO positions, depending upon having other specialized experience, education, or a combination of the two.

Additional qualifications are:

- U.S. citizenship

- a valid state driver's license

- successful completion of a written exam

- successful completion of a medical exam and drug test

- successful completion of a background investigation

- Immigration Agents, Border Patrol Agents, Detention Enforcement Officers, Deportation Officers and Criminal Investigators must be less than 37 years old when hired (if you have previously served in a federal civilian law enforcement position prior to age 37, you may be exempt from this requirement)

- successful completion of an oral board interview (Border Patrol Agents only)

- have, for three out of the last five years immediately prior to applying for these positions, resided in the United States; worked for the U.S. government as an employee overseas in a federal or military capacity; or been a dependent of a U.S. federal or military employee serving overseas.

TRAINING

All candidates for Border Patrol Agent, Immigration Agent, Criminal Investigator, Detention Enforcement Officer, Deportation Officer, and Immigration Inspector positions must complete a residential training program. INS Officer Corps trainees must complete a challenging training course at either the Immigration Officer Academy at the Federal Law Enforcement Training Center in Glynco, Georgia, or the Border Patrol Academy in Charleston, South Carolina. The length of training varies depending on the position. Detention Enforcement officers train for eight weeks; Immigration Agents, Immigration Inspectors, and Deportation Officers for sixteen to twenty weeks; Border Patrol Agents for eighteen weeks; and special agents for sixteen to twenty weeks.

APPLICATION PROCEDURES

Border Patrol applicants can apply anytime during an open period by calling 1-888-300-5500, Ext. 1000, or fill out an online application at http://www.usajobs.opm.gov. Open periods for the Border Patrol are scheduled several times a year and are announced by public notice. For more information, call 1-800-238-1945.

To inquire about job openings for Criminal Investigator, Immigration Agent, Immigration Inspector, and Deportation Officer and to get dates for the next open period, call (612) 725-3253.

To inquire about Detention Enforcement Officer job openings and to get dates for the next open period, call 612-725-3496.

Veterans who have served for more than 180 days of active duty, all or part of which occurred after August 4, 1964, and were discharged with other than a dishonorable discharge may be eligible for a Veteran's Readjustment Appointment (VRA). Reservists or guard members who have served for a period of less than 181 days of active duty may also be eligible for a VRA appointment under certain circumstances. If eligible for a VRA appointment, then those applying for Immigration Inspector, Immigration Agent, Criminal Investigator, Deportation Officer or Detention Enforcement Officer positions do NOT have to take the written test.

Graduates from an accredited four-year college or university with a grade point average of at least 3.45 (on a 4.0 scale) for all undergraduate courses, or graduates in the upper 10 percent of their class or major university subdivision, may qualify as an Outstanding Scholar. Outstanding Scholars do NOT have to take the written test if applying for Immigration Inspector or Criminal Investigator positions.

For additional information concerning VRA or Outstanding Scholar appointments and application procedures, call 612-725-3253.

For more information about Officer Corps career opportunities with the INS, visit the U.S. Immigration and Naturalization Service Web site at http://www.ins.usdoj.gov or send your inquiry to the INS Hiring Center at the following address:

U.S. Immigration and Naturalization Service
Career Opportunities Unit, 1 Federal Drive
Fort Snelling, Minnesota 55111-4055
For further information, contact:
U.S. Immigration and Naturalization Service
U.S. Department of Justice
Washington, D.C. 20536

INTERPOL-U.S. NATIONAL CENTRAL BUREAU

MISSION

The INTERPOL-U.S. National Central Bureau (USNCB) represents the United States in the International Criminal Police Organization (INTERPOL) and serves as the communications link between U.S. police and foreign police for the purpose of coordinating international criminal investigative matters. The broad range of offenses warranting investigative assistance through the USNCB includes murder and other violent crimes; robbery, drug trafficking, and other offenses; all forms of financial and economic fraud such as counterfeiting, money laundering, credit card and postal fraud; and terrorism matters, to name but a few. The USNCB also assists with tracing weapons, explosives, and misused licenses, and the location or identification of missing or deceased persons.

HISTORICAL REVIEW

Congressional approval for U.S. membership in INTERPOL was granted in 1938 when the Attorney General was authorized to interact with the Organization on behalf of the United States. World War II intervened, however, and U.S. participation was interrupted until 1947.

At that time, the authority for representing the United States was delegated to the Federal Bureau of Investigation. In 1950, the FBI discontinued the function and the Treasury Department continued an informal liaison with INTERPOL to maintain viable international contacts to assist in uncovering narcotics and currency violations.

In 1958, the Attorney General officially designated the Secretary of the Treasury as the U.S. representative to INTERPOL, and in 1969, the USNCB was established within the Treasury Department. In 1977, an arrangement between Justice and Treasury officials established dual authority in administering the USNCB. This Memorandum of Understanding designated the Attorney General as the permanent representative to INTERPOL and the Secretary of the Treasury as the alternate representative.

The Memorandum of Understanding was amended in 1981, designating the USNCB as an office within the Department of Justice, while oversight and management of USNCB functions and activities continue to be shared by both Justice and Treasury.

FUNCTIONS AND ACTIVITIES

The USNCB coordinates international criminal investigations through cooperation with federal, state, and local law enforcement agencies, forming an integral part of the U.S. efforts to confront the problem of international crime. Federal and state police entities detail senior investigators and special agents to the USNCB to staff the criminal, drugs, alien/fugitive, financial fraud, and state liaison divisions. These agents coordinate the exchange of criminal information between the United States and other members of INTERPOL to ensure that all relevant U.S. laws and regulations, as well as Department of Justice and INTERPOL policies guidelines, are met.

Agencies Represented at the USNCB

Participating agencies at the USNCB include the Federal Bureau of Investigation; U.S. Marshals Service; Drug Enforcement Administration; Immigration and Naturalization Service; Criminal Division of the Department of Justice; U.S. Customs Service; U.S. Secret Service; Internal Revenue Service; Bureau of Alcohol, Tobacco and Firearms; Office of the Inspector General, Department of Agriculture; U.S. Postal Inspection Service; Diplomatic Security Service, Department of State; the Financial Crimes Enforcement Network (FinCEN); U.S. Mint; and a State Police representative.

Liaison with State and Local Police

To better serve the criminal investigative needs of the state and local police, the USNCB implemented the INTERPOL/State Liaison Program in 1987. Through this program, state authorities designate a focal point within their police system to serve as the INTERPOL contact for the state. International leads developed in criminal investigations being conducted by a state or local police entity are pursued through the liaison office to the USNCB. Conversely, requests for criminal investigative assistance from abroad are funneled by the USNCB through the relevant state liaison office for action by the appropriate state or local agency. A state police representative is detailed to the USNCB to coordinate the State Liaison Program.

USNCB Sub-Bureaus

To effectively address the international law enforcement needs of U.S. territories, the USNCB has sub-bureaus in Puerto Rico, the U.S. Virgin Islands, and American Samoa.

For further information, visit the USNCB Web site at http://www.usdoj.gov/usncb or write to:
INTERPOL-USNCB
U.S. Department of Justice
Washington, D.C. 20530
Telephone: (202) 616-8006

OFFICE OF JUSTICE PROGRAMS

MISSION

The Office of Justice Programs (OJP) provides federal leadership, coordination, and assistance needed to make the nation's justice system more efficient and effective in preventing and controlling crime. OJP is responsible for collecting statistical data and conducting analyses, identifying emerging criminal justice issues, developing and testing promising approaches to address these issues, evaluating program results, and disseminating these findings and other information to state and local governments.

FUNCTIONS AND ACTIVITIES

The Office of Justice Programs is comprised of the following bureaus and offices:

- The Bureau of Justice Assistance (BJA), which provides funding, training, and technical assistance to state and local governments to combat violent and drug-related crime and help improve the criminal justice system

- The Bureau of Justice Statistics (BJS), which is responsible for collecting and analyzing data on crime, criminal offenders, crime victims, and the operations of justice systems at all levels of government

- The National Institute of Justice (NIJ), which sponsors research and development programs, conducts demonstrations of innovative approaches to improve criminal justice, and develops new criminal justice technologies

- The Office of Juvenile Justice and Delinquency Prevention (OJJDP), which provides grants and contracts to states to help them improve their juvenile justice systems and sponsors innovative research, demonstration, evaluation, statistics, replication, technical assistance, and training programs to help improve the nation's understanding of and response to juvenile violence and delinquency

- The Office for Victims of Crime, which administers victim compensation and assistance grant programs and provides funding, training, and technical assistance to victim service organizations, criminal justice agencies, and other professionals to improve the nation's response to crime victims

- The Violence Against Women Office, which coordinates legislative and other initiatives relating to violence against women and administers grant programs to help prevent, detect, and stop violence against women, including domestic violence, sexual assault, and stalking

- The Drug Court Program Office, which supports the development, implementation, and improvement of drug courts through technical assistance and training and grants to state, local, or tribal governments and courts

- The Corrections Program Office, which provides financial and technical assistance to state and local governments to implement corrections-related programs, including correctional facility construction and corrections-based drug treatment programs

- The Executive Office for Weed and Seed, which helps communities build stronger, safer neighborhoods by implementing the Weed and Seed Strategy, a community-based, multi-disciplinary approach to combating crime

■ The Office for State and Local Domestic Preparedness Support, which is responsible for enhancing the capacity of state and local jurisdictions to prepare for and respond to incidents of domestic terrorism involving chemical and biological agents, radiological and explosive devices, and other weapons of mass destruction

■ The Office of the Police Corps and Law Enforcement Education, which provides college educational assistance to students who commit to public service in law enforcement and scholarships with no service commitment to dependents of law enforcement officers who died in the line of duty

For further information, visit the OJP Web site at http://www.ojp.usdoj.gov or write to:

Department of Justice
Office of Justice Programs
810 Seventh Street, NW
Washington, D.C. 20531
Telephone: (202) 307-0703
E-mail: askocpa@ojp.usdoj.gov

U.S. MARSHALS SERVICE

MISSION

The U.S. Marshals Service is the nation's oldest federal law enforcement agency. The mission of the U.S. Marshals Service is to protect the federal courts and ensure the effective operation of the judicial system. Marshals and deputies of the Marshals Service operate as both officers of the federal courts and law enforcement agents of the Executive Branch within the ninety-four federal judicial districts and the Superior Court of the District of Columbia.

The Marshals Service provides direct support to the federal courts by protecting members of the judiciary, providing security for court facilities, executing court orders, and disbursing funds and collecting fees relating to court activities. In addition, the Marshals Service has custody of federal prisoners and provides for their appearance in court as well as their transportation to and between federal prison facilities.

The Marshals Service is also responsible for arresting federal fugitives, protecting endangered government witnesses and their families, and administering the National Asset Seizure and Forfeiture Program, which maintains custody and control of seized money and property acquired with the proceeds of certain illegal activities.

U.S. Marshals transport a fugitive felon. (Photo courtesy of U.S. Marshals Service, Department of Justice.)

HISTORICAL REVIEW

The positions of U.S. Marshal and Deputy Marshal were created by the first Congress in the Judiciary Act of 1789, the same legislation that established the Supreme Court and the federal judicial system. The marshals were given extensive authority to support the federal courts within their judicial districts and to carry out all lawful orders issued by judges, Congress, or the President.

Since their primary function was to support the federal courts, the marshals and their deputies served the subpoenas, summonses, writs, warrants, and other process issued by the courts, made all the arrests, and handled all the prisoners. The marshals paid the fees and expenses of the court clerks, U.S. Attorneys, jurors, and witnesses. They rented the courtrooms and jail space and hired the bailiffs, criers, and janitors. In effect, they ensured that the courts functioned smoothly.

Federal Representatives

Marshals also provided local representation for the federal government within their districts, and took the national census every ten years until 1880. They distributed Presidential proclamations, collected a variety of statistical information on commerce and manufacturing, supplied the names of government employees for the national register, and performed other routine tasks needed for the central government to function effectively.

For the American people, the marshals personified the authority of the federal government within their communities. The frequent outbursts of opposition to federal power were often first directed at individual marshals or deputies. The marshal was, in effect, the point of contact in the friction between the national government and the state and local communities. The Whiskey Rebels of 1794, for example, violently opposed the national tax on whiskey. They expressed that opposition by taking a marshal prisoner. Northern marshals enforced the bitterly resented Fugitive Slave Law of 1850. Every time they took an escaped slave into custody, they risked the wrath of angry mobs intent on freeing the fugitive. Southern marshals reconstructed the South and protected the rights of the newly freed slaves after the Civil War.

The civil rights movements of the twentieth century once again involved the U.S. Marshals. On the night of September 30, 1962, President John F. Kennedy sent military forces to Oxford, Mississippi, after a major riot erupted over the attempt by marshals to enforce the court-ordered enrollment of James Meredith, a black student.

At the Pentagon in October 1967, anti-Vietnam war demonstrators confronted a line of marshals blocking their path to the Defense Department. Behind the marshals stood regular army troops. In their position between the rioters and the army, the marshals symbolized the civilian power of the government which, when overcome, allowed the army to step into the fray. The marshals were on hand to make arrests, a civilian power not usually bestowed on the military. In a government based on the concept of civilian supremacy, the U.S. Marshals and their deputies provided the civilian enforcement power. The military was restricted to emergency support.

Selection

Traditionally, Presidents selected the marshals from the districts where they served. The individuals appointed as marshals usually had strong ties within the President's political party, thus ensuring that they were in sympathy with his policies. At the same time, they were prominent members of the communities where they served as Marshal. They understood the people, for they were dealing with their friends and neighbors. This was particularly important in the nineteenth century when lack of communications made the national government distant and seemingly foreign.

In addition, for most of their history, U.S. Marshals enjoyed independence in performing their duties. No headquarters or central administration existed to supervise the work of the marshals until the late 1950s. Even then, the Executive Office of the U.S. Marshals had no real power over the districts until it was transformed into the U.S. Marshals Service in 1969 and was given control of the district budgets and the hiring of deputies.

FUNCTIONS AND ACTIVITIES

Judicial Security

Protection of federal judicial officials, including judges, attorneys, and jurors, holds a high priority with the Marshals Service. Deputy marshals use the latest security techniques and devices at highly sensitive trials throughout the nation.

Fully trained contract officers comprise the agency's Court Security Officer Program. These specially deputized officers have full law enforcement authority and occupy a vital role in courthouse security. Deputies and Court Security Officers provide security at nearly 800 facilities with court operations.

The Marshals Service oversees each aspect of courthouse construction projects, from design through completion, to ensure the safety of federal judges, court personnel and the public.

Fugitive Investigations

Annually, the Marshals Service apprehends 55 percent of all federal fugitives. The agency executes more arrest warrants than all other federal law enforcement agencies combined. Working with law enforcement authorities at the federal, state, local, and international level, the Marshals Service apprehends thousands of dangerous felons each year. The Marshals Service has become the primary agency responsible for tracking and extraditing fugitives who are apprehended in other countries and wanted for prosecution in the United States.

The Marshals Service has representatives coordinating fugitive matters at the El Paso Intelligence Center in Texas, National Drug Intelligence Center in Pennsylvania, Sacramento Intelligence Unit in California, Missing and Exploited Children Task Force in Virginia, and at INTERPOL in Washington, D.C., and France.

International Operations

The Marshals Service has been designated by the Department of Justice as the primary U.S. agency to apprehend fugitives who are wanted by foreign nations and believed to be in the United States.

A witness under protection by U.S. Marshals. Masks, hoods, and other devices are used to hide a witness' identity during court testimony and before Congressional hearings. (Photo courtesy of U.S. Marshals Service, Department of Justice.)

Witness protection by U.S. Marshals. (Photo courtesy of U.S. Marshals Service, Department of Justice.)

Witness Security

The Marshals Service ensures the safety of witnesses who risk their lives testifying for the government in organized crime and other significant criminal activity cases. Since 1971, more than 6,500 witnesses have been protected, relocated, and given new identities by the Marshals Service. The successful operation of the Witness Security Program has been generally recognized as providing a unique and valuable tool in the government's war against major criminal enterprises.

Prisoner Services

The Marshals Service houses over 28,000 federal, unsentenced prisoners each day in federal, state, and local jails. Approximately 70 percent of the agency's prisoners are housed in 1,200 state and local jails. Another 30 percent are housed in Federal Bureau of Prisons facilities located around the country. Additionally, in areas where detention space is scarce, the Marshals Service uses Cooperative Agreement Program funds to improve local jail conditions and expand jail capacity in return for guaranteed space for federal prisoners.

Justice Prisoner and Alien Transportation System

In 1995, the air fleets of the Marshals Service and Immigration and Naturalization Service merged to create the Justice Prisoner and Alien Transportation System (JPATS). The merger created a more efficient and effective system for transporting prisoners and criminal aliens. Operated by the Marshals Service, JPATS is one of the largest transporters of prisoners in the world, handling hundreds of requests every day to move prisoners between judicial districts, correctional institutions, and other countries. Approximately 200,000 prisoner and immigrant movements a year are completed by JPATS via coordinated air and ground systems.

Asset Forfeiture Program

The Marshals Service is responsible for the management and disposal of seized and forfeited properties acquired by criminals through illegal activities. The agency currently manages nearly $1 billion worth of property. This program is a centralized, efficient management system that the Marshals Service uses to promptly dispose of assets seized by all Department of Justice agencies. A headquarters staff and three regional offices work to maximize the net return from seized property, reinvesting the property and proceeds for law enforcement use.

Special Programs

The Marshals Service carries out hundreds of special missions each year that are related to its broad law enforcement and judicial security responsibilities.

The Special Operations Group (SOG) is a highly-trained force of deputy marshals with the responsibility and capability of responding to emergency situations where federal law is violated or where federal property is endangered. Most SOG members are full-time deputy marshals in district offices throughout the nation, and remain on call 24-hours a day for SOG missions.

As part of the Missile Escort Program, specially trained deputy marshals provide security and law enforcement assistance to the Department of Defense and the U.S. Air Force when Minuteman and cruise missiles are moved between military facilities.

TRAINING

Training in the U.S. Marshals Service occurs at three levels (basic, advanced, and special operations). The Service operates the U.S. Marshals Service Training Academy at the Federal Law Enforcement Training Center (FLETC), Glynco, Georgia, and a second facility for its Special Operations Group and for other federal and nonfederal agencies at Camp Beauregard, Louisiana.

Basic Deputy Marshal Training

U.S. Marshal candidates must successfully complete fourteen weeks of intensive basic training at the Service's Academy. For the first eight weeks, candidates attend the Criminal Investigator Training Program, conducted for fifty-six different law enforcement organizations, including the U.S. Secret Service; the Naval Criminal Investigative Service; the Bureau of Alcohol, Tobacco and Firearms; the Internal Revenue Service; and the U.S. Customs Service.

Candidates who successfully complete the first training phase enter the Basic Deputy U.S. Marshal training, which is focused specifically on those skills required by the Service. This six-week portion of the program covers judicial protection, prisoner transportation, witness security, fugitive investigations and apprehensions, and execution and enforcement of court orders.

Specialized and Advanced Training

Within three years of entry on duty, deputy U.S. marshals receive additional training in key operational areas such as asset seizure and forfeiture, enforcement operations, court security, and witness security. Moreover, the Advanced Deputy U.S. Marshals Training Program is a four-week course designed to enhance the deputy's knowledge, skills, and proficiency in all operational areas.

The specialized Protective Services School is a two-week program dedicated to dignitary protection. This school was established to train personnel responsible for the Witness Security Program.

The Fugitive Course is a two-week training session focusing primarily on narcotic fugitive investigations, clandestine labs, and narcotics trafficking.

Special Operations—Camp Beauregard

Training for the Service's SOG members is conducted by Marshals Service personnel at the Service's facility in Camp Beauregard, Louisiana. SOG deputies are trained in varied disciplines, such as building entry and search techniques, helicopter operations (repelling and deployment), confrontation management (both urban and rural), operational planning, small unit tactics, bomb recognition, emergency care, etc.

Under the sponsorship of the Anti-Terrorism Assistance Program of the U.S. Department of State, nearly 300 police personnel from Mexico, Ecuador, Honduras, Costa Rica, Bolivia, the Philippines, and Colombia have received training in counterterrorism, advanced specialized police tactics, and personal protection from SOG personnel.

QUALIFICATIONS

To qualify as a deputy U.S. marshal, applicants must:

- be a citizen of the U.S.

- be between the ages of 21 and 36 (must not have reached the 37th birthday)

- have a bachelor's degree, three years of responsible experience, or an equivalent combination of education and experience

- successfully complete a written test

- successfully complete an oral interview

- be in excellent physical condition

- permit a background investigation

- complete a rigorous thirteen-week basic training program at the Federal Law Enforcement Training Center

For further information, visit the Marshals Service Web site at http://www.usdoj.gov/marshals or contact:

U.S. Marshals Service
Employment and Compensation Division
Field Staffing Branch
600 Army Navy Drive
Arlington, Virginia 22202-4210
Telephone: (202) 307-9408

NATIONAL INSTITUTE OF JUSTICE

The National Institute of Justice (NIJ), under the Office of Justice Programs, is the principal criminal justice research agency of the Department of Justice. NIJ sponsors and generates research about crime, its causes, and control. Priority is given to police-relevant research yielding new approaches and information for state and local agencies to use in preventing and reducing crime.

In addition, NIJ suggests new approaches, provides training and technical assistance, assesses new technology for criminal justice, and disseminates its findings to state and local practitioners and policymakers. A wide range of information is available for distribution to interested individuals and organizations through NIJ's National Criminal Justice Reference Service.

For further information, visit NIJ online at http://www.nij.usdoj.gov or contact:

Director
National Institute of Justice
810 Seventh Street, NW
Washington, D.C. 20531
Telephone: (202) 307-2942
Fax: (202) 307-6394

DEPARTMENT OF LABOR

EMPLOYMENT STANDARDS ADMINISTRATION

MISSION
Within the U.S. Department of Labor, the Assistant Secretary for Employment Standards is responsible for administering and directing employment standards dealing with minimum wage, overtime, and child labor standards; registration of farm labor contractors; determining prevailing wage rates to be paid on government contracts and subcontracts; nondiscrimination and affirmative action for minorities, women, veterans, and handicapped workers on government contracts and subcontracts; workers' compensation programs for federal and certain private employers and employees; and internal union democracy, financial integrity, and union elections, which protect the rights of union members.

The Wage and Hour Division, in addition to planning, directing, and administering programs dealing with a variety of federal labor legislation, has enforcement responsibility in ensuring that prevailing wages and overtime standards are paid in accordance with the provisions of the Davis-Bacon and related acts, such as the Service Contract Act, Public Contracts Act, and Contract Work Hours and Safety Standards Act.

FUNCTIONS AND ACTIVITIES
Wage-hour Compliance Officers inspect employers' time, payroll, and personnel records to ensure compliance with federal laws on minimum wages, overtime pay, employment of minors, and equal employment opportunity. They often interview employees to verify the employer's records and to check for complaints.

For further information, contact:
Employment Standards Administration
Office of Public Affairs
Department of Labor
Room S-3321, 200 Constitution Avenue NW
Washington, D.C. 20210
Telephone: (202) 693-0023

MINE SAFETY AND HEALTH ADMINISTRATION—METAL AND NONMETAL

MSHA inspectors check for violations. (Photo courtesy of the Mine Safety and Health Administration, Department of Labor.)

MISSION

The more than 14,000 mining and milling operations in the United States are under the authority of the Mine Safety and Health Administration (MSHA) of the Department of Labor, as established by the Federal Mine Safety and Health Act of 1977. This includes coal and lignite mines; metal and nonmetal minerals facilities, such as limestone and uranium mines, from small two-person operations to complex mines employing hundreds of workers. MSHA has designed its programs to help miners and mine operators control the special hazards associated with each, such as explosive methane gas, unstable mining structures, poisonous atmospheres, radiation, and harmful dusts.

To carry out this critically important mission, the agency uses an enforcement program complemented by training and education and technical and engineering assistance.

HISTORICAL REVIEW

1910—The Bureau of Mines is created in the Department of the Interior. Federal safety and health role is limited to research and investigation.

1941—The right of entry is given to federal inspectors to make annual or other inspections and investigations in coal mines to obtain information. No safety or health regulations are mandated.

1952—Federal Coal Mine Safety Act is passed. Emphasis is placed on preventing major disasters. Annual inspections are required at underground coal mines. Mandatory safety standards for underground coal mines are set, with more stringent standards for "gassy" mines. Federal inspectors are given authority to issue orders of withdrawal in situations of imminent danger as well as notices of violation. Also mandated are orders of withdrawal where less serious violations were not properly corrected. Enforcement of federal standards by state inspectors is allowed under the state plan system.

1969—The Federal Coal Mine Health and Safety Act of 1969 increases enforcement powers in coal mines. Surface mines are covered. Four annual inspections are required for each underground coal mine. Miners are given the right to request a federal inspection. State enforcement plans discontinued. Mandatory fines for all violations are set. Criminal penalties for knowing and willful violations are set. Safety standards for all coal mines are strengthened and health standards are adopted.

1973—Mining Enforcement and Safety Administration (MESA) is created as a new Interior Department agency. The new agency assumes safety and health enforcement functions formerly carried out by the Bureau of Mines.

1977—The Federal Mine Safety and Health Act of 1977 is created. The Act places coal mines and metal and nonmetal mines under a single law, with enforcement provisions similar to the 1969 Act and moves the enforcement agency to the Department of Labor, renaming it the Mine Safety and Health Administration (MSHA).

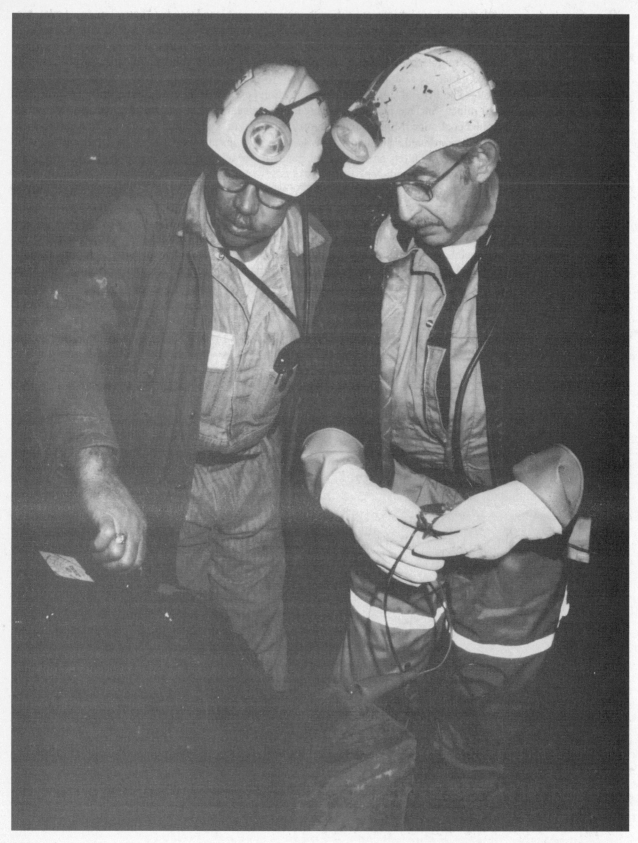

MSHA inspectors check for harmful gas. (Photo courtesy of the Mine Safety and Health Administration, Department of Labor.)

FUNCTIONS AND ACTIVITIES

Under the Federal Mine Safety and Health Administration Act of 1977, MSHA inspectors must issue a citation for each violation of a health or safety standard they encounter. Each citation entails a civil penalty. Usually, civil penalties are assessed against the mine operator. However, agents of corporate operators may individually be fined for violations they knowingly permitted. Individual miners can be fined for violating smoking prohibitions.

Several provisions of the act concern "significant and substantial" violations. A legal decision has defined a significant and substantial (or "S & S") violation as one that is reasonably likely to result in a reasonably serious injury or illness. In writing each citation, the MSHA inspector determines whether the violation is S & S or not.

In several situations, the law provides that MSHA may order miners withdrawn from a mine or part of a mine. Some of the most frequent reasons for orders of withdrawal are, imminent danger to the miners, failure to correct a violation within the time allowed; and failure to secure an area during an accident investigation.

If MSHA determines that a mine has a pattern of S & S violations, the law provides that the agency shall notify the operator. Subsequently, any S & S violation found within ninety days automatically triggers a withdrawal order. Each additional S & S violation means another order until the mine had a clean inspection with no S & S violations.

The law prohibits discrimination against miners, their representatives, or job applicants for exercising their safety and health rights. The MSHA investigates complaints of discrimination. If evidence of discrimination is found, the Labor Department can take the miner's case before the Federal Mine Safety and Health Review Commission, an independent judicial body.

The act provides for criminal sanctions against mine operators who knowingly and willfully violate safety and health standards. The MSHA initially investigates possible knowing and willful violations; if evidence of such violation is found, the agency turns over its findings to the Justice Department.

TRAINING

The MSHA maintains a fully staffed and extensively equipped training facility, the National Mine Health and Safety Academy, in Beckley, West Virginia, which offers courses in various aspects of mine safety and health for MSHA's inspectors, individuals from state and local government agencies and mine management and labor organizations. The Academy provides courses at its Beckley location and, when needed, in the field.

Publications, audiovisual programs, and other training materials are produced at the Academy and distributed to the mining community on request.

For further information, contact:
Mine Safety and Health Administration
Office of Information and Public Affairs
4015 Wilson Boulevard, Room 718
Arlington, Virginia 22203
Telephone: (703) 235-1452 or (703) 235-8480

OCCUPATIONAL SAFETY AND HEALTH ADMINISTRATION

MISSION

The enforcement responsibility of the Occupational Safety and Health Administration (OSHA) is to enforce the mandatory job safety and health standards that OSHA establishes.

HISTORICAL REVIEW

The Occupational Safety and Health Act (OSHAct) of 1970 was passed by a bipartisan Congress "...to assure so far as possible every working man and woman in the nation safe and healthful working conditions and to preserve our human resources."

FUNCTIONS AND ACTIVITIES

To enforce its standards, OSHA is authorized under the Act to conduct workplace inspections. Every establishment covered by the Act is subject to inspection by OSHA Compliance Safety and Health Officers. Similarly, states, with their own occupational safety and health programs, conduct inspections using qualified Compliance Safety and Health Officers.

Under the Act, "upon presenting appropriate credentials to the owner, operator or agent in charge," an OSHA Compliance Officer is authorized to:

- Enter without delay and at reasonable times any factory, plant, or establishment, construction site, workplace, or environment where work is performed by an employee of an employer

- Inspect and investigate during regular working hours, and at other reasonable times, and within reasonable limits and in a reasonable manner, any such place of employment and all pertinent conditions, structures, machines, apparatus, devices, equipment and materials therein, and to question privately any such employer, owner, operator, agent or employee

With very few exceptions, inspections are conducted without advance notice. There are, however, special circumstances under which OSHA may indeed give notice to the employer.

After an inspection tour, the Compliance Officer submits his report to the area director, who determines what citations, if any, will be issued and what penalties, if any, will be proposed. If an employer is convicted of a willful violation of a standard that has resulted in the death of an employee, the offense is punishable by a court-imposed fine, imprisonment, or both. A second conviction doubles these maximum penalties.

TRAINING

The OSHA Training Institute in Des Plaines, Illinois, provides basic and advanced training and education in safety and health for federal and state compliance officers, state consultants, other federal agency personnel, and private sector employers, employees, and their representatives. Institute courses cover areas such as electrical hazards, machine guarding, ventilation, and ergonomics.

For further information, visit OSHA's Web site at http://www.osha.gov or contact:
Occupational Safety and Health Administration
Office of Public Affairs
200 Constitution Avenue NW, Room N-3647
Washington, D.C. 20210
Telephone: (202) 693-1999

PENSION AND WELFARE BENEFITS ADMINISTRATION

MISSION

The Pension and Welfare Benefits Administration (PWBA) is charged with assuring the responsible management of nearly one million pension plans and 4.5 million health and welfare plans. PWBA is the national guardian of a vast private retirement and welfare benefit system that contains nearly $2 trillion in plan assets and accounts for almost 20 percent of all securities traded on the New York Stock Exchange.

HISTORICAL REVIEW

Since 1974, the U.S. Department of Labor's Pension and Welfare Benefits Administration has helped to protect the economic future and retirement security of working Americans. Established when the Employee Retirement Income Security Act (ERISA) was passed in 1974, PWBA has been at the center of protecting this system.

FUNCTIONS AND ACTIVITIES

PWBA's enforcement mission includes:

- conducting civil and criminal investigations related to plan operations and investments.

- performing investigations of employee benefit plans to ensure compliance with the fiduciary responsibility standards of ERISA

- coordinating and providing support in civil litigation and criminal prosecutions involving ERISA with various federal agencies (i.e., IRS, Justice Department, Pension Benefit Guaranty Corporation)

Investigators and auditors comprise the largest component of PWBA and are at the front line of enforcing the Employee Retirement Income Security Act. Investigators and auditors acquire detailed knowledge of program legislation and regulations as well as knowledge of auditing and investigative techniques. Among other duties, they conduct on-site audits or investigations by interviewing persons and reviewing records and prepare reports identifying and evaluating ERISA violations uncovered during an investigation.

TRAINING

On-the-job training and classroom training are provided.

QUALIFICATIONS

To be qualified as an investigator/auditor, candidates must have a combination of education and/or work experience in one or more of the following fields: accounting, finance/economics, law, investigative programs, employee benefit administration, or public administration.

For further information, visit PWBA online at http://www.dol.gov/dol/pwba or contact:
Administrative Officer
PWBA-Room N-5668
U.S. Department of Labor
200 Constitution Avenue NW
Washington, D.C. 20210
Telephone: (202) 219-6471 or (202) 219-8921 (Office of Public Affairs)

DEPARTMENT OF STATE

BUREAU OF DIPLOMATIC SECURITY

MISSION

The Bureau of Diplomatic Security (DS), an organization within the U.S. Department of State, has a broad scope of global responsibilities. In the United States, DS protects the Secretary of State, the U.S. Ambassador to the United Nations, and cabinet level foreign dignitaries who visit the United States. DS investigates passport and visa fraud violations, conducts personnel security investigations, and issues security clearances. Overseas, DS special agents advise chiefs of mission on all security matters and develop and implements effective security programs to safeguard all personnel who work in U.S. diplomatic missions around the world.

HISTORICAL REVIEW

Since 1916, the State Department has conducted investigations and provided personal protection. These responsibilities increased when the Bureau of Diplomatic Security was created by an Act of Congress in 1986. The Bureau was created to "provide a secure environment for the conduct of American diplomacy and the promotion of American interests worldwide" and to increase security awareness among all Americans living, working, and traveling abroad.

FUNCTIONS AND ACTIVITIES

Investigations

DS special agents investigate more than 4,000 passport and visa fraud investigations each year. These felonies are often committed in connection with other more serious crimes by individuals looking to change their identities and conceal their activities and movements. DS has investigated passport and visa fraud cases that have been connected to drug trafficking, international organized crime, money laundering, pedophilia, and murder. DS investigations help secure U.S. borders and protect the national security of the United States.

In addition, DS conducts protective intelligence investigations into threats made against the Secretary of State, other Department employees, facilities here and abroad, foreign dignitaries under our protection, and international missions in the United States. Since the East African bombings, DS has investigated thousands of threats directed at U.S. missions and personnel around the world.

DS also administers the interagency Rewards for Justice Program, which allows the Secretary of State to offer rewards of up to $5 million for information that either prevents or resolves acts of international terrorism against U.S. interests worldwide. This program is a key component of the U.S. government's fight against international terrorism.

In addition, the Bureau conducts personnel security investigations of ambassadorial nominees, employees, applicants, contractors, and others seeking access to State Department information or facilities. Each year, DS processes an average of 14,000 security clearances.

Protection

Diplomatic Security protects more dignitaries than any other agency in the U.S. Government. DS special agents guard the Secretary of State 24-hours a day, seven days a week, everywhere he goes in the world. DS also protects the U.S. Ambassador to the United Nations and foreign dignitaries below the level of head of state who visit the United States. Among those foreign dignitaries who have received DS protection are foreign ministers, former heads of state, members of the British royal family, representatives of the Middle East Peace Delegations, the Secretary General of NATO, Palestinian Authority Chairman Yassar Arafat, and the Dalai Lama. DS coordinates this protection with state and local police and with other federal law enforcement agencies in the cities to be visited.

The Bureau also assists foreign embassies and consulates in the United States with the security for their missions and personnel.

Abroad

DS special agents serving in Regional Security offices provide the first line of defense for U.S. diplomatic personnel, their families, U.S. diplomatic missions, and national security information. DS security officers advise chiefs of mission on all security matters, and develop and implement the programs that shield each U.S. mission and residence overseas from physical and technical attack.

DS special agents, in concert with other mission or post elements, formulate a number of subject specific action plans to deal with various emergency contingencies, ranging from hostage taking to evacuations. Often, in times of crisis and political instability, DS special agents rely on the U.S. military for assistance. Since the early 1990s, DS agents have worked closely with the military, especially the U.S. Marine Fleet Antiterrorism Security Teams, which have provided emergency force protection support for Department of State operations in a number of countries throughout the world when the host government was unable to do so.

In addition, special agents are the primary liaison with foreign police and overseas security services in an effort to obtain support for U.S. law enforcement initiatives and investigations. Much of the investigative and law enforcement liaison work done by special agents abroad is on behalf of other federal, state, and local agencies.

Through the Antiterrorism Assistance Program, DS arranges for civilian security personnel from friendly governments to be trained in police procedures focused on terrorism. Since the program's inception in 1983, more then 20,000 students from more than 200 countries have received training in bomb detection, crime scene investigation, airport and building security, maritime security, and dignitary protection.

The DS works with the U.S. private sector on security issues abroad through the Overseas Security Advisory Council (OSAC). The council, cochaired by DS, consists of 25 representatives from the U.S. Government and the American private sector who work together to promote open lines of communication between government and the U.S. business community on overseas security issues of mutual concern. The Council operates an electronic database that can be accessed via the Internet by OSAC's constituency. This database contains a directory of all Foreign Service posts by country, including regional security officers, police organizations, State Department travel advisories, security and crime situations, terrorism profiles, significant anniversary dates, and messages highlighting information of interest to American business travelers.

TRAINING

Six months of training begin with an orientation period in Washington, D.C., followed by basic and specialized training at the Federal Law Enforcement Training Center in Glynco, Georgia. Training continues at State Department facilities in the Washington, D.C., area. Candidates must pass all required tests at FLETC.

Initially, candidates are trained in personal protection techniques, criminal law and investigations, background investigations, first aid, firearms, and defensive driving. To prepare for specific overseas assignments, officers are trained in security management, post operations, counterintelligence, electronic security, and languages. Other instruction includes advanced firearms techniques, explosive devices, ordnance detection, arson investigation, and medical assistance.

QUALIFICATIONS

Candidates must be:

- U.S. citizens

- possess a B.A./B.S. degree at time of appointment

- 20 years of age to apply; candidates must be at least 21 years old but must not have reached their 37th birth date

- if required, register under the Military Selective Service Act

- successfully undergo written and oral assessment

- successfully undergo a thorough background investigation and qualify for a top secret security clearance

- pass a stringent medical exam, be available for worldwide assignment, and qualify for a Department of State Class 01 medical clearance

- pass physical fitness tests and be fit for strenuous physical exertion

- possess a valid U.S. drivers license

- be willing to carry, use, and qualify with firearms throughout career

- be willing to travel and accept assignments throughout the world; officers are required to live and work a substantial portion of their career overseas

- Successfully complete all aspects of 6-month training

Foreign language ability is desirable, but not mandatory. For further information, visit the DS Web site at http://www.ds.state.gov or contact:

U.S. Department of State
Bureau of Diplomatic Security
Attn: Recruitment Staff
2401 E Street, NW, Room H-518
Washington, D.C. 20522
Telephone: (202) 261-8940

DEPARTMENT OF TRANSPORTATION

FEDERAL AIR MARSHAL PROGRAM

FEDERAL AVIATION ADMINISTRATION

Federal Air Marshals are specially trained, armed federal law enforcement officers capable of rapid deployment, worldwide, on U.S. air carriers. The Air Marshal mission is one of strategic deterrence against criminal acts targeting civil aviation. The tactical objective is to save lives.

For further information, contact:
Federal Air Marshal Program
ACT-700, Building 201
FAA Technical Center
Atlantic City, N.J. 08405
Telephone: (609) 485-8700

TRAFFIC LAW ENFORCEMENT DIVISION

NATIONAL HIGHWAY TRAFFIC SAFETY ADMINISTRATION

MISSION

The mission of the Traffic Law Enforcement Division (TLED) of the National Highway Traffic Safety Administration is to assist national, state, and local law enforcement agencies in their efforts to improve traffic safety and reduce traffic crashes. Activities are based on current needs and demands of the national traffic safety and law enforcement community.

FUNCTIONS AND ACTIVITIES

The work of the Traffic Law Enforcement Division is compatible with other NHTSA program priorities in occupant protection, impaired driving, aggressive driving, bicycle safety, speed management, pedestrian safety, motorcycle safety, Emergency Management Service requirements, pupil transportation, and others to increase compliance with the transportation laws.

The TLED works with organizations such as the International Association of Chiefs of Police (IACP), the National Sheriffs' Association (NSA), National Organization of Black Law Enforcement Executives (NOBLE), International Association of Directors of Law Enforcement Standards and Training (IADLEST), the Hispanic American Police Command Officers Association (HAPCOA), and Operation C.A.R.E. to save lives, prevent injuries, and reduce traffic-related health care and other economic costs.

QUALIFICATIONS

For further information, visit the National Highway Traffic Safety Administration, Traffic Law Enforcement Division's Web site at http://www.nhtsa.dot.gov/people/injury/enforce/ or write to:

U.S. Department of Transportation
National Highway Traffic Safety Administration
Traffic Law Enforcement Division, NTS13
400 Seventh Street, SW
Washington, D.C. 20590
Telephone: (202) 366-4295
Fax: (202) 366-7721

U.S. COAST GUARD

U.S. Coast Guard helicopter pursues drug smugglers. (Photo courtesy of the U.S. Coast Guard, Department of Transportation.)

MISSION

As one of the nation's five armed forces, the U.S. Coast Guard is a military, multimission maritime service within the Department of Transportation. Its core role is to protect the public, the environment, and U.S. economic and security interests in any maritime region in which U.S. interests may be at risk, including international waters and America's coasts, ports, and inland waterways. The Coast Guard provides unique benefits to the nation because of its distinctive blend of military, humanitarian, and civilian law enforcement capabilities.

Maritime law enforcement involves the enforcement of all federal laws on the high seas and waters under U.S. jurisdiction, interdiction of smugglers moving drugs and illegal migrants, and enforcement of the Exclusive Economic Zone out to 200 miles at sea. The U.S. Coast Guard works closely with other law enforcement agencies in accomplishing these missions.

HISTORICAL REVIEW

In the early days, the Coast Guard's law enforcement responsibilities were to ensure that U.S. tariffs were not avoided, to protect shipping from pirates, and to intercept contraband. During colonial days and the War for Independence, smuggling was considered to be a patriotic duty of maritime America. Seamen, who circumvented King George's trade laws and later outran his fleet during the war, were admired.

After the War for Independence, a new respect for tariffs was needed. In 1790, Secretary of the Treasury Alexander Hamilton commissioned ten "revenue cutters" to enforce the new government's only source of income. These cutters and their crews became the United States Coast Guard.

Since its beginning, intercepting contraband has been a primary mission for the Coast Guard. As early as 1794, cutters were charged with preventing the shipping of slaves from Africa. Cutters helped to enforce the Embargo Act of 1807 by effectively closing all ports. During Prohibition in the 1920s, Coast Guard cutters confiscated illegal spirits being transported into the U.S. After Prohibition was repealed in 1933, the Coast Guard became involved in the search for illegal narcotics at sea. In the 1960s, the Coast Guard expanded beyond its interdictory role and established patrols to aid refugees from Cuba. Since that time, the Coast Guard has been involved with the search and rescue missions involving refugees and illegal immigrants attempting to enter the United States primarily from Cuba, the Dominican Republic, the People's Republic of China, and Haiti.

Today, the Coast Guard plays a primary role in the United States' war on drugs by interdicting vessels involved in narcotics smuggling.

USCG Canine Team searches for drugs. (Photo courtesy of the U.S. Coast Guard, Department of Transportation.)

FUNCTIONS AND ACTIVITIES

The basic element of the Coast Guard's operational law enforcement effort is the boarding team. This team is made up of members of a station's or cutter's crew that is specially trained and qualified to conduct boardings of vessels at sea. The Coast Guard also has Tactical Law Enforcement Teams whose job is to conduct boardings while embarked on U.S. Navy ships.

The Coast Guard Investigative Service (CGIS) is a federal investigative and protective program established to carry out the Coast Guard's internal and external criminal and personnel security investigations, assist in providing personal security services, and aid in maintaining the internal integrity of the Coast Guard. The CGIS's function is similar to a police/detective agency in a civilian community.

CGIS is managed by a professional criminal investigator who reports to the Assistant Commandant of Operations for the Coast Guard. CGIS is located outside the Coast Guard's operational chain of command, allowing consistency in investigative policy, procedure, training and education.

CGIS responsibilities include:

- criminal investigations of crimes relating to the maritime realm and Coast Guard missions

- investigations of fraud within the Coast Guard

- internal affairs investigations

- personal protective services

- counterintelligence investigations

- management of the Department of Transportation's hotline program relating to the Coast Guard .

- background investigations and national agency checks in support of granting security clearances to Coast Guard personnel

CGIS conducts investigations in the following areas:

- uniform Code of Military Justice (UCMJ)

- illegal immigration by sea

- drug smuggling

- environmental crimes

- assistance requested by other federal agencies

- other violations of the U.S. code

CGIS is made up of three groups of individuals: active duty warrant and petty officers, Reserve personnel, and full-time civilian agents. Active duty warrant and petty officers are of different specialties and ratings and rotate into CGIS for a tour of duty or consecutive tours of duty. They are selected for CGIS on a "best qualified" basis. Each summer, CGIS solicits for applicants to fill active duty positions.

Reserve personnel are warrant officers (Port Security Specialist) and petty officers serving in the Reserve Investigator rating (IV). Full-time civilian agents are hired from qualified civilian applicants. Generally, law enforcement experience is required. Job openings are announced under the title, "Criminal Investigator" on the U.S. Government's Office of Personnel Management Web site.

TRAINING

Many Coast Guard officers graduate from the Coast Guard Academy in New London, Connecticut. The Coast Guard Academy is the smallest service academy and the only one where acceptance is based strictly on merit competition.

Other officers graduate from the Coast Guard's Officer Candidate School in New London, Connecticut, after earning a college degree at a civilian university or distinguishing themselves through enlisted service.

Port Security men attend the Port Security Specialist "A" School at the Coast Guard Training Center, Yorktown, Virginia, for five weeks of intense training. This Coast Guard reserve course is designed to provide entry-level nonrated personnel with an introduction to the Port Security Specialist rating. Upon successful completion of this course, members are qualified for promotion to Port Security Specialist Third Class, provided time requirements are met. The skills covered include small arms familiarization, seaport security, antiterrorism, basic combat skills, military requirements, leadership, maritime defense, physical security, and others necessary for the rating. All Coast Guard enlisted members attend the Coast Guard Training Center, Cape May, New Jersey. Most Coast Guard personnel also attend advanced service schools and pursue advanced academic degrees.

QUALIFICATIONS

Boarding Teams and Boarding Officer positions are usually open to officers and petty officers at units that conduct law enforcement activities. Nonrated personnel (E-3 and below) may participate in boardings as boat crew or security. All Boarding Team members must:

- successfully qualify in firing the 9mm pistol and pass tests that determine judgmental skills regarding use of force

- meet certain physical fitness qualifications

- complete all training objectives

- be qualified by the unit's commanding officer to be on the team

Applicants for CGIS are screened and evaluated at the local command as well as by the Regional CGIS office. Final selection is made by the Director, Coast Guard Investigative Service.

The following are minimum qualifications for special agency duty. Applicants must:

- be a pay grade E-6 or higher

- have completed a minimum of one year of college (30 credit hours), verified by college transcript. A waiver to this requirement is considered if special circumstances warrant.

- be serving on active duty in the regular Coast Guard with at least six years active military service, two of which must be Coast Guard service, before selection for training. Before transferring for training, members must agree to reenlist or voluntarily extend for a period of at least four years from the convening date of the class

- be at least 21 years old

- have completed at least one year of sea duty. Commander (CGPC-epm) may waive this requirement

- be a U.S. citizen

- have no record of mental illness, alcoholism, or offenses involving moral turpitude.

- possess a valid state motor vehicle operator's license

- on application, be in excellent physical condition

- be eligible for a top secret security clearance and maintain eligibility throughout assignment to CGIS

For further information, visit the Coast Guard Web site at http://www.uscg.mil or contact:
Coast Guard Recruiter
Telephone: (877) 669-8724 or (202) 267-1587 (Office of Public Affairs)

DEPARTMENT OF THE TREASURY

FINANCIAL CRIMES ENFORCEMENT NETWORK (FINCEN)

MISSION

The mission of the Financial Crimes Enforcement Network is to support law enforcement investigative efforts and foster interagency and global cooperation against domestic and international financial crimes and provide U.S. policy makers with strategic analyses of domestic and worldwide money-laundering developments, trends, and patterns. FinCEN works toward those ends through information collection, analysis, and sharing; technological assistance; and innovative and cost-effective implementation of Treasury authorities.

Money laundering involves disguising financial assets so they can be used without detection of the illegal activity that produced them. Through money laundering, criminals transform the money generated by criminal activity—narcotics sales, arms trafficking, fraud, for instance—into funds that apparently come from a legal source.

HISTORICAL REVIEW

FinCEN is an organization established by the U.S. Department of Treasury to collect, analyze, and disseminate intelligence on financial crimes. Secretary of Treasury Nicholas F. Brady officially established FinCEN by an Executive Order dated April 25, 1990. This order set forth the FinCEN mission to provide a government-wide multisource intelligence and analytical network to support law enforcement and regulatory agencies in the detection, investigation, and prosecution of financial crimes.

FUNCTIONS AND ACTIVITIES

As reflected in its name, FinCEN is a network, a means of bringing people and information together to fight the complex problem of money laundering. Since its creation in 1990, FinCEN has worked to maximize information sharing among law enforcement agencies and its other partners in the regulatory and financial communities. Working together is critical in succeeding against today's criminals. No organization, agency, or financial institution can do it alone. Through cooperation and partnerships, FinCEN's network approach encourages cost-effective and efficient measures to combat money laundering domestically and internationally.

Law Enforcement

FinCEN's analysts use financial information and combine it with other government and public information to provide intelligence and analytical support to law enforcement. Through the innovative use of technology, FinCEN helps law enforcement build its investigations and plan new strategies to combat money laundering.

Regulatory

FinCEN uses anti–money laundering laws—the Bank Secrecy Act and amplifying rules and regulations—to require reporting and record keeping by banks and other financial institutions. These records and reports preserve a financial trail for investigators to follow as they track criminals and their assets.

International

FinCEN works to develop and foster global anti–money laundering strategies, policies, and programs, reaching out to assist countries in implementing these efforts. It also works to facilitate information among other centralized analytical agencies around the world to support law enforcement investigations.

To contact FinCEN for law enforcement support, call 1-800-SOS-BUCK (1-800-767-2825). For Bank Secrecy Act regulatory compliance questions/issues, call 1-800-949-2732. For further information, visit FinCEN's Web site at http://www.treas.gov/fincen or write to:

Department of the Treasury
Financial Crimes Enforcement Network
2070 Chain Bridge Road, Suite 200
Vienna, Virginia 22182-2536

Forensic Specialist dusts car bombing for fingerprints. (Photo courtesy of the Bureau of Alcohol, Tobacco and Firearms, Department of the Treasury.)

BUREAU OF ALCOHOL, TOBACCO AND FIREARMS

MISSION

The Bureau of Alcohol, Tobacco and Firearms (ATF) is a law enforcement organization within the U.S. Department of the Treasury with unique responsibilities dedicated to reducing violent crime, collecting revenue, and protecting the public. ATF enforces the federal laws and regulations relating to alcohol, tobacco, firearms, explosives, and arson by directing and working in cooperation with others to:

- suppress and prevent crime and violence through enforcement regulation and community outreach

- ensure fair and proper revenue collection

- provide fair and effective industry regulation

- support and assist federal, state, local, and international law enforcement

- provide innovative training programs in support of criminal and regulatory enforcement functions

HISTORICAL REVIEW

- 1791–Congress imposes the first federal tax on distilled spirits

- 1794–The Whiskey Rebellion—violent resistance to the established authority of the federal government to levy the excise tax on distilled spirits, takes place

- 1919–18th Amendment to the Constitution is ratified, ushering in the Prohibition Era, during which it was illegal to manufacture, sell, or transport intoxicating liquors for beverage purposes. Prohibition Unit established under the Commission of Internal Revenue.

- 1927–Prohibition Unit becomes the separate Bureau of Prohibition, under the Department of Justice

- 1933–21st Amendment to the Constitution ends the Prohibition Era

- 1934–National Firearms Act imposes criminal, regulatory, and tax laws on gangster-type weapons such as machine guns; the Bureau of Prohibition turns over its responsibilities to a newly created Alcohol Tax Unit within the Bureau of Internal Revenue

- 1935–Federal Alcohol Administration Act creates licensing and permit requirements and establishes regulations designed to ensure an open and fair marketplace to the legal businessman and the consumer

- 1938–Federal Firearms Act establishes regulations of the firearms industry and makes it a crime for felons and fugitives to receive firearms in interstate commerce

- 1952–As a result of tobacco tax duties being delegated to the Alcohol Tax Unit in 1951, the unit title is changed to the Alcohol and Tobacco Tax Division of the Internal Revenue Service (IRS)

- 1954–Through Internal Revenue Code, the Alcohol and Tobacco Tax Division gains jurisdiction over the regulation and tax collection on the alcoholic beverages, tobacco products, and firearms industries

■ 1968–The Gun Control Act creates stricter licensing and regulation of the firearms industry, establishes new categories of offenses involving firearms, and the first direct federal jurisdiction aimed at criminal use of explosives. responsibilities delegated to the Alcohol and Tobacco Tax Division

■ 1970–Title XI of the Organized Crime Control Act of 1970 contains provisions for industry regulations and establishes certain bombings and arsons as federal crimes; the Alcohol and Tobacco Tax Division name changes to the Alcohol, Tobacco and Firearms Division under the IRS

■ 1972–Alcohol, Tobacco and Firearms Division separates from the IRS and is given full Bureau status in the Treasury Department as the Bureau of Alcohol, Tobacco and Firearms

■ 1978–, In response to the millions of dollars being lost to the state by cigarette smuggling from low-tax to high-tax states, the ATF helps state enforcement agencies to improve their enforcement and revenue collection capabilities with the Contraband Cigarette Act. Bureau begins developing an entirely new federal effort against arson, an emerging crime problem

■ 1982–The Anti-arson Act amends the Explosives Control Act to include destruction of property by fire along with destruction by explosives

■ 1984–The Armed Career Criminal Act/Comprehensive Crime Control Act amends the 1968 Gun Control Act, establishing mandatory sentences for armed drug traffickers and violent career criminals

■ 1988–Alcohol Beverage Labeling Act requires the government warning statement to appear on alcoholic beverages distributed in the United States

■ 1992–Gang Resistance Education and Training (GREAT) establishes program for gang violence prevention

■ 1993–Brady Law creates a mandatory five-day waiting period for purchasing handguns. provision allows law enforcement to check the background of each handgun purchaser before delivery of any handguns are made by federal firearms dealers

■ 1994–Violent Crime Control and Law enforcement Act amends and strengthens current federal firearms and explosives laws enforced by ATF

■ 1996–Anti-Terrorism and Effective Death Penalty Act amends the federal explosives laws, including enhanced penalties for some explosives offenses, ATF enforcement of plastic explosives marking-detection requirement, and authorization to study the use of *taggants in certain explosive materials

---

*taggant.—a microscopic particle added to commercial explosive in order to facilitate law enforcement. Identification taggants carry a code making it possible to trace the batch of explosives, and the chain of legal distribution; they are intended to survive a bombing, be recovered from the debris, and assist in tracing the source of the explosives used. Detection taggants permit a suitable sensor to detect the presence of the taggants (and hence the explosives) through suitcases, packages, etc. –*U.S. Government Printing Office*

FUNCTIONS AND ACTIVITIES

Law Enforcement

The Bureau of Alcohol, Tobacco and Firearms has the primary investigative jurisdiction and the leading role among federal government agencies for the investigation of international arms trafficking, illegal arms movement, and illegal use of explosives. In addition to its substantial investigative authority, ATF has regulatory authority over the manufacture, possession, receipt, and transfer of firearms, destructive devices, and explosives.

ATF also regulates the firearms industry and is the primary federal law enforcement agency charged in the investigation and interdiction of major illegal firearms trafficking organizations. State and local law enforcement agencies and other federal law enforcement agencies utilize ATF's investigative and forensic expertise and experience to solve firearms crimes.

Compliance

ATF's compliance responsibilities include the licensing of nearly 248,000 firearms and explosives dealers, manufacturers, and importers. Inspection of firearms licensees' records assists ATF's investigative responsibilities. For example, during a task force on drugs in Miami, ATF inspection of licensee records identified 300 illegal sales, 450 potential traffickers, and 1,500 questionable purchases for further investigation

It is also ATF's responsibility to determine if criminals have infiltrated legal liquor businesses through hidden ownership, since organized crime often becomes involved in legitimate businesses in order to launder money from its criminal activities.

ATF protects the consumer in a number of ways, such as ensuring that alcoholic beverage labels accurately reflect the contents and include warning statements, monitoring liquor advertising for improprieties, conducting market area surveys to identify illegal trade practices, ensuring safe and secure storage of explosives by high-risk users, informing the nation about the fetal alcohol syndrome, working to eliminate foreign regulatory obstacles to U.S. wine exports, and conducting a nationwide sampling program to detect and remove potentially hazardous or adulterated liquor products from the marketplace.

National Response Teams

ATF has developed, equipped, and trained four National Response Teams (NRTs) capable of responding within 24 hours to assist in major bombing and arson investigations anywhere in the U.S.

Each team includes 10 ATF special agents trained in investigative techniques particular to arson and bombings, a forensic chemist, a cause-and-origin specialist, and an expert in explosives technology. In addition, trucks outfitted with state-of-the-art equipment can be driven to the scene or loaded aboard U.S. Coast Guard planes and flown to the site.

When an NRT arrives on the scene, a command center is established and immediate coordination with local authorities begins. ATF agents and fire officials start the tedious process of reconstructing the scene, identifying the seat of the blast, sifting debris, searching for evidence, canvassing the area for witnesses, tracking the purchase of the components, determining the cause of the fire, conducting on-scene interviews, and, often, making the arrests.

Evidence is sent to the ATF laboratory where specialists help to reconstruct the crime scene. The lab technicians also look for evidence linking the crime to a suspect. Laser equipment searches glass or plastic containers, doorknobs, or parts of the incendiary device for latent fingerprints. Materials handled or owned by a suspect are compared to materials found at the crime scene. ATF chemists pioneered many of the techniques used in forensic labs to detect accelerants.

ATF arson investigators sift through fire debris. (Photo courtesy of the Bureau of Alcohol, Tobacco and Firearms, Department of the Treasury.)

The Arson Task Force

The Arson Task Force concept consists of pooling the resources of state and local police, fire service personnel, and ATF special agents to provide a unified and concentrated attack on arson. Specialized training for task force participants addresses the latest techniques and skills associated with arson investigations.

Motives for arson vary, as does the degree of sophistication of arson-for-profit schemes, but the vast majority involve insurance fraud, revenge, and extortion. ATF's enforcement efforts are directed toward arson-for-profit schemes that tend to target industrial and commercial activities. Perpetrators of arson-for-profit may be members of organized crime, white-collar criminals, or members of organized arson rings.

Illegal Firearms Trafficking

ATF reduces the availability of black market firearms to criminals by identifying illicit sources of firearms and incarcerating illegal firearms traffickers. Overall goals include recommending illegal firearms traffickers for prosecution, preventing future firearms crimes, and reducing crime-associated costs by incarcerating illegal firearms traffickers.

Youth Crime Gun Interdiction Initiative

ATF developed the Youth Crime Gun Interdiction Initiative in response to increased crimes involving America's youths. This initiative enhances the Juvenile Firearms Violence Initiative, started in 1993, and the new Illegal Firearms Trafficking Project. The Youth Crime Gun Interdiction Initiative addresses illegal sources of guns for youths by providing additional resources and research to identify and investigate those sources.

Stolen Firearms

The passage of 18 U.S.Code Section 923(g)(6) requires the reporting to ATF of firearms thefts from Federal Firearms Licensees' inventories. The reports submitted to ATF detail a variety of thefts that result in federal legal violations and include other offenses such as homicide, robbery, and assault with intent to commit murder.

Prevent Criminal Misuse of Explosives

As an integral part of the Bureau's violent crime reduction strategy, ATF's arson and explosives projects focus on preventing arson and the criminal misuse of explosives and ensuring an effective post-incident response. The Bureau maintains information on the quantities of plastic explosives possessed by individuals, as mandated by the Anti-terrorism and Effective Death Penalty Act of 1996. In addition, ATF maintains the Explosives Incidents System, a computerized repository for historical and technical data on national explosives incidents. This system assimilates details on reported incidents helpful in determining motives. In addition, ATF is the focal point for other federal, state, and local law enforcement agencies to initiate traces of explosives.

Church Fires

ATF provides vital resources to local communities in the aftermath of arson and explosives incidents. In response to a dramatic increase in church arsons nationwide, ATF established a Church Fire Major Case Team. The team maintains a central repository for collecting, analyzing, and disseminating information while coordinating and monitoring all aspects of each investigation. The Church Fire Major Case Team became the foundation for the President's National Church Arson Task Force.

Accelerant-detecting Canine under training. (Photo courtesy of the Bureau of Alcohol, Tobacco and Firearms, Department of the Treasury.)

Canines

In 1989, ATF and the Connecticut State Police began a formal training program for accelerant-detecting canines to support state and local jurisdictions. Accelerant-detecting canines search for liquid catalysts that can be used to speed up the spread of fire. These canines are the only accelerant-detecting canines in this country that carry a federal certification and must be recertified annually by ATF.

Achilles

To remove the most dangerous armed career criminals and armed drug trafficking organizations from the streets, the Achilles Project uses specific federal firearms laws that provide for extended mandatory periods of incarceration. Possessing and using firearms becomes the Achilles heel of violent criminals. They are exposed to lengthy prison sentences under federal laws, and the firearms they possess yield valuable information regarding previous criminal acts and criminal associates. Further, through firearms tracing, the illicit firearms sources for these violent criminals are investigated under ATF's Illegal Firearms Trafficking project.

Violent Offenders

The Violent Offender Project serves as an early safety warning and notification system for law enforcement officers in the field. ATF personnel enter into the National Crime Information Center system preidentified violent career criminals who are currently free in society. When any law enforcement official encounters one of these individuals and runs a National Crime Information Center (NCIC) check on them, the officer receives a safety advisory that the person is a career offender and that ATF should be contacted if the offender is in possession of a firearm.

TECHNOLOGY

Firearms Tracing Center

ATF's Tracing Center, located in the suburbs of Washington, D.C., traces approximately 40,000 firearms a year for local, state, and federal law enforcement agencies. The tracing of firearms is an integral part of ATF's activities and has aided law enforcement in the identification of suspects involved in firearms, narcotics-related violations and homicide investigations.

National Laboratory Center

Located in Rockville, Maryland, ATF's National Laboratory Center supports both law enforcement and compliance activities.

Forensic chemists provide a full range of analyses using the latest scientific equipment and techniques. They examine intact and functional explosive devices and debris to identify their components. The findings are often relayed to agents still working the scene of a suspected arson or explosion.

New laser devices retrieve fingerprints that may have gone undetected using conventional methods. Portable hydrocarbon detectors, called "sniffers," allow the investigator to examine the scene for the presence of accelerants. Computer aid in the testing of fire-scene samples results in more accurate readings. The ATF National Laboratory also provides arson training for state and local chemists in arson accelerant detection.

The ATF Laboratory is also responsible for handling the chemical analysis of alcoholic beverages in order to protect the consumer and maintain the integrity of the alcoholic beverage industry.

National Explosives Tracing Center

To fulfill its responsibility for tracing explosives, ATF maintains liaison with the explosives industry. A trace involves checking with the manufacturer concerning explosive materials recovered at a crime scene.

Research Initiatives

Working in conjunction with the U.S. Army Corps of Engineers and the Defense Special Weapons Agency, ATF's Explosives Technology Branch and National Laboratory Center are researching the blast effects of large car bombs. The Dipole Might Project, started in 1994, is funded by the National Security Council. Its charter is to develop a computer software system to assist investigators in processing the scenes of large car bombs.

ATF is advancing the use of computerized fire modeling to calculate the physics of a fire and how a fire develops and spreads. A relatively new tool to the enforcement community, computer modeling has proven successful in the courtroom to verify witness testimony. ATF developed a comprehensive strategy to actively expand the use of fire research and computerized fire modeling with the criminal enforcement functions.

An Explosive Taggant Study Group is reviewing the feasibility and mechanics of using taggants in explosive materials to track criminal misuse in bombings and other incidents. If taggants prove feasible, they could help post-blast investigators determine the origin of explosive materials.

TRAINING

Special Agent training involves formal classroom instruction supplemented by on-the-job training. Appointees undergo approximately eight weeks of intensive training in general law enforcement and investigative techniques in Criminal Investigator School at the Federal Law Enforcement Training Center in Glynco, Georgia. Subjects of study include rules of evidence, surveillance techniques, undercover assignments, arrest and raid techniques, and the use of firearms.

Agents later attend New Agent Training, where they receive highly specialized training in their duties as ATF agents. Subjects relate to the laws enforced by ATF, case-report writing, firearms and explosives nomenclature, bomb scene search, arson training, and link analysis.

Successful completion of both training courses in mandatory for all newly hired ATF special agents.

ATF provides training in the investigation of complex, profit-motivated arson schemes for state and local law enforcement officers. The Advanced Arson for Profit Investigative Training program is also conducted at the Federal Law Enforcement Training Center at Glynco. The course concentrates on investigative techniques beyond the point of cause and origin determination and involves workshops and classes dealing with such topics as financial investigative techniques, motives of the arsonist, and the role of the insurance industry.

ATF also provides an undercover investigative techniques training program for state and local law enforcement officers at the training center at Glynco.

QUALIFICATIONS

ATF Special Agent must:

- be American citizens

- be between the ages of 21 and 37 at the time of appointment, unless they have had previous service in a federal civilian law enforcement position covered by special civil service retirement provisions, including early or mandatory retirement

- possess a current and valid automobile operator's license

- complete ATF Special Agent Applicant Questionnaire

- take and pass the Treasury Enforcement Agent examination

- complete a field panel interview; a writing sample will be required and an ATF Special Agent Applicant assessment will be administered at the time of the interview

- take and pass a polygraph examination

- take and pass a medical examination; applicants must be determined physically fit by an authorized federal government physician to perform strenuous and physically demanding duties

- at a minimum, meet an uncorrected distant vision minimum of at least 20/100 in each eye; corrected distant vision must test 20/20 in one eye and 20/30 in the other

- be proportionate in weight and height

- take and pass a drug test

- successfully pass a full field background investigation for a top secret clearance

- be registered with the Selective Service System, or be exempt from having to do so under Selective Service law (male applicants born after December 31, 1959)

- be able to carry a firearm and ammunition. (Persons who have been convicted of felonies and certain misdemeanors, including a misdemeanor crime of domestic violence (title 18, USC Section 922(g)(9)) are not eligible to possess a firearm.)

For further information, visit ATF online at http://www.atf.treas.gov, or contact:

Bureau of Alcohol, Tobacco and Firearms
650 Massachusetts Avenue, NW
Washington, D.C. 20226
Telephone: (202) 927-8500
Fax: (202) 927

INTERNAL REVENUE SERVICE

MISSION

The primary role of the Internal Revenue Service (IRS) is the collection of taxes in a fair and impartial manner. The IRS's goal is to achieve the highest possible degree of voluntary compliance with the internal revenue laws of the United States.

In support of the overall IRS mission, Criminal Investigation (CI) serves the American public by investigating potential criminal violations of the Internal Revenue Code and related financial crimes in a manner that fosters confidence in the tax system and compliance with the law.

The IRS mission is to "provide America's taxpayers top quality service by helping them understand and meet their tax responsibilities and by applying the tax law with integrity and fairness to all."

HISTORICAL REVIEW

The history of Criminal Investigation began shortly after the Revenue Act of 1913, which was the first income tax law enacted by Congress after the 16th Amendment was ratified. It imposed a modest tax of one percent on net incomes of individuals, estates, trusts, and corporations. Numerous internal revenue laws since that time have made changes in rates and other aspects of revenue assessment.

Tax evasion is not new. As early as 1919 many complaints concerning alleged tax frauds and dishonesty reached Commissioner of Internal Revenue, Daniel C. Roper. The Commissioner had previously served as First Assistant Postmaster General and was familiar with the work of the Post Office Inspectors, whose job was investigating frauds in the use of the mails and occasional cases of dishonesty among Post Office workers. The Commissioner decided to establish a group to make similar investigations in the Bureau of Internal Revenue.

With the approval of the Secretary of the Treasury and the Postmaster General, Commissioner Roper requested and transferred six experienced Post Office inspectors to the Bureau of Internal Revenue, and on July 1, 1919, these inspectors became the first special agents in the new Special Intelligence Unit.

Over the years, many underworld leaders have gone to prison on federal tax charges rather than for other crimes. Some of the famous names from past history whose convictions were brought about by Criminal Investigation include Al Capone, Frank Nitti, Jake and Sam Guzik, "Dutch" Schultz, Johnny Torrio, Albert Anastasia, and Frank Costello.

FUNCTIONS AND ACTIVITIES

When people or businesses try to corrupt the American system of taxation through illegal activities, IRS Criminal Investigation special agents enforce the tax and money laundering laws. The fact is that all income is taxable, even income earned through illegal sources.

Tax evasion, abusive trust schemes, health-care fraud, telemarketing fraud, and even drug trafficking are some examples of the types of crime that revolve around money. When a financial crime is committed, a financial investigation is the key to a conviction. In a financial investigation, traditional law enforcement investigative tools such as crime scene analysis and physical evidence can fall short in proving the crime. With no proof, there is no conviction. The techniques used in a financial investigation by CI special agents involve following the movement of money through paper and computerized records. The link between where the money comes from, who gets it, when it is received, and where it is stored or deposited can provide proof of criminal activity. CI special agents have earned the distinguished title, "Accountants with Convictions."

Focusing on Legal Source Tax Crimes

Legal source tax investigations involve taxpayers in legal industries and legal occupations who earned income legally but choose to evade taxes by violation of tax laws. Fraud in legal industries and legal occupations has been termed "white collar" crime because it involves income tax violations by individuals who are not involved in other criminal activity. Investigations and convictions in this area are the core of CI's efforts to encourage voluntary compliance with the tax laws. Legal source tax crimes include those cases that threaten the tax system, such as the Questionable Refund Program cases, unscrupulous return preparers, and frivolous filers/nonfilers who challenge the legality of the filing requirement. Publicity on convictions of individuals in legitimate professions sends a message to noncompliant associates that the IRS is serious about enforcing the tax laws.

Illegal Source Financial Crimes

The illegal source financial crimes cases involve money gained through illegal sources, such as dollars obtained through illegal gambling operations or double-billing health-care plans. This illegally obtained money is part of the untaxed underground economy, which is a threat to our voluntary tax compliance system and undermines the overall public confidence in our tax system.

When money is derived through illegal sources, the primary concern for the criminal is to legitimize the dollars. This process of "cleaning" the illegally obtained dollars is termed "money laundering." Money laundering activity is considered to be tax evasion in progress. CI is a major player in supporting the goals and objectives of the National Money Laundering Strategy.

Narcotics Related Financial Crimes

CI's involvement in investigating narcotics-related financial crimes is to reduce the profit and financial gains of narcotics trafficking and money laundering organizations that comprise a significant portion of the untaxed underground economy. Criminal Investigation seeks to identify, investigate, and assist in the prosecution of the most significant narcotics related tax and money laundering. Therefore, CI is committed to supporting the goals and objectives of the National Drug Control Strategy in conjunction with other law enforcement agencies.

Criminal drug organizations often go to great lengths to conceal the income earned and the source of their illegal income. Many top-level members of these organizations try to insulate themselves from the drugs and still profit from the drug proceeds. The drug proceeds are layered in financial transactions, and sometimes currency reporting requirements are manipulated to give the appearance of the money coming from several sources. This is where CI steps in to unravel the complex financial transactions leading from the crime to the criminal. Taking away the assets from the drug organizations hits them where it hurts the most—it takes away their profit.

TRAINING

Special agent candidates are required to attend a comprehensive training program at the Federal Law Enforcement Training Center in Glynco, Georgia. Training begins with a one-week orientation program sponsored by the National Criminal Investigation Training Academy. Students then attend a nine-week Criminal Investigation Training Program, which covers basic federal criminal investigation techniques, including federal criminal law, courtroom procedure, enforcement operations, interviewing, and firearms training that are common to all federal law enforcement agents. This segment of training includes new Treasury agents from Customs; Alcohol, Tobacco and Firearms; Secret Service; and other federal law enforcement agencies.

After the basic training is completed, the candidates begin CI's sixteen-week specialized training, which includes instruction in tax law, criminal tax fraud, money laundering, and a variety of financial fraud schemes. They are also introduced to agency specific undercover operations, electronic surveillance techniques, forensic sciences, court procedures, interviewing techniques and trial preparation and testifying.

The training emphasizes the development of both technical and behavioral skills. It incorporates a highly interactive methodology of course delivery coupled with a high expectation of trainee interaction throughout the program. It is designed to provide new agents with the opportunity to learn and practice progressively more complex tasks that are performed on the job. This is accomplished through a combination of practical exercises, simulated cases, and classroom-facilitated learning.

Computer Investigative Skills

Additional Opportunities for Specialized Computer Investigative Skills

With an increase in the automation of financial records, there is a need for CI special agents to be specially trained in recovering computer evidence. Those special agents interested in becoming a Computer Investigative Specialist (CIS) must complete a variety of computer courses which provide the agent with the tools and knowledge to perform forensic data recovery and analysis of electronic data. The training begins with a pre-basic two-week course, followed by a three-week Computer Evidence Recovery Training course at the University of North Texas. Finally, one year after a CIS's initial training, the agent attends a 21_-week Advanced Computer Evidence Recovery Training course to learn about computer network issues and more advanced data recovery.

Computer equipment seized for financial records may contain data that has been encrypted, password protected, or otherwise hidden. Agents use their investigative skills and specialized equipment to recover this data as substantial evidence to convict individuals on tax law or money laundering violations. Computer Investigative Specialists receive a laptop, two desktop computers, and numerous other equipment and software to assist in their investigations.

Assignments

There is a great amount of flexibility in locations within the United States. The U.S. is divided into six areas; each area encompasses a number of field offices. An office may have up to sixteen posts of duty. There are also a limited number of international assignments available. Electronic commerce has created a global economy where money laundering does not stop at the U.S. borders. Special agents have been permanently assigned to Hong Kong, Colombia, Mexico, Canada, and Germany, as well as at INTERPOL in Lyon, France. Strategically placing special agents on foreign soil is just one of the ways to stay one step ahead of global financial crimes.

Law Enforcement Team
CI Special Agents as Part of a "Bigger" Law Enforcement Team

Being a part of the IRS CI team means being a part of an enormous network of local, state, and federal law enforcement agencies. The IRS works closely with the Department of Justice, U.S. Attorneys, the FBI, U.S. Customs, the Drug Enforcement Administration, U.S. Postal Inspection Service, Inspectors General of all federal agencies, U.S. Marshals, and others. Many federal agencies rely on CI to unravel criminal activities by following the financial trail, which ultimately leads to violation of the tax laws and numerous other related financial crimes or other federal offenses. It is not unusual for a financial investigation to uncover motives for other serious crimes, such as corruption, embezzlement, extortion, or even murder.

For example, other law enforcement agencies tried to pin a crime on 1930s gangster Al Capone but failed. It was a CI special agent who penetrated the organized racketeering gangs, resulting in the tax evasion conviction of Capone and other reigning gangsters. Al Capone failed to report large profits from gambling, bootlegging, and various forms of racketeering. Al Capone's defense was the money came from illegal activities. Nevertheless, all income is taxable and must be reported.

Special Assignments

Special agents have numerous opportunities for diversity of work. They may participate in long- and short-term special assignments on multi-agency task forces, such as the Organized Crime Drug Enforcement Task Force (OCDEF), the U.S. Attorney's Telemarketing Fraud Task Force, presidential campaign protective assignments, or become a member of the undercover cadre or a Computer Investigative Specialist.

QUALIFICATIONS
Applicants must:

- be United States citizens

- be under the age of 37

- meet education and/or experience qualification requirements outlined below

- pass the IRS TEA examination, which consists of a written test and a skills assessment exercise; the skills assessment exercise consists of an accounting exercise, two writing exercises, and an oral panel interview, which assesses those skills necessary to be successful as a special agent

How to Apply

Applicants are encouraged to apply for all grades (GS-5, GS-7, or GS-9) for which they think they qualify. Applicants applying only for the GS-7 or GS-9 levels are considered for those levels only. Applicants applying for the GS-5 level are considered at the GS-5 and GS-7 level if they qualify for the GS-7 level.

NOTE: Application procedures are different for the GS-5/7 versus the GS-9 levels. Therefore, separate announcements with different instructions, depending on the grade, have been issued.

Applicants for the GS-5 and GS-7 special agents positions ONLY may call (212) 436-1403 and request an application package for this position. GS-9 special agent positions ONLY may call (212) 436-1436 and request an application package for the GS-9 level special agent position. Copies of the vacancy announcements are available online at http://www.irs.gov or as a Microsoft Word file. For further information or to request and application package or submit form OF0612 and a resume and statement addressing the knowledge/skills or abilities detailed in the vacancy announcements, applicants should contact:

Internal Revenue Service
Northeast Region Centralized Examining Unit
290 Broadway, 13ᵗʰ Floor
New York, New York 10007
Telephone: (212) 436-1436
or contact:
Office of Public Affairs
Chief, Media Relations
1111 Constitution Avenue, NW, Room 7032
Washington, D.C. 20224
Telephone: (202) 622-4000

OFFICE OF SECURITY

BUREAU OF ENGRAVING AND PRINTING

MISSION

The mission of the Office of Security is to provide around-the-clock protection of the Bureau of Engraving and Printing, where the nation's currency, stamps, and other securities are produced and also to safeguard its employees, visitors, and tourists by controlling, screening, and monitoring access to all Bureau property and entrances.

Additionally, the Office of Security is entrusted to provide security support to all Bureau components by developing, expounding, and enforcing Bureau security policies, procedures, standards and departmental regulations.

FUNCTIONS AND ACTIVITIES

The Bureau of Engraving and Printing manufactures the financial and other securities of the United States. Accordingly, the Bureau designs, prints, and finishes a large variety of security products including Federal Reserve notes, U.S. postage stamps, Treasury securities, identification cards, naturalization certificates, and other special security documents. All products are designed and manufactured with advanced counterfeit deterrence features to insure product integrity, and the Bureau advises other federal agencies on document security matters. The Bureau also processes claims for the redemption of mutilated currency.

For further information, visit the Bureau of Engraving and Printing online at http://www.bep.treas.gov and http://www.moneyfactory.com or contact:

Bureau of Engraving and Printing
Attn: Office of External Relations
14ᵗʰ and C Streets, SW
Washington, D.C. 20228
Telephone (202) 874-3019

U.S. CUSTOMS SERVICE

MISSION

The U.S. Customs Service is one of the United States government's major revenue producers and the lead federal agency in drug interdiction. Customs also monitors and protects the nation's perimeters to thwart attempts to bring all types of illicit merchandise into the country while enforcing more than 400 laws for more than 40 federal agencies.

An agency of the Department of the Treasury, the U.S. Customs Service operates more than 300 ports of entry. In addition to its headquarters in Washington, D.C., and offices in various U.S. embassies and consulates overseas, the U.S. Customs Service and has law enforcement offices throughout the country.

The Customs mission is to:

- assess and collect Customs duties, excise taxes, fees and penalties due on imported goods

- prevent fraud and smuggling

- control carriers, persons, and cargo entering and departing the United States

- intercept illegal high-technology exports to proscribed destinations

- cooperate with other federal agencies in suppressing the traffic in illicit narcotics and pornography

- enforce international transportation reporting requirements of the Bank Secrecy Act

- protect the American public by enforcing auto safety and emission control standards, flammable fabric restrictions, and animal and plant quarantine requirements on imports

- protect U.S. business and labor by enforcing laws and regulations dealing with copyrights, trademarks, and quotas

Early Customs inspectors. (Photo courtesy of U.S. Customs Service, Department of the Treasury.)

HISTORICAL REVIEW

Early Years

Soon after declaring independence in 1776, the United States faced imminent bankruptcy. Responding to the urgent need for revenue, the first Congress passed, and President George Washington signed, the Tariff Act of July 4, 1789, establishing a tariff system for collecting duties.

Customs districts, ports of entry, and the machinery for appointing Customs officers and prescribing their duties were established July 31, 1789—one day before the Tariff Act took effect. President Washington then nominated 59 Collectors of Customs and more than 40 other officers to staff the new Customs Service.

The entire service was later placed under the Treasury Department, where it remains today.

Customs was not only the first fully formed agency, but also for years it was the largest. By 1792, the Customs work force totaled nearly 500 people—80 percent of all Treasury employees and more than twice the number of the next largest agency, the Post Office.

For nearly 100 years, the Customs Service was virtually the only source of income for the U.S. Government. Customs revenues not only financed America's growth in its infancy but also succeeded in reducing the national debt to zero by 1835. Customs collections also built the U.S. military and naval academies as well as the city of Washington, D.C.

By 1860, Customs collections represented 90 percent of all monies raised for government operations. Passage of the 16th Amendment to the Constitution and the federal Income Tax Act in 1913 made the Internal Revenue Service the nation's number one revenue-producing agency, but even today the Customs Service contributes more than $20 billion a year to the national treasury.

Prohibition

With the passage in 1919 of the 18th Amendment prohibiting the importation, possession, and sale of liquor, smuggling in the U.S. reached a new high. Bootleggers worked the borders with boats, trucks, and planes, and when they were caught, Customs officers often confiscated the transport vehicles along with the liquor they carried. During Prohibition, the U.S. Customs air interdiction fleet consisted wholly of aircraft seized in the course of liquor smuggling.

The repeal of Prohibition in 1933 marked the eventual wane of bootlegging. However, "rum-running" continued for many years due to the high taxes which accompanied legal liquor. In 1935, Congress gave Customs and the Coast Guard increased authority to search and seize vessels. As liquor smuggling decreased, the illegal entry of narcotics and dangerous drugs increased, and the 1935 Act was applied once again.

Beginning in the 1960s and continuing to today, Customs officers have fought the influx of opium, heroin, cocaine, hashish, marijuana, amphetamines, and other illegal drugs into the United States.

FUNCTIONS AND ACTIVITIES

Within the U.S. Customs Service, two principal offices have an impact on the enforcement and regulatory operations of the agency. They are Field Operations and Investigations.

Office of Field Operations

In carrying out its border protection mission, Customs must balance the responsibility of enforcement with the requirement to facilitate the legitimate movement of passengers and cargo into the United States.

Working with the world trade community and the international transportation industry, Customs has implemented numerous automated systems and techniques to expedite the flow of commerce.

For example, Customs' Automated Commercial System (ACS) is a joint public/private sector computerized data processing and telecommunications system that links customhouses and members of the import trade community with the Customs computer.

Customs uses the data captured by the system in many ways, including the control and release of cargo; commodity classification and valuation decisions; collection of duty, taxes, fees and other revenue; and the enforcement of trade laws and regulations.

Trade Operations personnel collect fines and penalties and process seizures and forfeitures under the import laws and export control laws. Import specialists work with inspectors to enforce tariff and trade laws and prevent commercial fraud.

The Office of Laboratories and Scientific Services within the Office of Commercial Operations develops testing programs to enforce intellectual property rights, including rights that apply to copyrighted computers, software programs, and video game motherboards. Their work is often done in cooperation with private industry.

Field laboratories provide technical support for a number of specialized enforcement operations, such as counterfeit products, concentrating on textiles, steel, petroleum, or fasteners.

Customs' mobile laboratories expedite the movement of cargo through ports of entry without compromising enforcement.

Commercial Fraud

The Office of Fraud Investigations, part of the Office of Investigations, investigates textiles, steel, electronics, and quota fraud. It is a multidisciplined office whose primary function is to support the total Customs effort in combating commercial fraud.

The Carrier Initiative Program is a joint effort among air, sea, and land carriers and Customs to confront issues associated with smuggling.

Office of Passenger Operations

Protecting 96,000 miles of U.S. land, air, and sea borders and more than 300 ports of entry, the U.S. Customs Service performs many functions aimed at controlling carriers, persons, and articles entering and leaving the United States.

This phase of the Customs operation is the most visible and has the dual purposes of facilitating travelers and enforcing federal laws concerning international travel and commercial activity.

Customs Inspectors process persons, baggage, cargo, and mail, and assess and collect Customs duties, excise taxes, fees, and penalties levied on imported merchandise. Their efforts often uncover violations of federal law, such as drug smuggling and counterfeiting trademark items. Consequently, they work closely with the Customs Office of Investigations and other federal law enforcement agencies.

Canine Enforcement Officer searches vehicle. (Photo courtesy of U.S. Customs Service, Department of the Treasury.)

Canine Enforcement Program

With the growth of drug smuggling operations, Customs has turned to detector dogs to enhance the service's inspection effectiveness. Today, the Customs Canine Enforcement Program, which consists of more than 500 teams of dogs and handlers, is the most cost-effective narcotics interdiction program in the Customs Service, accounting for more than 120,000 narcotic seizures with a street value in excess of several billion dollars.

A dog and his handler can check 500 packages in 30 minutes; a Customs mail examiner would require several days to inspect as many. At border points, a dog can inspect a vehicle in about two minutes; the same search by a Customs Inspector would take at least 20 minutes.

The Customs Canine Enforcement Training Center, Front Royal, Virginia, has assisted more than 100 foreign, state, and local law enforcement agencies with managerial and handler training.

Office of Investigations

The Office of Investigations is responsible for enforcing the nation's import and export laws. Customs special agents delve into smuggling attempts, fraudulent entry of merchandise, undervaluation, cargo theft and pilferage, neutrality violations, the illegal export of sophisticated technology to restricted nations, money laundering activities, and cyber crime.

Customs special agents are cross-designated with DEA drug investigative authority to combat drug smuggling. Enforcement personnel utilize sources of information (informants), computers, electronic surveillance equipment, and polygraph examinations in support of their investigative activities. All enforcement offices are linked with one another, including inspectors, ports of entry, etc., through an enforcement computer network known as the Treasury Enforcement Communications System (TECS). This allows immediate access to critical information, the quick referral of investigative leads, and the rapid exchange of investigative information.

Customs Cybersmuggling Center

With the evolution of the Information Age and the availability of the personal computer with worldwide access to instantaneous communication via the Internet, traditional Customs interventions are being bypassed by the more sophisticated criminal elements. This environment, known as cyberspace, provides the criminal with a means to both communicate and conduct criminal activity that is beyond the realm of present day law enforcement techniques.

The U.S. Customs Service, Office of Investigations, has established the Cybersmuggling Center to more effectively focus Customs resources on Internet crimes. The Cybersmuggling Center brings together all U.S. Customs Service assets dedicated to the investigation of international criminal activity conducted on, or facilitated by, the Internet. The U.S. Customs Cybersmuggling Center's areas of responsibility include:

- international money laundering and offshore cyber-banking

- drug trafficking (including prohibited pharmaceuticals and steroids)

- intellectual property rights violations (including music and software)

- illegal arms trafficking and export of strategic and controlled commodities

- international child pornography investigations

- stolen antiquities/art

Stolen Antiquities/Art

Customs has formed the Art Recovery Team, comprised of Customs special agents, inspectors, Import specialists, and Customs attorneys. The team, stationed at Customs offices at the World Trade Center in New York City, was designed to expand an already successful art fraud program through the dedication of additional resources and better coordination of Customs' efforts in the interdiction and investigation of stolen and counterfeit art, antiquities, and cultural property.

The team provides specialized training to Customs officers involved in the processing of passengers and the examination of freight arriving in the United States and assists Customs offices nationwide in art-fraud–related matters. In addition, Customs attaches, located in twenty-six countries throughout the world, are provided with training tailored to address the specific threat relating to their particular areas of responsibility. The team works closely with the Customs Cybersmuggling Center in Fairfax, Virginia, to coordinate the investigation of art-fraud violations being perpetrated over the Internet via online auctions, Web sites, or other means.

The team conducts an outreach program to educate the New York City art community about Customs' interest, capabilities, and authority in this field, and provides a conduit for reporting suspicious activity nationwide.

Currency/Money Laundering Program

The Customs Financial Enforcement Program is comprised of Special Enforcement Programs (BUCKSTOP), Customs Joint Financial Task Forces, the Organized Crime Drug Enforcement Task Forces (OCDETF), Undercover Operations, the International Money Laundering Investigative Network, and the Commissioner's International Money Laundering Initiative (CIMLI).

BUCKSTOP is a national inbound/outbound currency enforcement program of the Office of Enforcement and the Office of Inspection and Control that is responsible for the interception of currency and negotiable monetary instruments in the process of being transported into or out of the United States without being properly reported.

Pornography Enforcement

In 1983, the President identified obscene and pornographic materials imported into the United States as a national enforcement priority, with special attention on the problem of child pornography. The Cybersmuggling Center is a national clearinghouse for the international enforcement of child pornography laws by the U.S. Customs Service. The CPPU has established a network of child pornography investigators who regularly work in task force groups in all Customs domestic and foreign field offices.

Export Enforcement

While Customs has been enforcing export laws since its inception, the Export Administration Act of 1979 has given Customs statutory authority to enforce export laws and exclusive jurisdiction over foreign investigations of export violations. This enforcement effort is a permanent part of Customs' mission, with both inspectors and investigative personnel dedicated to export enforcement activity.

Customs' most effective enforcement initiative to control the illegal export of valuable strategic technology to restricted nations is a proactive investigative stance involving carefully designed covert operations to disrupt smuggling conspiracies before they can harm national security. Covert operations have resulted in a number of high profile arrests and seizures involving major violations of the Arms Export Control Act (AECS) and the Export Administration Amendments Act (EAAA).

Customs surveillance plane. (Photo courtesy of U.S. Customs Service, Department of the Treasury.)

Aviation Program

The Air and Marine Interdiction Division's mission is to protect the nation's borders and the American people from the smuggling of narcotics and other contraband using an integrated and coordinated air and marine interdiction force.

To maintain the security of the border, air and marine branches and units are strategically located along the southern border of the United States and in Puerto Rico and the Virgin Islands. The primary focus of these branches is to detect, sort, and intercept suspect air and marine targets. U.S. Customs Service Cessna Citations and the Customs High Endurance Tracker (CHET) intercept and track air targets. The C-12M is equipped with surface search radar to detect and track marine targets. These aircraft work closely with USCS interceptor boats and U.S. Coast Guard vessels to apprehend suspected drug traffickers. Smuggling activities are videotaped and documented for subsequent use in criminal proceedings.

High performance, USCS intercept boats are operated in offshore waters along the eastern seaboard, the Gulf of Mexico, and the Caribbean. These boats work in conjunction with marine surveillance aircraft and boats to intercept, board, and search suspect vessels smuggling drugs into the United States. They also tow sensors alongside commercial ships to detect drug-laden containers attached to the hull.

Sikorsky Black Hawk apprehension helicopters are an integral part of the interdiction mission. The primary mission of the medium-lift helicopter is to support air, land, and marine interdiction efforts as an apprehension platform. Under this concept, it is used to acquire and interdict aircraft, vessels, and vehicles involved in smuggling. The Black Hawk also supports diversified missions, including relocation of evidence, insertion of agents serving search and arrest warrants, airspace security at designated special events, and humanitarian relief.

The Air and Marine Interdiction Division (AMID) is an essential element of the President's National Drug Control Policy. In addition to protecting the borders of the United States, USCS air and marine crews work in conjunction with the law enforcement agencies and military forces of other nations in support of their counternarcotic programs. The AMID provides detection interceptor support and coordinated training with military and law enforcement personnel of other countries. The Customs P-3 AEW airborne early warning (AEW) aircraft provide radar coverage over the jungles and mountainous regions of Central and South America. They also patrol the vast southwest border and international waters to monitor shipping lanes and air routes in search of smuggling activities. P-3 interceptor aircraft often augment the AEW aircraft to identify and track suspect targets.

The Air and Marine Interdiction Coordination Center (AMICC) in Riverside, California, is the only law enforcement facility of its kind in the nation. Information from a wide array of civilian and military radar sites, aerostats, airborne reconnaissance aircraft, and other detection assets is assimilated to provide 24-hour, seamless radar surveillance along the entire southern tier of the U.S., Puerto Rico, and the Caribbean. The AMICC provides communications and control to Customs air, marine, and ground units on patrol or engaged in special operations. It also integrates information systems with other domestic and international counterdrug centers and law enforcement agencies and serves as a focal point for tactical coordination between agencies.

TRAINING

Basic enforcement training is held at the U.S. Customs Service Academy at the Federal Law Enforcement Training Centers in Glynco, Georgia, and Marana, Arizona. Basic Special Agent school includes courses in such areas as fraud, smuggling, export investigations, and child pornography, as well as surveillance practices, physical fitness, and firearms.

Specialized training for Customs enforcement personnel includes training in undercover work, intelligence, physical surveillance, and marine and air law enforcement.

Training programs in basic supervisory skills for mid-level and senior managers, as well as programs in professional staff development are also offered by the Academy. In addition, a program on Officer Professionalism, which provides guidance on how to perform inspection duties in a businesslike and professional manner, is offered to all inspection personnel.

For Trade Operations, the Import Specialists receive basic, intermediate, and specialized training. Programs for Regulatory Auditors, Entry Unit personnel, Fines, Penalties, and Forfeiture Officers and Paralegals are also provided by the Academy.

The Academy's computer training facilities provide hands-on Automated Commercial System (ACS) instruction in all Customs major operational training programs. Legal training in such topics as border search, arrest authority, and major statutes enforced by Customs is routinely provided to Customs Officers.

Customs air and marine crews are made up of law enforcement officers who receive extensive training at the Federal Law Enforcement Training Center in Glynco, Georgia. Customs pilots are experienced aviators who have a minimum of 1,500 hours of flight time.

QUALIFICATIONS

Customs offers a number of career opportunities in the enforcement area. These include Special Agent, Inspector, Pilot, Canine Enforcement Officer, and other specialized positions that support enforcement.

To qualify, an applicant must:

- be a United States citizen

- be under 35 years of age (for Special Agent position)

- pass an appropriate physical examination

- pass a personal background investigation and drug test

- have at least one year of progressively responsible experience which demonstrates skill in effectively dealing with people, collecting pertinent facts, and writing reports

No less than four years (for special agents) and two years (for investigators) of specialized criminal investigative experience is also needed, plus the ability to analyze and evaluate evidence and make oral/written presentations of personally conducted investigations. Comparable experience in situations that call for tact, judgment, and resourcefulness is considered. One scholastic year of education above high school equals nine months of work experience. Educational achievement in accounting or criminal justice/law enforcement is desirable.

Candidates must successfully complete fourteen weeks of enforcement training at the Federal Law Enforcement Training Center in Glynco, Georgia. This consists of written and physical tests as well as graded practical exercises, including one on firearms proficiency.

Candidates must be willing to travel, work overtime, and work under stressful conditions and must be available for temporary and permanent assignments to a variety of geographic areas. They are also required to carry weapons and to qualify regularly with firearms.

To Apply:

Candidates who have never worked for the federal government in a civilian capacity must establish an eligibility rating on the Office of Personnel Management (OPM) register for the position and grade level for which they are qualified. For many positions, applicants are not required to take a written test. Instead, they are rated based on their education, experience, and background as reflected on their application forms. Contact the nearest OPM Federal Job Information Center (listed in the local telephone directory) for the latest information on establishing eligibility on the appropriate register and employment prospects.

Current or former federal employees should contact the division in the Office of Human Resources that recruits for the occupation in which they are interested in working. That office will be in the best position to advise of the availability of positions and application procedures.

Interested persons can also visit Customs' Web site at http://www.customs.gov for the latest information on recruiting initiatives. The career section of the Web site has extensive information about qualification requirements as well.

For the position of Special Agent, contact:
U.S. Customs Service
Office of Human Resources
Investigations Service Center
Attn: Special Agent
Washington, D.C. 20229
Telephone: (202) 927-2144

For the position of Inspector, contact:
U.S. Customs Service
Office of Human Resources
Staffing Services Division
Washington, D.C. 20229
Telephone: (202) 927-2816

For the position of Pilot, contact:
U.S. Customs Service
Office of Human Resources
Investigation Service Center
Washington, D.C. 20229
Telephone: (202) 927-3682

For the position of Canine Enforcement Officer, contact:
U.S. Customs Service
Office of Human Resources
Staffing Services Division
Washington, D.C. 20229
Telephone: (202) 927-2816

U.S. MINT POLICE

MISSION
A United States Mint Police Officer has the primary responsibility of protecting life and property; preventing, detecting, and investigating criminal acts; collecting and preserving evidence; making arrests; and enforcing federal and local laws. The authority of a Mint Police Officer extends to the buildings and land under the custody and control of the Mint, from the streets, sidewalks, and open areas in the vicinity of the facilities; to surrounding parking areas used by employees. U.S. Mint Police are also responsible for the protection of in-transit bullion, coins, dies, and other property and assets of, or in the custody of, the Mint.

HISTORICAL REVIEW
Established in 1792, the U.S. Mint police are one of the oldest federal law enforcement agencies in the nation. Responsible for establishing the standard "As secure as Fort Knox," Mint officers continue to meet that standard today.

FUNCTIONS AND ACTIVITIES
The U.S. Mint Police are responsible for protecting more than $100 billion in Treasury and other government assets stored in facilities located at Philadelphia, Pennsylvania; San Francisco, California; West Point, New York; Denver, Colorado; Fort Knox, Kentucky; and U.S. Mint headquarters in Washington, D.C.

TRAINING
Training begins at full pay at the Federal Law Enforcement Training Center (FLETC) in Glynco, Georgia, with ten weeks of intensive training in such areas as police procedures; psychology; criminal law; laws of arrest, search, and seizure; and physical defense techniques. After graduation

from FLETC, recruits return to their field facility for five weeks of additional training. They are assigned to a field-training officer and continue to develop their skills through on-the-job experience and continual in-service training. Some of the various areas stressed throughout an officer's career include professionalism, public relations, firearm proficiency, and physical fitness.

Assignments in the areas of Protective Services, Special Response Team, Instructional Training, Firearms, Bike Patrol, and other units exist for those who desire to enhance their career. Additionally, after two years with the Department, officers may compete in the promotional process when vacancies occur.

QUALIFICATIONS

Applicants must possess one year of specialized experience equivalent to the GS-4 in the federal service. Creditable experience may have been gained in work on a police force; through service as a military police officer; in work providing visitor protection and law enforcement in parks, forests, or other natural resource or recreational environments; in performing criminal investigative duties; in other work that provides the required knowledge and skills; or upon successful completion of a four-year course of study leading to a bachelor's degree in police science or comparable degree program related to the work of the position.

Applicants must also:

- be U.S. citizens

- possess a valid drivers license

- be in excellent physical health

- be a mature, responsible individual with a high degree of tact, motivated for police work, able to work with minimum supervision, and interested in assisting all employees and visitors

- not be involved in any pending criminal litigation

For further information, contact:
United States Mint Police
Recruiting Division, 8th Floor
801 9th Street, NW
Washington, D.C. 20220
Telephone: (202) 354-7300

U.S. SECRET SERVICE

MISSION

The mission of the Secret Service, an agency within the U.S. Department of the Treasury, encompasses both investigative and protective responsibilities. The protection of the President of the United States and of other dignitaries is the Service's primary responsibility. In addition, the U.S. Secret Service investigates the counterfeiting of U.S. currency, forgery of government bonds and other obligations, credit and debit card fraud, and computer crimes.

Secret Service operatives with President Woodrow Wilson. (Photo courtesy of the U.S. Secret Service, Department of the Treasury.)

HISTORICAL REVIEW

The Investigative Mission

The U.S. Secret Service is the oldest general law enforcement agency of the federal government. In 1861, the United States was faced with both a Civil War and a growing monetary crisis. At that time there was no national currency; state governments issued their paper money through banks within their own states. The notes were printed in numerous designs, and it was difficult for the public to become familiar with the wide array of paper money then in circulation. Estimates from that period indicate that as much as one-third to one-half of all paper currency in circulation was counterfeit.

In 1863, the U.S. Government introduced a new national currency that was uniform in design and printed with the very latest equipment. Treasury Department officials thought the new currency would be difficult for counterfeiters to duplicate and pass on to the public. They were wrong, however, and the new "greenbacks," as they were commonly called, were counterfeited and circulated extensively.

Despite the efforts of state and local law enforcement authorities and private investigators, counterfeiting continued to flourish. Although the U.S. Constitution empowered Congress to provide for the punishment of counterfeiters of the securities and current coin of the United States, there was no concentrated national effort to deal with the problem.

Consequently, on July 5, 1865, the Secret Service was created for the purpose of suppressing the counterfeiting of U.S. currency. William P. Wood was sworn in by Treasury Secretary McCulloch as the first Chief of the Secret Service Division, and Secret Service headquarters was established in Washington, D.C.

The scope of responsibilities assigned to the Secret Service broadened in 1867, when Congress provided funds for the purpose of "detecting persons perpetrating frauds against the government." The frauds in question initially involved back pay and county claims, but within a few years included investigations of the Ku Klux Klan, nonconforming distillers, smugglers, mail robbers, land frauds, and a number of other infractions against federal laws.

At the request of President Theodore Roosevelt in 1905, the Secret Service assisted the Department of Justice with an investigation that exposed widespread fraudulent homestead claims by western cattle barons and coal and lumber companies. Findings also disclosed that prominent and powerful politicians were involved in these fraudulent practices. As a result of the investigation, two members of Congress were indicted and millions of acres of land were recovered for the government.

Many politicians charged that the Secret Service had no right to investigate matters outside the realm of the Treasury Department and urged that action be taken to prevent other departments of the government from borrowing Secret Service agents for investigative purposes. Congress limited the Secret Service's activities by restricting their appropriations, and all investigations of the western land frauds were discontinued.

Seeking other ways to utilize the experienced Secret Service investigators for matters not related to Treasury business, President Roosevelt transferred eight of them to the Department of Justice on July 1, 1908, creating what is now known as the Federal Bureau of Investigation.

The Protective Mission

The assassination of President William McKinley in 1901 was the third such tragedy in U.S. history. The first occurred on April 14, 1865 when President Abraham Lincoln was shot by John Wilkes Booth. The second assassination ended the life of President James A. Garfield in 1881.

Following the death of President McKinley, the Secretary of the Treasury and the Secretary to the President directed the Secret Service to assume the responsibility of protecting the life of the President. Thus began the second mission of the Secret Service, a mission which today is the agency's primary responsibility. Permanent authority for this function did not come until years later.

World War II

Protective responsibilities expanded during World War II to include foreign dignitaries such as Norwegian Crown Princess Martha and her children, who came to the United States to escape the war. In the ensuing years, other foreign visitors who were protected included Prime Minister Winston Churchill of Great Britain, Madame Chiang Kai-shek of China, and Queen Wilhelmina of the Netherlands.

In December 1941, another wartime responsibility was added to the Service's agenda when the Declaration of Independence, the Constitution, the Gutenberg Bible, Lincoln's Second Inaugural Address, and the Lincoln Cathedral copy of the Magna Carta were safely transported by the Secret Service from Washington, D.C., to the government's heavily protected vaults at Fort Knox, Kentucky, where they were stored for the duration of the war.

Blair House Attack

During a period in 1950 when the White House was undergoing renovation, President and Mrs. Truman took up official residence in the Blair House, an historic home on Pennsylvania Avenue, close to the White House.

On the afternoon of November 1, 1950, two Puerto Rican nationalists attempted to assassinate the President. Although their attempt failed, a member of the White House Police was killed. Congress later passed legislation providing the Secret Service with permanent authority to continue its protective and investigative missions.

The assassination of President John F. Kennedy in Dallas, Texas, on November 22, 1963, greatly affected the way the Secret Service would operate on future protective missions.

Almost a year after the assassination, the President's Commission on the Assassination, more commonly known as the Warren Commission, submitted its report to President Lyndon B. Johnson. Those findings gave specific recommendations for the protection of Presidents. These included an increase in the number of special agents assigned to Presidential protection expansion of Special Agent training, further development of the protective intelligence function, and increased liaison with other federal agencies as well as with state and local law enforcement entities. The Service also added new technical security equipment, automatic data processing, and improved communications equipment.

Candidate Protection

The assassination of Robert F. Kennedy added presidential candidate protection to the roster of Secret Service activities. On June 5, 1968, after he had won the Democratic Presidential primary in California, Robert F. Kennedy had just given his victory speech at the Ambassador Hotel in Los Angeles. Private security guards were escorting the Senator through the hotel's kitchen when Sirhan Bishara Sirhan pointed a .22 caliber Iver Johnson revolver close to Kennedy's head and fired.

President Lyndon B. Johnson saw that the appropriate legislation was immediately passed for Secret Service protection of presidential candidates.

Uniformed Division officers standing post outside the White House. (Photo courtesy of the U.S. Secret Service, Department of the Treasury.)

The Uniformed Division

The thwarted attack on the life of President Truman in 1950 spotlighted the role of the Uniformed Division of the Secret Service, first known as the White House Police Force.

As early as 1860, the need for safeguarding the White House and its grounds was recognized. At that time, the force that protected the White House was made up of the military and a few members of the Washington, D.C., Metropolitan Police Department. This small protective unit was responsible to the White House Military Aide until 1922, when the White House Police Force was established at the request of President Warren G. Harding.

On May 14, 1930, Congress gave the supervision of the White House Police to the Chief of the Secret Service. This action was prompted by the entrance of an unexpected and unknown visitor to the White House dining room.

Another change occurred in March 1970, when the unit became known as the Executive Protective Service and its duties were enlarged to include the protection of diplomatic missions in the Washington, D.C., area. In 1974, Congress authorized the protection of the Vice President's immediate family and their residence, giving the Executive Protective Service further responsibility.

On November 15, 1977, the name of the uniformed force officially became the U.S. Secret Service Uniformed Division, conforming to the law enforcement status and authority of the organization.

Agents accompany President and Mrs. Bush during Inaugural Day ceremonies. (Photo courtesy of the U.S. Secret Service, Department of the Treasury)

FUNCTIONS AND ACTIVITIES

The Protective Function

Today, the Secret Service is authorized to protect the following persons:

- the President, the Vice President (or other officer next in order of succession to the Office of President), the President-elect, and Vice President-elect

- the immediate families of the above individuals

- former Presidents and their spouses for their lifetimes, with individuals elected to office after that time receiving protection for only 10 years after leaving office

- children of former Presidents until age 16

- visiting heads of foreign states or governments and their spouses traveling with them, other distinguished foreign visitors to the U.S., and official representatives of the U.S. performing special missions abroad

- major candidates for President and Vice President, and within 120 days of the general election, the spouses of such candidates

Protective Research

Protective research is inherent in all security operations. Protective research technicians and engineers develop, test, and maintain technical devices and equipment needed to secure a safe environment for the Service's protectees.

Agents and specialists assigned to protective research also evaluate information received from other law enforcement and intelligence agencies regarding individuals or groups who may pose a threat to protectees. Such information is critical to the Service's protective planning.

Candidate and Foreign Dignitary Protection

In 1968, Congress authorized the Secret Service to protect major candidates and nominees for President and Vice President of the United States. Under the law, eligibility for Secret Service protection is determined by a committee of House and Senate leaders who make recommendations to the Secretary of the Treasury. Protection is also authorized for the spouses of Presidential and Vice Presidential nominees for up to 120 days preceding the national election.

In 1971 Congress also authorized Secret Service protection for a visiting Head of State of a foreign government.

Case Illustrations

Two Assassination Attempts on President Gerald Ford

The first attempt on President Gerald Ford's life occurred in Sacramento, California, on September 5, 1975, as the President was walking across the State Capitol grounds to meet Governor Jerry Brown. Special Agent Larry Buendorf, accompanying the President, noticed a woman in a red cloak pushing her way through the crowd in an attempt to get closer to the President. Seeing her raise a gun and point it toward the President, Special Agent Buendorf grabbed the gun, pushed it down and disarmed the woman, who was later identified as Lynette "Squeaky" Fromme, a follower of convicted killer Charles Manson.

The second incident occurred 17 days later in San Francisco. Sara Jane Moore had been an informant for the FBI and other agencies and was an associate of extreme radicals. The Secret Service knew about Sara Jane Moore and had, in fact, interviewed her prior to the attempt. At the time of the interview, Ms. Moore was not thought to be a threat to the President. Less than 48 hours later, however, she attempted to shoot him. A bystander in the crowd viewing the President saw what Ms. Moore was about to do and grabbed at the gun, deflecting the shot.

The Reagan Assassination Attempt

On March 30, 1981, President Ronald Reagan had been speaking to representatives of the Building and Construction Trades Union at the Washington Hilton Hotel in Washington, D.C. As the President came outside to enter the limousine, John Hinckley, Jr. began shooting at him. Special Agent in Charge Jerry Parr pushed the President into the limousine and covered him with his own body. Then, seeing blood trickling from the President's mouth, Parr realized the President had been hit and directed the motorcade to proceed to nearby George Washington University Hospital. Two agents helped Mr. Reagan into the emergency room where he collapsed from post-injury shock and was immediately taken to surgery for removal of the bullet.

The Investigative Function

The Secret Service is the agency responsible for monitoring the integrity of U.S. currency, not only in the United States, but also abroad. It accomplishes this aspect of its mission through the services of its foreign liaison offices, which are now located in Paris, Rome, London, Bonn, and Bangkok.

As new methods and mechanisms evolve for handling financial transactions involving U.S. currency, the Service's investigative jurisdictions must expand. Computer crimes spawned by 20th-century technological advances are emerging as a major concern for law enforcement. In addition to investigating the counterfeiting of certain government identification documents and devices and theft and forgery of U.S. government checks and bonds, special agents today investigate major cases involving credit and debit card fraud, computer fraud, automated teller machine fraud, telephone fraud involving long distance calls, and electronic fund transfer fraud.

Two laws stemming from the 1984 Comprehensive Crime Control Act, commonly referred to as the Credit Card Fraud Act and the Computer Fraud Act, make it a federal violation to use "access devices" fraudulently. The term "access device" includes credit and debit cards, automatic teller machine (ATM) cards, computer passwords, personal identification numbers (PINs) used to activate ATM machines, credit or debit card account numbers, long-distance access codes, and, among other things, the computer chips in cellular car phones that assign billing.

In order to protect users of these transaction devices, Congress in 1986 empowered the Secret Service, along with other federal law enforcement agencies, to investigate fraud and related activities in connection with "federal-interest" computers.

Another area of high technology targeted by criminals is the telecommunications industry. Industry trade organizations estimate that fraud costs long-distance telephone companies about $500 million per year — or about one percent of the industry's total revenue.

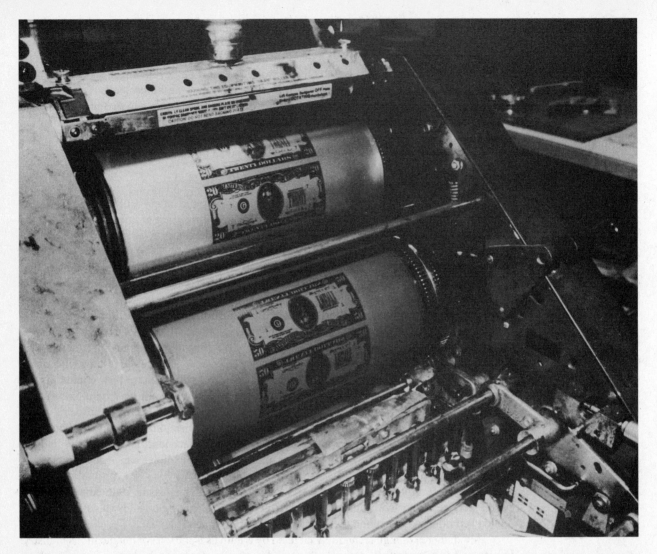

Printing press confiscated during a seizure. (Photo courtesy of the U.S. Secret Service, Department of the Treasury.)

Case Illustrations

Stolen Access Codes

The Service conducted an investigation of major marketers of stolen telephone long-distance access codes. The marketers were buying stolen access codes from hackers (individuals who obtain these codes through their personal computers). The marketers then sold the codes to innocent people and businesses. The group caused an estimated fraud loss of $125 million to the telecommunications industry. The Secret Service arrested 20 individuals, recovered 3,500 stolen access codes, and seized 12 computer systems.

Credit Card and Computer Crimes

Two separate credit card rings were operating in New York City, producing counterfeit Visa and Master Cards. The rings also had the potential to manufacture counterfeit American Express cards. Secret Service agents arrested 16 people and confiscated 100,000 credit cards with a street value of more than $500 million.

Other fraud cases have involved travel schemes. One concerned an airline company in Cincinnati. The airlines reported a loss of approximately $60,000 in ticket revenues through a credit card account number fraud scheme. As the investigation progressed, the Secret Service found that a number of airline personnel were involved, and suspects were found not only in the Cincinnati area, but also in Detroit, New York, and San Francisco. One search in the case took place in Cleveland, yielding approximately $90,000 in unused airline tickets and almost 2,000 credit card account numbers valued at $3 million.

Information Technology in the Service Today

In the 1970s, the Service developed the Master Central Index (MCI) to share information among its more than 100 locations around the country and the world. MCI allows the cross-referencing of all investigative data and provides access to other related databases within the Service and in other law enforcement agencies.

The Secret Service currently operates the Digital Encryption Signal-secured (DES), all-satellite, Very Small Aperture Terminal (VSAT) information network. Through this network, the Service staffs in field offices and resident agencies can access large, centralized databases of shared Secret Service information as well as the National Crime Information Center (NCIC) and the National Law Enforcement Telecommunications System (NLETS). The network also provides facsimile transmission and electronic mail capabilities.

Technical Security Division

The Technical Security Division (TSD) is comprised of special agents, security specialists, electronic technicians, and engineers. This operation supports headquarters, field offices, and the protective details through new concepts in lock, alarm and video systems, access control, bollards, and hydraulic gates. In its protection of the President and others, TSD handles chemical, biological, radiological, and nuclear concerns. It is involved in water security, fire protection, hazardous materials, and munitions countermeasures and is responsible for the Service's air space monitoring programs.

While providing the traditional physical security measures, TSD develops new investigative equipment for the field offices. Also, through its field support, it maintains, stores, and distributes equipment to the field as needed for protective and investigative missions.

An Examiner from the Forensic Services Division reviews evidence. (Photo courtesy of the U.S. Secret Service, Department of the Treasury.)

Forensic Services Division

The Forensic Services Division consists of four branches and includes specialists in fingerprinting, visual information, graphic arts, and audiovisual. In the division are document analysts, scientific/technical photographers, evidence control technicians, identification clerks, and special agent/polygraph examiners.

Today's FSD is monitoring technological developments that will allow computerized recognition of handwriting and is involved in the development of computerized voice recognition.

The Uniformed Division Today

The Uniformed Division is divided into three branches: the White House Branch, the Foreign Missions Branch, and the Administration and Program Support Branch.

Uniformed Division officers in the White House Branch are responsible for security at the Executive Mansion, the Treasury Building, the Treasury Annex and grounds, and the Old and New Executive Office Buildings. Uniformed Division officers clear all visitors, provide fixed posts, and patrol the White House grounds.

The Foreign Missions Branch of the Uniformed Division safeguards foreign diplomatic missions in the Washington, D.C., area. Officers maintain foot and vehicular patrols in areas where embassies are located. They are assigned to fixed posts at locations where a threat has been received or at installations of countries involved in tense international situations. This branch also provides security at the Vice President's residence and for foreign dignitaries in residence at the Blair House.

Uniformed Division officers have additional duties that closely involve them in almost every phase of the Service's protective mission.

The Administration and Program Support Branch officers support the entire Service and operate magnetometers at the White House and at other sites to prevent persons from taking weapons into secure areas.

Uniformed Division canine teams respond to bomb threats, suspicious packages, and other situations where explosive detection is necessary. The Uniformed Division Counter-sniper Team performs still other important security functions.

TRAINING

New agents begin their training as soon as they enter their first field office. There they become acclimated to the agent's way of life. Each field office designates experienced agents who are responsible for assisting the new agents.

The agents begin their structured training, as do all Treasury agents, at the Federal Law Enforcement Training Center in Brunswick, (Glynco) Georgia, as part of an eight-week general investigative training course.

They then attend a nine-week Special Agent Training Course at Special Agent Training and Employee Development Division Headquarters, Washington, D.C. There they learn about protection, investigations, and intelligence and participate in extensive simulation training and testing.

Once the new agents have successfully completed the Special Agent Training Course, they again return to the field office to complete their formal on-the-job training (OJT) program. At the end of the agent's first year, the Special Agent in Charge of the field office makes a determination whether or not to retain the new agent.

Officers attend the courses at Glynco and specialized training at the Secret Service training facilities at the James J. Rowley Training Center in Laurel, Maryland. Other training includes instruction in computer systems, management courses, and specialized instruction. Support personnel also receive training in these areas.

QUALIFICATIONS

Prior to being considered for a special agent position, candidates must pass the Treasury Enforcement Agent examination. Candidates may apply at the nearest U.S. Office of Personnel Management or at the nearest Secret Service field office. A limited number of qualified applicants will be called for a series of in-depth interviews. They must complete a polygraph examination as a condition of employment and may be asked to participate in a drug screening program.

Applicants must also undergo a thorough background investigation. Selected applicants should be prepared to wait an extended period of time for vacancies to occur. All appointees must be less than 37 years of age at the time of entrance on duty.

Since special agents must be in excellent physical condition, applicants must pass a comprehensive medical examination, provided by the Secret Service, prior to appointment. Weight must be in proportion to height. Vision must be at least 20/60 in each eye (uncorrected) or 20/20 in each eye (corrected).

A bachelor's degree from an accredited college or university in any field of study meets the minimum requirements for appointment at the GS-5 grade level. One additional year of specialized experience, superior academic achievement (defined as a grade point average of 2.9 or higher on a 4.0 scale), or one year of graduate study in a directly related field meets the requirements for appointment at the GS-7 grade level. In some cases, an applicant may be accepted with a minimum of three years of experience, two of which are in criminal investigation, or with a comparable combination of experience and education.

Uniformed Division officer receiving automatic weapon training. (Photo courtesy of the U.S. Secret Service, Department of the Treasury.)

Uniformed Division

Uniformed Division applicants must be United States citizens and have a high school diploma or its equivalent. They must possess a valid automobile driver's license and qualify for top secret clearance. Applicants must be less than 37 years of age when appointed to a Uniformed Division Officer position. Prior to being considered, they must pass a written exam. Qualified applicants will then receive a personal interview and must complete a polygraph examination as a condition of employment.

Applicants must also pass a comprehensive medical examination, which is provided at no cost to the applicant. Vision must be at least 20/60 in each eye, correctable to 20/20. Weight must be in proportion to height.

Selected applicants should be prepared to wait an extended period of time while a thorough background investigation is conducted.

For further information, visit the Secret Service online at http://www.treas.gov/usss or contact:

United States Secret Service
Personnel Division
950 H Street, NW
Washington, D.C. 20223
Telephone: (202) 406-5800

DEPARTMENT OF VETERANS AFFAIRS

VETERAN ADMINISTRATION POLICE AND THE OFFICE OF SECURITY AND LAW ENFORCEMENT

MISSION

The Veteran Administration (VA) Police's mission to maintain safety and security and enforce the law throughout its national health care system is based on Title 38 of the U.S. Code, the federal law that created and organized Veterans Affairs. Chapter 9 of that law gives the Secretary of Veterans Affairs the responsibility of prescribing rules and regulations "for the maintenance of law and order and protection of persons and property on Department property" and designating Department police officers to enforce them. The FBI has primary investigative jurisdiction on federal property and VA maintains a close relationship with the FBI at each location. Jurisdiction is concurrent at most locations, enabling prosecution of crimes in state, local, and federal courts.

Within this system of law enforcement, VA's Police remain dedicated to a philosophy that permeates VA training and policing: to prevent crime, work to defuse the threat, and take physical action.

HISTORICAL REVIEW

Since 1986, four VA police officers have been shot and killed in the line of duty. In addition, numerous other police officers were wounded by weapons or were involved in incidents that could have resulted in injuries. Although the force was unarmed until 1996, the need to arm police officers arose many years before. VA medical facilities are not immune to the growing incidence of violence. In response to the need to ensure a safe environment, the Secretary of Veterans Affairs directed that all VA police officers be trained and armed with VA-approved firearms.

Just two months after being armed, police officers at the Salisbury, North Carolina, Medical Center were able to stop a veteran who had shot a physician in the heart. When the VA officers responded to the scene, they found the physician lying on the floor, seriously wounded. When the officers approached the gunman and directed him to drop his firearm, he fired at them. The officers continued to try and persuade the gunman to drop the weapon but he continued firing at them. Police officers returned fire and killed the man. This incident brought into sharp focus the value that a properly trained and armed police force can bring to a facility and the importance of having the capability to protect patients and employees in volatile and unpredictable situations.

FUNCTIONS AND ACTIVITIES

The Office of Security and Law Enforcement

The Office of Security and Law Enforcement is responsible for providing guidance, consultation, and direct operational support for all elements of VA. Headed by the Deputy Assistant Secretary for Security and Law Enforcement, it is organized into three main sections:

- Police and Security Service: Headquartered at VA Central Office in Washington, D.C., the Police and Security Service conducts inspections of field Police and Security Units, conducts investigations, and provides direction, guidance, and support for law enforcement programs at VA medical centers and other VA facilities nationwide. The Police and Security Service also provides consultation and liaison services to all elements of VA and works closely with other federal law enforcement agencies.

- Emergency Management and Administration: This section provides direction and guidance to the disaster preparedness and emergency planning functions of VA. This section also manages the personnel and document security responsibilities of VA.

- VA Law Enforcement Training Center (LETC): This section provides training for VA police officers throughout the system.

Security and Safety of Utmost Concern

VA's philosophy in the use of firearms is to provide as much safety as possible, yet still be effective. VA leadership realizes there are concerns and that a firearm demands special responsibility and care. Consequently, VA is meticulous in its training program and evaluates each site for readiness before the officers are armed. A representative of the Office of Security and Law Enforcement (S&LE) conducts a pre-arming site visit to evaluate the facility's plan to arm its officers. Once a site has been approved for arming, LETC provides the initial 40 hours of firearm training and the S&LE certifies each officer prior to being armed. Following this initial training, each officer must complete continuing training on such subjects as the use of force, handgun retention, and reduced-light firing. They also must qualify on the range twice a year.

The Beretta 9 mm semiautomatic pistol was chosen for its special safety features. This double-action handgun was modified for VA to include a disconnecting device that renders it inoperable when the magazine is removed. This allows an officer to remove the magazine and make the pistol safe when entering certain areas of a hospital such as a psychiatric ward. The safety feature, along with a special security holster, greatly reduces the likelihood of the firearm being taken and used by an unauthorized person.

TRAINING

The VA Law Enforcement Training Center is located on the campus of the Central Arkansas Veterans Health Care System in North Little Rock, Arkansas. The LETC provides specialized training to all VA police officers, emphasizing VA policies and procedures and proper enforcement of federal law. Additionally, training prepares the police officers to deal with typical VA patients. This unique training program places special focus on community- and customer-oriented policing.

Each VA police officer is required to complete 80 hours of initial training and 160 hours of training at the LETC. Participants are instructed in a wide range of law enforcement topics, including criminal law, search and seizure, patrol techniques, personal protection, violence in the workplace, and techniques in managing potentially volatile situations. Special emphasis is placed on verbal skills and unique topics related to working in a health-care environment and other limited jurisdictional settings. The curriculum is current, timely, and responds to the needs of the community. Approximately 270 newly appointed VA police officers attend the basic course annually.

VA also offers training, on a fee-for-service basis, to other federal agencies such as Walter

Reed Army Medical Center, National Gallery of Art, Indian Health Service, Federal Emergency Management Agency, and the National Guard Bureau.

QUALIFICATIONS

VA police officers must have prior specialized law enforcement experience. Standards are set by the U.S. Office of Personnel Management and require experience with basic laws and regulations and law enforcement operations, practices, and techniques. Prior positions must include responsibility for protecting life and property and the maintenance of law and order. This experience may have been gained by serving as a police officer for a municipal, county, state, or federal agency; a military policeman; a parks or forest service policeman; or holding similar positions that require the necessary knowledge and skills in law enforcement. A degree in criminal justice may be substituted for some experience.

Additionally, each police officer is subjected to a background investigation and is required to take an entry physical examination and an annual physical examination to determine physical fitness and emotional stability.

For more information, see the Office of Security and Law Enforcement Web site at http://www.va.gov/osle or write to:

Department of Veterans Affairs
810 Vermont Avenue, NW
Washington, D.C. 20420
Telephone: (202) 273-5700

PART THREE

Law Enforcement Careers with Independent Agencies

INDEPENDENT AGENCIES

CENTRAL INTELLIGENCE AGENCY

MISSION

While not considered a law enforcement agency, the Central Intelligence Agency (CIA) supports the overall United States government effort to combat international terrorism by collecting, analyzing, and disseminating intelligence on foreign terrorist groups and individuals. It also conducts liaison with the intelligence and security services of friendly governments, sharing counterterrorism intelligence information with them and providing advice and training on request. The Agency's counterterrorism specialists participate actively in developing strategies aimed at combating terrorism, and intelligence resources worldwide provide significant support to U.S. efforts to solve this grave problem. The CIA also collects, produces, and disseminates intelligence on foreign aspects of narcotics production and trafficking.

HISTORICAL REVIEW

The United States has carried on foreign intelligence activities since the days of George Washington, but only since World War II have they been coordinated on a government-wide basis.

Even before Pearl Harbor, President Franklin D. Roosevelt was concerned about American intelligence deficiencies. He asked New York lawyer William J. Donovan to draft a plan for an intelligence service. The Office of Strategic Services (OSS) was established in June 1942, with a mandate to collect and analyze strategic information required by the Joint Chiefs of Staff and to conduct special operations not assigned to other agencies.

During the War, it supplied policymakers with essential facts and intelligence estimates and often played an important role in directly aiding military campaigns. But the OSS never received complete jurisdiction over all foreign intelligence activities. Since the early 1930s, the FBI had been responsible for intelligence work in Latin America, and the military services protected their areas of responsibility.

President Harry S. Truman established the Central Intelligence Group (CIG) in January 1946, directing it to coordinate existing departmental intelligence, supplementing but not supplanting their services. This was all to be done under the direction of the National Intelligence Authority (NIA) composed of a Presidential representative and the Secretaries of State, War, and Navy.

Twenty months later, the NIA and its operating component, the CIG, were disestablished. Under the provisions of the National Security Act of 1947 (which became effective on September 18, 1947), the National Security Council and the Central Intelligence Agency were established.

The 1947 Act charged the CIA with coordinating the nation's intelligence activities and correlating, evaluating, and disseminating intelligence that affects national security.

In order to protect intelligence sources and methods from disclosure, the 1949 Act further exempted the CIA from having to disclose its "organization, functions, names, officials, titles, salaries, or numbers of personnel employed."

Under these acts of Congress, the Director serves as the principal adviser to the President and the National Security Council (NSC) on all matters of foreign intelligence related to the national security. CIA's responsibilities are carried out subject to various directives and controls established by the President and the NSC.

Today, the CIA reports regularly to the Senate Select Committee on Intelligence (SSCI) and the House Permanent Select Committee on Intelligence (HPSCI), as required by the Intelligence Oversight Act of 1980. The Agency also reports regularly to the Defense Subcommittees of the Appropriations Committees in both houses of Congress. Moreover, the Agency also provides substantive briefings to the Senate Foreign Relations Committee, House Committee on Foreign Affairs, and the Armed Services Committees in both bodies as well as other Committees and individual members.

For further information, visit the CIA Web site at http://www.cia.gov or write to:

Director of Personnel
Central Intelligence Agency
Washington, D.C. 20505
(703) 482-0632 (Office of Public Affairs)

DIVISION OF ENFORCEMENT

SECURITIES AND EXCHANGE COMMISSION

MISSION
The enforcement mission of the Securities and Exchange Commission (SEC) is an aggressive and comprehensive program that enforces the federal securities laws essential to investor protection and investor confidence in the integrity, fairness, and efficiency of the securities markets. The enforcement program is designed to maintain a presence in all areas within the Commission's jurisdiction, concentrate on particular problem areas, and anticipate emerging problems.

The Commission is authorized to conduct investigations of potential violations of federal securities laws. Investigators may examine the conduct of individuals trading securities as well as the conduct of broker-dealers, municipal securities dealers, investment advisers, investment companies, transfer agents, and self-regulatory organizations.

HISTORICAL REVIEW
The *Handbook of Federal Police and Investigative Agencies,* by Donald A. Torres, states that the SEC was created under the Securities Exchange Act of 1934 in an effort by Congress to "police" and regulate securities and finance affecting the American public. Prior to 1934, very little was accomplished relative to protection or regulation of stock practices in the financial world. The enforcement of minimum regulatory inquiries had been assigned to the Department of Justice, although the area of selling or buying stocks and bonds was not a high priority for legislative restrictions prior to the Wall Street Crash of 1929. Only after the Crash did it become apparent that regulations and some restrictions were needed to prevent a similar event from reoccurring. After much debate and many Congressional hearings, the SEC was founded as a viable enforcement and regulatory tool in the corporate world.

FUNCTIONS AND ACTIVITIES
The Commission's enforcement activities are designed to secure compliance with the federal securities laws administered by the Commission and the rules and regulations adopted thereunder. These activities include measures to:

- compel obedience to the disclosure requirements of registration and other provisions of the acts

- prevent fraud and deception in the purchase and sale of securities

- obtain court orders enjoining acts and practices that operate as a fraud upon investors or otherwise violate the laws

- suspend or revoke the registrations of brokers, dealers, investment companies, and investment advisers who willfully engage in prohibited acts and practices

- suspend or bar from association persons associated with brokers, dealers, investment companies, and investment advisers who have violated any provision of the federal securities laws

- prosecute persons who have engaged in fraudulent activities or other willful violations of those laws

In addition, attorneys, accountants, and other professionals who violate the securities laws face possible loss of their privilege to practice before the Commission.

To this end, private investigations are conducted into complaints or other indications of securities violations. Evidence thus established is used in appropriate administrative proceedings to revoke registration or in actions instituted in federal courts to restrain or enjoin such activities. Where the evidence tends to establish criminal fraud or other willful violation of the securities laws, the facts are referred to the Attorney General for criminal prosecution of the offenders. The Commission may assist in such prosecutions.

QUALIFICATIONS

With the exception of the attorney category, positions are in the competitive civil service and are filled generally by selection from lists of eligible candidates established as a result of appropriate civil service examinations.

The Commission operates a college and law school recruitment program, including on-campus visitations for interview purposes.

For further information, visit the SEC Web site at http://www.sec.gov or contact:
Division of Enforcement
Securities and Exchange Commission
450 5th Street, NW
Washington, D.C. 20549-0801
Telephone: (202) 942-4500 or (202) 942-0020
E-mail: recruit@sec.gov

ENFORCEMENT AND COMPLIANCE ASSURANCE

ENVIRONMENTAL PROTECTION AGENCY

MISSION

The Office of Enforcement and Compliance Assurance (OECA), working in partnership with EPA regional offices, state governments, tribal governments, and other federal agencies, ensures compliance with the nation's environmental laws. Employing an integrated approach of compliance assistance, compliance incentives, and innovative civil and criminal enforcement, OECA and its partners seek to maximize compliance and reduce threats to public health and the environment.

Criminal Investigation Division

The mission of the EPA Criminal Investigation Division is to investigate the most significant and egregious violations of environmental laws that pose a significant threat to human health and the environment and to provide state-of-the-art training to EPA employees and partners in federal, tribal, state, local, and international law enforcement.

Enforcement/Clean Up

The Office of Regulatory Enforcement; the Office of Criminal Enforcement, Forensics, and Training; and the Federal Facilities Enforcement Office are responsible for conducting the regulatory enforcement program. The Office of Site Remediation Enforcement is responsible for enforcing cleanups at environmental sites.

Ar Enforcement Division

The Air Enforcement Division (AED), Office of Regulatory Enforcement, is responsible for judicial and administrative enforcement activities under the Clean Air Act (CAA) and the Noise Control Act (NCA).

HISTORICAL REVIEW

The Congress and the President responded to calls to protect future generations from the dangers of environmental pollution by creating the Environmental Protection Agency and by ensuring the swift passage of two landmark pieces of legislation—the Clean Air Act Amendments of 1970 and the Clean Water Act of 1972. In the years since then, many other environmental statutes have been passed. Over the years, EPA and the states have developed plans to abate pollution, issued permits governing industrial discharges, and taken enforcement actions to compel compliance with environmental laws.

Enforcement Accomplishments

In a recent year, a record 208 years of jail time were imposed on criminal defendants, including one sentence of thirteen years for a man responsible for dumping 4 million gallons of contaminated wastewater into the Tampa, Florida, sewer system and sending 170,000 pounds of hazardous sludge to the city's incinerator, which was not designed to dispose of hazardous materials. During the same year, polluters were required to spend more than $3.4 billion to correct violations and take additional steps to protect the environment. In the largest settlement in Clean Air Act enforcement history, seven heavy-duty diesel engine manufacturers will spend more than $1 billion to settle charges that they illegally released millions of tons of nitrous oxide (NOx) pollution into the air. The settlement resolved charges that these companies violated the CAA by selling an estimated 1.3 million engines equipped with "defeat devices"—software that allowed engines to meet EPA emission standards during testing but disabled the emission control system during normal highway driving. As part of the settlement, the companies will pay an $83.4 million civil penalty, the largest in environmental enforcement history, and undertake supplemental environmental projects (SEPs) costing $109.5 million to lower NOx emissions.

The FMC Corporation, Inc. (FMC) will spend a total of approximately $170 million to settle charges that it repeatedly violated the hazardous waste law at its phosphorus production facility in Pocatello, Idaho. The charges against FMC involved mismanagement of ignitable and reactive phosphorus wastes in surface ponds. The pond sediments burn vigorously and persistently when exposed to the air, and the wastes in these ponds generate phosphine and hydrogen cyanide, highly toxic gases that can cause serious health and environmental problems. It is also believed that migratory bird deaths in the area may be attributable to phosphine poisoning. FMC will close previously used surface ponds and construct a $40 million waste treatment plant to deactivate the phosphorus-bearing wastes. Costs associated with all the injunctive relief required under the settlement are expected to exceed $90 million. FMC also has committed to more than a dozen SEPs with a capital cost of $63 million, which will significantly improve air quality in the Pocatello region. As a final SEP, FMC will conduct a $1.65 million public health assessment and education program to investigate the effects of contaminants generated by FMC on human health and the environment, particularly within nearby tribal lands.

The Atlantic Richfield Company (ARCO) will spend $260 million, including a $1.8 million penalty, to clean up and restore natural resource damages caused by mine waste contamination in the Clark Fork River Basin. As part of the two settlements reached with the State of Montana and the Confederated Salish and Kootenai tribes of the Flathead Nation, ARCO will pay $80 million for the cleanup of the Silver Bow Creek and $20 million to restore wetlands, bull trout habitat, and other natural resources. ARCO has committed to perform additional restoration to create, restore, or enhance 400 acres of wetlands, primarily in the Anaconda area, which is estimated to cost $3.4 million.

Royal Caribbean Cruise Lines, Ltd. pled guilty to 21 violations of federal law and was fined $18 million for violating the CWA and the Oil Pollution Act (OPA) by dumping waste oil and hazardous chemicals into the ocean and for making false statements to the U.S. Coast Guard. Royal Caribbean will institute a five-year environmental compliance plan.

For further information, visit the OECA Web site at http://www.epa.gov or contact:

Office of Enforcement and Compliance Assurance
Environmental Protection Agency
1200 Pennsylvania Avenue, NW
Ariel Rios Building
Washington, D.C. 20460
Telephone: (202) 564-2119
(202) 564-2614

FEDERAL PROTECTIVE SERVICE

GENERAL SERVICES ADMINISTRATION

MISSION
The Federal Protective Service (FPS) is responsible for delivering a comprehensive physical security and law enforcement program in all General Services Administration (GSA)–owned and leased facilities. This involves providing protection services for more than a million federal workers and visitors to over 8,000 buildings nationwide.

HISTORICAL REVIEW
When the FPS was formed in 1971, largely in response to the growing number of demonstrations at federal facilities, it was primarily a guard service. Not long after, access control was increasingly delegated to contract guards, and FPOs became a mobile police force with wide law enforcement powers on GSA-controlled property.

FUNCTIONS AND ACTIVITIES
The FPS provides client or tenant federal agencies with a total security package that combines human, electronic, and educational elements. These include the FPS's own law enforcement, physical security, and investigative personnel; contract guards, electronic surveillance and entry control devices; and a widespread crime prevention awareness program.

FPS consists of a mobile police force of approximately 700 uniformed Federal Protective Officers (FPOs). These officers have all the police powers of sheriffs and constables, with the exception of serving civil processes. They are authorized to enforce laws and to make arrests on property under the jurisdiction of the U.S. General Services Administration.

An additional force of nonuniformed Criminal Investigators examines crimes ranging from theft of government property to homicide. Investigators coordinate their efforts, where appropriate, with other federal law enforcement agencies and with state and local groups.

Approximately 135 Physical Security Specialists perform physical security surveys and conduct crime prevention programs at client or tenant federal work sites around the country.

Nationwide coordination and support for the FPS is the responsibility of the U.S. General Services Administration (GSA), headquartered in Washington, D.C. Organizationally, the FPS is part of GSA's Public Buildings Service. Policy guidance comes from the Assistant Commissioner, Office of Physical Security and Law Enforcement.

In fulfilling the FPS mission, Uniformed Officers or other FPS personnel:

- provide mobile response to emergency calls

- conduct physical security surveys to assess facility risk and recommend appropriate security measures

- monitor intrusion, duress, and fire alarm systems

- advise and reinforce contract guards at building access points

- protect federal officials and foreign dignitaries when they are on GSA-controlled space

- direct control efforts, in cooperation with local police, in group demonstrations and riots

- respond to a direct attack on a federal facility

- investigate crime

- cooperate with other federal law enforcement agencies and with state and local law enforcement groups

- act as consultants to federal agencies with special security problems

- provide and maintain state-of-the-art electronic intrusion detection and security systems for GSA-controlled space

- conduct crime prevention awareness programs aimed at crime avoidance

- administer cardiopulmonary resuscitation (CPR) and first aid

TRAINING

Federal Protective Officers (FPOs) take a rigorous basic police training course at the Federal Law Enforcement Training Center, Glynco, Georgia. They also receive specialized training in crowd and riot control and in performing police functions with national security significance. Training is continuous and is designed to keep officers aware of changing security needs and procedures as well as developments in security technology.

QUALIFICATIONS

To be eligible, applicants must:

- be U.S. citizens

- pass a written test administered by the Office of Personnel Management

- meet required physical standards and pass a physical examination

- possess a valid automobile driver's license

- pass an extensive background investigation

- be willing to work shifts and weekends

- have two years of suitable experience (any type of military service may be credited toward meeting this requirement), three years of education at a school above high school, or any combination of education and experience totaling two years.

The FPS considers candidates solely on merit, regardless of race, creed, color, sex, national origin, or political affiliation.

For further information on the Federal Protective Service, visit the GSA Web site at http://www.gsa.gov or contact:

Federal Protective Service
General Services Administration
1800 F Streets NW, Room 2341
Washington, D.C. 20405
Telephone (202) 501-0907

POSTAL INSPECTION SERVICE

U.S. POSTAL SERVICE

MISSION

The protection of the U.S. Mail and the mail system is the responsibility of the Postal Inspection Service. As the law enforcement and auditing arm of the U.S. Postal Service, the Postal Inspection Service performs investigative, law enforcement, security, and auditing functions essential to a stable and sound postal system.

The Postal Inspection Service has jurisdiction in all criminal matters infringing on the integrity and security of the mail and the safety of all postal valuables, property, and personnel. Postal Inspectors are the fact-finding and investigative agents of the U.S. Postal Service.

Since the beginning of the postal system in the United States, criminal and administrative problems of the Postal Service have been interwoven. The Inspection Service plays an integral part in maintaining effective operations in the Postal Service by detecting and investigating crimes against the mail and postal revenue, establishing safe and efficient postal systems, protecting all postal properties, and assuring that the postal system is not criminally misused to the detriment of the public.

Security and enforcement functions of the Inspection Service provide assurance to American business for the safe exchange of funds and securities through the U.S. Mail and to postal customers regarding the sanctity of the seal in transmitting correspondence and messages to all parts of the world. Audits ensure stability to financial operations, help control costs, and promote increased efficiency in the Postal Service.

HISTORICAL REVIEW

The first significant date in the history of the Postal Inspection Service was 1737 when Benjamin Franklin was appointed Postmaster at Philadelphia and was assigned the additional duties of "regulating the several post offices and bringing the postmasters to account." In the performance of those duties he visited and audited the accounts of existing post offices, improved methods of transportation, devised better accounting methods, and established new post offices to keep pace with the growth of the colonies.

In 1753, Franklin was appointed Deputy Postmaster General but continued to be responsible for the "additional duties" previously assigned. In that year, he went on an inspection tour of the colonies and visited every post office in the country except Charleston, South Carolina, thus setting a precedent for periodic inspections of post offices, a practice which has lasted for more than 200 years.

In 1782, the colonial postal system created a new "Surveyor" position. These surveyors were the forerunners of today's Postal Inspectors and the organization that evolved became the Postal Inspection Service, the United States' first federal law enforcement agency.

The colonial postal system became the American Postal Service on July 26, 1775, when the Continental Congress elected Benjamin Franklin as Postmaster General.

In 1801, the title of Surveyor was changed to Special Agent and in 1830, a separate Office of Instructions and Mail Depredations was formed to be the investigative and inspection branch of the Post Office Department.

Congress enacted the Mail Fraud Statute in 1872 to combat a rash of swindles by mail that erupted after the Civil War. Prior to passage of this law, con artists, using the mails to defraud people throughout the land, were virtually safe from prosecution because local law enforcement officials were unable to obtain jurisdiction over the distant swindler.

As the West developed, the number and types of postal crimes increased, thus necessitating additional special agents. A law passed by Congress on June 11, 1880, established the title of Chief Post Office Inspector and changed the designation of Special Agent to Inspector.

The discovery of gold in the Yukon resulted in a tremendous surge in population and in the number of towns that suddenly arose in the wilderness. Mail service was hurriedly begun and inspectors were sent to establish post offices and were given the authority to appoint postmasters and hire contractors to carry the mail. Ultimately, inspectors established a line of post offices along the Yukon River from the Canadian border to the Bering Sea and provided mail service to the thousands of hopeful prospectors who crisscrossed Alaska in search of gold.

Expansion of the air transport industry in the 1950s and greater use of mail transport by air brought new challenges to the Inspection Service. When federal personnel investigated airplane crashes, teams of postal inspectors were also present to recover the mail, sort it, and arrange for it to be moved to its final destination. When the first bomb exploded on board an aircraft in 1955, the potential law enforcement problems surrounding the transportation of mail on aircraft became all too clear; inspectors determined the bomb had been in the mail. The inherent danger of mail bombs on aircraft established a greater need for inspectors specially trained in bomb investigations and a laboratory capability to assist them in the analysis of evidence from a bomb explosion.

Under the Postal Reorganization Act of 1971, the U.S. Postal Service became an independent establishment in the executive branch of the government. Other important events and changes which affected Inspection Service activities in the 1970s were:

- An Office of Security was established to implement the increased preventive responsibilities of the Inspection Service and to guide the activities of a newly created uniformed security force. Designed to patrol major postal facilities, escort shipments of valuable mail between postal terminals and airports, and provide security for postal employees, the Security Force was a key factor in an overall deterrent program that complemented the investigative efforts of inspectors aimed at reducing postal crimes.

- Through the Organized Crime Control Act of 1970, mail fraud was considered "racketeering activity" in some cases, and postal inspectors were assigned to work with special Department of Justice Strike Force teams in postal related investigations.

- New legislation increased the Inspection Service's responsibility in administering both the civil and criminal statutes pertaining to mailing sexually oriented advertisements.

As the Inspection Service has moved into the t21st century, its basic mission of maintaining the integrity and sanctity of the mail has remained unchanged.

FUNCTIONS AND ACTIVITIES

As the primary law enforcement arm of the U.S. Postal Service, the U.S. Postal Inspection Service is a highly specialized, professional organization performing investigative and security functions essential to a stable and sound postal system.

Congress empowered the Postal Service "to investigate postal offenses and civil matters relating to the Postal Service." Through its security and enforcement functions, the Postal Inspection Service provides assurance to American businesses for the safe exchange of funds and securities through the U.S. mail; to postal customers regarding the sanctity of the seal in transmitting correspondence and messages; and to postal employees for a safe work environment.

As fact-finding and investigative agents, postal inspectors are federal law enforcement officers who carry firearms, make arrests, execute federal search warrants, and serve subpoenas. Inspectors work closely with U.S. attorneys, other law enforcement agencies, and local prosecutors to investigate postal cases and prepare them for court. There are approximately 2,000 postal inspectors stationed throughout the United States who enforce more than 200 federal laws covering investigations of crimes that adversely affect or fraudulently use the U.S. mail and postal system.

Uniformed Postal Police Officers

To assist in carrying out its responsibilities, the Postal Inspection Service maintains a security force of 1,400 uniformed postal police officers who are assigned to critical postal facilities throughout the country. The officers provide perimeter security, escort high-value mail shipments, and perform other essential protective functions.

Laboratories

The Postal Inspection Service operates five forensic crime laboratories, strategically located in cities throughout the United States. The labs are staffed with forensic scientists and technical specialists who assist inspectors in analyzing evidentiary material needed for identifying and tracing criminal suspects and in providing expert testimony for cases brought to trial.

Other Personnel

The Inspection Service's 900 professional and technical employees, including forensic specialists, program analysts, financial analysts, information technology experts, and others, play a vital role in supporting the criminal investigation and security functions of the Postal Inspection Service. They perform a wide variety of tasks, including developing, maintaining and continually upgrading management systems; providing forensic examinations of evidence; developing, procuring, and deploying electronic security and surveillance equipment; publishing policy handbooks and consumer awareness guides and brochures; supplying photography and video services; and facilitating direct communications with Congress and the public.

Information Technology

The Postal Inspection Service's national information technology infrastructure supports over 4,300 users at more than 220 sites nationwide. Inspection Service offices are linked nationally via a dedicated frame-relay network, with online connections to the Postal Service, the National Crime Information Center, the National Law Enforcement Telecommunications System, and the Internet.

The Office of Inspections, operating with a staff of postal inspectors, an Assistant Inspector in Charge, four support employees, and postal police officers, has a three-fold mission. It ensures integrity and excellence within the Inspection Service by conducting independent internal investigations of its employees. The office oversees the quality and thoroughness of Inspection Service operations by conducting reviews at field divisions and headquarters units. Finally, it protects the safety of postal employees and customers by providing security and preventive service at national headquarters.

The Office of Counsel provides legal advice and services in support of Postal Inspection Service investigations, programs, and goals, and processes requests for access to Inspection Service records. The Counsel's office comprises inspector/attorneys and a support staff of paralegal specialists, information disclosure specialists, a labor relations specialist, a program specialist, and an administrative support specialist.

The U.S. Postal Inspection Service extends full cooperation to all federal, state, and local investigative and prosecutorial authorities in law enforcement matters to ensure greater protection to the public. Postal Inspectors regularly participate in joint task force cases with other agencies aimed at curtailing widespread criminal acts of an organized nature.

TRAINING

Basic training for postal inspectors, refresher courses, and specialized courses are conducted at the Postal Service's William F. Bolger Center for Leadership Development in Potomac, Maryland. The training academy has on-site dormitory, dining, classroom, fitness, and firearms facilities. All inspectors undergo fourteen weeks of basic training, which covers investigative techniques, defensive tactics, firearms, legal matters, search and seizure, arrest techniques, court procedures, postal operations, and a detailed study of the federal laws over which the Postal Inspection Service has jurisdiction. Postal police officers undergo a basic training course at the Federal Law Enforcement Training Center in Glynco, Georgia.

For more information, visit the Postal Inspection Web site at http://www.usps.govwebsites/depart/inspect. For qualifications and information concerning the positions of Postal Inspector and Postal Police Officer, contact:

U.S. Postal Inspection Service
Recruitment Specialist
Bolger Center for Leadership Development
9600 Newbridge Drive, North Building
Potomac, Maryland 20854-4436
Telephone: (301) 983-7413
(202) 268-5400 (Office of Congressional and Public Affairs)

TENNESSEE VALLEY AUTHORITY POLICE

MISSION

The Tennessee Valley Authority Police (TVAP) is committed to maintaining law and order on TVA properties and setting and upholding the highest standards of excellence and integrity while providing services and protection to the public and TVA employees.

HISTORICAL REVIEW

The TVA Police organization, federally commissioned in 1995 and accredited in 1998, evolved from a dozen-man property protection unit created in mid-1933. The following year the group's name was changed to Police, Fire, and Guide Service with fire prevention, traffic control, life and property protection, visitor escorts, and general policing responsibilities. In 1936 the name was changed again to Public Safety Service. During World War II, Public Safety Service members were sworn in as Civilian Auxiliary to the Military Police and charged with protection against sabotage at construction sites or power generating facilities. Nuclear plant construction and expanded outdoor recreation opportunities brought additional duties. Changing responsibilities and customer needs necessitated enhancing the quality and level of service provided. TVAP was created to fulfill these needs.

TVA Police officers and other local law enforcement agencies prepare for a demonstration by anti-nuclear protestors at the Watts Bar Nuclear Plant, Spring City, TN.

FUNCTIONS AND ACTIVITIES

The Tennessee Valley Authority Police (TVAP) is a federally commissioned, nationally accredited law enforcement agency that provides protection for TVA properties and employees as well as the 100 million annual users of TVA recreation facilities. It is divided into four districts that encompass a seven-state area. TVAP has motor, marine, bicycle, and mounted patrols, as well as investigative services personnel and victim witness representatives. They exemplify professionalism, integrity, and pride. Each officer is committed to service demonstrated through assistance to local law enforcement agencies, community volunteer efforts, and special events.

TRAINING

TVAP officers receive extensive training in all areas of law enforcement. All officers must successfully complete a rigorous sixteen-week course at the Federal Law Enforcement Training Center in Glynco, Georgia. In order to maintain a professional, well-qualified law enforcement unit, each officer must annually participate in 40 hours of in-service training. Officers are also encouraged to enhance their computer skills. In addition to in-service training, officers also receive specialized training from nationally recognized sources, including the FBI, the United States Coast Guard, and the Tennessee Wildlife Resources Agency.

TVA Police's Marine Operations provides protection and law enforcement services on the Tennessee River, its tributaries, and TVA lakes. Memorandums of Understanding with the United States Coast Guard and an agreement with the Tennessee Wildlife Resources Agency support TVAP's marine operations activities.

QUALIFICATIONS

Applicants must be at least 21 years of age, U. S. citizens without criminal conviction, and have an associate degree and two years related law enforcement experience or a bachelor's degree. Applicants must also successfully complete all required tests and a background investigation. Recruits must successfully complete a sixteen-week federal training program and a ten-week field training program.

For additional information, visit the TVA Police Web site at http://www.tva.gov/orgs/police/ or contact:

Tennessee Valley Police Authority
400 West Summit Hill Drive
Knoxville, Tennessee 37902-1401
Telephone: (865) 632-4762
(865) 63202101

QUASI-OFFICIAL AGENCIES

AMTRAK POLICE DEPARTMENT

NATIONAL RAILROAD PASSENGER CORPORATION

MISSION
The Amtrak Police Department is committed to improving Amtrak through customer-oriented policing. This is accomplished by building partnerships and making cost-effective security and enforcement decisions that increase ridership and customer satisfaction.

HISTORICAL REVIEW
The Department, established with the consent of Congress in 1976, is a vital component of the National Railroad Passenger Corporation. With a complement of police officers posted throughout sixteen states and the District of Columbia, the Department is charged with "protecting a nation in transit," and provides protection of passengers, employees, and Amtrak property. The Department is also responsible for the prevention of crimes, preservation of the peace, apprehension of offenders, and investigation of incidents and resolution thereof.

TRAINING
Amtrak police officers are duly appointed law enforcement officers who hold police commissions under state and federal statutes. Officer recruits undergo vigorous and challenging basic training courses prior to commissioning and a field training program.

Applicants who are eligible for appointment as an Amtrak Police Officer or Detective are subject to a twelve-month probationary period, beginning on the date that the member begins working. Probationary members must successfully complete a Basic Police Training and a Field Training Program for Recruits. The Amtrak Police Department is an Equal Opportunity Employer.

QUALIFICATIONS
Under applicable law, applicants must:

- be at least 21 years of age at the time of appointment

- be U.S. citizens or have the right to work in the United States

- be eligible for a valid drivers license; possession of a valid drivers license is required prior to appointment

- be able to pass all aspects of the selection process, including a job related physical and background investigation

Applicants must also possess one of the following:

- high school diploma or GED

- certification of successful completion of a basic training program at a state authorized police training academy

- current, related experience as a police officer or similar law enforcement experience

- an associate's degree or 60 hours/credits from an accredited college or university (an associate's degree is preferred)

For further information, visit Amtrak Police online at http://www.amtrak.com or contact:

Amtrak Police Department
15 South Poplar Street
Wilmington, Delaware 19801
Telephone: (302) 683-2218

NATIONAL ZOOLOGICAL PARK POLICE

SMITHSONIAN INSTITUTION

MISSION

The law enforcement function at the National Zoological Park in Washington, D.C., is the responsibility of the National Zoological Park Police. Within the park and perimeter areas, the Park Police protect life and property, prevent and detect crime, arrest violators, and enforce park rules and regulations. The enforcement duties of the uniformed officers include pedestrian and vehicle control, accident investigation, apprehension for criminal acts, location of lost children, protection of animals, and assistance to the visitors to the park.

HISTORICAL REVIEW

The National Zoological Park is a component of the Smithsonian Institution, officially established by Congress in 1890 with the appointment of 165 acres of Rock Creek Park to house a small group of animals in a natural habitat. Authority for operating the National Zoological Park was placed under the direction of the Smithsonian Institution. Metropolitan Police initially patrolled the area and between 1933 and 1966, a horse-mounted unit served as part of the Zoological Park Police.

FUNCTIONS AND ACTIVITIES

The National Zoological Park Police (NZPP) share concurrent arrest authority with the U.S. Park Police for offenses applicable in the National Capital Parks area. Police officers enforce regulations against several specific violations such as unlawfully destroying or damaging the park, killing or injuring animals, carrying deadly weapons or explosives, displaying or carrying placards, or participating in games for money or for other personal property.

TRAINING

All Park Police Officers attend the eight-week basic police officer course at the Federal Law Enforcement Training Center (FLETC), Glynco, Georgia. Officers also receive an additional three weeks of training in park policies, park regulations, firearms, and first aid before being assigned to foot patrol with a senior officer.

QUALIFICATIONS

There are no written tests for NZPP positions. Hiring is based on the applicant's experience and education. Specialized work, such as that of police officer, ranger, wildlife officer, game warden, military police officer, investigator, or other such work is acceptable experience. College study can be substituted for general or specialized factors.

Applicants must possess a valid driver's license. Candidates must also undergo an oral interview. Upon acceptance, a pre-employment physical is administered by the Zoological Park Police. (Information taken from *Handbook of Federal Police and Investigative Agencies* by Donald A. Torres, published in 1985 by Greenwood Press.)

For further information, visit the Zoological Park Police online at http://www.si.edu/natzoo or contact:

National Zoological Park Police
3001 Connecticut Avenue, NW
Washington, D.C. 20008
Telephone: (202) 673-4731

OFFICE OF PROTECTION SERVICES

NATIONAL GALLERY OF ART

MISSION

The mission of the Office of Protection Services is to ensure that the national collections and other properties entrusted to the National Gallery of Art are protected and secured; afford staff members and visitors a high degree of safety and security while permitting an appropriate level of public access to those collections and properties; and provide a proper level of occupational and medical service to staff members and emergency first aid to visitors.

HISTORICAL REVIEW

The National Gallery of Art was created for the people of the United States of America by a joint resolution of Congress. The Board of Trustees consists of four public servants serving ex officio and five private citizens. Under the policies set by the Board, the Gallery acquires and maintains a collection of paintings, sculpture, and graphic arts representative of the best in America's artistic heritage. Supported in its daily operations by federal funds, the Gallery is entirely dependent on the generosity of private citizens for the works of art in its collections.

FUNCTIONS AND ACTIVITIES

The Office of Protection Service is responsible for providing law enforcement and security services at the National Gallery complex. Officers carry out their responsibilities through a network of patrols, fixed posts, and electronic surveillance covering the West Building, the East Building, and the Sculpture Garden.

For further information, write to:

National Gallery of Art
4th Street and Constitution Avenue, NW
Washington, D.C. 20565
Telephone: (202) 737-4215 (Office of Public Affairs)

OFFICE OF PROTECTION SERVICES

SMITHSONIAN INSTITUTION

MISSION

Deriving its legal authority from Title 40, United States Code, Section 193, the Office of Protection Services' mission is to protect and secure the national collections and other properties entrusted to the Smithsonian Institution; ensure the safety and security of staff members and visitors; and permit an appropriate level of public access to collections and properties.

This office employs a force of more than 770, which uses an array of protection support services, including art escort, to provide maximum safe access to the Institution's collections for both scholars and the general public.

This office physically protects approximately 150 million objects of scientific, cultural, and historical interest belonging to the fourteen national museums in Washington, D.C., Maryland, New York City, and Panama. The Smithsonian Institution is the largest museum and research complex in the world. The Office of Protection Services keeps the museums open 364 days a year and provides protection services to the Smithsonian's 30 million visitors each year.

HISTORICAL REVIEW

Since the 1860s, the Protection Force has provided security for the Smithsonian's collections and the countless visitors who view them. The Smithsonian Institution is the bequest of James Smithson, an English chemist of the 1800s, who willed his estate to a country he had never seen, "to found at Washington, under the name of the Smithsonian Institution, an establishment for the increase and diffusion of knowledge among men." Congress accepted the bequest in 1836 in gold sovereigns and established the Smithsonian Institution on August 10, 1846.

The Smithsonian Institution is governed by a Board of Regents, composed of the Chief Justice, the Vice President, three members each from the U.S. Senate and the U.S. House of Representatives, and nine citizen members appointed by joint resolution of the U.S. Congress. The Smithsonian has developed the majority of its public museums along the National Mall between the Washington Monument and the Capitol Building. The National Gallery of Art on the Mall and the Kennedy Center are directed by separate boards of trustees. The National Gallery of Art and the National Zoological Park have separately operated protection forces.

FUNCTIONS AND ACTIVITIES

The Museum Protection Officers and their supervisors at the Smithsonian secure the tangible remnants of almost every major historic event in the nation and the world. Smithsonian officers protect such notable objects as the original Star Spangled Banner, the Hope Diamond, the Wright Flyer, the world's largest gold coin collection, and world famous paintings by, among others, James Whistler, Picasso, and Van Gogh. The officers work at one of the most culturally rich institutions on earth, manage numerous dignitary visits, and interact with visitors and scholars from around the world on a daily basis.

QUALIFICATIONS

For qualifications and further information, contact:

> Office of Protective Services
> Arts and Industries Building, Room 2480
> 900 Jefferson Drive, SW
> Washington, D.C. 20560
> Telephone: (202) 275-1058

LEGISLATIVE BRANCH DEPARTMENTS

LIBRARY OF CONGRESS POLICE

MISSION
The Library of Congress Police is responsible for protecting the life, property, and civil rights of staff and visitors by maintaining law and order, and for protecting Library property and collections.

HISTORICAL REVIEW
The Library of Congress was established under a law approved on April 24, 1800, that appropriated $5,000 "for the purchase of such books as may be necessary for the use of Congress..." The Library's scope of responsibility has been widened by subsequent legislation. The Librarian, appointed by the President with the advice and consent of the Senate, directs the Library.

FUNCTIONS AND ACTIVITIES
The Library of Congress Police Force is responsible for providing law enforcement and security services at the Library of Congress. The police carry out this responsibility by enforcing laws and regulations; patrolling buildings and grounds; controlling building access and conducting exit inspection; monitoring security and fire detection systems; preventing, detecting, and investigating crimes; and responding to safety and medical emergencies.

For qualifications and further information, visit the Library of Congress online at http://www.loc.gov or contact:

Director of Security
Library of Congress Police
101 Independence Avenue
Washington, D.C. 20540-9500
Telephone: (202) 707-9089
(202) 707-8708.

OFFICE OF SPECIAL INVESTIGATIONS

GENERAL ACCOUNTING OFFICE

MISSION
The Office of Special investigations (OSI) is a specialized unit within the General Accounting Office (GAO) that was created to meet the Congress' need for focused, quick responses to questions and issues of criminal activity, fraud, and abuse. Staffed with senior criminal investigators, its primary mission is to identify and investigate potential fraud, criminal misconduct, and serious wrongdoing involving federal funds, programs, and activities.

HISTORICAL REVIEW

OSI was established within GAO's Office of General Counsel in December 1986. OSI was set up to ensure that questionable matters involving possible violations of law uncovered in GAO's work are handled by trained, experienced criminal investigators.

FUNCTIONS AND ACTIVITIES

OSI assists the Congress in its oversight role through investigative work in areas as varied as Medicaid program abuses, money laundering schemes, and military justice. By identifying examples of fraud and abuse, OSI helps illustrate program weaknesses, demonstrates systemic problems, and supports findings and recommendations in GAO work.

During an audit, GAO analysts from other teams may find indicators that point to fraud or other wrongdoing. Analysts then refer these findings to OSI for preliminary investigation. Depending on OSI's preliminary assessment of the findings, OSI will develop a case-specific example to include in GAO's report to the Congress, refer the matter to the appropriate executive branch agency for further investigation, or determine that no basis for further investigation exists.

OSI also conducts independent investigations and works proactively to identify potential weaknesses that allow federal laws and regulations, such as Federal Communications Commission rules or federal firearms laws, to be circumvented. By testing suspected weaknesses, OSI can bring regulatory or operational flaws to the attention of the Congress and the Executive Branch before those weaknesses are exploited.

OSI also manages the GAO FraudNET, a hotline through which the public can report allegations of fraud and abuse online or by mail or telephone. OSI analysts evaluate allegations of abuse, which are either referred directly to the appropriate agency or investigated by an OSI special agent.

An OSI proactive investigation targeted security and public safety at federal buildings and airports and identified important security weaknesses. The Congress used this information in enacting the Enhanced Federal Security Act of 2000, making it a federal crime to enter or attempt to enter federal property or the secure area of an airport under false pretenses.

For further information, write to:
U.S. General Accounting Office
Office of Special Investigations
Room 6K175
441 G Street, NW
Washington, D.C. 20548
Telephone: (202) 512-7455

UNIFORMED POLICE BRANCH, PROTECTIVE SERVICES GROUP

U.S. GOVERNMENT PRINTING OFFICE

FUNCTIONS AND ACTIVITIES

The Government Printing Office (GPO) Police Force performs a variety of law enforcement duties such as patrols and inspections to prevent, detect, and deter incidents of crime; control access at entrances to the GPO; escort classified shipments of national defense security information; and conduct bomb searches. Officers also investigate vehicular accidents, robberies, thefts, assaults, and disturbances.

As part of the building perimeter security, they are required to monitor and regulate electronic alarms, fire protection devices, and access control systems. When the situation demands, they respond to emergencies and intrusion alarms, escorting medical personnel to the scene of medical emergencies and providing assistance when required.

In carrying out these duties, GPO police officers are empowered to make arrests.

TRAINING

Appointed GPO police officers are given an eleven-week intensive course of training in all phases of law enforcement at the Federal Law Enforcement Training Center in Glynco, Georgia. Included are courses in crisis intervention, officer safety and survival, patrol techniques, radio communications, report writing, criminal law, arrest techniques, cardiopulmonary resuscitation, defensive tactics, and defensive driving.

In addition to the required training at FLETC, GPO police officers are required to qualify in the use of a 9 mm semiautomatic pistol on a semiannual basis.

QUALIFICATIONS

To qualify, applicants must have one year of specialized experience for a PG-5 rating. Specialized experience is experience that provides knowledge of a body of basic laws and regulations, law enforcement operations, practices, and techniques and involved responsibility for maintaining order and protecting life and property. Creditable specialized experience may have been gained in work on a police force; through service as a military police officer; in work providing visitor protection and law enforcement in parks, forests, or other natural resource or recreational environments; in performing criminal investigative duties; or in other work that provided the required knowledge and skills. Certain related education can be substituted for the experience listed above.

For further information, contact the Employment Branch online at http://www.gpo.gov/employment or contact:

Employment Branch, Stop: PSE
U.S. Government Printing Office
732 North Capitol Street, NW
Washington, D.C. 20401
Telephone: (202) 512-1200

U.S. CAPITOL POLICE

MISSION

U.S. Capitol Police Officers are entrusted with the duty of preserving the peace, protecting life and property, preventing crime, detecting and investigating criminal acts, arresting violators of the law, and enforcing traffic regulations. In addition, the Capitol Police are authorized to protect, in any area of the United States, any member of Congress or officer of the Congress.

HISTORICAL REVIEW

At the direction of President John Quincy Adams, the United States Capitol Police was established in 1828 by an Act of Congress. Since that time, the Department has grown to include both uniformed and plainclothes officers who patrol approximately 250 acres of federal property that encompasses the U.S. Capitol, House and Senate office buildings, and the Capitol grounds.

The supervision of the U.S. Capitol Police is the responsibility of the Capitol Police Board, which is comprised of the Sergeant at Arms of the United States Senate, Sergeant at Arms of the U.S. House of Representatives, and the Architect of the Capitol. The Chief of Police oversees the daily operations of the Department.

FUNCTIONS AND ACTIVITIES

The U.S. Capitol Police has established a number of specialized units whose functions are to enhance the response, protective, and investigative capabilities of the Department.

The Capitol, House, Senate, and Patrol divisions are responsible for providing uniformed Officers to police the streets and parks of the Capitol complex. This area includes major thoroughfares and requires officers to enforce all traffic regulations and investigate motor vehicle accidents as well as interdict and deter criminal activity. Sector patrols are conducted on foot, on motorcycles, and in unmarked cruisers and marked scout cars. Undercover street tactical units are also used to suppress criminal activity.

The Containment and Emergency Response Team (CERT) was organized in 1978 to perform tactical operations during hostage/barricade situations within the Capitol complex. In addition, CERT assists the Drug Enforcement Unit and the Criminal Investigations Division in serving arrest or search warrants and provides the Protective Services Bureau with additional support during large-scale protective operations.

In the event a hostage/barricade incident does occur within a congressional building or on the Capitol grounds, members of the Hostage Negotiation Unit respond to the scene and attempt to defuse the situation through direct dialogue. Members of the unit are also trained to handle various volatile incidents that require negotiating skills.

The U.S. Capitol Police K-9 Explosive Detection Section is trained to detect a multitude of explosives. The handlers and their canines perform standard law enforcement duties and search areas prior to official visits or in response to bomb threats.   When a suspicious item is located within the Capitol complex, the members of the Hazardous Devices Unit are called. This unit has the responsibility of responding to, examining, rendering safe, and disposing of all suspicious items that pose a potential threat to life and property. The unit also conducts advance sweeps for visiting dignitaries, congressional delegations, and VIPs, including the President of the United States.

The Department has organized a special unit to provide security and protection to the exterior of the Capitol building. Known as the First Responder Unit, these officers respond to the area of any disturbance inside or outside the Capitol.

To handle large demonstrations, a group of officers was chosen to form the Civil Disturbance Unit. These officers are trained to control large groups of people during civil disobedience and mass arrest situations.

The Threat Assessment Unit conducts inquiries into all threats against members of Congress, their families, and staffs. U.S. Capitol Police detectives investigate all telephonic, written, and verbal threats in conjunction with the Federal Bureau of Investigation. If the threat is determined to be of such a serious nature that additional security is required, members of the Protective Operations Section will provide 24-hour protective services to the member anywhere in the United States.

The Electronic Countermeasures Section counters unauthorized electronic monitoring of Congressional offices, telephones, sensitive hearings, and conversations.

To provide an increased level of protection to members of Congress and to monitor the actions of visitors in the House and Senate public galleries, plainclothes officers assigned to the Gallery Security Section are placed at strategic locations around each chamber. These officers are also assigned with uniformed officers at all entrances to the Senate and House floors.

Detectives assigned to the Criminal Investigations Division conduct inquiries into all criminal acts committed within the Capitol complex. This division is composed of the Drug Enforcement Section, Office Thefts Section, and the General Assignments Section.

The Intelligence Section is responsible for collecting, processing, and disseminating information on criminal activities, subversive groups, terrorism, and civil disorders. Members of this section maintain close liaison with other federal, state, and local law enforcement agencies.

The Special Events Section is responsible for coordinating a wide variety of activities within the Capitol complex including dignitary visits, demonstrations, receptions, band concerts, choral performances, and VIP arrivals.

TRAINING

Training begins with a one-week orientation at the Capitol Police training facility in Washington, D.C. Recruits then spend approximately ten weeks at the Federal Law Enforcement Training Center (FLETC) in Glynco, Georgia. After graduation from FLETC, recruits return to the Capitol Police Training Division for an additional ten weeks of comprehensive training prior to assignment to the Field Training Officer (FTO). Upon completion of the FTO program, recruits receive their initial assignments.

QUALIFICATIONS

In accordance with current Department policy and availability of positions, applicants must successfully complete the following steps before being appointed:

- a written examination measuring reading comprehension

- a one-on-one interview with a background investigator

- a medical examination

- a psychological evaluation

- a background investigation

- a polygraph examination

Applicants must also:

- be between 21 and 37 years of age at time of appointment

- possess a high school diploma or GED equivalent

- be a U.S. citizen

- have vision of at least 20/100 uncorrected (correctable to 20/20 with either glasses or contact lenses)

- have no felony convictions, history of criminal or improper conduct, or poor driving record

- not be involved in any pending criminal or civil litigation(s)

For further information, visit the Capitol Police online at http://www.aoc.gov or contact:

Recruiting Section
U.S. Capitol Police Headquarters
Room 601-P, 119 D Street NW
Washington, D.C. 20510
Telephone: (202) 224-9820

JUDICIAL BRANCH

PROBATION OFFICERS, FEDERAL CORRECTIONS AND SUPERVISION DIVISION

ADMINISTRATIVE OFFICE OF THE U.S. COURTS

MISSION

U.S. Probation Officers play an integral part in the federal criminal justice process. Simply stated, their mission is to investigate and supervise offenders whom the courts have conditionally released to the community on probation, parole, or supervised release. By serving as the court's fact-finder, controlling the risk offenders may pose to public safety, and providing offenders with correctional treatment, officers help ensure that persons previously convicted of crime choose a law-abiding lifestyle rather than further criminal behavior. Their responsibilities require them to work not only with federal judges and other court professionals, but with U.S. attorneys, defense attorneys, Federal Bureau of Prisons and U.S. Parole Commission officials, state and local law enforcement agents, treatment providers, and community leaders. Officers deliver services that benefit the court, the community, and the offender.

FUNCTIONS AND ACTIVITIES

Officers conduct presentence investigations, gathering and verifying important information about the offender and the offense. By order of the court, the officers conduct thorough presentence investigations into the circumstances of the offenses and the offender's criminal background and characteristics. The officers gather information in two ways: by conducting interviews and by reviewing documents. The cornerstone of the investigation is the interview with the offender, during which officers inquire about such things as the offender's family, education, employment, finances, physical and mental health, and alcohol or drug abuse. The officers also conduct home visit to assess the offenders' living conditions, family relationships, and community ties and to detect alcohol or drugs in the home.

Besides interviewing the offender, the officers interview other persons who can provide pertinent information about the offender and the offense, including the defense counsel, the prosecutor, law enforcement agents, victims, the offender's family and associates, employers, school officials, doctors, and counselors. The officers also review various records and reports, including court records, financial records, criminal history transcripts, probation/parole/pretrial services records, birth/marriage/divorce records, school records, employment records, military service records, medical records, and counseling and treatment records. The officers verify the information gathered, interpret and evaluate it, and present it to the court in an organized, objective report called the pre-sentence report.

The officer prepares a pre-sentence report that helps the court determine the appropriate sentence. The presentence report contains information about the offense, the offender, the impact of the offense on the victim, and sentencing options under the federal sentencing guidelines. It also includes information about the offender's ability to pay fines and restitution. The primary purpose of the report is to provide information that enables the court to impose a fair sentence that satisfies the punishment, deterrence, and corrective goals of sentencing. The officers consider applicable statutes and the federal sentencing guidelines, apply them to the facts of the case, and come up with a recommended sentence and a justification for it.

The report assists the following:

- Federal Bureau of Prisons–In choosing the institution where the offender will serve the sentence, selecting prison programs that will help the offender, and making the offender's release plans

- U.S. Sentencing Commission– by providing information useful for monitoring sentencing guidelines application and research

- U.S. Probation Officer supervising the offender–in assessing the risk the offender poses and assessing the offender's needs

The officers recommend the conditions under which offenders are released to the community and propose conditions of release in the presentence report. These conditions help structure the offender's movement and behavior in the community. They address many areas of the offender's life, including personal, financial, and health issues. The court imposes two kinds of conditions: standard and special. Standard conditions apply to all offenders. For example, they forbid the offender to commit another federal, state, or local crime; require the offender to report as directed to the probation officer; and prohibit the offender's use of alcohol or drugs. Special conditions give officers the authority to administer additional sanctions, provide correctional treatment, and address specific risks the offender may present to himself or herself, others, and the community in general. For example, special conditions may require the offender to serve a period of home confinement, undergo drug testing or treatment, or disclose financial information.

The officers supervise offenders in the community to make sure they comply with court-ordered conditions of release. Officers supervise or monitor all offenders who are conditionally released to the community by the federal courts, the U.S. Parole Commission, and military authorities. Community supervision gives officers the means to carry out the court's sentence and to accomplish offender rehabilitation and public safety goals.

The officers control the risk offenders may pose to themselves and others by providing correctional treatment to help offenders become productive members of the community.

Officers provide correctional treatment that helps offenders live law-abiding lives. These are activities designed to rehabilitate offenders by changing behavior that contributes to criminality and to reintegrate offenders into the community. Correctional treatment encompasses many services, including drug or alcohol treatment, mental health treatment, educational or vocational training, medical care, and employment assistance. The officer's job is to locate and use community resources to address offender needs in these areas or to arrange for services.

The officers use special skills, work with particular caseloads, and take on specialized responsibilities to further investigation, supervision, or officer safety goals.

Some officers hold specialist positions or perform special duties that require certain skills or expertise. Experience, on-the-job training, and training received from outside sources prepare officers for such positions. For example, drug and alcohol treatment specialists closely supervise drug- or alcohol-dependent offenders, require them to undergo drug testing and treatment, and arrange for appropriate treatment such as detoxification or counseling. Mental health treatment, home confinement, community service, sentencing guidelines, financial investigation, employment, and firearms are some other specialty areas.

For further information, contact:
Federal Corrections and Supervision Division
Administrative Office of the U.S. Courts
One Columbus Circle, NE
Washington, D.C. 20544
Telephone: (202) 502-1600

SUPREME COURT OF THE UNITED STATES POLICE

MISSION
The Supreme Court of the United States Police (SCUSP) has the statutory authority to:

- police the Supreme Court building and grounds and adjacent streets for the purpose of protecting persons and property

- protect the Chief Justice, Associate Justices, and any official guest of the Supreme Court in any part of the United States

- protect employees while engaged in official duties

- make arrests for any violation of U.S. law in the performance of its protection authority

In addition, the SCUSP assist the more than 1 million visitors to the Supreme Court each year.

HISTORICAL REVIEW
The Supreme Court of the United States is provided for in Article III, Section 1, of the Constitution. It was established by authority of the Judiciary Act of 1789. The Court first assembled on February 2, 1790, in New York City, which was then the nation's capital.

The SCUSP was overseen by the Marshal of the Supreme Court, whose responsibilities included maintaining suitable order and decorum within the building and the immediate outside vicinity and protecting persons and property of the Court. The United States Capitol Police provided some security for the Supreme Court justices during the time the Court met in the Capitol from 1800 until 1935. The initial guard force consisted of 33 deputized guards. There are now more than 100 officers on the independent force of the SCUSP.

The SCUSP was officially established by statute on August 18, 1949. In 1981, Congress passed legislation authorizing the SCUSP to protect justices and other designated persons outside the Court premises. This new legislation provided specific statutory authority to carry firearms and expanded SCUSP jurisdiction to "any part of the United States." This legislation has since been amended and expanded several times. Subsequent significant changes include authority to carry weapons off duty and entitlement to law enforcement retirement benefits.

TRAINING
Each SCUSP Officer attends the eight-week basic police officer course given at the Federal Law Enforcement Training Center (FLETC), Glynco, Georgia. After completing the course, officers receive on-the-job training from senior officers to enhance their knowledge of the position and attend extensive additional on- and off-site training throughout their careers.

QUALIFICATIONS
Selection for the SCUSP begins with a standard written examination. The position requires a high school education; prior law enforcement experience and/or a college degree; good oral communication skills; a medical examination; a valid driver's license, and a background investigation. Although the SCUSP does not use the GS position classification system, the basic Police Officer position is comparable to a GS-7 grade level.

For further information, visit the Supreme Court of the United States Police online at http://www.supct.law.cornell.edu/supctl or contact:

Supreme Court of the United States
Washington, D.C. 20543
Telephone: (202) 479-3341

PART FOUR

Offices of Inspectors General

INTRODUCTION

Inspectors General (IG) have existed in government since the founding of the Republic. The IG's traditional role was to determine the operational readiness of U.S. combat forces. Civilian IGs, however, are a relatively recent and different concept. These IGs have far-reaching auditing and investigative responsibilities that promote the economy, efficiency, and effectiveness of federal operations and prevent and detect fraud, waste, and mismanagement. Inspectors General conduct investigations of contractors, program participants, and government employees that can lead to prosecution and may result in convictions that carry penalties such as prison terms, fines, settlements, and recoveries to the government.

The Secretary of Agriculture created the first civilian IG in 1962. The auditing and investigative resources of ten major programs were consolidated into a single Office of Inspector General (OIG), which reported directly to the Secretary. Ten years later, the Department of Housing and Urban Development established a second civilian IG by administrative action.

Although these agencies experimented with adapting the IG concept to civilian use, the IGs' lack of independence from program officials interfered with their effectiveness and credibility. Congressional hearings explored ways these problems might be corrected, while disclosures of widespread fraud, waste and abuse, and scandals in agricultural, health, and welfare programs lent impetus to their efforts.

Subsequently, Congress established the first statutory IG at the former Department of Health, Education, and Welfare (HEW), which is now the Department of Health and Human Services. In addition to assigning this IG overall responsibility for the Department's auditing and investigative activities, the implementing legislation required the IG to report to the Congress as well as to the agency head.

The establishment of the IG at HEW in 1976 marked the beginning of the IG concept as it is known today. When the Department of Energy was created in 1977, Congress included an IG based on the HEW model.

The Inspector General Act of 1978 and subsequent amendments institutionalized the IG concept. The Act established new statutory IGs at the Departments of Agriculture, Commerce, Housing and Urban Development, Interior, Labor, and Transportation; the Community Services, General Services, National Aeronautics and Space, Small Business, and Veterans Administrations; and the Environmental Protection Agency. (The Community Services Administration no longer exists.)

The 1978 Act has been amended to include IGs at the Department of Education (1979), the Agency for International Development (1981), the Department of Defense (1982), and the United States Information Agency (1986). In addition, separate legislation was passed to establish IGs at the Railroad Retirement Board (1983) and the Department of State (1985). By law, the Inspector General is to have unfettered access to all agency records, information, or assistance when engaged in an investigation or audit. Today, there are fifty-seven statutory IGs—fifteen executive branch departments, thirty-eight independent agencies, two quasi-official agencies, one legislative branch department, and one Commission.

Inspector General Act of 1978

The purpose of the Inspector General Act of 1978 was "to create independent and objective units" to:

- conduct and supervise audits and investigations relating to agency programs and operations

- provide leadership and coordination of activities designed to promote economy and efficiency in the administration of agency programs and operations and prevent and detect fraud and abuse in such programs and operations

- provide a means for keeping the head of the agency and the Congress fully and currently informed about problems and deficiencies

The 1978 Act provides IGs with substantial autonomy. The Act states that IGs are to be appointed by the President and confirmed by the Senate. By law, they are appointed solely on the basis of integrity and demonstrated ability in accounting, auditing, financial analysis, law, management analysis, public administration or investigations, without regard to political affiliation. The law provides that they report not to any lower-level official, but directly to the agency head or principal deputy. This grants them broad powers to initiate and carry out audits and investigations.

Like the IGs at the Department of Health and Human Services and the Department of Energy, the IGs established under the 1978 Act regularly report to the agency head and to the Congress, thereby assuring public disclosure of IG findings and IG independence from agency pressures. This dual reporting requirement is key to the critical components of insuring public disclosure of program weaknesses and the objectivity and independence of the reporting office. The current IG authority also relieves program managers and agency executives from being solely responsible for gathering objective data and evidence in those circumstances where wrongdoing is suspected and where intense scrutiny is needed and controversy exists.

Semiannual reports of each IG must be furnished to the head of the agency who, in turn, is required to transmit the reports to the appropriate Congressional committees or subcommittees.

These reports describe programmatic and administrative problems, list the current and pending recommendations, summarize prosecutorial referrals and convictions made during the reporting period, and contain other information on IG activities. The reports are widely distributed and are available to the public. The Act also contains special requirements for the immediate reporting of particularly serious or flagrant problems, abuses, or deficiencies.

All IGs must have auditing organizations, which perform audits of agency programs and operations and investigative organizations, which perform investigations that can lead to criminal, civil, and administrative penalties. Although not required to do so, a number of IGs also have inspection units that conduct evaluations of facility or office management or perform management studies that assess the administration of programs and the delivery of services.

IGs are required by law to review existing and proposed legislation and regulations relating to programs and operations of their respective agencies. The objectives of this review include making recommendations concerning the impact of the laws and regulations on the economy, efficiency, and effectiveness of agency programs and operations and their susceptibility to fraud and abuse.

IGs are also engaged in other prevention activities, such as providing early advice on the design or redesign of agency programs and operations; operating and publicizing hotlines for reporting fraud, waste or mismanagement; and carrying out integrity-awareness efforts.

Inspectors General and management pursue the same ultimate objective—the efficient and effective operation of programs and delivery of services. IGs function as part of the agency head's senior management team. They act as independent fact-gatherers, with no vested interest in particular programs or operations, and serve as technical advisers in such areas as financial management systems and internal controls.

Inspectors General work cooperatively with other organizations in order to accomplish their missions, except when such a relationship would compromise OIG independence. Often, they develop close working relationships with the major components of their departments in order to coordinate efforts and to combine expertise shared by both groups. As part of these close working relationships, program managers are frequently involved in the formulation of the OIG work plan and may request that specific audits, investigations, or studies be done by the IG.

The Inspector General Act Amendments of 1988 established Inspectors General to be appointed by their respective federal agencies. This group complements the Inspectors General at the larger agencies who are appointed by the President. The two groups have virtually identical powers and mandates.

EXECUTIVE BRANCH DEPARTMENTS

DEPARTMENT OF AGRICULTURE

The U.S. Department of Agriculture's (USDA) mission is to enhance the quality of life for the American people by supporting production agriculture; ensuring a safe, affordable, nutritious, and accessible food supply; caring for public lands and helping people care for private lands; supporting sound sustainable development of rural communities; providing economic opportunities for farm and rural residents; expanding global markets for agricultural and forest products and services; and working to reduce hunger in America and throughout the world.

OFFICE OF INSPECTOR GENERAL

USDA's Office of Inspector General (OIG), the first civilian OIG in the Federal Government, was established by the Secretary of Agriculture in 1962 to conduct audits and investigations in USDA, and is now one of the largest OIGs in the federal government. The Inspector General Act of 1978 strengthened OIG's auditing and investigative authority, and the Agriculture and Food Act of 1981 granted law enforcement authority to OIG criminal investigators.

OIG has a two-pronged mission. The auditing mission is to conduct and supervise audits to prevent or detect fraud, waste, or abusive activity and to improve the effectiveness of USDA programs by recommending changes that will increase efficiency and reduce wasteful and fraudulent activities. The investigative side of OIG is the law enforcement arm of USDA and, as such, conducts investigations of significant criminal activity in and affecting the Department's programs, and carries out other law enforcement activities in support of the Department. This mission is carried out by approximately 650 professional and administrative staff members who are located throughout the country.

Investigative Initiative

Operation Talon was designed and implemented by USDA OIG to locate and apprehend fugitives, many of them violent offenders, who are current or former food stamp recipients. Operation Talon has resulted in well over 7,000 arrests of fugitive felons during joint OIG, state, and local law enforcement operations throughout the country. Serious crimes perpetrated by those arrested included homicide-related offenses (murder, attempted murder, manslaughter), sex offenses (child molestation, rape, attempted rape), kidnapping/abduction, assault, robbery, and drug/narcotics violations. Operation Talon was made possible by the Welfare Reform Act of 1996 and was designed to locate and arrest fugitive felons by matching law enforcement agencies' felony fugitive files with the state social services agencies' food stamp recipient files.

Auditing Initiative

USDA OIG initiated a series of audits to determine whether USDA's meat and poultry inspection program remained effective under the science-based Hazard Analysis and Critical Control

Point (HACCP) System. OIG reviewed HACCP, laboratory analyses, foreign imports, and the compliance program that carried over from the previous system. Positive steps had been taken, but more needed to be done in all four of the reviewed areas. Maximum advantage needs to be taken of the expanding role science now plays as a control over the meat, poultry, and egg products that enter the marketplace. Moreover, oversight had been reduced short of what is prudent and necessary for the protection of the consumer. OIG made recommendations to correct the cited shortcomings and ensure that the intent of the HACCP program is met.

Audit-Investigative Joint Initiative

Operation "Kiddie Care" is USDA OIG's nationwide initiative to identify, remove, and prosecute unscrupulous sponsoring organizations of the Child and Adult Care Food Program (CACFP). Forty-seven CACFP sponsors, who were receiving about $82.7 million annually, were found seriously deficient in their operation of the program. Twenty-nine of these sponsors, who received about $52.9 million annually, were terminated because they did not take sufficient action to correct the deficiencies. Sixty-four individuals were indicted or named in criminal information documents for defrauding CACFP, and 51 pled guilty or have been convicted. In Michigan, the owner of a multicenter day care operation was sentenced to nine years in prison and ordered to pay more than $23.5 million in combined fines and restitution, as well as forfeit more than $1.1 million in cash and three properties.

Careers in Investigations

As designated federal law enforcement officers, special agents carry firearms, make arrests, and conduct searches. The highest degree of integrity, reliability, impartiality, good judgment, communication skills, resourcefulness, tact, and diplomacy is necessary.

Special agents in USDA OIG plan and conduct investigations relating to alleged or suspected violations of federal law, particularly as they pertain to the programs and operations of the Department. Investigations involve obtaining physical and documentary evidence, interviewing witnesses, examining files and records, and performing undercover and surveillance work, which may sometimes be dangerous. Investigative reports are used to assist prosecuting attorneys and special agents often testify and assist at criminal trials and civil hearings. Special agents in USDA OIG also provide security for the Secretary and Deputy Secretary of Agriculture.

Work Environment

Criminal investigators may work on cases involving fraud against the government, bribery, food tampering, conflict of interest, improper and/or false claims, collusion, misuse of loan/grant funds, or embezzlement. The performance of these duties frequently requires working irregular hours, exposure to inclement weather, considerable overnight travel, and arduous exertion under adverse conditions. Applicants must possess and maintain a valid state driver's license to operate a motor vehicle.

Applicants must meet the requirements set forth in the Law Enforcement Availability Pay Act of 1994 and related OIG policies. As such, they must, at a minimum, work an average of two hours of unscheduled duty in excess of each regular workday, on an annual basis (i.e., work an average of 10 hours, rather than an average of eight hours, on every workday). In compensation, the annual salary is increased by 25 percent.

Benefits

Salary levels are competitive and are adjusted for areas with a higher than average cost of living. In addition, some locations have special pay rates for investigators. Specific details of any special pay rates may be obtained from vacancy announcements. As a federal employee, benefits include:

■ opportunities for advancement

■ liberal law-enforcement retirement benefits, including retirement eligibility at age 50 with 20 years of service or at any age with 25 years of service

■ group health insurance and life insurance

■ thirteen days of annual (vacation) leave each year; annual leave increases periodically to the maximum of 26 days per year after 15 years of government service

■ thirteen days of sick leave annually, which accumulates without limitation

■ ten paid holidays per year

QUALIFICATIONS

Special agents must be at least 21 years of age and not over 37 years of age at the time of appointment; be in good physical condition and maintain a prescribed level of physical fitness; pass a preemployment urinalysis test to screen for illegal drug use; agents are subject to random drug testing after appointment Specific details of the requirements of the position may be obtained from vacancy announcements.

Applicants for the GS-5 level must have a minimum of 3 years of general work experience of a progressively responsible nature that required the ability to work with individuals and groups; skill in collecting and assembling facts; the ability to prepare clear, concise reports; and the ability and willingness to accept responsibility. A bachelor's degree may be substituted for general experience.

Applicants for the GS-7 level must have one year of specialized experience that has equipped them with the particular knowledge, skills, and abilities to successfully perform the duties of a criminal investigator. The specialized experience must have been equivalent to the GS-5 level in the federal service.

TRAINING

Special agents spend their first several months in developing professional skills and becoming familiar with the new job. During this period, new agents attend the basic eight-week Criminal Investigator Training Program at the Federal Law Enforcement Training Center in Glynco, Georgia.

Classroom instruction covers such matters and investigative techniques, criminal law and procedure, and the rules of evidence.

Practical exercises cover surveillance techniques, fingerprinting, raids and apprehension, courtroom testimony and demeanor, and crime scene examinations.

Physical specialties include conditioning and instruction in unarmed self-defense. Firearms training includes the proficient use of weapons and survival under various tactical conditions.

Diversified training assignments to develop technical and supervisory capabilities follow, along with specialized training in subjects including white-collar crime, program investigations, supervision, firearms, and risk management.

Advancement in OIG is rapid for those individuals who possess excellent skills and are highly motivated. Qualified persons are eligible for promotion each year, without competition, to the GS-12 grade level. Promotions above the GS-12 level require further competition.

Careers in Auditing

Auditors review, examine, and evaluate the operational and financial policies, systems, and procedures of the Department's agencies and programs and report findings and recommendations for corrective action to management or render audit opinions on financial information.

Auditing includes the examination of program documents for conformity to Departmental regulations and sound business practices, the determination of the existence and application of proper administrative controls, the appraisal of existing program and administrative policies for adequacy and effectiveness, and the examination of financial data for accuracy and conformance to standards. Auditors must be able to locate, verify, and analyze detailed program and financial data and information for the preparation of accurate audit reports. OIG audits are performed in accordance with generally accepted government auditing standards.

Work Environment

Most new employees work on several different audits so they are exposed to the different programs that OIG audits and become familiar with OIG's auditing techniques.

Some of the fieldwork typically performed includes field inspections of agricultural crops, visits to food stamp retailers, measuring crop residue, reviewing crop insurance loss claims, reviewing Forest Service special use permits to ski resorts, measuring grain at grain elevators, reviewing controls at meat packing plants, and analyzing financial statements and reports. Fieldwork is completed in a variety of ways.

Benefits

Federal employee benefits include:

- opportunities for advancement

- liberal retirement benefits

- group health insurance and life insurance

- thirteen days of vacation leave each year; annual leave increases periodically to a maximum of 26 days per year after fifteen years of government service

- thirteen days of sick leave annually, which accumulates without limitation

- ten paid holidays per year

QUALIFICATIONS

OIG is seeking highly qualified candidates for entry-level auditor positions at the GS-5 and GS-7 levels. To be eligible, applicants must have a bachelor's degree with a major in accounting or a minimum of 24 hours of accounting and/or auditing courses (can include 6 hours of business law). Salary levels are competitive and are adjusted for areas with a higher than average cost of living. In addition, some locations have special pay rates for auditors. Specific details of the requirements of the position and any special pay rates may be obtained from vacancy announcements.

Entry and Advancement

Entry-level auditors spend their first months fine-tuning their professional skills in a governmental auditing environment and becoming more knowledgeable of OIG operations and the Department of Agriculture's programs. Although classroom and on-the-job training are provided throughout an individual's career, all entry-level auditors attend an intensive and highly innovative multiweek training course at the OIG Audit Academy, which is designed to provide both broad-based and job-specific training to entry-level auditors. Throughout an individual's career, diversified assignments provide the opportunity to further develop skills in financial, programmatic, or ADP auditing.

Advancement in OIG is rapid for those individuals who possess excellent skills and are highly motivated. Once hired, auditors are eligible for promotion each year, without competition, to the GS-12 grade level. If their work meets certain criteria, they may be eligible for promotion to the GS-7 level after six months on the job. Promotions above the GS-12 level require further competition.

Many auditors are certified public accountants, certified government financial managers, certified internal auditors, or certified information systems auditors.

How To Apply

USDA OIG vacancy announcements are available through USA JOBS, a World Wide Web site operated by the Office of Personnel Management. For additional information, visit the USDA OIG online at http://www.usda.gov/oig or contact:

U.S. Department of Agriculture
Office of Inspector General
Human Resources Management Division
USDA STOP 2319
1400 Independence Avenue, SW
Washington, D.C. 20250-2319
Telephone: (202) 720-3079 (Voice)
 (202) 720-3090 (TDD)
Fax: (202) 720-4321
(800) 384-8708 (toll-free vacancy hotline)

DEPARTMENT OF COMMERCE

The U.S. Department of Commerce encourages, serves, and promotes the nation's international trade, economic growth, and technological advancement. Within this framework and a policy of promoting the national interest through the encouragement of the competitive free enterprise system, the Department offers assistance and information to increase America's competitiveness in the world economy; administers programs to prevent unfair foreign trade competition; provides social and economic statistics and analyses for business and government planners; provides research and support for the increased use of scientific, engineering, and technological development; works to improve our understanding of the benefits of the Earth's physical environment and oceanic resources; grants patents and registers trademarks; develops policies and conducts research on telecommunications; provides assistance to promote domestic economic development; promotes travel to the United States by residents of other countries; and assists in the growth of minority businesses.

OFFICE OF INSPECTOR GENERAL

Under the Inspector General Act of 1978, the IG is responsible for conducting audits, inspections, and investigations relating to Department of Commerce programs.

OIG Initiatives

The OIG is conducting an assessment of the Department's implementation of Presidential Decision Directive 63, which was created in part to address the growing cyber-threat. This directive establishes a national program to assure the security of cyber-based systems essential to the operations of the U.S. economy and government. Protecting the Department's computer systems from cyber-attack is a significant challenge today and will continue to be so in the future. The number of cyber-attacks on the nation's computer systems has increased dramatically over the last few years and is projected to grow at an even faster rate in the future. In addition, the sophistication of such attacks also continues to increase, posing a severe threat to computer system security. Industry and government research has shown that cyber-attacks are carried out not just by hackers, but by foreign governments and organized criminal and terrorist groups with harmful intent. An increasing number of interconnected, widely distributed computer systems support vital Commerce operations and provide essential services to the public. As the Department's systems have become more widely distributed and interconnected, security vulnerabilities have also increased, creating a need to improve procedural and technical security measures. Strong computer security measures are vital to protect the secrecy and privacy of information, the integrity of computer systems and their networks, and the availability of services to users.

Recognizing the need to focus more attention on improving the security of U.S. overseas facilities, in 1997, Congress appropriated $24.8 million to the State Department for security improvements. U.S. & Foreign Commercial Service (US&FCS) received $9.4 million of that supplemental appropriation to improve the security of its forty-five overseas facilities located outside embassies and consulates (referred to as noncollocated facilities). After the bombing of the U.S. embassies in Kenya and Tanzania in August 1998, State received another $627 million in FY 1999 emergency funding for reconstructing the embassies and conducting other security-related activities. US&FCS received $8 million of the funding for its overseas facilities. The OIG conducted an inspection of US&FCS's overseas security program, including the accounting for the use of the FY 1997 and 1999 funds, after questions were raised about how those funds were spent. The review identified weaknesses in ITA's and the Department's management of the program and the management of and accounting for program funds.

A senior National Institute of Standards and Technology (NIST) scientist agreed to pay the United States $30,000 to resolve charges that he had violated the False Claims Act and federal conflict of interest law in connection with the development of a robotic device by his division. An OIG investigation found that the scientist owned a patent for a stabilized lifting platform, which was an integral part of a robotic crane being developed at NIST. He committed government funds allocated to his division to develop and fine-tune the crane and thereby enhance the value of his own patent, without disclosing his financial interest in the platform to the Department. When the scientist's ownership of the platform patent came to the Department's attention, he agreed to sell the patent to the government. OIG investigators concluded that, by failing to disclose that he had used government resources to develop the platform, the scientist made false statements to the Department's Office of General Counsel when he was negotiating the sale of his patent. The scientist disputed the OIG's findings, but entered into a settlement agreement after being notified of the government's intention to prosecute its claims through a civil lawsuit.

A former National Oceanic and Atmospheric Administration (NOAA) secretary entered into a pretrial diversion agreement to settle charges that she had used a government credit card to make more than $4,300 of personal purchases. A Massachusetts state court ordered the former employee to repay the money to the government within one year and complete 25 hours of community service or face a sentence of up to 2 years' imprisonment and a $25,000 fine for the theft.

A National Marine Fisheries Service (NMFS) employee was suspended for 30 days for misuse of a government vehicle. Although the vehicle was observed at his residence on multiple occasions, the employee claimed that he had only stopped there briefly while working in the field. An OIG investigation revealed, however, that there was no work-related reason for him to have been driving in the area of his residence at any of the times in question.

A National Wildlife Service (NWS) employee resigned from federal service in the face of his proposed demotion and reassignment for use of a government vehicle for other than official purposes, including home-to-work transportation on a regular and recurring basis.

TRAINING

Training, qualifications, and application procedures are similar to those found under the Department of Agriculture. For further information, visit the Department of Commerce OIG Web site at http://www.oig.doc.gov or contact:

U.S. Department of Commerce
Office of Inspector General
Room 7099C, HCHB
14th Street and Constitution Avenue, NW
Washington, D.C. 20230
Telephone: (202) 482-4661

DEPARTMENT OF DEFENSE

The Department of Defense (DoD) is responsible for providing the military forces needed to deter war and protect the security of the United States.

The major elements of these forces are the Army, Navy, Marine Corps, and Air Force. Under the President, who is also the Commander in Chief, the Secretary of Defense exercises direction, authority, and control over the Department, which includes the separately organized military Departments of Army, Navy, and Air Force; the Joint Chiefs of Staff, providing military advice; the unified and specified combatant commands; and various defense agencies established for specific purposes.

OFFICE OF INSPECTOR GENERAL

The Defense Criminal Investigative Service (DCIS), established by the Secretary of Defense in 1981, is the investigative arm of the Office of Inspector General (OIG), Department of Defense (DoD). The DCIS investigates allegations of criminal, civil, and administrative violations and promotes economy, efficiency, and effective operations within the DoD. The investigations conducted by DCIS primarily involve contract and procurement fraud, antitrust violations, bribery, corruption, large-scale thefts of government property, health-care fraud, and computer crimes. DCIS is one of four Defense Criminal Investigative Organizations (DCIOs) within the DoD. The other three are the U.S. Army Criminal Investigation Command, the Naval Criminal Investigative Service, and the Air Force Office of Special Investigations.

The DCIS's mission and jurisdiction is derived from Public Law 95-452; Title 10, Section 1585a (The Inspector General of the Department of Defense); and DoD Directive 5106.1, which assigns duties and responsibilities to the IG to conduct, supervise, monitor, and initiate investigations relating to fraud within DoD and other investigations deemed appropriate by the OIG. DoD Instruction 5505.2 (Criminal Investigations of Fraud Offenses) provides guidance for determining DoD criminal investigative jurisdiction for fraud offenses among DCIS and the Military Criminal Investigative Organizations.

OIG Initiatives

Environmental Crimes Program

The DoD, through its Defense Environmental Restoration Program, is committed to correcting environmental damage caused by its activities. The Comprehensive Environmental Response, Compensation and Liability Act of 1980 and the Superfund Amendments and Reauthorization Act of 1986 gave DoD the authority for certain cleanup activities at former DoD sites in the United States and its territories, known as Formerly Used Defense Sites (FUDS). The U.S. Army Corps of Engineers is DoD's manager for the FUDS program. To date, DoD has identified more than 8,700 sites throughout the U.S. and its territories that have or are receiving restoration funding. DCIS is working in conjunction with the OIG Assistant Inspector General for Audit to ensure that the facilities receive the work they contract to be done and to identify any fraudulent activity.

The Environmental Protection Agency has primary jurisdiction for matters involving hazardous waste spills or other hazardous situations and environmental crimes. DCIS also works with the Environmental Protection Agency in investigating fraud in the DoD environmental programs, including contract fraud with regard to the removal, transport, and disposal of hazardous material from DoD installations.

Examples of Environmental Crimes Investigations

A Kingsville, Missouri, waste management firm entered a guilty plea with regard to having violated its permit specification for waste disposal under federal waste disposal regulations. The company illegally disposed of obsolete military M13 gas mask filters and committed insurance fraud resulting from a fire caused by the illegal processing of commercial and military aerosol waste products. The company was sentenced to 36 months probation and ordered to pay a $50,000 fine. In addition, the company paid a $230,850 civil penalty to the state of Missouri to settle alleged violations of the Missouri Hazardous Waste Management Law, Missouri Solid Waste Law, and Missouri Clean Water Law for the same DoD waste products it disposed of illegally.

The president of a company pled guilty to interstate transportation of money obtained by fraud, mail fraud, and obstruction of justice and was sentenced to twenty-one months imprisonment, followed by three years supervised release, and was ordered to pay $681,104 in restitution and a $400 special assessment fee. He was also directed to pay $600,000 to the defrauded insurance company and $81,104 to the Defense Reutilization and Marketing Service.

Computer Crimes Program

In addition to the investigation of computer-related crimes, DCIS is responsible for investigating incidents of unauthorized access involving the Defense Information Infrastructure (DII). DCIS consolidated computer intrusion and forensic specialties under its Computer Crimes Program to form a coordinated and efficient approach to Internet and computer-related crimes. DCIS computer intrusions personnel provide an immediate criminal investigative response to suspected computer intrusions against the DoD; develop and disseminate criminal intelligence to assist in protecting the DII; coordinate with DoD and other government agencies; and provide assistance in assessing, reporting, and correcting vulnerabilities in the DII.

Some DCIS special agents are trained to properly seize, protect, and analyze computer evidence. These Seized Computer Evidence Recovery Specialists (SCERS) work closely with the primary case agent to ensure the computer searches are complete, thorough, and relevant to the matter being investigated. When needed, SCERS agents are prepared to testify in court as experts in computer forensics.

Example of Computer Intrusion Case

Charges were filed against a Boston, Massachusetts, individual with one count each of interfering with a DoD computer system, computer fraud, and intercepting electronic communications. An investigation was conducted into the individual's alleged computer hacking into numerous computers around the U.S. after law enforcement authorities learned of an illegal intrusion into a computer owned by an online marketing service in Washington state, causing significant damage to the service's computer system. The intrusion initially appeared to originate from a DoD computer in Virginia. However, the DoD computer was used in an attempt to conceal the hacker's true identity. The hacker is alleged to have illegally accessed a computer owned by NASA in Maryland. Once connected to the NASA computer, the hacker used it to launch attacks against other computer systems, to include the defacement of the Department of Interior Web page. DCIS special Agents, NASA, the FBI, the Immigration and Naturalization Service, and the Department of Interior executed a search warrant of the hacker's residence. He was later arrested on charges relating to his computer hacking activities.

Examples of Other Investigative Initiatives

An investigation of a West Virginia manufacturer of chemical biological suits, known as BDO's (Battle Dress Outer garments), worn by the military, revealed that the garments failed testing, and were intentionally defectively produced. The company manufactured various military uniforms and other types of military apparel under five contracts awarded by the Defense Supply Center in Philadelphia, Pennsylvania. The former president of the company pled guilty to one count of conspiracy to defraud the government and stealing an explosive material from a licensed dealer. He was sentenced to four months detention (followed by three years supervised release) and ordered to pay a $4,000 fine and restitution of $195,417. The former vice president of the company pled guilty to one count of conspiracy to defraud the government, was sentenced to six months and one day detention (followed by two years supervised release) and ordered to pay a $40,000 fine. The company's former production manager pled guilty to one count of conspiracy to defraud the government, was sentenced to six months home detention (followed by three years probation) and ordered to pay a $20,000 fine. The company's former plant manager pled guilty to three counts of filing a false official certificate and was sentenced to two years probation and ordered to pay a $5,000 fine. The company pled guilty to one count of conspiracy to defraud the government and was sentenced to three years probation and ordered to pay a $266,825 fine.

A national tire and rubber company in St. Mary's, Ohio, agreed to pay $453,000 in civil restitution and deliver 5,000 alternative T-130 track shoe assemblies to the U.S. Army to settle allegations that it manufactured T-107 track shoe assemblies that did not conform to contractual specifications. T-107 track shoe assemblies are used on the M-88 Armored Recovery Vehicle.

An aluminum heat treating company in La Mirada, California, improperly treated and falsified quality testing on parts used in numerous DoD aircraft and space programs for the

NASA Space Shuttles and Space Station, as well as on commercial aircraft. Following a two-week trial, the company and its officers were convicted of conspiracy to make false statements, and six counts of making false statements to the DoD. The company paid a $1,638,000 fine, its president paid a $74,968 fine and served four months home confinement (followed by three years probation), and its vice present was sentenced to serve 55 months confinement (followed by three years probation).

Health-Care Fraud

DCIS has the responsibility for national health-care fraud investigations involving programs administered by the Assistant Secretary of Defense (Health Affairs). The programs provide health care to active duty dependents, retired military personnel and their dependents, and survivors of military personnel through a health insurance program known as TRICARE. Investigations have found an increase in fraud in the delivery of health-care services, including those provided by hospitals, clinics, and private practitioners.

Example of Health-Care Fraud

DCIS, FBI, Health and Human Services Office of Inspector General, and the Department of Labor conducted a five-year investigation that resulted in a $486 million global settlement with a medical-care company headquartered in Lexington, Massachusetts. The company had conspired to defraud the government through the submission of false claims and kickback payments. The allegations included billings for unnecessary laboratory tests and nutritional services, falsification of documents, and double billing of laboratory services. The health-care company provided services and supplies for patients with end stage renal disease.

Financial Crimes

The investigation of financial crimes focuses on cases where financial gain is the sole motivation. These cases are usually accomplished by defrauding or abusing pay systems, such as the Defense Finance and Accounting Service (DFAS).

Examples of Financial Fraud Cases

A general supply specialist with the Defense Logistics Agency in Battle Creek, Michigan, submitted a claim for reimbursement of moving expenses in connection with his relocation from Columbus, Ohio. He falsely claimed his wife and children had accompanied him on various dates when they had not, and that he was paying rent and breach of lease payments on an apartment in Ohio. He pled guilty to making a false claim against the government and was sentenced to six months home detention (followed by five years probation) and ordered to pay $24,041 in restitution.

An investigation disclosed that a former DFAS employee issued 53 U.S. Treasury checks to various individuals, including several of his relatives. He pled guilty to possession of pornographic images of children and mail fraud, was sentenced to 27 months incarceration (followed by three years of supervised release) and ordered to pay $91,264 in restitution.

Contractor/Subcontractor Kickbacks and Bribery

Since the Anti-Kickback Act of 1986 was passed, the number of subcontractor kickback investigations in the DCIS inventory has increased dramatically. The utilization of informants and undercover operations has been particularly successful in these cases and has uncovered culpable DoD and contractor employees.

Example of Kickback and Bribery Case

A former government expediter at the Defense Distribution Depot in Susquehanna, Pennsylvania (DDDSP), solicited bribes from a government supplier in return for increased and continued business with the DDDSP. Following initiation of the investigation, the expeditor retired. He pled guilty to accepting a bribe, was sentenced to one year of incarceration (followed by three years probation) and ordered to pay $36,535 in restitution.

TRAINING

Training, qualifications, and application procedures are similar to those found under the Department of Agriculture. For further information, visit the OIG-DCIS Web site at www.dodig.osd.mil/dcis or contact:

> Office of Inspector General
> Department of Defense
> Defense Criminal Investigative Service
> 400 Army Navy Drive, Room 901E
> Arlington, Virgina 22202
> Telephone: (703) 604-8300

DEPARTMENT OF EDUCATION

The Department of Education is the Cabinet-level department that establishes policy for, administers, and coordinates most federal assistance to education. The Department of Education was created by the Department of Education Organization Act, with the first Secretary of Education sworn in on December 6, 1979. Its mission is to ensure equal access to education and promote educational excellence throughout the nation.

OFFICE OF INSPECTOR GENERAL

Like most federal OIGs, Education's Office of Inspector General addresses both audits and investigation. Investigation Services is responsible for all investigative activities relating to the Department's programs and operations, and includes conducting, supervising, and coordinating investigations of suspected fraudulent activity by participants in Department programs or employee misconduct.

Investigation Services is also responsible for the direction of programs for the protection of classified information for the Department and for establishing the necessary procedures for coordination with the Department of Justice on all criminal matters dealing with departmental programs and operations. This office coordinates with other components of the OIG to ensure the effective, efficient, and economical utilization of resources.

INVESTIGATIVE INITIATIVES

A former financial aid director at Middle Tennessee State University (MTSU), Murfreesboro, Tennessee, pled guilty to official misconduct and the theft of more than $10,000. The investigation revealed that he had obtained more than $250,000 in Federal Family Education Loans to which he was not entitled for himself and several family members. He concealed the loans from the university as well as state and federal officials by not entering the loans into MTSU's loan tracking system. He further concealed the loans by picking up the loan checks directly from the banks that issued them. The subject was ordered to pay restitution of $10,400 for scholarship funds that he illegally received from MTSU and repay more than $250,000 in illegally received student loans.

Two school owners were indicted for operating an ineligible campus of the American Welt Testing Schools in Pasadena and Beaumont, Texas. The Beaumont campus was not Title IV eligible; however, more than $1 million in federal aid was alleged to have been disbursed there by processing the aid through the Pasadena campus.

A school owner in Lexington, Kentucky, was indicted for allegedly misapplying more than $258,000 by funneling financial aid for her four ineligible campuses through her one eligible campus.

The former owner of the Midwest Career College in Indianapolis, Indiana, was sentenced to forty-one months of incarceration and ordered to make restitution of $205,000 for obtaining Pell Grants for students who did not attend the school and for failure to refund the unearned grants.

The former director of admissions at Lincoln Technical Institute in Oak Lawn, Illinois, was sentenced to twenty-one months of incarceration and ordered to pay $123,519 in restitution. The director had falsified high school diplomas and GED certificates for students who did not have them, and ordered other admission representatives under his supervision to do the same.

A school director for the Travel and Trade Center Institute in Orange, California, was sentenced to ten months of incarceration and ordered to pay restitution of $83,000. The director drew Pell Grants for students who did not exist.

Auditing Initiatives

Seven states were audited to establish compliance with the provisions of the Gun-Free Schools Act. West Virginia, Wisconsin, Texas, Maryland, Colorado, New Mexico, and California were selected to participate in this audit. The OIG concluded that five of the states were generally in compliance with the Act. Weaknesses were identified in the following areas:

- Possible noncompliance in two states: The Colorado state law may not require mandatory expulsions for a period of at least one year for students who bring a firearm to school, while in California, the state law may not require mandatory expulsions of students who bring explosives to school.

- Collection and reporting of data: In California, Maryland, Wisconsin, and New Mexico, the OIG found weaknesses in the collection and reporting of data that resulted in errors reported by the state departments of education. Most of the errors in reporting were due to confusion over what weapons qualify as firearms. Most of the states concurred with the findings and recommendations, and many are taking action to address the weaknesses identified.

- Security control weaknesses noted: A recent OIG audit on the Department's security posture, policies, and plans for its fourteen mission-critical systems revealed that the Department has significant control weaknesses. They include a lack of security plans and reviews for six mission-critical systems, no process to ensure resolution of identified security deficiencies, and a lack of technical security training for many employees responsible for overseeing the Department's computer security. The absence of these controls heightens the risk that those Department systems and data are vulnerable to security threats. Implementing IG recommendations will enable the Department to greatly enhance the security of its financial management and other mission-critical systems.

TRAINING

Training, qualifications, and application procedures are similar to those found under the Department of Agriculture. For further information, visit the Department of Education Office of Inspector General's Web site at http://www.ed.gov/offices/oig or contact:

Office of the Inspector General
U.S. Department of Education
400 Maryland Avenue, SW
Washington, D.C. 20202-1510
Telephone: (202) 205-5439

DEPARTMENT OF ENERGY

The Department of Energy, in partnership with its customers, is entrusted to contribute to the welfare of the nation by providing the technical information and the scientific educational foundation for the technology, policy, and institutional leadership necessary to achieve efficiency in energy use, diversity in energy sources, a more productive and competitive economy, improved environmental quality, and a secure national defense.

OFFICE OF INSPECTOR GENERAL

The Office of Inspector General for DOE is organized into three areas: The Office of Audit Services, the Office of Inspections, and the Office of Investigations.

The Office of Audit Services conducts and/or coordinates all auditing activities for the Department's programs and operations, including those done under contract as well as those performed by Department employees.

The Office of Investigations conducts investigations into allegations of fraud, waste, and abuse in programs and operations of the Department of Energy. Priority is given to investigations of suspected violations of criminal and civil statutes as well as serious administrative misconduct.

The Office of Inspections conducts reviews of management issues, administrative allegations, and certain types of whistleblower reprisal complaints. The Office of Inspections also maintains the Inspector General Hotline to facilitate the reporting of allegations and processes referrals of administrative allegations to Department management.

Auditing Initiative

The DOE, through its Stockpile Stewardship Program, is responsible for ensuring the safety, security, and reliability of the nuclear weapons stockpile. During an audit, DOE concluded that aging and deteriorating weapons production facilities had created a $422 million maintenance and repair backlog. In light of this situation, the DOE OIG conducted an audit to determine whether the Department had maintained the nuclear weapons production infrastructure to meet current and future goals of the Stockpile Stewardship Plan. The audit disclosed that despite data suggesting that current military requirements were being met, the deterioration of the infrastructure resulted in delays in weapons modification, remanufacture, dismantlement, and surveillance testing of nuclear weapons components. It was also determined that current and future goals of the Stockpile Stewardship Program were at risk. DOE officials within the National Nuclear Security Administration (NNSA) estimated that DOE must invest $5 billion to $8 billion more than the currently budgeted amounts over the next 10 years to offset the effects of a delayed or neglected infrastructure.

The OIG recommended that the administrator of NNSA develop an overall infrastructure restoration plan based on individual site plans and current and planned stockpile workload requirements. The administrator concurred with the OIG recommendations and advised that Phase II of the Facilities and Infrastructure Initiative study, now underway, would address each of the OIG's recommendations.

Investigative Initiatives

An OIG investigation disclosed evidence that the president of a subcontractor authorized the submission of false bioassay data under a contract with the Sandia National Laboratory. The company provided bioassay services to Sandia. Bioassay involves the testing of urine for potential exposure to nuclear materials. Accurate reporting alerts authorities to potentially excessive radiation exposure. The U.S. Attorney's Office for the District of New Mexico pursued criminal prosecution. The president of the company was indicted on 136 counts of false claims and false statements. The defendant entered a guilty plea and was sentenced to three months in a Bureau of Prisons halfway house; three months of electronic monitoring and two years supervised probation; paid more than $122,000 in restitution and a $40,000 fine; and was barred (along with his company) from government contracting for ten years.

The U.S. Attorney's Office in Syracuse, New York, requested assistance from the OIG in investigating allegations of a gas pipeline company's violations of the Clean Water Act. Also participating in the investigation were the Federal Bureau of Investigation, the Criminal Investigation Division of the Environmental Protection Agency, and the U.S. Army. The pipeline company pled guilty in federal court to four felony violations of the Clean Water Act. The company agreed to pay $22 million in fines and penalties and $800 in court costs; perform remedial action at identified streams and wetlands; implement a ten-year safety plan to monitor, identify, and remediate potential damage to the pipeline; and implement a backfill stability monitoring and maintenance plan. Four senior officials with the pipeline company also pled guilty in federal court to violations of the Clean Water Act.

The OIG conducted an investigation that substantiated irregularities with costs claimed by a contractor under a cooperative agreement with the Department's Savannah River Operations Office. The OIG recommended that management consider issuing a notice of intent to disallow approximately $718,000 in costs improperly claimed by the contractor. Management concurred, and the Department received $720,000 from the contractor in final settlement of the disputed costs claimed under the agreement.

In an effort to combat cyber–attacks, intrusions, and other crimes involving technology within DOE, the OIG established a Technology Crimes Section (TCS). The TCS has special agents highly skilled in detecting and investigating cyber-crimes. One TCS case involved a joint investigation with the Federal Bureau of Investigation that resulted in the arrest of a hacker who was charged with intrusion into two financial computer systems at the Lawrence Livermore National laboratory. The hacker was indicted on violation of Title 18, U.S.C. 1030 (fraud and related activity in connection with computers).

Inspection Initiative

At the request of the Secretary of Energy, the OIG reviewed the sale to a Chinese national and the repurchase of an INTEL Paragon XPS supercomputer (Paragon) by Sandia National Laboratories (Sandia). The Paragon had originally been purchased in 1993, in part, because it was a "cutting edge research instrument essential to the Department's nuclear weapons program." If reassembled after disposal, the Paragon could have been one of the 100 fastest computers in the world. Concerns were raised that the sale of the supercomputer could be detrimental to the national security of the United States. The process used to sell the Paragon was seriously flawed. Notably, Sandia did not treat the Paragon as a high-risk property, and thus, did not perform an evaluation of the Paragon for any significant risks to national security and nuclear nonproliferation as required by the Property Management Regulations. In addition, Sandia sold the Paragon with approximately 130 unclassified data storage disks that were not sanitized prior to sale. A fundamental weakness in the sale of the Paragon was that senior-level management officials were not aware of the sale. Therefore, these officials were not afforded the opportunity to exercise management judgment on how to dispose of this high-risk property. The OIG recommended that the Albuquerque Operations Office address weaknesses in Sandia's high-risk property control process and Sandia's property management process. The OIG also recommended that the general counsel issue an opinion on whether Department contractors may inquire into the possible foreign ownership of companies that bid on excess property. Department management concurred with the recommendations.

TRAINING

Training, qualifications, and application procedures are similar to those found under the Department of Agriculture. For further information, visit the DOE-OIG Web site at www.ig.doe.gov or contact:

Office of Inspector General
U.S. Department of Energy
1000 Independence Avenue, SW, Room 5D-039
Washington, D.C. 20585
Telephone: (202) 586-4393

DEPARTMENT OF HEALTH AND HUMAN SERVICES

The Department of Health and Human Services (HHS) is the Cabinet-level department of the federal executive branch that is most concerned with people and the nation's human concerns. Whether it is mailing out social security checks or making health services more widely available, HHS touches the lives of more Americans than any other federal agency.

OFFICE OF THE INSPECTOR GENERAL

The primary responsibility of the Office of Inspector General (OIG), Office of Investigations (OI) is to detect and prevent waste, fraud, and abuse within more than 200 departmental programs. In an effort to fulfill this mission, special agents with the OI conduct various criminal, civil, and administrative investigations.

The skyrocketing cost of our nation's health care requires OI special agents to spend a significant amount of their time investigating fraud committed against the Medicare and Medicaid programs. The United States spends in excess of $1 trillion a year on health care, making these programs prime targets for fraud.

In addition to health-care fraud, OI special agents conduct investigations of wrongdoing committed against various agencies within the Department. These agencies include the Administration for Children and Families, the Centers for Disease Control and Prevention, the Public Health Service, the Food and Drug Administration, and the National Institutes of Health. OI special agents also conduct internal investigations involving allegations of misconduct by departmental employees.

The OIG has made the investigation of absent parents who fail to pay court-ordered child support a high priority. The OI is part of multiagency, multijurisdictional investigative task forces that are responsible for identifying and investigating the most egregious violators of federal and state child support laws.

A significant number of OI investigations are conducted in conjunction with other law enforcement agencies, such as the Federal Bureau of Investigation, the U.S. Postal Inspection Service, the U.S. Marshals Service, the Internal Revenue Service, and the various state Medicaid Fraud Control units.

OI special agents ensure the safety and protection of the Secretary of HHS. Special agents in the field supplement the OI's Secretarial Protection Operations staff when the secretary is traveling or when there is a specific threat which necessitates additional protection.

Investigative Initiatives

As the result of a joint effort by investigators, auditors, and multiple law enforcement agencies, the government reached a multimillion dollar Medicare fraud settlement with the world's largest provider of kidney dialysis products and services. The company agreed to a global resolution under which three subsidiaries pled guilty and the company agreed to pay $486 million to resolve criminal and civil aspects of the case.

A Florida physician was sentenced to prison for conspiracy to dispense and distribute controlled substances outside the course of professional medical practice, conspiracy to defraud the Medicare program, and conspiracy to solicit and receive kickbacks in return for ordering Medicare services and for referring Medicare beneficiaries. A pharmacist was also sentenced to prison for his role in filling and dispensing hundreds of invalid prescriptions written by the physician for highly addictive pain medication.

A former professional basketball player was sentenced for failing to pay child support for his 15-year-old son living in Massachusetts. Prior to sentencing, he paid a total of $160,210 to become current in this case and four other child support orders. Previously, he also pled guilty and was sentenced for failing to pay support for two other children who live in Georgia.

A man was sentenced for failing to pay child support for his two daughters who reside with their mother in New York. The man is a career criminal whose record includes violations in several states, such as various narcotics violations, robbery, assault, use of a handgun in a felony, resisting arrest, passing false documents, criminal mischief, and other crimes.

The University of Minnesota agreed to pay $32 million to resolve its civil liability for the sale of an unlicensed, experimental drug over a period of more than twenty years. The lawsuit sought recovery of profits and damages for alleged violations of Food and Drug Administration regulations prohibiting the commercial sale of unlicensed drugs and departmental rules governing the handling of program income earned with grant funds.

The city and state of New York agreed to pay HHS $49 million to settle charges that a city agency had misused $39 million in HHS grant funds over a four-year period. The agency had not provided required foster care services, such as developing case plans and conducting periodic case reviews for children in foster care.

TRAINING

Training, qualifications, and application procedures are similar to those found under the Department of Agriculture. Office of Investigation position vacancies can be found online at http://www.psc.gov/spo/sw.shtml. For further information, visit the OI online at http://oig.hhs.gov/oi or contact:

Office of Inspector General
Department of Health and Human Services
330 Independence Avenue, SW, Cohen Bldg., Rm. 5409
Washington, D.C. 20201
Telephone: (202) 619-3148

DEPARTMENT OF HOUSING AND URBAN DEVELOPMENT

The mission of the Department of Housing and Urban Development (HUD) is to provide a decent, safe, and sanitary home and suitable living environment for every American. HUD is primarily concerned with creating opportunities for home ownership; providing housing assistance for low-income persons; working to create, rehabilitate, and maintain the nation's affordable housing; enforcing the nation's fair housing laws; helping the homeless; spurring economic growth in distressed neighborhoods; and helping local communities meet their development needs.

OFFICE OF INSPECTOR GENERAL

The Office of Inspector General was administratively established by HUD in 1972 and statutorily mandated in 1978 when the Congress passed the Inspector General Act. Under the requirements of this Act, the IG is responsible for, among other things, reviewing existing and proposed legislation and regulations relating to HUD programs and operations and making recommendations concerning their impact on the administration of HUD programs and the prevention and detection of fraud and abuse; recommending policies and coordinating relationships between HUD and other federal agencies, along with state and local government agencies, concerning the prevention and detection of fraud and abuse in HUD program; and conducting, supervising, and coordinating audits and investigations relating to the programs and operations of HUD. As such, the Inspector General has access to all records, reports, reviews, documents, papers, or other materials relating to the Department.

OIG Initiatives

Operation Safe Home is a campaign to combat violent crime in public and assisted housing, fraud in the administration of public housing programs, and equity skimming in Federal Housing Administration (FHA) insured multifamily housing. These three types of wrongdoing represent particularly high risks to HUD's programs and to the well-being of residents of public, assisted, and insured housing. The OIG's role in Operation Safe Home entails significant departures from the IG's traditional auditing and investigative activity. Notably, Operation Safe Home is proactive rather than reactive. It focuses on violent crime as well as other types of wrongdoing; involves an unprecedented level of OIG collaboration with federal, state, and local law enforcement agencies; and employs new methodologies such as direct auditing and/or investigative referral of civil cases to the Department of Justice and U.S. Attorneys.

Examples of Operation Safe Home results in each of the three areas of emphasis include the following:

The South Jamaica, New York Task Force, consisting of the New York City Police Department, HUD OIG, and the Queens County District Attorney's Office Narcotics Investigation Bureau, was established in July 1998 to target drug trafficking, violent crime, and gang activity in and around the South Jamaica public housing development. Three individuals were recently sentenced to a total of more than eighteen years in prison. A fourth person was sentenced to life in prison. All four were members of the "Chomp Crew," a violent gang that controlled a $3-million-per-year drug trafficking enterprise in and around the South Jamaica development. To date, the Task Force has executed twenty-five search warrants in the development and has seized 290 glassines of heroine; 298 vials, 453 ziplock bags, and 17 ounces of cocaine; 6 ounces of heroin; 4 ounces of marijuana; more than $71,000 in cash; one shotgun, four pistols, one revolver, one stun gun, one imitation pistol, 220 live rounds of ammunition, and two bullet-resistant vests; and 8 vehicles. More than 100 gang members and associates have been arrested by the task force. Thirty persons have been either evicted from the development, terminated from tenancy, permanently excluded from the New York City Housing Authority, or placed on probation by the Authority's Anti-Narcotics Strike Force. In addition, the task force has been responsible for dismantling three violent gang organizations.

The Executive Director (ED) of the Lakewood, New Jersey Housing Authority and the Lakewood Tenants Rental Assistance Program (and owner of the Brick Towers multifamily housing development) pled guilty to a felony charge of preparing a false tax return. The charges pertained to funds the ED diverted from Brick Towers. BTA Properties, Inc. also pled guilty to false statement charges and was ordered to pay more than $300,000 in restitution and fines. In addition, the company was ordered to be dissolved. The ED entered into a separate civil settlement agreement by which he paid $1 million to HUD. He was also barred for five years, relinquished his position as ED of the Housing Authority, deeded Brick Towers over to HUD, was sentenced to three years probation and two months confinement, and fined $5,000. The HUD OIG, FBI, and IRS conducted this investigation.

In Tampa, Florida, 10 individuals and one partnership pled guilty to criminal equity skimming and obstruction of investigations and audits in their efforts to defraud HUD of more than $1.16 million. The schemes resulted in the diversion of funds from seventeen HUD-insured multifamily properties. Guilty pleas were entered by the property owners and their agents, the property management owners and their agents, a certified public accountant, and a roofing contractor who worked on the properties. They were each sentenced to probation ranging from three to five years, home detention ranging from two to four months, a total of $31,000 in fines, and $949,641 in restitution. This investigation, conducted by the FBI and HUD OIG, resulted in the first ever prosecution of property management fee–splitting and accounting fee–splitting under the equity skimming statute.

The Housing Fraud Initiative (HFI) is a proactive law enforcement effort using a unified approach to the detection and prosecution of fraud in HUD programs. The concept combines OIG auditing and investigative resources together with FBI agents and Assistant U.S. Attorneys for the sole purpose of rooting out corruption and fraud in all HUD funded activities within targeted federal judicial districts. HFI arose out of concern by members of the House Appropriations Subcommittee on Veterans Affairs, HUD, and independent agencies that HUD funds may not be reaching those needing federal assistance due to pervasive fraud. The following federal judicial districts have been designated as HFI sites: the Eastern District of New York, the District of Maryland, the District of Columbia, the Northern District of Illinois, the Central District of California, and Northern District of Texas.

A former HUD Single Family Housing specialist in Santa Ana, California, was sentenced to two years incarceration (and three years supervised release) and ordered to pay $1.4 million in restitution to HUD. The specialist was also ordered to stop working in any capacity which would involve HUD business after it was revealed that, since her termination from HUD, she had been working as a mortgage consultant doing quality control work on FHA loans for lenders. The specialist previously pled guilty to one count of accepting a bribe and two counts of tax evasion. A joint investigation by the FBI, HUD OIG, and the IRS Criminal Investigation Division disclosed that the specialist sold eighty-two HUD properties valued by HUD at approximately $9.1 million to various individuals for a total of $2 million, resulting in a loss to HUD of more than $7 million. The specialist sold twenty of these homes to a real estate agent for about $700,000. These properties were appraised at $2.1 million. The agent resold the properties for $2.2 million. The specialist received more than $80,000 in bribe payments and a BMW convertible from the agent. The specialist's BMW and bank account with $7,200 were seized. Forty-six of the eighty-two properties have also been seized.

In Chicago, Illinois, 20 individuals were charged in a sixteen-count indictment relating to a $10 million, eighty property flipping scheme. Those named in the indictment included an attorney, 2 paralegals, 2 mortgage brokers, 2 real estate appraisers, 2 real estate agents, mortgagor recruiters, investors, and mortgagors. Approximately $3 million of the $10 million included FHA-insured mortgages with losses exceeding $750,000. The alleged scheme, which included mail fraud, wire fraud, and false statements to HUD, involved the individuals buying and selling properties on the same day, whereby the inflated second sale would actually fund the first purchase with cash. This amounted to the buyer's closing on a property that the seller had not yet purchased. The defendants purportedly reaped the benefits of the fraudulent appraisals on the second sales and split the proceeds through a variety of pay-offs. In virtually every instance, the second sale would require a variety of fraudulent loan documents, including fictitious identities, occupancy affidavits, W-2s, verifications of deposit and employment, pay stubs, and gift letters. The FBI and HUD OIG conducted this investigation.

Training, qualifications, and application procedures are similar to those found under the Department of Agriculture. For further information, visit the HUD OIG online at http://www.hud.gov/oig/oigindex.html or contact:

Office of the Inspector General
Department of Housing and Urban Development
451 7th Street, SW
Washington, D.C. 20410
Telephone: (202) 708-0430

DEPARTMENT OF THE INTERIOR

The mission of the Department of the Interior is to protect and provide access to our nation's natural and cultural heritage and honor our trust responsibilities to Native American tribes. The Department manages the nation's public lands and minerals, national parks, national wildlife refuges, and western water resources and upholds federal trust responsibilities to Native American tribes. It is responsible for migratory wildlife conservation, historic preservation, endangered species, surface mine lands protection and restoration, mapping, and geological, hydrological, and biological science.

OFFICE OF INSPECTOR GENERAL

To cover the Department's many and varied activities, the Office of Inspector General (OIG) has auditing and investigative positions along with other positions that provide management support. These employees are under the direction of the Assistant Inspectors General for Audits, Investigations, Management, and Policy and Program Integrity and are assigned to the headquarters office in Washington, D.C., and field offices.

Coordinated auditing and investigative work provides management with information and recommendations to improve operations and detect and deter illegal activities. The efforts of these two distinct functions are consolidated under the leadership of the Inspector General. OIG activities that foster coordination between audits and investigations include annual planning conferences, input into the auditing work plan by investigative staff, and intra-office referrals.

Auditing Investigative Initiatives

Several major oil, gas, and coal companies were investigated by the OIG for systematically underreporting the value of gas, crude oil, and coal extracted from federal and Native American lands for more than ten years. The companies agreed to resolve claims under the False Claims Act by entering settlement agreements. To date, the settlement agreements total more than $330 million.

The OIG investigated allegations that several individuals stole approximately $2.6 million from the Oglala Lakota College (OLC), an Oglala Sioux Tribe college located in Kyle, South Dakota. The investigation resulted in the convictions of 6 individuals on 128 criminal counts, including conspiracy, embezzlement, theft, money laundering, and asset forfeiture. The scheme to defraud the OLC involved the theft of checks belonging to the OLC, followed by an elaborate scheme to create eight fictitious companies. The conspirators then opened bank accounts in the fictitious companies' names and used the accounts to launder the embezzled OLC funds for the personal benefit of the conspirators. Among the defendants were 2 former vice presidents for business affairs at OLC and several local businessmen. The convictions resulted in a maximum sentence of 151 months for one of the defendants. All of the defendants were ordered to pay $2.6 million in restitution.

An investigation conducted jointly by the Office of Investigations and Audits uncovered a two-year embezzlement scheme by a former Minerals Management Service accountant that resulted in the theft of nearly $400,000 of government money. The accountant created fictitious vendors that purportedly performed government services and then authorized payment for the services allegedly provided. The accountant then caused the U.S. Treasury to make electronic transfers to both her bank accounts and those of her associates. The investigation identified forty-six such transactions, ranging from approximately $2,000 to $39,000. As part of her plea agreement, the accountant was sentenced to eighteen months in prison and agreed to repay $266,000 to the government.

A joint audit and investigation determined that a U.S. Fish and Wildlife Services (FWS) employee mishandled the collection of refuge fees and misused government property. As a result, the FWS agreed to cease the practice of keeping collected fees, which cost the U.S. Treasury approximately $6.8 million in revenues. This also resulted in the issuance of policy by the Department's Assistant Secretary for Policy, Management and Budget governing the collection and use of fees Departmentwide. In addition, the Department is studying fee collection practices to ensure that the use of fees collected complies with legal and policy requirements. The employee was disciplined for his actions.

A joint audit and investigation found that an Native American tribal school had inflated mileage claims for buses used to transport students to school. To resolve the allegations, which covered a five-year period, the school agreed to pay the government about $4.5 million.

The U.S. Fish and Wildlife Service had paid a contractor about $231,000 to construct a brook stock test facility and drainage system at a fish hatchery before the contract was terminated for default. The contractor filed a $416,000 claim for equitable adjustment that it attributed to a government shutdown, differing site conditions, and weather delays. Based on the OIG audit, the service disallowed over $411,000 of the claimed amount.

Training, qualifications, and application procedures are similar to those found under the Department of Agriculture. For further information, contact:

Office of Inspector General
U.S. Department of the Interior
1849 C Street, NW, Mail Stop 5341
Washington, D.C. 20240
Telephone: (202) 208-5745

DEPARTMENT OF JUSTICE

As the largest law firm in the nation, the Department of Justice serves as counsel for its citizens. It represents them in enforcing the law in the public interest. Through its thousands of lawyers, investigators, and agents, the Department plays the key role in protection against criminals and subversion, ensuring healthy competition of business in our free enterprise system, safeguarding the consumer, and enforcing drug, immigration, and naturalization laws.

OFFICE OF INSPECTOR GENERAL

The Office of the Inspector General is a statutorily created independent entity in the Department of Justice (DOJ) whose mission is to detect and deter waste, fraud, abuse, and misconduct in DOJ. In addition, the OIG assists managers in promoting the integrity, economy, efficiency, and effectiveness of DOJ programs and operations. The OIG carries out its mission through the Investigations, Audit, Inspections, and Management and Planning Divisions and the Special Investigations and Review Unit.

The OIG Investigations Division investigates allegations of bribery, fraud, abuse, civil rights violations, and violations of other laws and procedures that govern Department employees, contractors, and grantees. The division develops cases for criminal prosecution or civil and administrative action. In many instances, the OIG refers to the internal affairs offices of other components within the Department (such as the Immigration and Naturalization Service Office of Internal Audit, U.S. Marshals Service Office of Internal Affairs, or the Federal Bureau of Prisons Office of Internal Affairs) for the investigation of and appropriate responses to non-criminal or administrative allegations against lower-level employees. In the more important cases that are referred, the division reviews their findings and the disciplinary actions taken.

Attorney General Order 1931-94, Jurisdiction for Investigation of Allegations of Misconduct by Department of Justice Employees, dated November 8, 1994, defines the respective jurisdictions of the Department's Office of Professional Responsibility (OPR) and the OIG to conduct investigations of allegations of employee misconduct. Specifically, the order gives DOJ OPR the primary function of investigating "allegations of misconduct by Department attorneys that relate to the exercise of their authority to investigate, litigate, or provide legal advice." The order retains the authority of FBI OPR and DEA OPR to conduct internal investigations of their respective employees. The order gives the OIG authority to investigate all other allegations of misconduct by any Department employee, or allegations of waste, fraud, or abuse by any contractor, grantee, or other person doing business with or receiving benefits from the Department. The order also allows the OIG to request permission from the Deputy Attorney General to take responsibility for an investigation from any of the OPRs.

On January 29, 1990, and continuing to date, the Attorney General conferred upon and delegated to the DOJ Inspector General certain law enforcement authorities and directed that all individuals designated as special agents within the OIG be deputized as Special Deputy United States Marshals. Under this deputation, OIG special agents seek and execute arrest warrants and make warrantless arrests, seek and execute search warrants, serve subpoenas and other legal writs, perform undercover roles, and carry firearms. OIG special agents carry out law enforcement functions in the same manner as other special agents within the DOJ, including FBI and DEA agents.

All OIG special agents are graduates of a basic criminal investigator training program at either the Federal Law Enforcement Training Center (FLETC) or equivalent training centers such as those run by the DEA and FBI.

Investigative Initiatives

An INS supervisory asylum officer was arrested and convicted on charges of bribery and obstruction of justice. The investigation revealed that the supervisory asylum officer altered hundreds of decisions in the INS's computer system, causing the original assessments written by asylum officers to change from a court referral to a grant of political asylum. Albanian and Yugoslavian nationals paid civilian middlemen $1,000 to $4,000 for each political asylum decision fraudulently granted by the asylum officer. Four middlemen and four Albanian and Yugoslavian nationals were arrested on charges of bribery, conspiracy, and document fraud. As a result of this investigation, the INS revised its computer security by instituting procedures specifically designed to deter and detect internal fraud and abuse.

An INS immigration inspector was arrested, convicted, and sentenced to more than twelve years in prison on federal racketeering charges, alien smuggling, and importation of controlled substances. The investigation revealed that the immigration inspector used his official position to permit entry of certain designated vehicles and individuals into the United States from Mexico without proper inspection and examination in exchange for money. The investigation led to the apprehension of 23 aliens who the immigration inspector allowed to enter the country without proper inspection documents. In addition, the immigration inspector allowed four separate loads of marijuana totaling more than 3,500 pounds to enter the United States. In return for these acts, the immigration inspector was paid $350,000.The marijuana shipments were later intercepted.

A Bureau of Prison correctional counselor was arrested and convicted by a jury trial for sexually abusing female inmates while he was employed at the Federal Transfer Center in Oklahoma City. An OIG investigation led to an indictment alleging that on numerous occasions the correctional counselor engaged in abusive sexual contact with multiple female inmates. He was convicted on all counts and sentenced to more than twelve years of incarceration.

Training, qualifications, and application procedures are similar to those found under the Department of Agriculture. For further information, contact:

Office of the Inspector General
U.S. Department of Justice
950 Pennsylvania Avenue, NW, Suite 4706
Washington, D.C. 20530
Telephone: (202) 514-3435

DEPARTMENT OF LABOR

The Department of Labor administers a variety of federal labor laws guaranteeing workers' rights to safe and healthful working conditions, a minimum hourly wage and overtime pay, freedom from employment discrimination, unemployment insurance, and workers' compensation. The Department also protects workers' pension rights, provides for job training programs, helps workers find jobs, works to strengthen free collective bargaining, and keeps track of changes in employment, prices, and other national economic measurements.

OFFICE OF INSPECTOR GENERAL

The Office of Inspector General (OIG) of the Department of Labor (DOL) serves the American worker and taxpayer by conducting audits, investigations, and evaluations that result in improvements in the effectiveness, efficiency, and integrity of programs and operations. In conducting investigations, the OIG uses the full range of investigative techniques and works closely with other law enforcement agencies. Under its program fraud responsibility, the OIG conducts criminal, civil, and administrative investigations relating to alleged violations concerning DOL programs and personnel. OIG investigations address criminal activity, program fraud and abuse, employee misconduct, and unethical behavior by recipients of program benefits administered by DOL, including grant and contract funds.

In addition, the Department of Labor has the only federal OIG dedicated to combating the influence of organized crime in the nation's labor unions, a cooperative effort with the U.S. Department of Justice. Formed in response to concern over the growth of organized crime, the history of the labor racketeering program can be traced back to the beginning of the Organized Crime Strike Forces created in the 1960s. Attention is not only directed to the more traditional *La Cosa Nostra* organized crime families, but also toward other emerging crime groups engaged in labor racketeering. The OIG conducts criminal investigations primarily in three areas: internal union affairs, employee benefit plans, and labor-management relations. Activities of concern include extortion, embezzlement of union or employee benefit funds, kickbacks to benefit plan officials, and illegal payments between management and union officials.

Investigative Initiatives

The former president and vice president of an international union in Fort Lauderdale, Florida, were cumulatively sentenced to five years of imprisonment and six years of probation for their convictions on racketeering and conspiracy charges. The joint investigation with the FBI and DOL's Pension and Welfare Benefits Administration (PWBA) and Office of Labor-Management Standards (OLMS) revealed that the former officials engaged in threatened and actual violence and economic injury to union members and employers. For example, rank-and-file members who opposed the officials in union elections were threatened, along with their families, with physical beatings and shootings, while other members were demoted, fired, or denied work referrals through the union hiring hall. Similarly, employers who were in the position to enter into collective bargaining agreements with the union were subjected to physical beatings as well as damage to expensive machinery by fire, explosives, shooting with firearms, and by placing sand in machinery oil or hydraulic fluid.

Following his guilty plea to a fraud charge, the former general president of an international union resigned his position and was suspended for two years from the practice of law in Rhode Island. In addition to his sentence of two years of probation and $100,000 in restitution, the former union president was barred from holding any future position with the union and from being an employee of any labor union for a period of five years. This investigation was conducted jointly with the FBI and OLMS.

Two owners of a Michigan brokerage firm pled guilty to charges of RICO conspiracy and paying kickbacks to two union pension fund trustees through a money laundering operation in the Cayman Islands, Great Britain, and the Isle of Man. In return, the trustees for the pension funds of two union locals in Chicago used their positions to select investment advisers who would direct pension fund trades for the benefit of the brokerage firm. The joint investigation with the FBI and PWBA revealed that the defendants made payoffs totaling approximately $1 million to the trustees over a three-year period.

A prominent New Mexico doctor was sentenced to nineteen years of imprisonment and two years of probation and ordered to pay more than $23 million in restitution and forfeit $11 million and his residence. Following the joint investigation with the FBI, IRS CID, and Postal Inspection Service, a jury found the physician and 8 coconspirators, including his accountant and attorney, guilty of conspiracy, mail fraud, and money laundering. The scheme to defraud DOL's Office of Workers' Compensation Program and other insurance programs involved the submission of false and excessive billings through several medical-related businesses in Texas, Mexico, and the Cayman Islands.

Following an OIG investigation, DOL terminated a $30.6 million annual contract with a Texas educational foundation which, for over thirty years, had administered the second largest Job Corps Center in the U.S. The investigation revealed that the president of the foundation conspired with a subcontractor to circumvent the DOL contract approval process. The investigation also found that the subcontractor, a pharmacy, overbilled the Job Corps Center up to five times the average cost for medications over a four-year period.

The former lead accountant and bookkeeper of a Seattle nonprofit organization that was partially funded by DOL's Employment and Training Administration was sentenced to 2 _ years of incarceration and three years of probation and ordered to pay more than $1.8 million in restitution. The joint investigation with the IRS CID, EPA-OIG, and FBI determined that the absence of internal controls facilitated the five-year embezzlement scheme, allowing the former accountant to issue checks to himself and members of his family.

Training, qualifications, and application procedures are similar to those found under the Department of Agriculture. For further information, visit the OIG DOL online at http://www.oig.dol.gov or contact:

Office of the Inspector General
U.S. Department of Labor
200 Constitution Avenue NW, Room S-1303
Washington, D.C. 20210
Telephone: (202) 693-5100

DEPARTMENT OF STATE

The Department of State advises the President in the formulation and execution of foreign policy and promotes the long-range security and well-being of the United States. The Department determines and analyzes the facts relating to American overseas interests, makes recommendations on policy and future action, and takes the necessary steps to carry out established policy. In so doing, the Department continuously consults with the American public, the Congress, other U.S. departments and agencies, and foreign governments; negotiates treaties and agreements with foreign nations; speaks for the United States in the United Nations and other international organization in which the United States participates; and represents the United States at international conferences.

OFFICE OF INSPECTOR GENERAL

The Office of Inspector General is an independent office that audits, inspects, and investigates the programs and activities of all elements of the Department of State and the Broadcasting Board of Governors for International Broadcasting. The Inspector General reports directly to the Secretary, the Broadcasting Board of Governors, and the Congress on the results of this work and makes recommendations to promote economy and efficiency and to detect and prevent fraud, waste, and mismanagement in the Department's programs and operations.

The Office of Investigations conducts criminal, civil, and administrative investigations, usually to follow up on allegations of wrongdoing received from State Department management and employees, other OIG units, the Inspector General of other agencies, the Congress, the OIG Hotline, and the general public. The types of investigations conducted by OIG cover a wide range of criminal and civil misconduct. In addition, because of the worldwide nature of State Department operations, OIG investigative activities take place in locations across the United States and around the world.

Investigative Initiatives

As a result of a joint investigation between OIG and Diplomatic Security, a foreign service officer and a foreign national were arrested in Illinois and Florida for the sale of U.S. visas at a U.S. embassy. In addition, $1.8 million in cash, gold bars, and other assets representing the proceeds of the visa sales were seized. Prosecution of both the officer and the foreign national is pending. The officer has resigned from the Foreign Service and has been incarcerated since his arrest. The investigation also determined that three foreign service nationals employed by the embassy also were involved in the visa sales and were subsequently terminated from employment.

OIG conducted a joint investigation with the FBI based on information that a school principal in Colorado had been engaged in a scheme to assist Russian nationals in fraudulently obtaining visas to enter the United States. The investigation developed evidence that this individual had used his position as an educator to submit letters to the U.S. Embassy in Moscow in support of applications for tourist visas. In these letters, he falsely claimed the applicants would participate in cultural and educational activities in the United States. Investigators determined that the principal submitted false information over a period of four years, that he had been aware that most applicants did not plan to return to Russia, and that he had accepted fees from the applicants for obtaining the visas. The principal was sentenced to ten months of imprisonment.

OIG conducted an investigation into allegations that a Foreign Service Officer wrote bad checks to the U.S. embassy of assignment. The loss to the government was about $15,000. The officer was sentenced to three years of probation, four months of home detention, and ordered to make full restitution to the U.S. government.

Training, qualifications, and application procedures are similar to those found under the Department of Agriculture. For further information, visit the OIG-State Department Web site at http://www.oig.state.gov or contact:

Office of Inspector General
Department of State
2201 C Street, NW, Room 6817
Washington, D.C. 20520-6817
Telephone: (202) 647-9450

DEPARTMENT OF TRANSPORTATION

The U.S. Department of Transportation establishes the nation's overall transportation policy. Under its umbrella there are ten administrations whose jurisdictions include highway planning, development, and construction; urban mass transit; railroads; aviation; and the safety of waterways, ports, highways, and oil and gas pipelines. Decisions made by the Department, in conjunction with the appropriate state and local officials, strongly affect other programs, such as land planning, energy conservation, scarce resource utilization, and technological change.

OFFICE OF INSPECTOR GENERAL

The Department's Office of Inspector General has given top priority to several transportation issues, including aviation safety and the investigation of suspected unapproved aircraft parts (SUP), the DOT's Motor Carrier Safety Program, and the Hazardous Material (HazMat) Transportation Safety Program. In addition, through the Transportation Equity Act, (TEA-21), DOT is infusing $217 billion into the economy to rebuild the nation's surface transportation infrastructure.

OIG Initiatives

Aviation Safety and Suspected Unapproved Aircraft Parts (SUP)

Because of the serious safety risks associated with SUPs, Congress made it a federal crime to intentionally misrepresent the condition of an aircraft part. SUPs include counterfeit aircraft parts and parts not repaired or manufactured according to Federal Aviation Administration (FAA)– approved standards. OIG works with the FBI, U.S. Customs, and the Defense Criminal Investigative Service to conduct proactive undercover sting operations along with traditional investigations to combat the SUP problem. OIG also works closely with the FAA, which has regulatory oversight of the aviation industry.

On April 5, 2000, the Wendell H. Ford Aviation Investment and Reform Act for the 21st Century was signed into law. Section 506 of the Act, titled Prevention of Frauds Involving Aircraft or Space Vehicle Parts in Interstate or Foreign Commerce, substantially increased the criminal penalties for those convicted of trafficking in substandard aircraft parts.

Motor Carrier Safety Program

Statistics show that over 5,000 people are killed each year in accidents involving large trucks. Many such accidents have been attributed to driver fatigue, unsafe vehicles, and unqualified operators.

To help protect the safety of the traveling public, the inspection program of the Department's Federal Motor Carrier Safety Administration (FMCSA) enforces the Federal Motor Carrier Safety Regulations with civil remedies. Among these regulations are laws governing the amount of time a driver can operate a commercial motor vehicle without rest, requirements for obtaining a commercial driver's license, maintenance of large trucks, and testing of commercial drivers for drug and alcohol abuse.

In furtherance of FMCSA's inspection program, OIG special agents investigate allegations that companies and individuals have violated criminal statutes relative to the Motor Carrier Safety Regulations.

Contract/Grant Fraud Investigations

The Transportation Equity Act (TEA-21) is infusing billions of dollars into the economy to rebuild the nation's surface transportation infrastructure. Another program, the Aviation Investment and Reform Act will commit an additional $40 billion for modernization and stability of our nation's aviation system. To protect the integrity of these and other transportation-related programs against fraud, waste, and abuse, the OIG has made investigating contract and grant fraud one of its top priorities.

OIG has designated a national contract/grant fraud coordinator and regional specialists to coordinate fraud prevention, detection, and investigation efforts with DOT components, such as the Federal Highway Administration, the Federal Transit Administration, and the Federal Aviation Administration. These specialists also coordinate efforts to combat contract and grant fraud with state DOTs and grantees that manage TEA-21, AIR-21, and other transportation-related funds.

Hazardous Materials Safety Investigations

The Office of Hazardous Materials Safety, which is within DOT's Research and Special Programs Administration (RSPA), is responsible for coordinating a national safety program for the transportation of HazMat by air, rail, highway, and water. In addition to RSPA, there are several other DOT Administrations involved in HazMat-related matters, including the Federal Aviation Administration, the U.S. Coast Guard, and the Federal Railroad Administration

Most criminal violations of HazMat regulations involve falsification and misrepresentation of documentation used to identify products being shipped. Misrepresenting the actual product being shipped can jeopardize the safety of the traveling public. In combating this serious safety-related problem, OIG special agents work with FBI, EPA/CID, and other federal and state officials to investigate these matters and report them to the Department of Justice for prosecution.

Investigative Initiatives

A former Federal Highway Administration official was sentenced in U.S. District Court in Alexandria, Virginia, to twenty-seven months in prison and twenty-four months of probation and ordered to pay $73,000 in restitution following his guilty plea to bribery and wire fraud charges. His wife previously pled guilty to paying a kickback and served thirty days in jail, sixty days of home detention, and was ordered to pay $23,000 in restitution. The official had authority over FHWA contractors who performed transportation research and engineering projects under multi-million dollar government contracts. In return for awarding contracts, the official and his wife solicited and received approximately $150,000 in personal loans and consulting contracts and used a series of pass-through companies and a business name to conceal their activity.

A citizen of Puerto Rico was placed on thirty-six months of probation and eight months of home confinement and ordered to pay $5,214 in restitution to American Airlines by a U.S. District Court judge in Brooklyn for illegally offering hazardous materials to an air carrier for shipment. He utilized curbside check-in at New York's LaGuardia Airport in an attempt to ship a box containing flammable liquids aboard an American Airlines flight to Florida. Investigation revealed that he concealed the box's DOT-required hazardous materials placard and that he falsely declared to a skycap that the box contained books. Baggage handlers detected a solvent-type odor and discovered the box to be leaking.

A former general manager of Tam Metal Products, Inc., of Mahwah, New Jersey, was convicted of conspiracy to commit wire fraud for his role in a scheme involving aircraft parts and was placed on twelve months of probation and fined $5,000 by a U.S. District Court judge in Trenton. In 1996, Menasco Aerospace of Ontario, Canada, ordered metal parts from Tam Metal products for Boeing 757 wheel assemblies, specifying that the parts were to be heat-treated by a Boeing-authorized treater. The Tam Metal official falsely represented that the parts had been heat-treated when some were not. Without heat-treating, aviation parts may crack and jeopardize the traveling public.

A truck driver for Extec USA in Lester, Pennsylvania, was sentenced to five months in jail and fined $2,500 in U.S. District Court in Philadelphia after pleading guilty to falsifying his daily driver's log book. He was involved in a fatal accident in May 1999. At the time of the fatal accident, his log book reflected he was off duty when, in fact, he was driving without a rest break.

Training, qualifications, and application procedures are similar to those found under the Department of Agriculture. For further information, visit the DOT/OIG Web site at http://www.oig.dot.gov or contact:

Office of Inspector General
Department of Transportation
400 - 7th Street, SW, Room 9210
Washington, D.C. 20590
Telephone: (202) 366-1959

DEPARTMENT OF THE TREASURY

The Department of the Treasury performs four basic functions: formulating and recommending economic, financial, tax, and fiscal policies; serving as financial agent for the U.S. Government; enforcing the law; and manufacturing coins and currency.

The Department's mission is to promote prosperous and stable American and world economies, manage the government's finances, protect our financial systems and our nation's leaders, foster a safe and drug-free America, and continue to build a strong institution for the future.

OFFICE OF INSPECTOR GENERAL

The Inspector General Act Amendments of 1988 consolidated the Treasury's existing OIG and those portions of the Offices of Internal Affairs in the Bureau of Alcohol, Tobacco and Firearms (ATF); the U.S. Customs Service; and Office of Inspection in the U.S. Secret Service that were engaged in auditing activities. The amendments provided that the Inspector General would initiate, conduct, and supervise internal audits and investigations within the Department. The amendments also provided that the Inspector General would oversee internal investigations made by the Offices of Internal Affairs and Inspection in the ATF, Customs, and Secret Service and internal audits and investigations of IRS' Inspection Service.

The OIG performs reviews of Treasury's many roles, which include such diverse functions as striking commemorative medals, enforcing national firearms and explosives laws, and investigating financial institution fraud. Treasury, as one of the oldest federal agencies, performs some of the most fundamental governmental activities, including collecting and borrowing the money to run the United States government and enforcing federal laws.

Investigative Initiatives

The OIG investigated the theft of Customs and FLETC equipment from FLETC that was worth thousands of dollars. Following the investigation, a FLETC employee and a Customs employee were arrested and convicted in connection with the theft. The Customs employee was sentenced to three years in prison and a $500 fine; the FLETC employee was sentenced to six months in prison and received 30 months of probation. A third defendant, a nonfederal employee, was arrested on a federal bench warrant, convicted, and sentenced to three years in prison and a $500 fine. State charges were filed against a fourth individual, a former FLETC employee. As a result of the investigation, stolen property was recovered, including television sets, videotapes, office supplies, and a camera.

An IRS District Counsel used government resources to write a book about the IRS for personal monetary gain. He spent a large portion of his official work time drafting and editing the book on a government computer. He also directed IRS employees to photocopy the book on a government copy machine. The District Counsel resigned after receiving a notice of proposed adverse action for reduction in grade.

An Office of the Comptroller of the Currency (OCC) employee contacted the OIG in regard to the suspicious activity of another OCC employee. An OIG investigation found that a senior performance development specialist falsely certified OCC contractor's invoices. The employee, who was serving as the contracting officer's technical representative (COTR) on the contract, falsely certified that the contractor rendered services that had not been provided to the OCC. Although the employee stated she made the certifications to ensure the availability of funding and not for personal gain, her actions nonetheless resulted in $41,990 of improper payments to the contractor. Investigation led to the employee's termination.

An OIG investigation disclosed that a GS-14 Senior Intelligence Research Specialist improperly used his official position, time, and government computer resources. The analyst gathered and solicited information about the Church of Scientology and acted as an unpaid tax consultant to members of a group opposed to Scientology while on official duty. He also actively assisted in the creation of an Internet Web site designed to discredit members of the Church of Scientology while on official duty. The analyst also used his position to conduct twenty-seven unauthorized queries/searches of the Treasury Enforcement Communications System (TECS) to obtain information on himself and several Indian nationals with whom he maintained a personal relationship. The investigation also revealed that the analyst violated agency ethics policies regarding approval for outside employment when he provided written articles for a monthly newsletter on countering money laundering published by an associate in the United Kingdom. In addition, he used official time and government computer resources to access the Internet for personal reasons for significant periods of time while on duty and paid overtime. While the U.S. Attorney's Office declined prosecution in this matter, investigation did result in the employee's resignation.

Auditing Initiative

Audits at departmental offices of the Office of Financial Enforcement (OFE), IRS, Customs, and the Office of the Comptroller of the Currency identified several areas where implementation of the Bank Secrecy Act (BSA) could be improved. For example, OFE had a backlog of 200 civil penalty referrals and cases for noncompliance with BSA's reporting and record-keeping requirements and the IRS needed to improve processing and security controls to ensure that all BSA documents were complete and correct, processed on time, and adequately safeguarded. In addition, Customs needed to improve methods for controlling, submitting, processing, and correcting BSA documents and examiners at the Comptroller of the Currency had inconsistently reported BSA violations identified during bank examinations.

Training, qualifications, and application procedures are similar to those found under the Department of Agriculture. For further information, visit the Treasury OIG Web site at http://www.treas.gov/oig or contact:

Office of Inspector General
Department of the Treasury
1500 Pennsylvania Avenue NW, Room 2412
Washington, D.C. 20220
Telephone: (202) 622-1090
Fax: (202) 622-2151

Office of the Treasury Inspector General for Tax Administration

In July 1998, the Congress passed the Internal Revenue Service Restructuring and Reform Act of 1998 (RRA98) and created the newest statutory Office of Inspector General, the Treasury Inspector General for Tax Administration (TIGTA).

This latest amendment to the Inspector General (IG) Act of 1978 added the TIGTA to execute all duties and responsibilities of an Inspector General with respect to the Department and the Secretary of the Treasury and all matters relating to the Internal Revenue Service (IRS), including those of the IRS Oversight Board and the IRS Office of Chief Counsel.

This change in the IG Act, effective January 18, 1999, transferred to TIGTA all the powers and responsibilities of the former IRS Office of Chief Inspector, except for conducting background checks of and providing physical security to IRS employees.

The TIGTA Office of Inspector General provides leadership and coordination and recommends policy for activities designed to:

- promote economy, efficiency, and effectiveness in the administration of the internal revenue laws

- prevent and detect fraud and abuse in the programs and operations of the IRS and related entities

The TIGTA is also responsible for:

- conducting and supervising independent and objective audits and investigations relating to IRS programs and operations

- protecting the IRS against external attempts to corrupt or threaten its employees

- reviewing and making recommendations regarding existing and proposed legislation and regulations relating to the programs and operations of the IRS

- recommending actions to resolve fraud and other serious problems, abuses, and deficiencies in the programs and operations of the IRS

- informing the Secretary and the Congress of these problems and the progress made in resolving them

Authorities

The Treasury Inspector General for Tax Administration has all the authorities granted under the Inspector General Act of 1978. In addition, the TIGTA has access to tax information in the performance of its responsibilities and the authority to report criminal violations directly to the Department of Justice. The TIGTA and the Commissioner of the IRS have established policies and procedures delineating responsibilities to investigate offenses under the internal revenue laws.

The TIGTA provides a program of comprehensive auditing and investigative services of IRS operations and activities. This includes a national integrity program, which emphasizes deterrence and detection approaches to assist the IRS in ensuring the highest degree of integrity and ethics in its workforce.

Resources from the TIGTA Offices of Audit, Investigations, and Information Technology are jointly utilized to:

- inform IRS executives and managers of the importance of established internal controls both to protect government assets and revenue from fraud and to protect IRS employees from temptations

- proactively identify additional violators of fraud based on profiles of existing crimes

- identify for investigation suspicious instances of computer browsing through comparisons against established computerized patterns

- report to the Secretary of the Treasury, the IRS Commissioner, and the IRS Oversight Board internal control weaknesses that resulted in fraud, along with recommendations to correct the deficiencies

Training, qualifications, and application procedures are similar to those found under the Department of Agriculture. For further information, visit the TIGTA Web site at http://www.treas.gov/tigta or contact:

Treasury Inspector General for Tax Administration
IG:IG, 700A
1125 15th Street, NW
Washington, D.C. 20005
Telephone: (202) 622-6500

DEPARTMENT OF VETERANS AFFAIRS

The Department of Veterans Affairs (VA) was established March 15, 1989, with Cabinet rank, succeeding the Veterans Administration and assuming responsibility for providing federal benefits to veterans and their dependents. Headed by the Secretary of Veterans Affairs, VA is the second-largest department in the federal government and operates nationwide programs of health care, assistance services, and national cemeteries. VA's mission is to serve America's veterans and their families with dignity and compassion and to be their principal advocate in ensuring that they receive the care, support, and recognition earned in service to the United States.

OFFICE OF INSPECTOR GENERAL

VA OIG agents executive arrest/search warrants. (Photo courtesy of the Office of Inspector General, Department of Veterans Affairs.)

The Inspector General Act of 1978 established a statutory Inspector General in VA responsible for recommending policies designed to promote economy and efficiency in the administration of, and to prevent and detect fraud and abuse in, the programs and operations of VA. Special agents of VA OIG derive their federal law enforcement authority through an appointment as a Special Deputy United States Marshal. In performing its mandated oversight function, VA OIG conducts criminal, civil, and administrative investigations, audits, and health-care inspections of all VA activities. VA OIG investigators also work closely with VA Police in pursuing individuals responsible for committing a wide range of criminal offenses at VA facilities around the country, including assault, robbery, and illicit drug distribution. VA OIG agents often conduct investigations in cooperation with other federal, state, and local agencies and participate in a number of Benefits Fraud, Healthcare, and Drug Task Forces throughout the nation. Close liaison is maintained with the Department of Justice and the various offices of the U.S. Attorney, as well as state and local prosecutors.

VA OIG investigations originate from information developed by field and headquarters agents, and from complaints received at the VA OIG Hotline concerning allegations of fraud, waste, and abuse in the programs and operations of the Department. The hotline receives complaints from the general public, VA employees, veterans, Congress, the General Accounting Office, and other federal agencies.

Investigative Initiatives

A seven-year murder investigation by VA OIG agents and health-care inspectors, along with the Office of the U.S. Attorney and other agencies, led to the guilty plea of a doctor responsible for administering lethal injections of toxic substances to three patients at the VA Medical Center (VAMC) in Northport, N.Y. A fourth victim/patient survived the doctor's poison attack. The investigation involved an extensive records review, laboratory studies, and interviews with hundreds of witnesses in the United States and Africa. Prior to criminal charges being filed, the doctor fled the country and was hired as a physician in Zimbabwe, Africa, where he proceeded to administer lethal injections of toxic substances to two additional patients at Mnene Hospital. These patients survived and the doctor was suspended. Agents arrested the doctor in Chicago while he was en route from Africa to Saudi Arabia, where he had again been hired to work as a physician in a hospital. The doctor was sentenced to three consecutive life terms without parole for the Northport murders.

VA OIG agents and State Police making buy/bust in drug diversion investigation. (Photo courtesy of the Office of Inspector General, Department of Veterans Affairs.)

A joint investigation by VA OIG, FBI, IRS, and the Food and Drug Administration revealed that the director of an import/export company committed procurement fraud when he purchased nonmedical grade latex gloves and deceptively repackaged, labeled, and sold them as medical–grade gloves. The VA purchased more than 8 million mislabeled gloves and distributed them to fourteen VA Medical Centers nationwide. The defendant was charged with mail fraud and filing a false income tax statement. He was sentenced to forty-one months of incarceration, three years of supervised release, 300 hours of community service and ordered to pay restitution of more than $3 million to victims of the scheme.

A VA OIG investigation disclosed that a church pastor, acting as the president of a non-profit organization whose mission was to improve the quality of life for persons living in the area of the church, applied for a $500,000 VA Homeless Providers and Per Diem grant, which was to be used to provide transitional housing and vocational skills to homeless veterans. The application was approved and VA forwarded the first $200,000 to be used specifically to purchase and rehabilitate a building slated to be a veteran's living skills center. It was later determined that the pastor committed contract fraud as he never purchased the building and used more than $118,900 for purposes unrelated to the project.

Body exhumation under direction of Veterans Administration OIG agents in suspicious death investigation. (Photo courtesy of the Office of Inspector General, Department of Veterans Affairs.)

A former nurse was convicted of murdering four patients during her employment with the VA Medical Center (VAMC) in Northampton, Massachusetts. The five-year investigation by VA OIG and Massachusetts State Police commenced with the report of suspicious deaths at the VAMC. Exhumations and extensive laboratory and record analysis were conducted. The investigation determined that the nurse had injected each victim/patient with a lethal dose of epinephrine. The Attorney General authorized the Federal Prosecutor to seek the death penalty in this case. However, the nurse was sentenced to four consecutive life terms for the murder charges, two consecutive twenty-year terms for assault with intent to kill, and twenty- and ten-year concurrent terms for assaulting two other patients.

A VA Supervisory Claims Examiner was arrested by VA OIG agents after an investigation determined the employee created a fictitious computerized record of a 100 percent disabled veteran who were entitled to substantial benefits. Coworkers unwittingly authorized the fraudulent disability ratings. As a result of this scheme, monthly VA payments of $5,011 and ten special one-time payments were placed into an account that was controlled by the defendant. Total loss to VA was over $615,000. The employee was tried and convicted sentenced to a prison term, and ordered to make restitution.

Auditing Initiatives

An audit was performed to evaluate how effectively VA Medical Centers (VAMC) managed their pharmaceutical inventories. In a fiscal year, VAMC pharmaceutical purchases totaled $951 million. At any given time that year, the value of VAMCs' inventories was about $41 million. As a result of the successful transition to a pharmaceutical prime vendor distribution program over the past several years, VAMCs have substantially reduced their pharmacy inventories from levels previously maintained under VA's centralized depot system. However, inventories still exceeded current operating needs for many pharmaceutical items. Auditing coverage at four VAMCs with combined pharmaceutical inventories valued at $1.7 million found that about $820,000 (48 percent) was excess inventory. The excess inventories occurred because VAMCs relied on informal inventory methods and cushions of excess stock as a substitute for more structured inventory management. Inventory managers had not consistently or systematically determined their current inventory requirements based on item demand, safety requirements, and replenishment cycles. It was estimated that better management could reduce VAMC pharmaceutical inventories by $25 million and $6 million could be freed up by eliminating unnecessary year-end spending.

A review was conducted to identify opportunities to enhance oversight and review and implement cost containment measures to reduce costs associated with Workers Compensation Program (WCP) claims at one of VA's Veterans Integrated Service Networks (VISN). Selected claims were reviewed and network facility WCP specialists were assisted in identifying required case management actions. The review found additional effort was needed to strengthen case management to assure the appropriateness of some claims. It identified opportunities for the network to reduce annual costs by about $2.9 million, with an estimated lifetime benefit cost reduction of more than $37.9 million. The review also identified ten claims that were potentially fraudulent.

Training, qualifications, and application procedures are similar to those found under the Department of Agriculture. For further information, visit the VA Web site at http://www.va.gov/oig or contact:

Office of Inspector General
Office of Investigations
801 I Street, NW
Washington, D.C. 20420
Telephone: 202/565-7702

INDEPENDENT AGENCIES

AGENCY FOR INTERNATIONAL DEVELOPMENT

The Agency for International Development (AID) carries out economic assistance programs designed to help the people of developing countries to enhance their human and economic resources, increase their productive capacities and improve their quality of life, and to promote economic and political stability in friendly countries.

AID administers programs in areas such as agriculture, rural development and nutrition, health and population planning, housing and urban development, education and human resource development, energy, selected development activities, and private enterprise.

OFFICE OF INSPECTOR GENERAL

Investigations are carried out worldwide in response to complaints or allegations regarding violations of federal law, as well as certain noncriminal and civil matters. Criminal violations are referred to U.S. or host-government prosecuting officials for appropriate judicial consideration, and administrative irregularities are referred to cognizant USAID missions or AID/Washington management for administrative action.

In addition to criminal investigations, special agents conduct proactive inspections designed to seek out fraud, abuse, and areas of systemic weakness in AID programs and operations. When indicators of fraud are uncovered, full criminal investigations follow. When systemic weaknesses conducive to fraud are uncovered, they are brought to the attention of mission or AID/Washington management with recommendations for improvements to prevent future problems.

Investigative Initiatives

The OIG and eighteen other federal agencies participated in a joint investigation of a large consulting firm that yielded a settlement of $1,900,000. The investigation determined that the consulting firm had violated the Federal Acquisition Regulation through a practice of billing the federal government for subcontractor services prior to actually paying the subcontractors. The extent of the practice was revealed by a Defense Contract Agency audit, which disclosed that the firm had prematurely billed its government clients by an average of thirty-seven days 74 percent of the time. The consulting firm cooperated during the investigation and implemented measures to remedy the problem in the future.

The OIG resolved a case involving apparent violations of the Foreign Corrupt Practices Act that resulted in a civil penalty of $400,000 and $50,000 for government investigative costs. The investigation revealed that a large U.S. environmental firm had provided benefits to the chairman of a foreign organization to influence that individual to support the award of $36 million in contracts to the firm by USAID. The foreign organization, an instrument of the government of the United Arab Republic of Egypt, is responsible for operating sewage and waste-water treatment facilities in Egypt.

An OIG investigation resulted in the removal of a Foreign Service National employee after that individual attempted to smuggle computer parts and equipment into Bolivia using a USAID-issued airport pass. The employee was an expediter and had been issued the pass to gain entry to secured areas of the airport to facilitate incoming and outgoing shipments and customs clearance of private and U.S. government property. Due to the employee's extended length of service, the individual was allowed to resign in lieu of termination.

An OIG investigation resulted in the conviction of two companies (one German and one American) on one felony count each for participating in a criminal conspiracy to manipulate or rig bids on USAID-funded construction contracts in violation of the Sherman Antitrust Act. In sentencing each company, the Federal District Court noted both the depth of the involvement and degree of participation of each company in the scheme. The court then took into consideration each company's remorse as exhibited through its willingness to cooperate with the ongoing investigation. The result was a $30 million criminal fine imposed upon the German company and a $4.2 million criminal fine and $500,000 civil restitution payment imposed upon the American company. The investigation was conducted in coordination with the U.S. Department of Justice, Antitrust Division, Atlanta Field Office, and required coordination of extensive investigative activities in six countries on three continents. It required the use of a broad array of investigative techniques. These included the extensive use of Inspector General and grand jury subpoenas, the collection of documentary evidence in unprecedented amounts and in diverse overseas locations, the analysis of complex financial records, and the unprecedented use of an international search warrant.

Auditing Initiatives

USAID awarded more than 921 active contracts valued at approximately $1 million over a three-year period. Though the Federal Acquisition Streamlining Act of 1994 requires federal agencies to consider past performance as a factor when awarding new contracts, the OIG found that USAID had not implemented an effective program to evaluate contractor performance; less than 10 percent of the contractors had been evaluated. USAID has taken steps to implement an information system that would provide procurement officials with secure access to contractor past performance information. It would also allow USAID officials to obtain information from eight other federal agencies through the existing Internet-based system.

Responding to four OIG audits that identified computer security vulnerabilities, USAID has undertaken a course of action to improve computer security. USAID has crafted a Model Information System Security Program that provides a framework for identifying and disseminating to other agencies a complete set of best practices for implementing an effective computer security program. Recognized by the Chief Information Officers Council, General Services Administration, and others as an innovative and comprehensive approach, USAID's model is beneficial to the entire federal government.

TRAINING

Training, qualifications, and application procedures are similar to those found under the Department of Agriculture. For further information, contact:

Office of Inspector General
Agency for International Development
1300 Pennsylvania Avenue, NW, Room 6.06D
Washington, D.C. 20523
Telephone: (202) 712-1150

CENTRAL INTELLIGENCE AGENCY

The Central Intelligence Agency (CIA) collects, evaluates, and disseminates vital information on foreign political, military, economic, scientific, and other developments needed to safeguard national security.

OFFICE OF INSPECTOR GENERAL

As described in *CIA Entrance Examination* by John Quirk (ARCO, 1988), "the Inspector General (IG) is the investigative arm of the Director of Central Intelligence (DCI) and assists him and the heads of offices and directorates in improving the performance of CIA offices and personnel. The IG endeavors to assure that CIA activities are consistent with the laws and regulations that govern them. The IG conducts inspections of all CIA components to examine how well each carries out its function, whether organizational changes are in order, and the quality and performance of the personnel involved. He also makes special investigations and studies directed by the DCI."

The CIA's statutory Office of Inspector General was established in 1989 by amendments to the CIA Act of 1949. In addition to other duties, the OIG conducts investigations to prevent and detect fraud, waste, and abuse in CIA programs and operations.

For further information, contact:
Central Intelligence Agency
Room 2X30 New Headquarters
Washington, D.C. 20505
Telephone: (703) 874-2555

ENVIRONMENTAL PROTECTION AGENCY

The mission of the Environmental Protection Agency (EPA) is to protect human health and to safeguard the natural environment —air, water, and land—upon which life depends. EPA's purpose is to ensure that federal laws protecting health and the environment are enforced fairly and effectively and that efforts to reduce environmental risks are based on the best scientific information.

OFFICE OF INSPECTOR GENERAL

The mission of the Office of Inspector General is to promote economy, effectiveness, and efficiency within the EPA and to prevent and detect fraud, waste, and abuse in agency programs and operations. The Office of Investigations conducts criminal, civil, and administrative investigations in the areas of program integrity, contracts and procurement, assistance agreements, employee integrity, and computer forensics. The current emphasis is on initiatives to uncover criminal activity in the award and delivery of EPA assistance agreements and contracts and in the conduct of laboratory work by contractors. The criminal investigation of computer intrusions that affect EPA's systems is another top priority.

Investigative Initiatives

A private utility company and its corporate president pleaded guilty to a criminal charge of violation of the Clean Water Act. In the plea agreement, the defendants admitted to not disclosing to government officials that the wastewater discharged by the utility directly into a Florida bay was not properly treated. As part of the plea, the utility company and the corporate president paid a total of $1.75 million in restitution and fines. Of that amount. $1.2 million was paid directly to three different Florida environmental trust funds for environmental restoration and enhancement projects.

A Virginia company entered into an agreement with the United States to pay $415,000 to settle civil claims arising under the federal False Claims Act. The Federal Acquisition Regulations (FAR) prohibit government contractors from billing the government for subcontractor costs prior to actually paying those costs (Paid Cost Rule). The company allegedly billed the EPA, the Department of Defense, and the National Aeronautics and Space Administration prematurely for subcontractor costs and other direct costs. The company denied any criminal act but acknowledged that certain billings did not fully comply with the Paid Cost Rule. The company, therefore, agreed to compensate the government for the interest it lost as a result of the premature billings and for a portion of the cost of the investigation, for a total of $415,000. The settlement agreement incorporated separate administrative proceedings conducted by the EPA, Office of Suspension and Debarment, as lead agency.

The former lead accountant of a nonprofit organization was sentenced to a thirty-month prison term and ordered to pay $1.8 million in restitution for his role in various embezzlement schemes. His daughter received five years of probation as a result of her involvement, following her pleading guilty to wire fraud. The organization was funded by the EPA as a nonprofit organization whose mission is to serve the needs of older Asian and Pacific Americans throughout the United States through employment and training programs. The lead accountant devised various schemes in which he issued thousands of payroll and travel advance checks to himself and immediate family members, embezzling in excess of $1.8 million. He also failed to report the income from the embezzled funds on his federal income tax returns, resulting in a tax loss of $609,083. His daughter devised and executed a scheme to obtain a home mortgage loan. In application papers, she claimed to be employed by a fictitious company, variously claiming earnings of $4,800 and $5,700 per month. She also sent, via wire facsimile, a copy of her checking account monthly statement showing deposits of more than $10,000, knowing that all the deposits were actually derived from funds provided by her father.

A state regulatory agency received assistance agreement funds from the EPA to enforce federal and state air quality laws. The former executive director of the agency agreed to accept $169,750 from a regulated entity for advising them on pending applications before the state agency. This former executive director was convicted for accepting an unlawful gratuity and conspiracy to defraud the United States. Several accomplices were also convicted for aiding and abetting in the acceptance of an unlawful gratuity and conspiracy to defraud the United States.

Two representatives of an Native American environmental coalition each pleaded guilty to a one-count criminal misdemeanor for embezzling from a tribal organization. The coalition's executive director and office manager used a coalition credit card for personal expenses and other unauthorized purposes, such as cashing in earned leave/ compensatory time without permission to do so. The coalition receives part of its funding from U.S. government agencies, including the EPA.

A contractor employee admitted that he created a shell company to receive the kickbacks paid by vendors who subcontracted with his employer, a government contractor. The vendors paid more than $2.6 million in kickbacks to the employee and his coconspirators in exchange for favorable treatment. Approximately $800,000 of the kickbacks were in connection with government contracts. The employee pled guilty to a two-count criminal charge of conspiracy to violate the Anti-Kickback Act of 1986 and with filing a false federal income tax return. His codefendants pled guilty to a two-count criminal charge of violations of the Anti-Kickback Act and aiding the employee in filing a false tax return.

Training, qualifications, and application procedures are standard for GS-1811 special agents. For further information, contact:

Environmental Protection Agency
Office of Inspector General
Office of Investigations
1200 Pennsylvania Avenue, Mail Code 2431
Washington, D.C. 20460
Telephone: (202) 260-1109

FEDERAL EMERGENCY MANAGEMENT AGENCY

The Federal Emergency Management Agency is the central agency within the federal government that is responsible for emergency planning, preparedness, mitigation, response, and recovery. Working closely with state and local governments, the agency funds emergency programs, offers technical guidance and training, and deploys federal resources in times of catastrophic disasters. These coordinated activities ensure a broad-based program to protect life and property and provide recovery assistance after a disaster.

OFFICE OF INSPECTOR GENERAL

Congress enacted the Inspector General Act in 1978 to ensure integrity and efficiency in government. A 1988 amendment to the Act (Public Law 100-504) created the position of Inspector

General in FEMA, a position that is subject to presidential appointment and senatorial confirmation. Before April 16, 1989, when the law became effective, the OIG was established administratively and the Director of FEMA appointed the Inspector General.

The statute conferred new authorities and responsibilities on the OIG, including the power to issue subpoenas, responsibility for various reports, and authority to review relevant proposed laws and regulations to determine their potential impact on FEMA programs and operations. The law also mandates that the OIG audit and investigate FEMA programs.

Investigative Initiatives

A former cabinet member of the Virgin Islands (V.I.) government was convicted in a jury trial of two counts of filing false claims (18 U.S. Code 287) for disaster-related expenses. The official hired a contractor without competitive bids to repair the roofs of two different buildings that had been damaged as a result of Hurricane Marilyn. The contractor did not perform repairs to either roof, but submitted invoices totaling more than $130,000, which the cabinet member certified and approved. The contractor was sentenced to twenty-one months in prison and thirty-six months of supervised probation, fined $40,000, and ordered to make immediate restitution of $113,000. The former official was sentenced to thirty months in prison and thirty-six months of supervised probation, fined $50,000, and ordered to make immediate restitution of $80,000.

A local county commissioner caused false claims to be filed for disaster recovery operations in a north Georgia county. The claims filed for certain debris removal projects showed equipment rental costs for several pieces of equipment. Because the costs appeared excessive, an investigation was conducted, revealing that these were not rental costs, but rather purchase agreements with vendors. The case was ultimately resolved through an administrative resolution where FEMA recovered $100,000 in disaster funds that were applicable to the equipment rental costs overcharges.

Auditing Initiatives

The California Office of Emergency Services awarded $41.8 million to the Los Angeles City Police Department to cover a variety of law enforcement activities during the civil unrest that started in April 1992. The Department claimed $41.8 million. The claim included $3,717,193 in questionable costs (federal share [FS] $2,787,895) resulting from unrelated force account labor with benefits and unsupported costs.

FEMA awarded $15.9 million to the metropolitan government of Nashville-Davidson County, Tennessee, for debris removal, emergency protective measures, and road repairs as a result of an April 1998 tornado. The county claimed $15.2 million. The claim included questionable costs of $519,976 (FS $389,982) resulting from excessive equipment and contract charges, unsupported costs, unauthorized activities, and duplicate charges.

The California Office of Emergency Services awarded $1.7 million to the city of Oxnard to assist in the recovery from severe rainstorms, wind, flooding, and mud slides in February 1992. The city claimed $1.7 million. The claim included $376,550 in questionable costs (FS $282,413) resulting from nondisaster-related costs, unsupported project costs, and amounts covered by FEMA's administrative allowance.

Training, qualifications, and application procedures are similar to those found under the Department of Agriculture. For further information, contact:

Office of Inspector General
Federal Emergency Management Agency
500 C. Street SW, Room 505
Washington D.C. 20472
Telephone: (202) 646-3910

GENERAL SERVICES ADMINISTRATION

The General Services Administration (GSA) establishes policy and provides the government with an economical and efficient system for the management of its property and records, including construction and operation of buildings; procurement and distribution of supplies; utilization and disposal of property; transportation, traffic, and communications management; stockpiling of strategic materials; and the management of the government-wide automatic data processing resources program.

OFFICE OF INSPECTOR GENERAL

The GSA Office of Inspector General (OIG) was established on October 1, 1978, as one of the original twelve OIGs created by the Inspector General Act of 1978. The OIG's five components work together to perform the missions mandated by Congress.

The OIG provides nationwide coverage of GSA programs and activities. The components include:

- The Office of Audits, an evaluative unit staffed with auditors and analysts who provide comprehensive coverage of GSA operations through program performance reviews, internal controls assessments, and financial and compliance audits. The office also conducts external reviews in support of GSA contracting officials to ensure fair contract prices and adherence to contract terms and conditions. In addition, the office provides advisory and consulting services to assist agency managers in evaluating and improving their programs.

- The Office of Investigations, an investigative unit that manages a nationwide program to prevent and detect illegal and/or improper activities involving GSA programs, operations, and personnel

- The Office of Counsel, an in-house legal staff that provides legal advice and assistance to all OIG components, represents the OIG in litigation arising out of or affecting OIG operations, and manages the OIG legislative/regulatory review functions

- The Internal Evaluation Staff, a multidisciplinary staff that plans and directs field office appraisals and conducts internal affairs reviews and investigations

- The Office of Administration, an in-house staff that provides information systems and budgetary, administrative, personnel, and communications services

Investigative and Auditing Initiative

A U.S. District Court entered a $5.6 million civil judgment for the United States against a partitions supply firm. The court found that the firm had defrauded the government. A joint audit and investigation disclosed that the contractor falsified laboratory test results in order to obtain its GSA contract. Independent laboratory tests confirmed that partitions sold to federal agencies contained a cheap, flammable cardboard filler, rather than the fire-retardant material specified in the contract. Previously the company and its president had been convicted on conspiracy, submitting false claims, and preparing false statements. The company and its president were each fined $365,000. In addition, the president was sentenced to nine years in prison (five years suspended) and five years of probation. Both parties were also barred from doing business with the government for a three-year period.

OIG Initiative

Telecommunication Fraud

The OIG is a principal participant in the New York Electronic Crimes Task Force (NYECTF). NYECTF members include the Secret Service, Department of Defense, Department of Justice, New York City Police, and telecommunications industry representatives. The purpose of the task force is to investigate telecommunications fraud, primarily involving federal facilities within the New York metropolitan area. GSA is the principal provider of telecommunications services for these facilities. The OIG is a permanent member of the NYECTF and frequently is the lead agency in the investigations.

The task force investigates several types of telecommunications fraud, including cloned cellular telephones, stolen calling card numbers, and intrusions of Private Branch Exchange (PBX) telephone switches. Cellular telephones are cloned through the use of electronic devices that capture the electronic signatures of the telephones. These signatures are programmed into other cellular telephones, which are then used to illegally make unauthorized telephone calls. Calling card numbers are stolen either through the use of electronic devices, which intercept the caller's use of the number, or by "shoulder surfing" which is the simple act of watching someone dial in the card numbers. PBXs, or telephone switches, are usually breached through their voice mail systems. Individuals may use their computers to locate and break into mailboxes that can be used to make outgoing telephone calls. In all of these scenarios, access is often sold to other individuals who make telephone calls around the world until the misuse is detected.

Two individuals pled guilty to charges related to fraudulent access of the White House Communications Agency (WHCA) telephone system. One individual, a U.S. Army Sergeant assigned to WHCA, pled guilty pursuant to a plea agreement in the U.S. District Court.

The investigation disclosed that several individuals had used their telephone lines to illegally access the PBX of WHCA. The investigation identified the sergeant as having supplied at least one individual with access numbers to the WHCA PBX. These numbers allowed that individual to access and make telephone calls from the WHCA system.

The OIG's goal is to prevent such crimes by vigorously prosecuting offenders.

PROTECTION OF FEDERAL FACILITIES AND PERSONNEL

Building Security

GSA's Federal Protective Service (FPS) has had an increased responsibility for security and law enforcement in federal facilities since the 1995 bombing of the federal building in Oklahoma City. Because of the heightened importance of the Agency's security mission, the OIG has directed several reviews toward major activities within the FPS, and aspects of those reviews have been highlighted in semiannual reports over the past several years.

Contract Security Guard Program

GSA contracts with private security firms for both armed and unarmed guards at federal facilities. Currently, there are almost 7,000 contract security guards nationwide. FPS is attempting to create a national program and has determined that five program areas must be standardized in all regional guard contracts. These include guard training, weapons and ammunition, guard eligibility, a basic written examination, and suitability and certification requirements.

Training, qualifications, and application procedures are similar to those found under the Department of Agriculture. For further information, contact:

Office of Inspector General
General Services Administration
1800 F Street, NW, Room 5340
Washington, D.C. 20405
Telephone: (202) 501-0450

NATIONAL AERONAUTICS AND SPACE ADMINISTRATION

The National Aeronautics and Space Administration conducts research for the solution of problems of flight within and outside the earth's atmosphere and develops, constructs, tests, and operates aeronautical and space vehicles. It conducts activities required for the exploration of space with manned and unmanned vehicles and arranges for the most effective utilization of the scientific and engineering resources of the United States with other nations involved in space activities for peaceful purposes.

OFFICE OF INSPECTOR GENERAL

The Office of Inspector General is a diverse, multidisciplinary workforce located at headquarters and in offices at all NASA Centers, the Jet Propulsion Laboratory (JPL), and other sites throughout the country. The current organizational structure focuses resources on those areas representing the agency's highest vulnerabilities, especially safety, procurement, information technology (IT) security, and export of sensitive technology controls and processes. Under the general direction of the Inspector General, the Assistant Inspectors General (AIG's) and managers for the OIG's four major program offices (Office of Audits, Office of Criminal Investigations, Network and Advanced Technology Protection Office, and Office of Inspections, Administrative Investigations, and Assessments) develop, implement, and manage their respective programs.

The Counsel to the Inspector General and the OIG legal staff provides advice and assistance on a variety of legal issues and matters relating to the OIG's reviews of agency programs and operations. The AIG for Management and External Relations (AIGMER) serves as the congressional liaison and coordinates outreach activities; advises the Inspector General and all other OIG managers and staff on administrative, budget, and personnel matters; and oversees OIG adherence to management policies.

Its two criminal investigative units, the Network and Advanced Technology Protection Office (NATPO) and the Office of Criminal Investigations (OCI) conduct the NASA OIG's law enforcement activities. NATPO, staffed with investigators who specialize in cyber-crimes and computer forensics professionals, investigates statutory violations of the agency's electronic data processing and advanced technology programs. Incidents of computer intrusion are increasing in frequency and sophistication. NATPO not only detects criminal computer intrusions, but also works with other elements of the OIG and agency management to assist in protecting the integrity and enhancing the security of NASA's IT systems. OCI, consisting of trained special agents and support staff, focuses its efforts and resources on preventing and detecting waste in NASA's procurement activities, fraud, and other criminal activities. Like other OIG units, OCI conducts a vigorous outreach and awareness program aimed at preventing and detecting crimes against NASA.

Investigative Initiatives

Following an investigation conducted by special agents of the OIG's NATPO and the Federal Bureau of Investigation, a New York man pled guilty to five counts of gaining unauthorized access to nonpublic computers, unauthorized interception of communications, and unauthorized possession of access devices (credit card numbers and usernames/passwords) after he gained unauthorized access to computers at a NASA Center. Investigators also found that the hacker possessed credit card numbers, usernames, and passwords for other computer systems. As a result of his guilty plea, the man faced a maximum sentence of twenty-seven years in prison and fines totaling $900,000.

In another case, OIG OCI special agents investigated allegations of a kickback scheme perpetrated by individuals representing an industrial supply vendor and five former contractor employees. The vendor paid kickbacks to six employees of a former NASA prime contractor at one of NASA's installations to obtain noncompeted subcontract awards. The scheme caused NASA to order millions of dollars worth of materials that were not needed. In some instances, the materials were subsequently stolen and resold to NASA. The vendor pled guilty to paying kickbacks, 3 prime contractor employees pled guilty to kickback conspiracy charges, and 3 employees pled guilty to felony theft of NASA government property.

Other NASA OIG Organizations

The Office of Audits (OA) provides a broad range of professional auditing and advisory services that focus on key issues impacting the NASA mission. OA reports address program and operational areas with a high vulnerability of risk and impact on NASA operations, internal control weaknesses, and other management concerns. OA's goal is to enhance the protection of NASA personnel and resources through published reports, consulting engagements, commentary on NASA policies, and deterrence of crime, fraud, waste, and abuse. OA activities have included numerous audits of the International Space Station, contractor exports of controlled technologies, information technology systems, and a variety of other topics.

The Office of Inspections, Administrative Investigations, and Assessments (IAIA) provides timely and constructive evaluations of agency programs, projects, and organizations. The IAIA staff conducts assessments of policies, processes, programs, and operations to determine whether resources are effectively managed and applied toward accomplishing NASA's missions. The IAIA staff also conducts administrative investigations involving noncriminal allegations of administrative wrongdoing. These investigations include misuse of government equipment and other resources, violations of the Standards of Conduct, and other forms of misconduct. IAIA evaluation reports have been published on a wide range of subjects, including astronaut medical transport aircraft, physical security processes, the agency's use of the metric measurement system, and contract management processes.

IAIA and other OIG staff members include professional aerospace technologists, attorneys, auditors, computer specialists, management analysts, operations research analysts, procurement specialists, and professionals in other fields. The IAIA staff provides technical expertise in various specialties, such as procurement, information technology security, personnel, and aerospace technology to OIG auditors, attorneys, and other staff members.

Training, qualifications, and application procedures are similar to those found under the Department of Agriculture. Vacancy announcements, as well as more information about NASA OIG activities, can be found at the NASA OIG Web site at http://www.hq.nasa.gov/office/oig/hq/ or by contacting:

Personnel Officer
Code W
Office of the Inspector General
National Aeronautics and Space Administration
300 E Street, SW
Washington, D.C. 20546
Telephone: (202) 358-1220

NUCLEAR REGULATORY COMMISSION

The Nuclear Regulatory Commission licenses and regulates civilian use of nuclear energy to protect public health and safety and the environment. This is achieved by licensing persons and companies to build and operate nuclear reactors and other facilities and to own and use nuclear materials. The Commission makes rules and sets standards for these types of licenses. It also carefully inspects the activities of the persons and companies licensed to ensure that they do not violate the safety rules of the Commission.

OFFICE OF INSPECTOR GENERAL

The Office of the Inspector General supports the public health and safety mission of the NRC by carrying out its mandate to independently and objectively conduct and supervise audits and conduct investigations concerning NRC's programs and operations; to prevent and detect fraud, waste, and abuse; and to promote economy, efficiency, and effectiveness in NRC programs and operations.

The Inspector General serves under the general supervision of the NRC Chairman, and keeps the Chairman and Congress fully and currently informed about significant problems disclosed by its audits and investigations, recommends corrective actions, and monitors NRC's progress in implementing these actions.

Investigative Initiative

OIG conducted an investigation into a complaint from an NRC contractor who alleged that she was receiving obscene and threatening electronic mail (e-mail) messages from an unknown individual on her government computer. OIG's investigation included issuing NRC OIG subpoenas and a Maryland Circuit Court Grand Jury subpoena to determine the source of the e-mails. Consequently, OIG identified and interviewed the individual who made the threatening e-mails. The individual admitted sending the e-mails to the contractor. The subject was arrested and prosecuted for electronic mail harassment under Maryland state law and was found guilty.

The subject was sentenced to six months in jail (suspended) and 12 months of probation, fined $250, and ordered to undergo psychiatric evaluation and perform twenty hours of community service. The subject was also terminated from this employment.

Criminal Investigator Positions

Criminal Investigators perform investigative activities related to the integrity of the NRC's programs and operations. The majority of investigative activities focus on violations of law and misconduct by NRC employees and contractors as well as allegations of irregularities or abuse in NRC programs and operations.

Candidates for criminal investigator positions should have knowledge of the basic principles and techniques of investigating, skill in conducting interviews and applying investigative techniques, experience in planning and conducting criminal investigations, and the ability to effectively communicate, both orally and in writing, the fact and circumstances of these investigations.

Criminal investigators are subject to physical and medical qualification standards, satisfactory completion of an eight-week basic training program, and drug testing; there is a maximum entry age of 37. Criminal investigators are also subject to frequent travel in the performance of their duties and the successful granting of a security clearance.

Criminal investigators are required to work an average of ten hours per day to perform their investigative activities for which they are eligible to receive law enforcement availability pay.

Training, qualifications, and application procedures are similar to those found under the Department of Agriculture. For further information, contact:

U.S. Nuclear Regulatory Commission
Office of the Inspector General
Mail Stop T5 D28
Washington, D.C. 20555
Telephone: (301) 415-5930

OFFICE OF PERSONNEL MANAGEMENT

The Office of Personnel Management (OPM) administers a merit system for federal employment that includes recruiting, examining, training, and promoting people on the basis of their knowledge and skills, regardless of their race, religion, sex, political influence, or other nonmerit factors. The office's role is to ensure that the federal government provides an array of personnel services to applicants and employees. Through a range of programs designed to develop and encourage the effectiveness of the government employee, the office supports government program managers in their personnel management responsibilities and provides benefits to employees and to retired employees and their survivors.

OFFICE OF INSPECTOR GENERAL

In outlining his thoughts on the role of Inspectors General, OPM's Inspector General Patrick E. McFarland stated, "The most significant aspect of becoming an Inspector General is the realization that I must now perform my duties as if I were the eyes and ears of every citizen. To be nominated by the President and confirmed by the Senate is an honor that must be cherished and repaid through hard work and high standards. Accountability is everyone's responsibility. It is the job of the Inspector General to insure that government personnel and programs are held strictly accountable for their actions. To this end, the Office of Inspector General must be exemplary in its own programs, goals, and aspirations."

"The Inspector General position was not created to be only a reactive force in finding fraud, waste, and abuse. I feel there is a clear mandate for Inspectors General to give of their institutional knowledge and management skills in an effort to assist the leadership of the organization to identify and remedy improper management practices and thereby prevent problems. I believe it to be inconsistent with the intent of the 1978

Inspector General Act for someone in a high position of public trust, such as an Inspector General, to only react when wrongdoing occurs, and otherwise be complacent about providing help, guidance, and counsel."

"If the 1978 Inspector General Act exemplifies one concept, it is that of independence. A major challenge confronting any Inspector General is the steadfastness that is necessary to maintain independence. Simply an aura of independence is not sufficient. It must be practiced every day. For independence to be effective, it must be supported by the presence of quality and objectivity in each and every audit and investigation that is undertaken. "

Investigative Initiative

The Office of Investigations within the Office of Inspector General was established to investigate allegations of waste, fraud, and abuse against the programs administered by OPM. These programs include the Civil Service Retirement System, the Federal Employees Retirement System, the Federal Employee Health Benefit Program (FEHBP), and the Federal Employees Group Life Insurance Program trust funds. These trust fund programs currently cover approximately 9.5 million current and retired federal civilian employees, including their family members, and disburse about $61 billion annually. Another responsibility of OPM includes the administration of the Combined Federal Campaign.

The Office of Investigations spends the majority of its resources investigating allegations of health-care fraud and abuse against the FEHBP. The FEHBP is the third-largest health-care expenditure for the federal government and the largest employer-sponsored health benefits program of its kind. Allegations of fraud and abuse against the federal employees' retirement programs, as well as misconduct by OPM employees, are also investigated. The misconduct cases primarily involve the theft of government funds and property. However, OPM also examine instances of bribery involving federal officials or financial conflicts of interest.

The special agents assigned to the Office of Investigations are criminal investigators (government series 1811s) who perform similar work and receive the same basic and advanced law enforcement training as criminal investigators in other federal law enforcement agencies charged with investigating white collar fraud, such as the Internal Revenue Service, U.S. Secret Service, U.S. Customs Service, and others.

Training, qualifications, and application procedures are similar to those found under the Department of Agriculture. For further information, contact:

Office of Inspector General
U.S. Office of Personnel Management
1900 E Street, Room 6400
Washington, D.C. 20415-0001
Telephone: (202) 606-1200

RAILROAD RETIREMENT BOARD

The Railroad Retirement Board (RRB) is an independent agency in the Executive Branch of the federal government. The RRB is headed by a three member board appointed by the President of the United States and subject to the advice and consent of the Senate. One member is appointed upon the recommendation of railroad employers, one is appointed upon the recommendation of railroad labor organizations, and the third, the chairman, is appointed to represent the public interest.

The agency administers comprehensive retirement/survivor and unemployment/sickness insurance benefit programs for the nation's railroad workers and their families, under the Railroad Retirement and Railroad Unemployment Insurance Acts. Under the Social Security Act, the RRB also has administrative responsibilities for certain benefit payments and Medicare coverage for railroad workers.

OFFICE OF INSPECTOR GENERAL/OFFICE OF INVESTIGATIONS

The Railroad Retirement Solvency Act of 1983 established the Office of Inspector General at the RRB by naming the agency as one of "such establishments" identified under Section 2 of the Inspector General Act of 1978. The Inspector General Act Amendments of 1988 added the RRB to the list of agencies covered by the Inspector General Act.

The Inspector General must submit semiannual reports to the Chairman of the Railroad Retirement Board and to the U.S. Congress. This dual reporting requirement helps to ensure the public disclosure of program weaknesses as well as OIG independence.

The Office of Inspector General, Office of Investigations (OI) focuses on RRB benefit program fraud. OI's primary objective is to identify, investigate, and refer for prosecution and monetary recovery action cases of waste, fraud, and abuse in RRB programs. The OI consists of criminal investigators/special agents who conduct OI investigations. Through its investigations, the OI also seeks to prevent and deter program fraud. In order to maximize the effectiveness of its resources, OI continues to pursue cooperative investigative activities and coordination with other Inspectors General and law enforcement agencies.

Investigative Initiatives

An individual in the Southern District of Texas pled guilty to six counts of forgery and one count of theft of government funds. The individual stole, forged, and negotiated six monthly government annuity checks totaling $8,495.84, made payable to a U.S. Railroad Retirement Board annuitant after the annuitant had died. The individual was sentenced to one-year of imprisonment and three years probation and ordered to pay restitution of $8,495.84.

An individual in the District of Nebraska pled guilty to one count of theft of government funds. The individual failed to report and attempted to hide his employment from the RRB while receiving a monthly disability annuity from the RRB. The individual had his employer make his paychecks payable to his wife, believing that his employer was using his wife's social security number for reporting his income. Unknown to the individual, however, the employer used his social security number for reporting his income, not his wife's number. The individual received $25,330.14 from the RRB to which he was not entitled. The individual was sentenced to twelve months and one day of imprisonment and three years of probation and ordered to pay restitution of $25,330.14.

A jury in the state of Indiana convicted an individual of one count of felony theft and one count of felony welfare fraud. The individual falsely claimed and received unemployment benefits from the RRB totaling $3,276.00 while being gainfully employed. The individual was sentenced to eighteen days of time served in jail, three years in prison (suspended), and three years of probation and ordered to pay restitution of $3,276.00.

A railroad in the state of Alaska pled guilty to two counts of failing to report compensation of railroad employees to the RRB. In order to avoid greater tax liability under the railroad retirement system, the railroad falsely reported the railroad employees as nonrailroad employees through a temporary personnel company. The railroad was sentenced to three years of probation, ordered to pay a fine of $75,000, restitution of $278,443.68, investigative costs of $24,118.20, and an additional $278,443.68 in civil settlement for submitting false annual compensation reports, for a total $656,005.56.

Training, qualifications, and application procedures are similar to those found under the Department of Agriculture. For further information, contact:

Office of Inspector General
Railroad Retirement Board
844 N. Rush Street, Room 450
Chicago, Illinois 60611
Telephone: (312) 751-4690

SMALL BUSINESS ADMINISTRATION

The fundamental purposes of the Small Business Administration are to aid, counsel, assist, and protect the interests of small businesses; ensure that small business concerns receive a fair portion of government purchases, contracts, subcontracts, and sales of government property; make loans to small business concerns, state and local development companies, and the victims of floods or other catastrophes, or of certain types of economic injuries; and license, regulate, and make loans to small business investment companies.

OFFICE OF INSPECTOR GENERAL

The Office of Inspector General (OIG) is an independent and objective oversight office created within the Small Business Administration (SBA) by the Inspector General Act of 1978. The Investigations Division of OIG manages a nationwide program to prevent and detect illegal and/ or improper activities involving SBA programs, operations, and personnel. The criminal-investigative staff carries out a full range of traditional law enforcement functions, such as conducting interviews, gathering and reviewing records to develop evidence, executing arrest and search warrants, and conducting consensual electronic monitoring.

The Investigations Division's mission is includes more than conducting criminal investigations. The IG Act specifies that the Inspector General will:

- detect and prevent fraud and abuse

- conduct and supervise investigations relating to the agency's programs and supporting operations

- report violations of law to the U.S. Attorney General

- promote economy and efficiency through maintaining effective working relationships with other federal, state, and local governmental agencies and nongovernmental entities regarding the mandated duties of the Inspector General

- inform the SBA Administrator and Congress of serious problems and recommend corrective actions and implementation measures

The special agents investigate allegations of wrongdoing and identify the proper venue for a successful resolution that could include criminal prosecution, civil proceedings, administrative action, or combinations thereof. If systemic weaknesses are identified, the special agents prepare a report outlining the weaknesses and potential remedies for correction. All aspects of this process require working closely with the Department of Justice, U.S. Attorney offices, the Federal Bureau of Investigation, other law enforcement agencies, other OIGs, SBA program staff, and other elements of SBA OIG.

Investigative Initiative

An investigation disclosed that an individual who headed the SBA division of a bank, while in his official capacity at the bank, received money both directly and indirectly from the proceeds of a $1 million SBA-guaranteed loan made to a brokerage firm head to purchase a gas station and mini-mart business. The bank employee failed to disclose that he owned 50 percent of the business or that he was going to receive at least $65,000 of the loan proceeds for his personal use. Also, he received approximately $2 million in incentive bonuses and commissions from the bank's secondary-market sale of SBA-guaranteed loans, plus a base salary that eventually reached $250,000. During his years at the bank, at least 17 borrowers submitted fraudulent documents, including falsified copies of tax returns, seeking SBA-guaranteed loans. He admitted that he accepted a $24,000 automobile from a loan brokerage firm as a reward for its business with the bank. This case resulted in 19 individuals being charged in federal court and an additional 6 persons were charged in a companion investigation of another loan broker with whom the bank employee did business.

Training, qualifications, and application procedures are similar to those found under the Department of Agriculture. For further information, contact:

Office of Inspector General
Small Business Administration
409 3rd Street SW, Suite 7150
Washington, D.C. 20416
Telephone: (202) 205-6586

SOCIAL SECURITY ADMINISTRATION

The Social Security Administration (SSA) manages the nation's social insurance program, consisting of retirement, survivors, and disability insurance programs, commonly known as Social Security. It also administers the Supplemental Security Income program for the aged, blind, and disabled. The SSA is responsible for studying the problems of poverty and economic insecurity among Americans and making recommendations on effective methods for solving these problems through social insurance. The SSA also assigns Social Security numbers to U.S. citizens and maintains earnings records for workers under their Social Security numbers.

OFFICE OF INSPECTOR GENERAL

The Office of Inspector General (OIG) improves the Social Security Administration's programs and operations by protecting them against fraud, waste, and abuse by conducting independent and objective audits, evaluations, and investigations. They provide timely, useful, and reliable information and advice to administration officials, Congress, and the public.

By conducting independent and objective audits, investigations, and evaluations, they strive for continuous improvement in the Social Security Administration's programs, operations, and management.

The OIG conducts and coordinates investigative activities related to fraud, waste, abuse, and mismanagement in SSA's programs and operations. It investigates wrongdoings by applicants, beneficiaries, contractors, physicians, interpreters, representative payees, third parties, and SSA employees. The office also frequently conducts joint investigations with other federal, state, and local law enforcement agencies.

The OIG also conducts comprehensive financial and performance audits of SSA's programs and operations and makes recommendations to ensure that program objectives are achieved effectively and efficiently. The OIG also conducts management and program evaluations that identify and recommend ways of preventing program fraud and maximizing efficiency.

Investigative Initiatives

OIG components have partnered in a number of initiatives to capitalize on the skills of staff members and to make the most of limited resources. Where appropriate, they work with other federal and state agencies. Perhaps one of the most significant activities is the continuing effort in the Social Security number (SSN) misuse and identity theft area.

OIG's Office of Audit (OA) provides SSN misuse and identity theft leads that have been uncovered during the course of OA's reviews to the Office of Investigations (OI). These leads, for the most part, evolve into investigations that are easily prosecutable.

OIG's Identity Theft Task Force members are active in the intergovernmental work groups that review the extent of the identity theft problem and initiate programs to solve these problems. One of these is the Department of Justice Identity Theft Subcommittee of the Law Enforcement Initiatives Committee of the Attorney General's Council on White-Collar Crime. This subcommittee gauges whether new law enforcement initiatives or strategies are needed.

Bribery of a Corrupt Public Official

A former SSA employee in Fresno, California, processed more than 300 fraudulent applications for SSN cards. Three coconspirators sold the SSN cards for between $400 and $1,400 to people who could not otherwise obtain them legally. SSA subsequently mailed the fraudulent SSN cards to mail drops. The investigation was based on information provided by the manager of the SSA Southeast Fresno District Office and the SSA Security Integrity Team after a security review revealed that SS-5 applications processed by the employee were missing. The former SSA employee was sentenced to twelve months of incarceration and thirty-six months of supervised release after pleading guilty to bribery of a public official. He was ordered to forfeit the $12,400 in cash that he accepted as a bribe to fraudulently process the SSN applications.

SSA Employee and Municipal Government Employee Conspire with More than 20 Individuals to Defraud SSA

The New York Field Division, the Federal Bureau of Investigation, and the U.S. Postal Inspection Service conducted an investigation in Puerto Rico of an SSA employee and his co-conspirator, an employee of the Las Piedras Municipal Government, Las Piedras, Puerto Rico, who conspired with 20 individuals to illegally obtain approximately $369,085 in SSA Old-Age, Survivors and Disability Insurance (OASDI) benefits. The investigation revealed that the co-conspirator recruited the individuals to file fraudulent OASDI applications and provided some of the individuals with fake baptismal certificates. The employee illegally accessed SSA's system to change the date of birth of the individuals and then processed the OASDI applications. The employee and his coconspirator received approximately $70,832 for their services from the 20 individuals. Both pled guilty to conspiracy. The employee was sentenced to five months of home detention and two years of supervised release. The coconspirator is scheduled to be sentenced.

Two individuals Bribe an SSA Employee to Illegally Process SSNs

The Boston Field Division and the Connecticut Organized Crime Drug Enforcement Task Force conducted an investigation of an SSA employee who accepted bribes to fraudulently process SSN card applications. The investigation identified 131 fraudulent SSN card applications processed by the employee and determined that two individuals paid the employee to process the fraudulent SSN card applications. The employee pled guilty to accepting a bribe and was incarcerated. The two individuals who paid the employee to process the fraudulent SSN applications pled guilty to bribery of a public official. They were incarcerated and ordered to perform 100 hours of community service. All three were ordered to pay a total fine of $14,400.

Auditing Initiative

The Social Security Act provides benefits to the children of retired, deceased, or disabled workers. Generally, these children are entitled to Social Security benefits until they marry or reach age 18. However, children who are full-time students may continue to receive benefits until they reach age 19 or complete their secondary education, whichever occurs first. The act does not provide for benefits to child beneficiaries over age 18 if they are neither students nor disabled.

An audit was conducted to determine whether SSA paid benefits to child beneficiaries who were age 18 or over and neither students nor disabled. The review disclosed that 390 (85.7 percent) of the 455 child beneficiaries in the U.S. population were age 18 or over and neither students nor disabled. These individuals were ineligible for Social Security benefits under the act. The remaining 65 individuals represented child beneficiaries who, based on subsequent information obtained by SSA, were entitled to benefits. It was determined that 390 child beneficiaries who were not entitled to benefits received $435,282 in Social Security. The OIG recommended and SSA agreed to:

- modify its automated system to terminate benefits to child beneficiaries at age 18 if they are neither disabled nor full-time students

- generate alerts for employees to review complex cases, recalculate benefit amounts, and adjust payments due other individuals in the same family, if necessary

- evaluate the feasibility of automating benefit increases for other individuals in the same family when the benefits for child beneficiaries who are neither students nor disabled are terminated at age 18

Training, qualifications, and application procedures are similar to those found under the Department of Agriculture. For further information, contact:

Office of Inspector General
Social Security Administration
6401 Security Boulevard
Suite 300, Altmeyer Building
Baltimore, Maryland 21235
Telephone: (410) 966-8385

DESIGNATED FEDERAL ENTITIES

AMTRAK

The National Railroad Passenger Corporation (Amtrak) was established to develop the potential of modern rail service in meeting the nation's intercity passenger transportation needs. The National Railroad Passenger Corporation was incorporated under the District of Columbia Business Corporation Act in accordance with the provisions of Section 301 of the Rail Passenger Service Act of 1970. The Act specifically provides that:

> "The Corporation shall be operated and managed as a profit corporation, the purpose of which shall be to provide intercity and commuter rail passenger service, employing innovative operating and marketing concepts so as to fully develop the potential of modern rail service in meeting the Nation's intercity and commuter passenger transportation requirements. The Corporation will not be an agency ... or establishment of the U.S. Government. It shall be subject to the provisions of this Act and, to the extent consistent with this Act, to the District of Columbia Business Corporation Act."

Amtrak operates an average of 212 trains per day, serving more than 540 station locations in forty-five states, over a system of approximately 24,500 route miles.

OFFICE OF INSPECTOR GENERAL

The Department of Internal Affairs (Office of Inspector General) at Amtrak was formed April 1, 1989, pursuant to the provisions of the Inspector General Act Amendments of 1988. The Act required that Amtrak, as a "designated federal entity," establish an Office of Inspector General to supervise and conduct audits and investigations of waste, fraud, and abuse within the company.

On May 1, 1989, internal procedures were promulgated mirroring the scope and authority of the IG as delineated in the IG Act. Amtrak's IG is independent and reports only to the president of Amtrak. The IG also provides quarterly reports to Amtrak's Board of Directors Audit Committee to notify it of significant auditing activity. The IG is authorized full access to all company records, property, and other material related to the performance of its duties. Management is ultimately responsible for ensuring that audit findings and investigative reports are properly acted upon, and all management personnel are required to respond to IG recommendations within thirty days from receipt of the audit or investigative report.

Investigative Initiatives

OI received an allegation that an ATS access code issued to an Amtrak employee was compromised and a large volume of telephone calls were placed using the stolen ATS code. As a result of the OI investigation, 14 Amtrak employees were identified to have used a total of ten ATS codes not assigned to them to place unauthorized telephone calls.

A Midwest hotel billed Amtrak, through Corporate Lodging Corporation (CLC), for more than 1,100 unused rooms that were not specifically provided for by contract. The OI investigation initially recovered partial repayment from the hotel and CLC. An additional monetary recovery from the hotel is anticipated upon conclusion of the investigation.

OI received information that an Amtrak employee submitted questionable payment request forms to Amtrak's Accounts Payable Department. OI confirmed that the employee was forging authorization signatures on the payment requests, keeping money from employees that was given to him to purchase food, and submitting payment requests for personal hotel stays and then arranging to have his personal bills paid by Amtrak. The employee was terminated from employment and restitution is being sought through the courts.

OI determined that Amtrak equipment was being sold on the Internet without Amtrak authorization. An OI investigation determined that an Amtrak employee had on several occasions removed from Amtrak property and sold the equipment without the knowledge or permission of his supervisors. The matter was reported to management for appropriate disciplinary action.

OI received information that a corporate credit card of an Amtrak manager had been used in the area of his prior assignment without his permission. The total charged against the credit card was ultimately reimbursed by Amtrak as a result of a fraudulent payment request. OI determined that an Amtrak director had obtained the credit card number from a previously submitted expense report, and then used the card number to purchase railroad memorabilia under the cardholder's name. The director was terminated from Amtrak employment.

Auditing Initiative

The OIG devoted significant resources to a review of the security and reliability of Amtrak's networks and its proprietary business information. Overall, it was determined that improvements are needed. Risk assessment of this critical area noted Amtrak's core business activities had become increasingly dependent on its data network, Web sites, and client/server applications. Amtrak's local area and wide area networks supported approximately 7,000 users and 8,000 devices, such as computers and printers, in 250 locations around the country. In addition, connectivity to the Internet, wide availability and increasing sophistication of hacker tolls, proliferation of software with security weaknesses, and an increasingly complex technology environment had contributed to the security risk. The review indicated that Amtrak's servers hosting critical business applications were vulnerable to attack by unauthorized users. An intruder could gain the highest administrator-level access on the servers and disrupt critical corporate headquarters and station automation networks. Similarly, some limited vulnerabilities were observed with respect to Amtrak Web sites, and management was advised that the dial-in modems posed a significant risk to data network since the remote access bypasses access controls such as firewalls and Windows NT domain authentication. It was noted that Amtrak's security controls promulgated through its policies and procedures and the enforcement of such controls need to be strengthened.

Training, qualifications, and application procedures are similar to those found under the Department of Agriculture. For further information, contact:

National Railroad Passenger Service
Office of Inspector General
10 G Street, NE, Suite 3W-300
Washington, D.C. 20002-4285
Telephone: (202) 906-4863

APPALACHIAN REGIONAL COMMISSION

The Appalachian Regional Commission (ARC) was established as an independent agency by the Appalachian Regional Development Act of 1965. The Act authorizes a federal/state partnership designed to promote long-term economic development on a coordinated regional basis in the thirteen Appalachian states. The Commission represents a unique experiment in partnership among the federal, state, and local levels of government and between the public and private sectors. It is composed of the governors of the thirteen Appalachian states and a federal representative who is appointed by the President. The federal representative serves as the federal cochairman, with the governors electing one of their number to serve as the states' cochairman.

Through joint planning and development of regional priorities, ARC funds are used to assist and encourage other public and private resources to address Appalachia's unique needs. Program direction and policy are established by the Commission (Appalachian Regional Commission Code) by a majority vote of the state members and the affirmative vote of the federal cochairman. Emphasis has been placed on highways, infrastructure development, business enterprise, and human resources programs.

OFFICE OF INSPECTOR GENERAL

The ARC Office of Inspector General became operational on October 1, 1989, with the appointment of an Inspector General and provision of budgetary authority for contracted auditing and/or investigation activities. The Inspector General is responsible for keeping the head of the Commission and Congress fully informed about the problems and deficiencies in ARC programs and operations and the need for corrective action. The Inspector General has authority to inquire into all ARC programs and activities as well as the related activities of persons or parties performing under grants, contracts, or other agreements. The inquiries may be in the form of audits, surveys, criminal and other investigations, personnel security checks, or other appropriate methods. The two primary purposes of these inquiries are to assist all levels of ARC management by identifying and reporting problem areas, weaknesses, or deficiencies in procedures, policies, program implementation, and employee conduct; and to recommend appropriate corrective actions.

Emphasis is placed on surveys of ARC operations and programs; initiation of grant audits by contractors; liaison and communications with ARC, state, and other OIG officials; identification of audit inventory; strategic planning; and assessment of resource needs.

Auditing Initiatives

During the past ten years, priority OIG efforts have been directed at improved grant management. Based on audit recommendations and agency initiatives, more than $25 million of previously mismanaged funds have been made available for additional economic development projects.

Grant audits and OIG technical assistance have significantly contributed to improved financial systems and internal controls, accountability for ARC funds, and compliance with grant requirements. Consequently, there have been significant reductions in the extent of questioned costs with respect to grantor administration of ARC projects.

Compliance audits of an ARC-sponsored program to ensure the availability of medical service in Appalachia through the use of foreign physicians have identified problems with respect to use of physicians at unapproved sites and failure to provide the required primary care. These reviews have contributed to substantial program improvements that have had positive benefits for Appalachian health services.

Training, qualifications, and application procedures are similar to those found under the Department of Agriculture. For further information, contact:

Office of Inspector General
Appalachian Regional Commission
1666 Connecticut Avenue, NW, Suite 215
Washington, D.C. 20235
Telephone: (202) 884-7675

BOARD OF GOVERNORS OF THE FEDERAL RESERVE SYSTEM

Congress established the Federal Reserve System (System) as the nation's central bank in 1913. The System is structured to give it a broad perspective on the economy and economic activity in all parts of the nation. It is a federal system, composed basically of a central, governmental agency——the Board of Governors—in Washington, D.C., and twelve regional Federal Reserve banks and their branches, located in major cities throughout the nation. These components share responsibility for supervising and regulating certain financial institutions and activities, providing banking services to depository institutions and to the federal government, and ensuring that consumers receive adequate information and fair treatment in their business with the banking system.

A major component of the System is the Federal Open Market Committee (FOMC), which is made up of the Board of Governors, the president of the Federal Reserve Bank of New York, and the presidents of four other Federal Reserve banks, all of whom serve on a rotating basis. The FOMC oversees open market operations, which are the main tools used by the Federal Reserve to influence money market conditions and the growth of money and credit.

The Board of Governors of the Federal Reserve System (Board) was established as a federal agency. It is made up of seven members who serve fourteen-year, staggered terms. The Chairman and Vice Chair of the Board each serve four-year terms, which can be renewed. Board members are appointed by the President of the United States and confirmed by the U.S. Senate. The Board has three primary mission areas: monetary policy, banking supervision and regulation, and oversight of Reserve Bank operations and payment systems.

The Federal Reserve is responsible for promoting a safe, sound, competitive, and accessible banking system and stable financial markets. To achieve this mission, the Board supervises and regulates state-chartered banks, bank holding companies, international branches of member banks, Edge Act agreement organizations, and domestic activities of foreign banks; acts as a lender of last resort; and implements regulations designed to inform and protect consumers. The Board has delegated a portion of its supervisory and regulatory functions to the Federal Reserve banks, including commercial bank examinations, bank holding company inspections, and approval of certain types of applications. The Board also coordinates many of its supervisory activities with other federal, state, and foreign regulators.

OFFICE OF INSPECTOR GENERAL

The Office of Inspector General (OIG) was established by the Board in July 1987. The OIG became statutorily mandated in April 1989 by the IG Act, which legislated specific duties and responsibilities and reporting relationships. Specifically, the IG Act states the Inspector General will:

- provide police direction for and conduct, supervise, and coordinate audits and investigations relating to the programs and operations of the Board

- review existing and proposed legislation and regulations relating to the programs and operations of the Board and make recommendations concerning the impact of such legislation or regulations on the economy and efficiency in the administration of programs and operations administered or financed by the Board or the prevention and detection of fraud and abuse in such programs and operations

- recommend policies for and conduct, supervise, or coordinate relationships between the Board and other federal, state, and local government agencies and nongovernmental entities with respect to all matters relating to the promotion of economy and efficiency in the administration of and the prevention and detection of fraud and abuse in programs and operations administered or financed by the Board, as well as the identification and prosecution of participants in such fraud or abuse

- keep the Chairman and Congress fully and currently informed concerning fraud and other serious problems, abuses, and deficiencies relating to the administration of programs and operations administered or financed by the Board; recommend corrective actions; and report progress made in implementing corrective actions.

In addition, the Federal Deposit Insurance Act (FDI Act) requires the OIG to conduct reviews of certain failed depository institutions whose failure results in a material loss to the bank insurance funds.

Investigative Initiatives

The OIG also receives requests for investigations from within the Board and from outside sources and makes referrals to other law enforcement organizations as appropriate. The OIG's prevention and detection strategy is designed to identify causes of fraud and abuse, to provide a mechanism for the early detection of fraud and abuse, to minimize any potential damage or loss, and to help the board resolve such problems and prevent their recurrence, if possible.

The investigative services program received seventeen allegations that were referred to the OIG from Board program staff, OIG audit activities, and other sources. As a result of these allegations, the OIG opened ten additional formal investigations, and incorporated seven of those allegations into ongoing review of fictitious-instrument fraud complaints. Fictitious-instrument fraud schemes are those in which promoters promise very high profits based on fictitious instruments that they claim are issued, endorsed, or authorized by the System or a well-known financial institution.

Auditing Initiatives

During the reporting period, OIG participated with the audit departments of each Reserve Bank in a review of compliance with the Federal Reserve System's *Information Security Manual* (ISM) provisions for vulnerability assessments and penetration testing. This project is part of a system-wide effort to help ensure a uniform approach to ISM compliance and to identify common vulnerabilities as well as best practices. Plans are to brief Board management on the results of the review and participate in any additional system-wide auditing activity that may result from this initial data gathering effort.

The Office of the Comptroller of the Currency closed the First National Bank of Keystone (FNB Keystone), Keystone, West Virginia. The Federal Deposit Insurance Corporation (FDIC) has estimated that this failure may cost the FDIC's Bank Insurance Fund between $500 and $800 million. The Treasury OIG issued the report *Material Loss Review of the First National Bank of Keystone,* as required by the FDI Act, since the Office of the Comptroller of the Currency was Keystone's primary regulator. The OIG is studying the Treasury's OIG report on the problems that resulted in the losses and the supervision of FNB Keystone to determine if any issues identified in the report can help enhance the supervisory efforts of the Federal Reserve System. Information learned about this bank failure, along with a study of recent bank supervisory initiatives undertaken in response to the failure, may also assist in planning future auditing efforts.

The OIG initiated a review of the Board's frequent flyer policy. The overall objectives are to evaluate alternatives for implementing an economic, efficient, and effective frequent flyer program to help the Board maximize the benefit of employee participation in airline frequent flyer programs and to evaluate compliance by frequent travelers with the current Board policy.

Training, qualifications, and application procedures are similar to those found under the Department of Agriculture. For further information, contact:

Office of Inspector General
Federal Reserve Board
Mail Stop 300
20th Street and Constitution Avenue, NW
Washington, D.C. 20551
Telephone: (202) 973-5003

COMMODITY FUTURES TRADING COMMISSION

The Commodity Futures Trading Commission (CFTC) was established in 1974 as an independent agency to regulate commodity futures and options trading in the U.S. The CFTC is based in Washington, D.C., with additional offices in Chicago, New York, Kansas City, Los Angeles, and Minneapolis. The basic objectives of the CFTC are to prevent manipulation of the markets, abusive trade practices, and fraudulent activities; to maintain effective oversight of the markets and self-regulatory organizations (SROs); and to enforce the Commodity Exchange Act and Commission rules.

The CFTC regulates the futures trading activities of brokerage firms, salespersons, floor brokers, commodity pool operators, commodity trading advisers, introducing brokers, and leverage transaction merchants. In addition, the agency ensures the effective enforcement of exchange rules, reviews the terms and conditions of proposed futures contracts, reviews the registration of firms and individuals who provide advice or handle customer funds, and oversees the activities of the National Futures Association (NFA).

OFFICE OF INSPECTOR GENERAL

The Office of the Inspector General in the CFTC was created in accordance with the amended Inspector General Act of 1978. The first Inspector General was appointed in September 1989. The OIG was established to create an independent unit to promote economy, efficiency, and effectiveness in the administration of CFTC programs and operations and to detect and prevent fraud and abuse in such programs and operations; conduct and supervise audits and, where necessary, investigations relating to the administration of CFTC programs and operations; and to keep the chairman and Congress fully informed about any problems or deficiencies in the administration of CFTC programs and operations and provide recommendations for correction of these problems and deficiencies.

Auditing Initiative

The OIG conducted an audit to determine if the CFTC was complying with the requirements of the lease of space for its headquarters office in Washington, D.C. The particular focus was on the appropriateness of all base rental and escalation payments made under the lease. The OIG issued an audit report finding that the system of internal controls for the procedure for receiving invoices, approving and paying lease invoices, and documenting each stage of the process has been functioning properly. However, the OIG also concluded from the absence of some key records that more attention was needed to oversee the creation and retention of records.

Investigative Initiative

The OIG reviewed the legal advice given to a senior-level employee on the requirements under the ethics rules for recusal from matters in which he had an interest, for divestiture of prohibited holdings, and of his compliance with that advice. Although the OIG found that the official immediately complied in good faith with the legal advice he received, his experience pointed to the absence of a comprehensive system to ensure the proper execution of the CFTC ethics program. The Office of General Counsel indicated that it was in the process of redefining the administration of the ethics program to ensure that, in the future, employees are promptly and correctly informed of their ethical obligations, records of advice given are created and maintained in a manner which permits secure storage and easy retrieval, and that responsibility for carrying out the program is fixed on identified individuals. The OIG concurred that such an effort is needed.

Legislative and Regulatory Reviews

The staff of the CFTC proposed a rule that would allow certain foreign futures and options brokers to directly receive foreign futures and options orders from sophisticated U.S. customers. The OIG raised questions and offered suggestions. The staff provided clarifying answers and adopted several suggestions.

The staff proposed amendments that would require rate-of-return performance measures used by Commodity Trading Advisers (CTAs) to be computed by dividing net performance by the nominal account size. Previously, the CFTC had required that actual deposited funds be used in the denominator. The OIG urged the staff to consider using a focus group to determine the relative values of disclosure of the two methods. The trading and markets staff is currently reviewing public comments.

The CFTC staff proposed an amendment to Rule 1.41 that would permit contract markets to place new rules and rule amendments into effect on the business day following their receipt by the CFTC, subject to certain conditions. OIG supported the staff action and recommended approval to the Commission

Training, qualifications, and application procedures are similar to those found under the Department of Agriculture. For further information, contact:

Commodity Futures Trading Commission
Three Lafayette Centre
1155 21ˢᵗ Street, NW
Washington, D.C. 20581
Telephone: (202) 418-5110

CONSUMER PRODUCT SAFETY COMMISSION

The U.S. Consumer Product Safety Commission (CPSC) was established is 1973 as an independent agency to protect the public against unreasonable risks of injuries associated with consumer products. CPSC's headquarters is located in Bethesda, Maryland. Regional centers that oversee the activities of the field personnel stationed throughout the country are located in New York, Chicago, and Oakland. Under the Consumer Product Safety Act, Congress granted CPSC broad authority to issue and enforce standards prescribing performance requirements, warnings, or instructions regarding the use of consumer products. CPSC also regulates products covered under three other acts: the Flammable Fabric Act, the Federal Hazardous Substance Act, and the Refrigerator Act. CPSC is headed by three Commissioners appointed by the President with advice and consent of the Senate. The President designates the chairman.

OFFICE OF INSPECTOR GENERAL

The Office of Inspector General (OIG) is an independent office established under the provisions of the Inspector General Act of 1978, as amended by the Inspector General Act Amendments of 1988 (P.L.100-504). The Inspector General Act gives the Inspector General the authority and responsibility to:

"Conduct and supervise audits, inspections, and investigations of CPSC's programs and operations; provide leadership, coordination, and recommend policies for activities designed to promote economy, efficiency, and effectiveness in the administration of CPSC's programs and operations; provide a means for keeping the chairman of the agency and Congress fully and currently informed about problems and deficiencies relating to CPSC's programs and operations, and provide recommendations for corrective actions."

The OIG investigates complaints and information received concerning possible violations of laws, rules, and regulations; mismanagement; abuse of authority; and waste of funds. These investigations are in response to allegations, complaints, and information received from employees of CPSC, other government agencies, contractors, and other concerned individuals.

Training, qualifications, and application procedures are similar to those found under the Department of Agriculture. For further information, contact:

Office of Inspector General
U.S. Consumer Product Safety Commission
Room 701
4330 East West Highway
Bethesda, Maryland 20814-4408
Telephone: (301) 504-0573

CORPORATION FOR NATIONAL AND COMMUNITY SERVICE

The Corporation for National and Community Service engages Americans of all backgrounds in community-based service that addresses the nation's educational, public safety, environmental, and other human needs to achieve direct and demonstrable results. In so doing, the Corporation fosters civic responsibility, strengthens the ties that bind us together as a people, and provides educational opportunity for those who make a substantial service contribution.

The Corporation oversees three major service initiatives: AmeriCorps, Learn and Serve America, and the National Senior Service Corps. The Corporation was established on October 1,

1993, by the National and Community Service Trust Act of 1993 (42 U.S.C. 12651 *et seq.*). In addition to creating several new service programs, the act consolidated the functions and activities of the former Commission on National and Community Service and the federal agency ACTION.

The goal of the Corporation is to address the nation's most critical problems in the areas of education, the environment, public safety, and other human needs, while fostering a service ethic in participants and beneficiaries.

The Corporation is a federal corporation governed by a 15-member bipartisan Board of Directors, appointed by the President with the advice and consent of the Senate. The Secretaries of Agriculture, Defense, Education, Health and Human Services, Housing and Urban Development, Interior, and Labor; the Attorney General; the Environmental Protection Agency Administrator; the Peace Corps Director; and the Chief Executive Officer of the Corporation serve as *ex officio* members of the board. The board has responsibility for overall policy direction of the Corporation's activities and has the power to make all final grant decisions, approve the strategic plan and annual budget, and advise and make recommendations to the President and the Congress regarding changes in the national service laws.

AmeriCorps

AmeriCorps, the domestic Peace Corps, engages more than 40,000 Americans in intensive results-oriented service. Most AmeriCorps members are selected by and serve with local and national organizations like Habitat for Humanity, the American Red Cross, Big Brothers/Big Sisters, and Boys and Girls Clubs,

Learn and Serve America

Learn and Serve America helps support nearly one million students from kindergarten through college who meet community needs while improving their academic skills and learning the habits of good citizenship. In addition to providing grants to schools and community organizations, the Corporation for National and Community Service also promotes student service through the President's student service challenge.

National Senior Service Corps

Through the National Senior Service Corps (Senior Corps), nearly half a million Americans age 55 and older share their time and talents to help solve local problems. As foster grandparents, they serve one-on-one with young people with special needs; as senior companions, they help other seniors live independently in their homes; and as volunteers with the Retired and Senior Volunteers Program (RSVP), they help meet a wide range of community needs.

OFFICE OF INSPECTOR GENERAL

The Corporation's Office of Inspector General is authorized by the amended Inspector General Act of 1978 to conduct independent and objective audits and investigations; promote organizational economy, efficiency, and effectiveness; prevent and detect fraud, waste, and abuse; review and make recommendations regarding existing and proposed legislation and regulations relating to CNS programs and operations; and keep the Chief Executive Officer, the Corporation's Board of Directors, and the Congress fully and currently informed of problems in agency programs and operations.

Investigative Initiative

An investigation was opened when Corporation management reported that several AmeriCorps members might have falsified their time sheets with the knowledge of the program director, allowing them to earn an educational award without completing the required number of service hours. Current and former AmeriCorps members were interviewed. The majority of these admitted to performing service that would not count as credible volunteer service. All of the AmeriCorps members claimed they relied on instructions provided to them by the program director or program staff members. Several former staff members were also interviewed. These interviews substantiated the statements provided by the AmeriCorps members. The U.S. Attorney's Office declined to prosecute or pursue civil recovery. The Corporation received $237,189.68 from the State Commission as reimbursement for unearned education awards already paid for questioned grant costs.

Auditing Initiative

OIG's audit of the Corporation's procurement operations determined that the Corporation is still vulnerable to fraud, waste, and abuse, and the auditors classify the Corporation's procurement operations as a material weakness. An OIG audit of costs claimed by one Corporation contractor resulted in questioned costs in excess of $1.1 million.

Training, qualifications, and application procedures are similar to those found under the Department of Agriculture. For further information contact:

Office of Inspector General
Corporation for National and Community Service
1201 New York Avenue, NW, Suite 8100
Washington, D.C. 20525
Telephone: (202) 606-5000

CORPORATION FOR PUBLIC BROADCASTING

The Corporation for Public Broadcasting (CPB) is a private, nonprofit organization created by Congress in 1967 to facilitate the development and distribution of high-quality public service programs for all Americans. CPB is funded by federal appropriations and private funds and is accountable to the Congress for its performance. The Corporation's directors are private citizens, not employees or officers of the government. They are appointed by the President of the United States and confirmed by the Senate.

CPB's principal task is to initiate and finance the production of high-quality educational, informational, instructional, and cultural programs of greater than local interest that are not available from other sources. As it performs this task, the Corporation must balance the requirements of creative discretion, fiduciary responsibility for the use of appropriated funds, and protection of program content from extraneous interference or control.

OFFICE OF INSPECTOR GENERAL

The objective of the Office of Inspector General (OIG) is to prevent and detect fraud, waste, and abuse in CPB's programs and operations and to assist management in the effective execution of its fiduciary responsibilities for funds appropriated for public broadcasting.

Auditing Initiatives

During a six-month period, the OIG issued thirty-two audit reports which covered thirty-two CPB-supported public broadcasting stations, three independent contractors, and one internal audit of Corporate travel. The thirty-two issued audit reports included a total of thirty-seven recommendations for management action.

Each year, CPB reports to the Congress on the amount of nonfederal financial support (NFFS) generated by public broadcasting to qualify for annual appropriated funds. This summary report is based on the CPB annual financial reports submitted by each CPB-supported television and radio station and by other public broadcasting entities. Annual system NFFS is approximately $1 billion. The twenty-eight-station audit reports indicated there were no instances noted in which CPB funds were misused or unaccounted for.

Training, qualifications, and application procedures are similar to those found under the Department of Agriculture. For further information, contact:

Office of Inspector General
Corporation for Public Broadcasting
401 Ninth Street, NW
Washington, D.C. 20004-2129
Telephone: (202) 879-9660
Fax: (202) 879-9699

EQUAL EMPLOYMENT OPPORTUNITY COMMISSION

The purpose of the Equal Employment Opportunity Commission is to ensure equality of employment opportunity by enforcing federal laws prohibiting employment discrimination.

EEOC enforces the following laws:

- Title VII of the Civil Rights Act of 1964, which prohibits discrimination based on race, color, religion, sex, and national origin

- Age Discrimination in Employment Act, which prohibits discrimination against individuals 40 years of age or older

- Sections of the Civil Rights Act of 1991

- Equal Pay Act

- Title I of the Americans with Disabilities Act, which prohibits discrimination against people with disabilities in the private sector and state and local governments

- Rehabilitation Act of 1973, which prohibits against disability discrimination in the federal government

The Commission also promotes voluntary action programs by employers, unions, and community organizations to make equal employment opportunity an actuality.

OFFICE OF INSPECTOR GENERAL

EEOC Office of Inspector General's audits, investigations, and evaluations focus on the prevention, identification, and elimination of waste, fraud, and misuse of Agency resources; violations of laws, rules, or regulations; and misconduct, mismanagement, and inefficiencies of all EEOC programs and operations.

OIG exercises the right to perform audits, investigations, and evaluations on activities undertaken by others on contract with EEOC. OIG provides leadership and coordination and recommends policies for activities designed to promote economy, efficiency, and effectiveness in the administration of EEOC programs.

OIG is responsible for ensuring Agency compliance with the following laws: Government Performance and Results Act, Government Management Reform Act, Federal Financial Management Improvement Act, the Clinger-Cohen Act (formerly the Informative Technology Management Reform Act), Government Information Security Reform Act, Chief Financial Officers Act, and the Inspector General Act.

Investigative Initiatives

An investigation found that a field office employee misused a government credit card, stole and attempted to cash a charging party's settlement check, and made false statements on an employment application and academic record. The employee resigned and the case was referred to the United States Attorney for criminal prosecution.

An investigation into allegations of assorted mismanagement, ethics violations, and possible criminal conduct involving a senior management official was completed. The evidence substantiated the allegations, and OIG reported its findings to appropriate management officials and referred the criminal matters to the Department of Justice, which declined prosecution. The employee was removed from service and appealed to the Merit Systems Protection Board, where the Agency's decision was upheld.

OIG completed an investigation, and referred for criminal prosecution, a matter involving the theft of two agency laptop computers by an EEOC employee. As a result of efforts by OIG and the Federal Protective Service, the matter was accepted for prosecution. The employee pled guilty to a charge of theft of government equipment and was removed from government service.

Auditing and Evaluation Initiatives

OIG conducted a review of a contractor's wage determination rates related to a contract. The review involved the evaluation and analysis of the contract to determine whether the contractor's request for additional contract payment was in accordance with the Fair Labor Standard Act and Service Contract Act-Price Adjustments. OIG determined that an additional payment had to be made to the contractor due to the increase in wage and fringe benefits, social security, unemployment taxes, and workers' compensations insurance.

OIG performed a workflow analysis of business processes between the agency's field and headquarters offices and its Payment and Receipts Management Division. OIG provided observations and suggestions regarding vendor master file maintenance, customer service shortfalls, management controls over funds, and office director financial management accountability.

OIG issued a report to Congress addressing the agency's practice of obtaining personal identifiable information from those individuals who access the agency's Web site. Based upon information provided by agency personnel, as well as OIG's own independent tests, EEOC does not employ any procedures to track personal identifiable information of users visiting the agency's official Internet site.

Training, qualifications, and application procedures are similar to those found under the Department of Agriculture. For further information, contact:

Office of Inspector General
Equal Employment Opportunity Commission
1801 L Street, NW, Suite 3001
Washington, D.C. 20507
Telephone: (202) 663-4379

FARM CREDIT ADMINISTRATION

The Farm Credit Administration (FCA or Agency), an independent agency in the executive branch of the U.S. government, regulates and examines the banks, associations, and related entities that constitute the Farm Credit System (FCS), including the Federal Agricultural Mortgage Corporation (Farmer Mac). The FCS is a network of borrower-owned cooperative financial institutions and related service organizations that serve all fifty states and the Commonwealth of Puerto Rico. These institutions specialize in providing credit and related services to farmers, ranchers, producers, harvesters of aquatic products, and farmer-owned cooperatives. They make loans for agricultural processing and marketing activities; rural housing; certain farm-related businesses; agricultural, aquatic, and public utility cooperatives; and foreign and domestic entities in connection with international trade. The FCS raises its loan funds by selling securities in the national and international money markets. The U.S. government does not guarantee these securities.

OFFICE OF INSPECTOR GENERAL

The Office of Inspector General provides independent and objective oversight of agency programs and operations through audits, inspections, investigations, and the review of proposed legislation and regulations. The Inspector General is appointed by and works under the general supervision of the chairman of the agency. The OG keeps the chairman of the agency and the Congress fully and currently informed and makes recommendations concerning the impact on the economy and efficiency of programs and operations administered by FCA and the prevention and detection of fraud and abuse.

Investigative Initiative

An investigation disclosed that an employee had stolen a government credit card and used it to purchase expensive goods. The employee confessed to the crime and the investigation resulted in criminal convictions.

Auditing Initiative

Recently, the OIG issued an audit of performance budgeting. The audit found the agency needed a more streamlined and cohesive planning process. The OIG recommended that the agency consolidate individual planning documents to enable the board to have more comprehensive information linking office resources and goals to the agency's strategic plan and performance measures. The OIG also found the agency needed to address financial planning and human capital planning in its planning process.

Training, qualifications, and application procedures are similar to those found under the Department of Agriculture. For further information, visit the FCA OIG's Web site at http://www.fca.gov/oig or contact:

Farm Credit Administration
1501 Farm Credit Drive
McLean, Virginia 22102
Telephone: (703) 883-4030

FEDERAL COMMUNICATIONS COMMISSION

The Federal Communications Commission (FCC) is an independent regulatory agency exercising authority delegated to it by Congress under the Communications Act of 1934 as amended by the Telecommunications Act of 1996. The FCC is charged with regulating interstate and international communications by radio, television, wire, satellite, and cable. The FCC's jurisdiction covers the fifty states, the District of Columbia, and U.S. possessions. The mandate of the FCC under the Communications Act is to make available to all people of the United States a rapid, efficient, nationwide, and worldwide wire and radio communication service. The FCC performs four major functions to fulfill this charge:

- spectrum allocation

- creating rules to promote fair competition and protect consumers where required by market conditions

- authorization of service

- enforcement

OFFICE OF INSPECTOR GENERAL

Within the FCC, the Office of Inspector General (OIG) was established by an order adopted on March 29, 1989. The OIG is an independent office within the Commission, reporting directly to the chairman.

The OIG has dedicated itself to assisting the Commission as it continues to improve its efficiency and effectiveness. OIG personnel continue to work with the FCC Security Officer to evaluate overall building security and develop recommendations as appropriate to best ensure the safety and integrity of FCC staff and operational systems.

Auditing and Investigative Initiatives

The OIG audited the FCC Headquarters Imprest Fund's handling of local travel and other expenses. The audit was designed to review the policies, procedures, and controls in place to protect the Imprest Fund from fraud, waste, and abuse, and to review the actual fund activity. While the auditors found no instances of fraud, waste or abuse, they did find the need for improvement in the operations of the Imprest Fund (i.e., revision/clarification of the FCC Imprest Fund instructions), close adherence to the requirements contained in the existing instructions, and training of the cashiers to aid them in the performance of their duties.

The OIG initiated an investigation based on allegations that a supervisory FCC employee routinely utilized his computer workstation to access pornographic sites on the Internet, actions that are in violation of FCC regulations and provisions of the Code of Federal Regulations concerning use of government equipment and use of official time. Through investigation, the employee was found to have accessed the sites in question in violation of the applicable standards. Disciplinary action was taken against the employee and the matter was closed.

The Computer Security Officer of the Commission's Information Technology Center (ITC) notified the OIG that due to an apparent misuse of the Commission's electronic mail system by an employee, the Commission's outbound electronic mail system shut down on two recent occasions. It was determined that the employee did use his commission computer to conduct a music business. Disciplinary action was taken against the employee and the matter was closed.

Training, qualifications, and application procedures are similar to those found under the Department of Agriculture. For further information, visit the FCC-OIG Web site at http://www.fcc.gov/oig or contact:

Office of Inspector General
Federal Communications Commission
445 12th Street, SW, Room 2-C762
Washington, D.C. 20554
Telephone: (202) 418-0470

FEDERAL DEPOSIT INSURANCE CORPORATION

The Congress created the Federal Deposit Insurance Corporation (FDIC) through the Banking Act of 1933 to provide protection for bank depositors and to foster sound banking practices. The FDIC insures deposits at more than 10,100 of the nation's banks and savings associations. In cooperation with other federal and state regulatory agencies, the FDIC promotes the safety and soundness of these institutions and the U.S. financial system by identifying, monitoring, and addressing risks to which the deposit insurance funds are exposed.

OFFICE OF INSPECTOR GENERAL

The Office of Inspector General at the FDIC was established on April 17, 1989 by the FDIC Board of Directors pursuant to the Inspector General Act Amendments of 1988 (Public Law 100-504). The Resolution Trust Corporation Completion Act, enacted December 17, 1993, provides that the FDIC Inspector General be a presidential appointee confirmed by the Senate. In April 1996, Gaston L. Gianni, Jr., became the FDIC's first Inspector General appointed by the president and the third Inspector General since the office was established.

The Office of Inspector General accomplishes its mission by conducting independent audits, investigations, and evaluations, and by keeping the FDIC chairman and the Congress fully and currently informed of the FDIC OIG's work. Five core values drive the work of the OIG: independence, effectiveness, integrity, quality, and respect.

The FDIC OIG acts as an agent of positive change, striving for continuous improvement in and protection of FDIC programs, operations, and management. The OIG is committed to the Congress and the American public to promote good government and to create an environment where employees with diverse backgrounds have an opportunity to learn, excel, and be proud of the work they do.

The OIG's Office of Investigations (OI) is responsible for carrying out the investigative mission of the OIG. Staffed with agents in Washington D.C., Atlanta, Dallas, Chicago, and San Francisco, OI conducts investigations of alleged criminal or otherwise prohibited activities impacting the FDIC and its programs. As is the case with most OIG offices, OI agents exercise full law enforcement powers as special deputy marshals under a blanket deputation agreement with the Department of Justice. OI's main focus is the investigation of criminal activity that may harm, or threaten to harm, the operations or the integrity of the FDIC and its programs. In pursuing these cases, OI's goal, in part, is to bring a halt to the fraudulent conduct under investigation, protect the FDIC and other victims from further harm, and assist the FDIC in recovery of its losses. Another consideration in dedicating resources to these cases is the need to pursue appropriate criminal penalties not only to punish the offender but also to deter others from participating in similar crimes.

OI works closely with U.S. Attorneys' offices throughout the country in attempting to bring individuals who have defrauded the FDIC to justice. Support and cooperation among other law enforcement agencies is also a key ingredient for success in the investigative community. The OI frequently partners with the Federal Bureau of Investigation (FBI), Internal Revenue Service (IRS), Secret Service, and other law enforcement agencies in conducting investigations of joint interest.

Investigative Initiatives

Based on a request from the U.S. Attorney's Office in Tampa, Florida, the OIG investigated an allegation that registered representatives of a joint venture formed by a major bank and a large investment brokerage company marketed some investment products to customers of the bank by falsely representing, among other things, that the investments were FDIC-insured. The investigation disclosed a systemic pattern of false and fraudulent misrepresentations and material omissions during the sales presentations to bank customers regarding two proprietary ten-year closed-end bond funds the company marketed. The customers were mostly elderly and extremely risk-averse but often unsophisticated with respect to investment experience. Using the information obtained during the investigation, the U.S. Attorney's Office negotiated separate civil settlements with the joint venture partners. The bank contributed $11.5 million to a victim reimbursement fund established for the funds' investors and paid a civil monetary penalty of $6.75 million to the United States. Additionally, the bank paid U.S. Attorney's Office costs and a portion of FDIC OIG investigative costs. The investment brokerage company contributed $3 million into the victim reimbursement fund and paid the U.S. Attorney's expert witness costs and the remainder of FDIC OIG investigative costs.

Based on evidence obtained by a multiagency task force that included special agents of the FDIC OIG, FBI, and IRS, two officials of the now defunct First National Bank of Keystone, Keystone, West Virginia, were charged, tried, and convicted on charges of obstructing an examination of the bank. Among the actions taken to obstruct the examination was the burial of several dump truck loads of bank documents and microfilm on a ranch owned by one of the convicted officials and her husband. A search of the ranch by investigators resulted in the recovery of buried bank records that filled 370 file boxes. Following her conviction, the former senior executive vice president of the bank and president of Keystone Mortgage Company, a subsidiary of the bank, was sentenced to fifty-seven months of imprisonment and fined $100,000. The former executive vice president of the mortgage company was sentenced to fifty-one months of imprisonment and fined $7,500. Both were sentenced to probation for a period of 3 years following their incarcerations. The defendants received maximum sentences under the federal sentencing guidelines, in part, for lying under oath.

After the OIG learned of an attempted intrusion of the FDIC Web site, special agents from the OIG obtained information that permitted them to identify the source of the attack. The information revealed that the attack had originated from a computer owned by an information technology company that had considered seeking a contract to provide Internet security services to the FDIC. An employee of the information technology company launched the hack of the FDIC Web site to determine whether the FDIC's computers were vulnerable to a series of well-known hacker techniques. The information technology company failed to notify the FDIC of the origin of the hack. As a result of the expenses incurred by the FDIC in investigating the hack and resecuring the server, the information technology company agreed to pay $44,841 in damages to the FDIC.

Training, qualifications, and application procedures are similar to those found under the Department of Agriculture. For further information, contact:

Federal Deposit Insurance Corporation
Office of Inspector General
801 17th Street, NW, Room 1096
Washington, D.C. 20434
Telephone: (202) 416-2026

FEDERAL ELECTION COMMISSION

The Federal Election Commission (FEC) is an independent, regulatory agency responsible for administering and implementing the Federal Election Campaign Act (FECA). The FEC is one of thirty-three designated agencies required to have an Inspector General under the 1988 amendments to the Inspector General Act of 1978 (P.L. 100-504).

The FEC is composed of six commissioners who are appointed for six-year terms by the President with the advice and consent of the Senate. The FECA also established the position of Staff Director and General Counsel, who are appointed by the commissioners. The Staff Director serves as general manager of the FEC and ensures that the policies and directives of the Commission are implemented. The General Counsel serves as the chief legal adviser and litigator for the FEC and also serves as an advocate on compliance matters presented to the commissioners for their decision. The Inspector General reports directly to the six commissioners.

OFFICE OF INSPECTOR GENERAL

The responsibilities of the Inspector General, as stated in P.L. 100-504 are to conduct and supervise audits and investigations relating to the Federal Election Commission's programs and operations; provide leadership, coordination, and recommend policies for activities designed to promote economy, efficiency, and effectiveness in the administration of Commission programs and operations; prevent and detect fraud, waste, and abuse in these programs and operations; and keep the commissioners and Congress fully and currently informed about problems and deficiencies and the need for and progress of corrective actions.

The Office of Inspector General is under the supervision of the Inspector General who provides overall direction to the staff. The staff consists of four full-time employees: the Inspector General, the Special Assistant to the Inspector General, and two senior auditors.

Training, qualifications, and application procedures are similar to those found under the Department of Agriculture. For further information, contact:

Federal Election Commission
Office of Inspector General
999 E Street, NW, Room 940
Washington, D.C. 20463
Telephone: (202) 694-1015

FEDERAL HOUSING FINANCE BOARD

The Federal Housing Finance Board (Finance Board) was established by the Federal Home Loan Bank Act, as amended by the Financial Institutions Reform, Recovery, and Enforcement Act of 1989 (FIRREA) (12 U.S.C. 1421 *et seq.*), as an independent regulatory agency in the executive branch. The Finance Board succeeded the Federal Home Loan Bank Board for those functions transferred to it by FIRREA.

The Finance Board is managed by a five-member board of directors. Four members are appointed by the President with the advice and consent of the Senate for seven-year terms; one of the four is designated as chairperson. The Secretary of the Department of Housing and Urban Development is the fifth member and serves in an *ex officio* capacity.

The Finance Board supervises the twelve Federal Home Loan Banks created in 1932 by the Federal Home Loan Bank Act and issues regulations and orders for carrying out the purposes of the provisions of that act. Savings associations, commercial banks, savings banks, credit unions, insurance companies, and other institutions (specified in section 4 of the act that make long-term home-mortgage loans) are eligible to become members of the Federal Home Loan Banks. The Finance Board supervises the Federal Home Loan Banks and ensures that they carry out their housing finance and community investment mission, remain adequately capitalized and able to raise funds in the capital markets, and operate in a safe and sound manner.

OFFICE OF INSPECTOR GENERAL

The Office of Inspector General (OIG) is responsible for ensuring that the audits and investigations at the Finance Board are conducted in accordance with generally accepted government auditing standards and investigative standards. OIG may also conduct auditing or investigative activities at the twelve FHL Banks and other related entities when requested to do so by the Chairman; necessary to obtain information on the Finance Board's administration of its programs; and when they are aimed at detecting fraud or inefficiency in the administration or operation of Finance Board programs.

The investigative work focuses on resolving each case expeditiously and illuminating control weaknesses that may have contributed to possible fraud or abuse. This investigative activity was performed in accordance with Quality Standards for Investigations issued by the President's Council on Integrity and Efficiency (PCIE) and the Executive Council on Integrity and Efficiency (ECIE). By the end of the reporting period, OIG had two investigations in process.

The OIG maintains liaison with Finance Board officials, in efforts to identify and correct management problems; external auditors, to facilitate timely and accurate reporting on Finance Board operations; and the Inspector General community, to keep it apprised of evolving issues that affect the Finance Board. Specifically, the OIG continues to monitor management efforts to improve the agency's financial management system and management's efforts to enhance the agency's automated capabilities. They also continue to coordinate with the General Accounting Office and other financial regulatory agencies on audits and reviews impacting the Finance Board. In addition, OIG participates in activities involving the entire Inspector General community. As part of their affiliation with the ECIE, they coordinate and enhance the process for ECIE members' peer reviews and provide comments on various legislative proposals affecting the Inspector General community.

Training, qualifications, and application procedures are similar to those found under the Department of Agriculture. For further information, contact:

Federal Housing Finance Board
Office of Inspector General
1777 F Street, NW
Washington, D.C. 20006
Telephone: (202) 408-2544
Fax: (202) 408-2972

FEDERAL LABOR RELATIONS AUTHORITY

The Federal Labor Relations Authority (FLRA), an independent entity within the Executive Branch, oversees the labor-management relations program of the federal service. The FLRA administers the law that protects the right of employees of the federal government to bargain collectively and to participate through labor organizations of their own choosing in decisions affecting many conditions of their employment. The FLRA ensures compliance with the statutory rights and obligations of federal employees and the labor organizations that represent them in their dealings with federal agencies.

OFFICE OF INSPECTOR GENERAL

The Office of the Inspector General at the FLRA was formally established on March 24, 1989, and the first Inspector General was appointed on September 25, 1989. Under the authorizing legislation, the OIG was established to conduct and supervise audits and investigations; provide leadership and coordination; recommend policies which promote economy, efficiency, and effectiveness in agency programs and operations; prevent and detect fraud and abuse in those same areas; and keep the chairman and the Congress fully informed regarding problems and deficiencies.

The OIG investigates allegations of fraud or other integrity violations in FLRA operations and programs. Any violation of criminal statutes is reported to the Department of Justice. The OIG also conducts sensitive inquiries and noncriminal investigations. Since the FLRA does not administer grants and entitlement programs as do many other agencies with statutory Inspectors General, most of the audits conducted by the OIG are directed primarily toward improving program management and ensuring efficient operations.

For further information, contact:
Office of the Inspector General
Federal Labor Relations Board
607 14th Street, NW, Room 240
Washington, D.C. 20424
Telephone: (202) 482-6570

FEDERAL MARITIME COMMISSION

The Federal Maritime Commission (FMC) is responsible for the regulation of ocean-borne transportation in the foreign commerce of the United States.

The principal statutes or statutory provisions administered by the FMC are the Shipping Act of 1984, the Foreign Shipping Practices Act of 1988, section 19 of the Merchant Marine Act, 1920, Public Law 89-777, and the Ocean Shipping Reform Act of 1998.

The FMC ensures that United States international trade is open to all nations on fair and equitable terms and protects against unauthorized, concerted activity in the ocean-borne commerce of the United States. This is accomplished through review of operational and pricing agreements among ocean carriers and marine terminals to ensure that they do not have excessively anticompetitive efforts.

The FMC also reviews service contracts between ocean-faring common carriers and shippers and investigates discriminatory rates, charges, classifications, and practices of common carriers, terminal operators, and licensed ocean transportation intermediaries operating in the foreign commerce of the United States.

OFFICE OF INSPECTOR GENERAL

The Office of Inspector General was established pursuant to the Inspector General Act Amendments of 1988. The OIG is relatively small and relies, for the most part, on a memorandum of understanding with the OIG at the Social Security Administration for criminal investigative assistance. Administrative investigations are conducted by the legal counsel to the Inspector General.

The OIG is authorized to receive and investigate complaints from FMC employees, the general public, and other external sources concerning the Commission of illegal acts, mismanagement, violation of a regulation, abuse of authority, or any other allegation of wrongdoing dealing with the waste or misappropriation of agency funds. Because the FMC is a regulatory agency, most of the audits conducted are directed primarily towards improving management and ensuring efficient operations.

For further information, contact:
Office of Inspector General
Federal Maritime Commission
800 North Capitol Street, NW, Suite 1072
Washington, D.C. 20573-0001
Telephone: (202) 523-5863

FEDERAL TRADE COMMISSION

The objective of the Federal Trade Commission (FTC) is to maintain competitive enterprise as the keystone of the American economic system and prevent the free enterprise system from being fettered by monopoly or restraints on trade or corrupted by unfair or deceptive trade practices. The (FTC) is charged with keeping competition both free and fair.

OFFICE OF INSPECTOR GENERAL

The Inspector General is authorized by the IG Act to receive and investigate allegations of fraud, waste, and abuse occurring within FTC programs and operations. Matters of possible wrongdoing come to the OIG in the form of allegations or complaints from a variety of sources, including FTC employees, other government agencies, and the general public.

Reported incidents of possible fraud, waste, and abuse can give rise to administrative, civil, or criminal investigations. OIG investigations might also be initiated based on the possibility of wrongdoing by firms or individuals outside the agency when there is an indication that they are or were involved in activities intended to improperly affect the outcome of a particular agency enforcement action. Because this kind of wrongdoing strikes at the integrity of the FTC's consumer protection and antitrust law enforcement missions, the OIG places a high priority on investigating it.

In conducting criminal investigations during the past several years, the OIG has sought assistance from, and worked jointly with, other law enforcement agencies, including other OIG's, the Federal Bureau of Investigation (FBI), the U.S. Postal Inspection Service, the U.S. Secret Service, the U.S. Marshals Service, the Internal Revenue Service, Capitol Hill Police, as well as state agencies and local police departments.

Investigative Initiative

Several investigations have been conducted by the OIG since the office was established in 1989. Some significant cases related to allegations of employee misconduct, including theft of government property, while others concerned the obstruction of government proceedings. Several investigative outcomes were reported to FTC management officials responsible for taking corrective action. Two cases were referred to the Department of Justice for criminal prosecution.

Auditing Initiative

Civil penalties represent cash payments received from either a person, partnership, or corporation for violation of an agency order or trade rule. Penalties can amount to $10,000 per violation and are deposited in the U.S. Treasury after collection. Civil penalty collection responsibility rests solely on the FTC when it acts as plaintiff in a case. This responsibility is usually delegated to the lead attorney on the case, as there exists no independent centralized receivable system within the agency to record, report, and follow up on such collections. Thus, if a lead attorney should ever fail to personally verify the deposit of a civil penalty payment or to aggressively pursue a past due collection, the government could suffer an unnecessary loss.

Training, qualifications, and application procedures are similar to those found under the Department of Agriculture. For further information, contact:

Office of the Inspector General
Federal Trade Commission
600 Pennsylvania Avenue, NW, Room 494
Washington, D.C. 20580
Telephone: (202) 326-2800

GOVERNMENT PRINTING OFFICE

For more than a century, the Government Printing Office's mission under the public printing and documents statutes of Title 44, U.S. Code, has been to fulfill the needs of the federal government for information products and to distribute those products to the public.

Formerly, GPO's mission was accomplished through the production and procurement of traditional printing technologies. However, a generation ago, GPO began migrating its processes to electronic technologies, and in 1993 Congress amended Title 44 with the GPO Electronic Information Access Enhancement Act (P.L. 103-40), which requires GPO to disseminate government information products online. This act is the basis of GPO Access, the GPO Internet information service.

Today, GPO is dedicated to producing, procuring, and disseminating government information products in print, CD-ROM, and online formats. In GPO, the government has a unique asset that combines a comprehensive range of conventional production and electronic processing, procurement facilitation, and multiformat dissemination capabilities to support the needs of Congress, federal agencies, and the public.

GPO provides print and electronic information products and services to Congress and federal agencies through in-plant processes and the purchase of information products from the private sector. For Congress, GPO maintains a capability to fully support the information products needs of the legislative process, working in close cooperation with leadership offices, committees, members, and staffs in each Chamber.

GPO disseminates government information to the public in print and electronic formats through a low-priced sales program and a reimbursable program, and to federal depository libraries nationwide, where the information may be used by the public free of charge. GPO catalogs and indexes government information products so they can be identified and retrieved by users.

GPO also disseminates a massive volume of information online via the Internet with GPO Access. Recent data shows that the public retrieves more than 21 million documents every month using this system. GPO strongly supports the increased dissemination of government information in electronic formats, and GPO Access is one of the leading federal sites on the Internet. The GPO home page, at http://www.access.gpo.gov, provides free public access to more than seventy federal databases from all three branches of the government, a growing number of agency government information locator service (GILS) sites, and associated locator and pathway aids.

OFFICE OF INSPECTOR GENERAL

The Office of Inspector General was created by the Government Printing Office Inspector General Act of 1988, Title II of Public Law 100-504 (October 18, 1988). Title I of that Public Law, known as the Inspector General Act Amendments of 1988, created offices of Inspectors General in designated federal entities. Because GPO is a legislative branch agency, the GPO OIG was established separately. However, the GPO Inspector General shares the same duties, responsibilities, and authority as the Inspectors General in the designated federal entities, except that there is no statutory prohibition against assigning program operating responsibilities to the GPO Office of Inspector General. Another exception is that Public Law 104-316, the General Accounting Office Act of 1996, provides that the GPO Inspector General conducts audits under the direction of the Joint Committee on Printing, and conducts annual audits of the GPO financial statement when requested by the Joint Committee on Printing.

The mission of the OIG is to prevent and detect fraud, waste, and abuse as well as to promote economy, efficiency, and effectiveness in GPO's programs and operations. To meet these responsibilities, the OIG conducts audits and investigations through its Office of Audits (OA) and Office of Investigations (OI). The Inspector General has been a member of and active in the President's Executive Council on Integrity and Efficiency (ECIE) since the Council was established in 1992 by Executive Order 12805.

Investigative Initiatives

In a case brought in the Southern District of Ohio, a printing company agreed to a settlement under the False Claims Act by which GPO will receive a $300,000 recovery. The company settled potential charges that it presented false and fraudulent claims to the United States for payment in connection with illegally subcontracting the predominant production function of at least 607 GPO contracts.

Seven corporate and private entities were charged with common law fraud, negligent representation, breach of contract, unjust enrichment, conversion, and violations of the False Claims Act. A settlement was reached between the parties and the USAO, Baltimore, Maryland, in which $9,000 would be repaid to the GPO. However, the parties have failed to make payment and the USAO is in the process of demanding the full penalty of $40,000.

The OI conducted two separate investigations of a GPO employee regarding allegations of the submission of false information on a job application, and providing sensitive/confidential information to two other employees without proper authority.

An investigation of a GPO Region 4 contractor regarding the alleged submission of false claims/statements to the GPO has resulted in debarment proceedings being initiated against two companies and their corporate officials. In addition, civil action by the U.S. Attorney's Office, Atlanta, Georgia, has been initiated. This matter alleges that the companies were unjustly awarded 244 GPO printing contracts worth approximately $380,000.

Auditing Initiative

The OA conducted a performance audit on the adequacy, efficiency, and effectiveness of management controls over property within GPO. The audit found that GPO's Property Management program did not reflect the current operating procedures, controls, and responsibilities of GPO offices and the current instruction was not followed by management officials. For instance, the Comptroller, the designated Property Management Officer, did not maintain a complete records system for both capitalized and noncapitalized property as required by the instruction. Instead, the Comptroller concentrated on maintaining a records system for capitalized property only. As a result, the property custodians could not always use the records system as a management tool to account for the property assigned to their cost codes. The report's seven recommendations to the Comptroller should strengthen the internal controls over administering GPO's Property Management Program. The report's remaining three recommendations to the Production Department's Production Manager, the Superintendent of Documents, the Printing Procurement Department's Manager, and the Comptroller should strengthen the internal controls over the accounting of property.

Training, qualifications, and application procedures are similar to those found under the Department of Agriculture. For further information, contact:

Office of the Inspector General
Government Printing Office
North Capital and H Streets, Room C551
Washington, D.C. 20401
Telephone: (202) 512-0039

LEGAL SERVICES CORPORATION

The Legal Services Corporation is a private, nonprofit organization established by the Legal Services Corporation Act of 1974 to provide financial support for legal assistance in noncriminal proceedings to persons financially unable to afford legal services.

The Corporation is governed by an eleven-member Board of Directors, appointed by the President with the advice and consent of the Senate.

The Corporation provides financial assistance to qualified programs that furnish legal assistance to eligible clients and makes grants to and contracts with individuals, firms, corporations, and organizations for the purpose of providing legal assistance to these clients.

The Corporation establishes maximum income levels for clients based on family size, urban and rural differences, and cost-of-living variations. Using these maximum income levels and other financial factors, the Corporation's recipient programs establish criteria to determine the eligibility of clients and priorities of service based on an appraisal of the legal needs of the eligible client community. The Corporation also conducts research and technical assistance activities.

OFFICE OF INSPECTOR GENERAL

The Legal Services Corporation (LSC) Office of Inspector General (OIG) was established pursuant to the Inspector General Act Amendments of 1988. The OIG has two principal missions: to assist management in identifying ways to promote efficiency and effectiveness in the activities and operations of LSC and its grantees and to prevent and detect waste, fraud, and abuse.

The OIG's primary tool for achieving these missions is fact-finding through financial, performance, and other types of audits and reviews, as well as investigations into allegations of wrongdoing. Its fact-finding activities enable the OIG to develop recommendations to LSC and grantee management for actions or changes that will correct problems, better safeguard the integrity of funds, improve procedures, or otherwise increase efficiency or effectiveness.

In addition to the missions shared by all OIGs, Congress, starting with LSC's fiscal year 1996 appropriation, directed that the primary tool for monitoring grantee compliance with legal requirements would be the annual grantee audits conducted by independent public accountants under guidance developed by the OIG, thus adding participation in monitoring compliance to the role of the OIG.

Training, qualifications, and application procedures are similar to those found under the Department of Agriculture. For further information, visit the LSC OIG online at http://www.oig.lsc.gov or contact:

Office of the Inspector General
Legal Services Corporation
750 First Street, NE
Washington, D.C. 20002
Telephone: (202) 336-8830
Fax: (202) 336-8859

NATIONAL ARCHIVES AND RECORDS ADMINISTRATION

The National Archives and Records Administration (NARA) ensures ready access to essential evidence for the citizens, public servants, the President, Congress, and the courts.

By preserving the nation's documentary history, NARA serves as a public trust on which our democracy depends. It enables citizens to inspect for themselves the record of what the government has done. It enables officials and agencies to review their actions and helps citizens hold them accountable. It ensures continuing access to essential evidence that documents the rights of American citizens, the actions of federal officials, and the national experience.

Federal records reflect and document America's development over more than 200 years and are great in number, diverse in character, and rich in information. These holdings include more than 4 billion pages of textual materials; over 112,000 reels of motion picture film; more than 4 million maps, charts, and architectural drawings; over 200,000 sound and video recordings; more than 9 million aerial photographs and nearly 7 million still pictures; and over 14,000 electronic files from more than 200 agencies and bureaus.

In addition, NARA involves millions of people in its public programs, which include exhibitions, tours, educational programs, film series, and genealogical workshops. NARA publishes the *Federal Register* and other legal and reference documents that form a vital link between the federal government and those affected by its regulations and actions. Through the National Historical Publications and Records Commission, NARA helps to preserve and publish nonfederal historical documents that also constitute an important part of our national heritage. NARA also administers the Nixon Presidential Materials Staff and ten Presidential libraries, which preserve the papers and other historical materials of all past presidents since Herbert Hoover.

OFFICE OF INSPECTOR GENERAL

The Office of Inspector General ensures that NARA provides the American people with ready access to the history of America.

The IG Act of 1978, as amended, established the OIG's independent role and general responsibilities. The IG reports to both the Archivist and the Congress. The OIG evaluates NARA's performance, makes recommendations for improvements, and follows up to ensure economical, efficient, and effective operations and compliance with laws, policies, and regulations. In particular, the OIG:

- assesses the effectiveness, efficiency, and economy of NARA programs and operations

- recommends improvements in policies and procedures to enhance operations and correct deficiencies

- recommends cost savings through greater efficiency and economy of operations, alternative use of resources, and collection actions

- investigates and recommends legal and management actions to correct fraud, waste, abuse, or mismanagement

OIG Initiative

The OIG advised the Archivist of the United States that the physical security of NARA facilities, employees, researchers, and visitors may have been be at risk. The OIG came to this conclusion after performing a preliminary assessment of security measures in place at Archives I and II. As criteria for making this assessment, the OIG reviewed security procedures issued by NARA as well as security procedures issued by the Department of Justice (DOJ). They also reviewed an internal memorandum that outlined steps NARA should take to improve physical security, but found that many of these recommendations had not been completed. For some recommendations, NARA had not initiated action.

Investigative Initiatives

The OIG investigated two reported thefts. In one case, an employee admitted taking $300 in cash receipts. That employee resigned pending administrative action. In addition, the IG investigated a theft of computer software, but closed the case administratively due to a lack of investigative leads.

The OIG investigated an allegation that World War II records concerning Nazi war criminals were removed and possibly destroyed. During the investigation, the records were located. The investigation was closed.

The OIG investigated an allegation regarding missing POW/MIA records. The investigation identified administrative deficiencies, but did not find any evidence of missing records.

The OIG received a letter threatening the detonation of nuclear devices at numerous NARA and Department of Defense (DoD) facilities, beginning December 31, 1999. The return address on the envelope indicated that the letter was from an institution for the criminally insane in Louisiana. The OIG subsequently notified authorities at the DoD; the U.S. Postal Service; the Bureau of Alcohol, Tobacco, and Firearms; and the Federal Bureau of Investigation (FBI) Bomb Task Force. The FBI assumed the investigation.

Auditing Initiative

The OIG completed field work on an assessment of the policies and procedures for backing up computer programs and files at NARA facilities. The overall purpose of the assessment, requested by management, was to determine if agency backup procedures are adequate for ensuring that lost computer files can be recovered, and that operations could be continued in the event of a disaster. Specifically, the OIG determined whether successful backup copies of all server files are created at frequent intervals, backup copies are maintained in a secure location at a site away from the server facility, and backup procedures are documented.

Training, qualifications, and application procedures are similar to those found under the Department of Agriculture. For further information, visit the NARA Web site at http://www.nara.gov or contact:

Office of the Inspector General
National Archives and Records Administration
8601 Adelphi Road
College Park, Maryland 20740-6001
Telephone: (301) 713-7300

NATIONAL CREDIT UNION ADMINISTRATION

The National Credit Union Administration (NCUA) was established as an independent, federal regulatory agency on March 10, 1970. The agency is responsible for chartering, examining, supervising, and insuring federal credit unions. It also insures state-chartered credit unions that have applied for insurance and have met National Credit Union Share Insurance requirements. NCUA is funded entirely by credit unions; it does not receive any tax dollars. As of December 31, 2000, the NCUA was supervising and insuring 6,336 federal credit unions and insuring 3,980 state-chartered credit unions, a total of 10,316 institutions. This represents a loss of 230 federal and 82 state-chartered institutions since late 1999, for a total loss of 312 credit unions nationwide.

NCUA operates under the direction of a board composed of three members appointed by the President and confirmed by the Senate. They serve six-year terms. Terms are staggered so that one term expires every two years. The board is responsible for the management of the National Credit Union Administration, the NCUA Share Insurance Fund, the Central Liquidity Facility, and the Community Development Revolving Loan Program.

OFFICE OF INSPECTOR GENERAL

The Office of the Inspector General was established at the NCUA in 1989 under the authority of the Inspector General Act of 1978, as amended in 1988. The staff consists of the Inspector General, an Assistant Inspector General for Investigations/Counsel, a Senior Special Agent, an Assistant Inspector General for Audits, two senior auditors, a senior information technology auditor, and an office administrator.

The Inspector General reports to, and is under the general supervision of the NCUA Board. The Inspector General is responsible for:

■ conducting, supervising, and coordinating audits and investigations of all NCUA programs and operations

■ reviewing policies and procedures to ensure efficient and economic operations as well as preventing and detecting fraud, waste, and abuse

■ reviewing existing and proposed legislation and regulations to evaluate their impact on the economic and efficient administration of agency programs

■ keeping the NCUA Board and the Congress apprized of significant findings and recommendations

Investigative Initiative

The OIG conducted an investigation of alleged misuse of funds. It was found that internal controls were weak, funds were disbursed without proper approval or authority, and ethical misconduct had taken place. Administrative action was taken.

Auditing Initiative

NCUA's financial system, SAP, is primarily used to perform online payment and accounting of agency financial transactions. The purpose of the IG's review was to access controls and recommend corrections for any deficiencies. The review identified several internal control weaknesses in the SAP security configuration. Because SAP is utilized to process financial accounting information including purchasing, accounts payable, accounts receivable, general ledger, and human resources, security breaches in this area could lead to unauthorized, undetected access to confidential financial and employee data. The most significant findings were:

■ duties within the purchasing process had not been adequately segregated. As a result, personnel could possibly gain control of the entire purchasing cycle, resulting in errors, irregularities, or fraud.

■ a large number of users had been granted inappropriate authorities in the financial accounting and controlling modules.

The OIG reported that NCUA should take immediate action to conduct a thorough review of user access in order to ensure that user access is appropriately restricted and that incompatible duties are segregated. NCUA's consolidated response to the report's forty-two recommendations was extremely positive. NCUA has either implemented or agreed to implement all of the report's recommendations.

Training, qualifications, and application procedures are similar to those found under the Department of Agriculture. For further information, contact:

Office of Inspector General
National Credit Union Administration
1775 Duke Street
Alexandria, Virginia 22314-3428
Telephone: (703) 518-6350

NATIONAL ENDOWMENT FOR THE ARTS

The goal of the National Endowment for the Arts (NEA) is to foster professional excellence of the arts in America, to nurture and sustain them, and to help create a climate in which they may flourish so they may be experienced and enjoyed by the widest possible public audience.

OFFICE OF INSPECTOR GENERAL

The Office of Inspector General for NEA was established in compliance with the Inspector General Act Amendments of 1988.

Auditing Initiatives

Audits and other reviews conducted by OIG personnel during the current and prior periods have disclosed a few instances of deficient financial management practices in some organizations that received NEA grants. Among these were:

- reported grant project costs did not agree with the accounting records, i.e., financial status reports were not prepared directly from the general ledger or subsidiary ledgers or from worksheets reconciled to the accounts;

- personnel costs charged to grant projects were not supported by adequate documentation, i.e., personnel activity reports were not maintained to support allocations of personnel costs to NEA projects;

- the amount allocated to grant projects for common (indirect) costs which benefited all projects and activities of the organization was not supported by adequate documentation

- grantees needed to improve internal controls, such as ensuring a proper separation of duties to safeguard resources and including procedures for comparing actual costs with the budget

In order to assist in correcting or preventing the common deficiencies identified, the OIG finalized two *Financial Management Guides*, one for nonprofit organizations and the other for state and local organizations. The guides serve the following purposes:

- to provide a description of the most common financial management deficiencies identified through audits and surveys of NEA grantees

- to provide a description of certain elements which are necessary for adequate administration of federal grant projects and includes sample documentation forms which could be used to support certain types of costs such as salaries, travel, and in-kind contributions

- to include a self-evaluation questionnaire that will identify whether or not the grantee's management system includes any of the more common deficiencies that contribute to audit/survey findings

- to describe the independent financial audits required by OMB Circular A-133, Audits of States, Local Governments, and Non-Profit Organizations

For further information, visit the National Endowment for the Arts OIG online at http://www.arts.endow.gov/learn/oig/contents.html or contact:

Office of the Inspector General
National Endowment for the Arts
1100 Pennsylvania Avenue, NW, Room 601
Washington, D.C. 20506
Telephone: (202) 682-5402

NATIONAL ENDOWMENT FOR THE HUMANITIES

The National Endowment for the Humanities (NEH) is an independent agency created by Congress in 1965 to support exemplary work in all disciplines of the humanities. NEH provides grants to individuals and institutions for projects in the humanities. These include research and educational opportunities for college professors, independent scholars, and elementary and secondary school teachers; the writing and publication of scholarly texts; translations of important works in the humanities; museum exhibitions; television and radio programs; and a variety of other programs to make the humanities accessible to the general public.

The Endowment is directed by a chairman who makes policy and is responsible for day-to-day administration. Advising the Chairman is a National Council of 26 distinguished private citizens. Both the Chairman and the National Council are appointed by the President and approved by the Senate.

OFFICE OF INSPECTOR GENERAL

The NEH's Office of Inspector General was established on April 9, 1989, in accordance with the Inspector General Act Amendments of 1988, Public Law 100-504. In this legislation, Congress established Offices of Inspector General in several departments and in thirty-three agencies, including NEH. The NEH IG is appointed by the Chairman. The independence of the IG is an important aspect of the Act. For example, the IG:

- cannot be prevented from initiating, carrying out, or completing an audit or investigation, or from issuing any subpoena

- has access to all records of the agency

- reports directly to the Chairman, and can only be removed by the Chairman, who must promptly advise Congress of the reasons for the removal

- reports directly to congress

The Act states that the Office of Inspector General is responsible for conducting audits and investigations, reviewing legislation, recommending policies to promote efficiency and effectiveness, and preventing and detecting fraud, waste, and abuse in the operations of the agency. The Inspector General is also responsible for keeping the Chairman and Congress fully and currently informed of problems and deficiencies in the programs and operations.

The OIG staff consists of the IG, a Deputy IG for Audits, two auditors, and a secretary. The OIG and the Office of General Counsel (OGC) have a Memorandum of Understanding detailing the procedures for the OIG to be provided with OGC legal services. Investigations are handled by the IG, an auditor and, as required, by the agency's Deputy General Counsel.

The IG Act provides the authority for the OIG to investigate possible violations of criminal and civil laws, administrative regulations, and agency policies which relate to the programs and operations of NEH. The OIG Hotline, e-mail address, and regular mail are efficient, effective means of receiving allegations or complaints from employees, grantees, contractors, or the general public. The OIG has obtained assistance from other OIGs, the Federal Bureau of Investigation, the Postal Inspection Service, and other investigative entities, as applicable.

Training, qualifications, and application procedures are similar to those found under the Department of Agriculture. For further information, contact:

Office of Inspector General
National Endowment for the Humanities
1100 Pennsylvania Avenue NW, Room 419
Washington, D.C. 20600
Telephone: (202) 606-8350

NATIONAL LABOR RELATIONS BOARD

The National Labor Relations (NLRB) is an independent federal agency created by Congress in 1935 to administer the National Labor Relations Act, the primary law governing relations between unions and employers in the private sector. The statute guarantees the right of employees to organize and to bargain collectively with their employers or to refrain from all such activity. Generally applying to all employers involved in interstate commerce (other than airlines, railroads, agriculture, and government), the Act implements the national labor policy of ensuring free choice and encouraging collective bargaining as a means of maintaining industrial peace.

Through the years, Congress has amended the Act and the Board and courts have developed a body of law drawn from the statute.

OFFICE OF INSPECTOR GENERAL

The Office of Inspector General (OIG) is an independent office created within the NLRB by the Inspector General Act Amendments of 1988. As set forth in the Act, the OIG is to prevent and detect fraud, waste, abuse, and mismanagement and promote economy and efficiency in government. OIG carries out its responsibilities by conducting audits, administrative and criminal investigations, and other inquiries relating to NLRB programs and operations. OIG also reviews proposed and existing laws, regulations, and internal guidance concerning NLRB. In order to maintain independence, OIG is prohibited from performing any agency program functions. This does not prohibit OIG from participating in "prevention" activities, such as the development of agency policy or serving in an advisory capacity on committees.

Training, qualifications, and application procedures are similar to those found under the Department of Agriculture. For further information, contact:

Office of Inspector General
National Labor Relations board
1099 14th Street, NW, Suite 9820
Washington, D.C. 20570
Telephone: (202) 273-1960

NATIONAL SCIENCE FOUNDATION

The National Science Foundation is an independent agency created by the National Science Foundation Act of 1950, as amended (42 U.S.C. 1861-1875).

The purposes of the Foundation are:

- to increase the nation's base of scientific and engineering knowledge and strengthen its ability to conduct research in all areas of science and engineering

- to develop and help implement science and engineering education programs that can better prepare the nation for meeting the challenges of the future

- to promote international cooperation through science and engineering

In its role as a leading federal supporter of science and engineering, the agency also has an important role in national policy planning.

OFFICE OF INSPECTOR GENERAL

The Foundation's Office of Inspector General is responsible for conducting and supervising audits, inspections, and investigations relating to the programs and operations of the Foundation, including allegations of misconduct in science.

The NSF's Office of Inspector General was established by the Inspector General Act Amendments of 1988. The IG reports to the National Science Board, the policy-making body of the agency. In addition, to be effective, the Foundation's OIG must employ scientists able to grasp the implications of proposed policy initiatives, respond to allegations of misconduct in projects funded by the agency, and monitor the administration of scientific programs. These endeavors require equipment and highly trained staff.

Investigative Initiatives

After being notified of three separate incidents involving alleged computer crimes and unauthorized intrusions into NSF computer systems, the National Science Foundation Office of Inspector General is developing a Computer Incident Response Team (CIRT). This team, like other CIRT teams in the federal government, will be able to rapidly respond to computer intrusions to protect NSF's systems and carefully gather the evidence necessary for possible civil or criminal prosecutions. The NSF CIRT team will be multidisciplinary, incorporating management and law enforcement capabilities and possessing technical and forensic skills.

The OIG worked with DOJ and another federal agency's IG offices in an investigation of a government contractor that resulted in a $1.9 million civil settlement. These funds will go to the U.S. Department of the Treasury. It was alleged that the contractor billed seventeen federal agencies for subcontractor and consultant charges that it had not yet paid, a violation of the Federal Acquisition Regulation. The investigation determined that over a ten-year period, the contractor prematurely billed the government an average of thirty-seven days prior to payment of funds about 75 percent of the time, thereby depriving the government of the use of these funds for this period of time.

A chemistry professor at a large West Coast university who allowed a large number of personal telephone calls to be charged to his NSF grants agreed with the U.S. Attorney's Office to pay $65,000 in a civil settlement resolving this matter. The subject's university identified the questionable telephone charges during a university audit. In an investigation coordinated with the university's internal auditing department, the IG found that the subject directed that all charges for use of his university-issued calling card be charged to his NSF grants and that his wife used the calling card to make personal telephone calls. The subject claimed that he was unaware of most of his wife's telephone charges. However, after he learned about the calls, he continued to allow telephone billings to be charged to the grant. He claimed he had been tracking the expenses with the intention of reimbursing the grant. As part of the civil settlement, the subject and his university agreed to restrict the subject's authority to administer research funds for three years. The subject also agreed to pay the university $3,400 for other questionable expenditures charged to his research accounts. In addition, a university disciplinary committee suspended the subject without pay for six months.

The OIG assisted local law enforcement authorities in a southeastern state in investigating a complaint that a high school teacher invited students to participate in a research project and then sexually assaulted them during the project. The subject told the students his project was sponsored by NSF, but in fact the subject never received any research funds from NSF and had no connection with NSF or any NSF-funded research. The subject was arrested and subsequently pled guilty to state charges of sexual assault.

Auditing Initiatives

The OIG reported on reviews of two research institutes. The reviews focused on strategies to decrease NSF funding, because the institutes are expected, over time, to replace federal funds with outside funding. They reviewed their active awards and proposed budgets, including one located at a large northern state university. They recommended budget revisions related to the proposed revenue and inflationary estimates, the electronic distribution of a newsletter and overhead slides, and charges for dinners and other refreshments. The institute agreed to implement the OIG recommendations in a revised version of the proposal, resulting in $659,205 of funds put to better use.

Based on the results of a previous audit of an eastern university, NSF agreed that $158,743 of the university's claimed costs were unallowable and not adequately supported. The Foundation required the university to repay $70,744 and offset $87,999 against future unbilled costs. NSF and the university satisfactorily resolved other compliance and internal control issues.

Responding to an audit of a midwestern university, NSF agreed that $97,418 of the university's claimed costs were unallowable and not adequately supported. NSF required the university to repay $24,437 and offset $72,981 against future unbilled costs. NSF and the university satisfactorily resolved other compliance and internal control issues.

Training, qualifications, and application procedures are similar to those found under the Department of Agriculture. For further information, contact:

Office of Inspector General
National Science Foundation
4201 Wilson Boulevard, Room 1135
Arlington, VA 22230
Telephone: (703) 292-7100
E-mail: oig@nsf.gov

PEACE CORPS

The purpose of the Peace Corps is to promote world peace and friendship, help the peoples of other countries in meeting their needs for trained manpower, promote a better understanding of the American people on the part of the peoples served, and promote a better understanding of other peoples on the part of the American people. In 1977, the Peace Corps Act was amended to emphasize the Peace Corps' commitment toward programming to meet the basic needs of those living in the poorest areas of the countries in which the Peace Corps operates.

OFFICE OF INSPECTOR GENERAL

Congress established an Office of Inspector General (OIG) in 1978 to prevent and detect fraud, waste, abuse, and mismanagement, and to promote economy, effectiveness, and efficiency in government. In 1988, Congress extended the law to most other federal agencies, including the Peace Corps. The Peace Corps established its OIG in February 1989.

The OIG is an independent entity within the Peace Corps. The Inspector General reports directly to the Peace Corps Director. In addition, the IG reports to Congress biannually with data on OIG activities.

OIG investigators respond to allegations of criminal or administrative wrongdoing by Peace Corps personnel, including experts and consultants, and by those who do business with the Peace Corps, including contractors.

OIG auditors review Peace Corps functional activities, such as contract compliance and financial and program operations, to ensure accountability and to recommend improved levels of economy and efficiency.

OIG evaluators analyze Peace Corps management and program operations at both overseas posts and domestic offices. They identify best practices and recommend program improvements and means to comply with Peace Corps policies.

In their on-site visits, OIG staff members encourage post self-evaluations, identify problem areas, and recommend corrective actions. They conduct inspections focused on administrative compliance with rules and regulations. In addition, they review the safety and security of volunteers and staff members, particularly overseas. More broadly, OIG staff members identify common problems and trends from post to post and offer guidance for quality improvements agency-wide.

The OIG serves as the law enforcement arm of the Peace Corps and works closely with the Department of State, the Department of Justice, and other federal agencies.

The following are examples of offenses that should be reported to the OIG when they involve Peace Corps staff members, volunteers, trainees, contractors, experts, and consultants or funds, including Peace Corps' appropriations; host country contributions; SPA, PASA, IAA, and Partnership support; and any other agency funding sources:

- theft or embezzlement
- fraud
- unexplained deficiencies in federal funds
- misuse or mismanagement of federal funds
- illegal mutilation or destruction of a public record
- false statements, involving federal funds, accounts, or documents
- illegal drug use
- selling or importing/exporting narcotics, controlled drugs, or contraband in violation of federal law
- arson or vandalism
- bribery, attempted bribery, or unlawful gratuities involving a government official
- conflict of interest and other ethics violations
- misuse of government vehicles, property, or transportation requests
- significant violations of Peace Corps regulations
- sexual harassment/abuse by a co-worker or supervisor
- violent crimes, including sexual assault and rape
- kidnapping

■ disappearance

■ death (by any means, including suicide)

■ acts of terrorism and actions endangering the public health and safety.

For further information, contact:
Peace Corps
Office of Inspector General
P.O. Box 57129
Washington, DC 20037-7129
Telephone: 1-800-233-5874
Fax: (202) 692-2901
E-mail: oig@peacecorps.gov

PENSION BENEFIT GUARANTY CORPORATION

The Pension Benefit Guaranty Corporation (PBGC or Corporation) was established under Title IV of the Employee Retirement Income Security Act of 1974 (ERISA), as amended, 5 U.S.C. § 1301 - 1461, as a self-financing, wholly owned federal government corporation to administer the pension insurance program. ERISA requires that PBGC encourage the continuation and maintenance of voluntary private pension plans, provide for the timely and uninterrupted payment of pension benefits to participants and beneficiaries, and maintain premiums at the lowest level consistent with carrying out PBGC's obligations.

For about 43 million Americans, the PBGC provides assurance that their retirement benefits are safe now and for the future. The PBGC protects the pensions of participants in certain defined benefit pension plans (i.e., plans that promise to pay definitely determinable retirement benefits). Such defined benefit pension plans may be sponsored individually or jointly by employers and by unions.

OFFICE OF INSPECTOR GENERAL

The Inspector General is authorized to receive and investigate complaints from PBGC employees, the public, and other sources concerning violations of laws, rules, or regulations; mismanagement; gross waste of funds; abuse of authority; or a substantial and specific danger to the public health and safety. Individuals may disclose information or make complaints to the Inspector General through the OIG Hotline. The Inspector General has a policy to protect the legal rights of whistleblowers and complainants. At all times, the Inspector General takes reasonable precautions not to disclose the identity of the complainant without that person's consent.

One of the strategic goals of the Office of Inspector General (OIG) is to assist the PBGC in operating more efficiently and effectively by identifying ways to improve PBGC's programs. To accomplish this goal, the OIG conducts agency audits, inspections, and investigations and makes recommendations to PBGC management. In addition, the OIG is statutorily required to inform the agency head of fraud and other serious problems, abuses, and deficiencies relating to the programs and operations administered or financed by the PBGC, recommend corrective action concerning such problems, and report on the progress made in implementing corrective actions.

Investigative Activities

Upon investigation, it was determined that a senior-level employee had misused a government credit card for improper cash advances and for personal items purchased locally and while traveling. It was discovered that the employee engaged in multiple abuses relating to government travel, including conducting personal travel under the guise of official government travel, abuse of travel bonus programs, and solicitation of loans from a subordinate employee. Because the offenses involved violations of criminal statutes, this matter was referred to the District of Columbia Office of the United States Attorney for possible prosecution.

It was determined that a pension plan participant had filed a forged waiver of spousal retirement benefits. In this case, the husband forged his wife's signature on a document that gave up her right to any future retirement benefits. Upon determination of the fraud, the matter was referred to the agency to correct the records regarding the wife's entitlement to a spousal benefit and to recoup benefits overpaid to the husband as a result of the fraud.

It was determined that a senior-level employee abused official travel privileges, engaged in a pattern of false statements and false claims on the employee's travel vouchers, and accepted gratuities from prohibited sources while on travel. Because the offenses involved violations of criminal statutes, this matter was referred to the District of Columbia Office of the United States Attorney for possible prosecution. Once the United States Attorney's Office determined that the evidence did not support a finding of bribery in violation of 18 U.S.C. §201, it declined other criminal prosecution in lieu of administrative action. The case was referred back to the OIG for further investigation of the multiple ethics and travel violations. Though the defendant terminated employment with this agency during the course of the investigation, the employee was still a government employee. Therefore, a Report of Investigation was issued to agency officials to recoup monies owed the federal government, and a copy was sent to the Inspector General at the employee's current federal agency.

Auditing Initiatives

The OIG contracted with a team from the Technology Risk Services practice of PricewaterhouseCoopers, LLP, to perform a security review of the UNIX server that hosts the Corporation's performance accounting system. The review evaluated the security controls to determine whether only those with authorization had access to the sensitive information in the performance accounting system. A team specializing in UNIX technical controls conducted a risk-based review of the UNIX server. As the report contains sensitive information, its release is restricted.

A network security penetration assessment was performed to determine the extent to which someone could obtain unauthorized access to PBGC's systems through external or internal sources. Weaknesses in access controls over PBGC systems included the IPA's ability to gain administrator access to the PRISM system. In response to the reported findings, PBGC stated that the benefit payment process was not at risk because the controls within PRISM would prevent creation of unauthorized benefit payments. To test PBGC's assertions, the OIG engaged an IPA and a technology expert to assist in evaluating the effectiveness of PRISM's controls surrounding benefit payments. The team developed specific and realistic scenarios that would test controls to determine whether unauthorized benefit payments could be made. The scenarios were tested in both OIG and PBGC computer test labs. The PRISM evaluation identified system vulnerabilities and determined that certain types of unauthorized payments could be generated. Control weaknesses were identified and it was suggested that PBGC enhance access controls by implementing formal auditing, monitoring, reviewing, and logging procedures for system actions impacting on benefit payments. In addition to the written report, a live demonstration of the vulnerabilities was provided. Because the report contained sensitive information, its release was restricted.

Training, qualifications, and application procedures are similar to those found under the Department of Agriculture. For further information, contact:

Office of Inspector General
Pension Benefit Guaranty Corporation
1200 K Street, NW
Washington, D.C. 20005
Telephone: (202) 326-4030

SECURITIES AND EXCHANGE COMMISSION

The Securities and Exchange Commission (SEC) provides for the fullest possible disclosure to the investing public and protects the interests of the public and investors against malpractice in the securities and financial markets.

OFFICE OF INSPECTOR GENERAL

The mission of SEC's Office of Inspector General is consistent with the IG Act of 1978 as amended. There are no additional legislative authorities, and the scope of the OIG's investigation activity focuses on internal affairs matters related to staff misconduct. Examples of investigations range from the unauthorized disclosure of nonpublic documents (e.g., communications between the Commission and its attorneys) and conflicts of interest to payroll irregularities, embezzlement, and theft of relatively minor amounts.

Because the Securities and Exchange Commission does not give out grants, loans, or loan guarantees, nor award major contracts, the Office of Inspector General focuses on internal audits and investigations. As such, the office generally functions as an internal affairs unit. The Commission's Division of Enforcement is responsible for conducting investigations of securities fraud within the securities industry and for bringing civil and administrative proceedings as appropriate.

Auditing Initiatives

Because of the materiality of revenue collection by the Commission (approximately $250 million annually), the OIG initiated a "system development life cycle" audit of the development of a fee collection system. The objective of this type of audit is to identify audit concerns early in the development process so they can be addressed efficiently rather than making required changes after implementation. The audit found unfocused responsibility, authority, and accountability that resulted in delays in resolving several fundamental planning issues in the project. In response to this finding, management developed a division of responsibility to help resolve the problems. In addition, management agreed to develop explicit task plans, issue monthly progress reports, and establish improved project management procedures. The audit also identified weaknesses in contract administration. Existing procedures that were satisfactory for administering fixed-price contracts were inadequate for monitoring labor-hour contracts used for system development. Since the Commission accepts all risk if the project exceeds the budget or if the work products do not satisfy the Commission's needs, recommendations were made to strengthen contract administration procedures to insure successful development of the system.

Based on a report to OIG, the office tested and confirmed an alleged weakness in the security of the Commission's headquarters building. The audit recommended limited modifications to procedures and equipment involving access to the headquarters building and detection of intruders.

Training, qualifications, and application procedures are similar to those found under the Department of Agriculture. For further information, contact:

Office of the Inspector General
Securities and Exchange Commission
450 5th Street NW
Washington, D.C. 20549
Telephone: (202) 942-4461

SMITHSONIAN INSTITUTION

The Smithsonian Institution is both publicly supported and privately endowed. The governance is vested in an independent Board of Regents composed of the Chief Justice of the United States, the Vice President, three members each from the United States Senate and House of Representatives, and nine private citizens. The Board appoints the Secretary, who is the chief executive officer of the Institution.

The National Gallery of Art, the Woodrow Wilson International Center for Scholars, and the John F. Kennedy Center for the Performing Arts are statutory bureaus of the Institution but are administered under separate boards of trustees. Consequently, management and oversight of programs and operations rests within those organizations.

OFFICE OF INSPECTOR GENERAL

The Institution's OIG was established on April 17, 1989, in accordance with the Inspector General Act of 1978, as amended in 1988. The office is headed by the Inspector General, who reports directly to the Secretary of the Smithsonian Institution. The IG has authority to review all Institution programs and operations as well as related activities of persons or parties performing under grants, contracts, or other agreements. The reviews may be in the forms of audits, investigations, surveys, criminal or other investigations, or other appropriate action.

Investigative Initiatives

An OIG report of a worker's compensation investigation was referred to the U.S. Attorney in 1989. Although the U.S. Attorney declined prosecution, an administrative notice of overpayment was issued to the subject of the investigation. The Department of Labor sought repayment of about $14,300 from the subject. In addition, the Department of Labor's OIG and an Assistant U.S. Attorney of the Department of Justice explored the possibility of seeking civil damages from the subject.

Smithsonian Institution management requested an audit of a collection when heirs submitted a tax form and a curator indicated that there was a discrepancy between an independent appraisal and the curator's assessment of the size of the collection. The auditing staff found that forty-five shells that were previously accounted for were missing. Audit staff cited inadequate internal controls of the collection and requested investigative assistance to recover six of the more valuable shells. Investigative efforts resulted in the recovery of three shells valued at $300.

A museum curator identified a Smithsonian-owned model boat in the possession of a private citizen. Coordinated efforts by the OIG resulted in the return of the boat to the National Collection.

Auditing Initiatives

Significant backlogs in processing valuable objects into the collections of the Department of Anthropology existed. As a result, adequate inventory control was not being exercised over the backlogged objects. Recommendations were made to improve systems for recording items acquired for the Department's collections and monitoring the status of backlogs.

The OIG found that many physical and programmatic deficiencies were preventing the disabled public from gaining full access to Smithsonian Institution buildings, facilities, and programs. The OIG recommended major improvements in the central coordination and administration of the Smithsonian Institution accessibility program.

Improvements were needed in the maintenance of accession, deaccession, and inventory files for the museums' collections. The OIG made recommendations to improve the maintenance of these files.

The OIG found that the National Zoological Park (NZP) needed to fully comply with the Smithsonian Institution safety policy and procedures and improve the management of the NZP construction program.

Training, qualifications, and application procedures are similar to those found under the Department of Agriculture. For further information, contact:

Office of the Inspector General
Smithsonian Institution
Victor Building, Suite 4200
750 Ninth Street, NW
Washington, D.C. 20560
Telephone: (202) 275-2244

TENNESSEE VALLEY AUTHORITY

The Tennessee Valley Authority (TVA), a federal corporation, is the nation's largest electric power producer, a regional economic development agency, and a national center for environmental research. TVA's statutory responsibilities include management of the nation's fifth-largest river system.

TVA's mission is to develop and operate the Tennessee River system to minimize flood damage, improve navigation, and provide energy and related products and services safely, reliably, and at the lowest feasible cost to residents and businesses in the multistate Tennessee Valley Region.

TVA's programs fall into two separate but interrelated activities: the power program and the resource management programs.

TVA's power system consists of eleven coal-fired plants, three nuclear plants, twenty-nine hydroelectric dams, and a pumped storage plant. These plants provide over 28,000 megawatts of net dependable generating capacity. TVA's electric power business is entirely self-funding.

TVA's major functions include multiple purpose management of the Tennessee River system; generation, sale, and transmission of electricity to wholesale and large industrial customers; investment in economic development activities that generate a higher standard of living for citizens of the Tennessee Valley; stewardship of TVA assets and provision of recreation opportunities on federal lands entrusted to TVA; and research and technology development that addresses environmental problems related to TVA's statutory responsibilities for river and land management and power generation.

OFFICE OF INSPECTOR GENERAL

The TVA Board of Directors administratively established the Office of Inspector General (OIG) in October 1985. When the Inspector General Act Amendments of 1988 were enacted, TVA's OIG became one of the statutory offices whose Inspector General is appointed by the agency head. TVA's Inspector General is independent and subject only to the general supervision of the Board of Directors.

The OIG consists of an auditing unit and an investigative unit. The OIG's auditing operations unit consists of three departments. One is devoted to contract-related audits, both pre-award and post-award reviews; the two other departments focus on performance and special projects and financial and ADP-related issues, respectively.

The OIG's investigative operations unit consists of two investigative departments (Financial Investigations and Internal Investigations). Both departments work a variety of cases, including employee integrity and environmental issues. Financial Investigations focuses on contract and workers' compensation cases, while Internal Investigations focuses on employee conduct issues and benefits and entitlements programs. In addition, an Investigative Services and Hotline group reports to the Assistant Inspector General for Investigations.

Investigative Initiatives

An explosive device, consisting of dyno-unigel and a homemade timer, was found affixed to a breaker at a TVA substation in Erin, Tennessee. Although the device malfunctioned and failed to detonate, had it exploded, it would have resulted in a significant regional electric power outage, equipment destruction, and environmental damage. After an extensive joint OIG and TVA Police investigation, a Clarksville, Tennessee, man was indicted in federal court on four charges of destruction of government property by means of an explosive device.

The OIG participates in ECJTF, which is comprised of members from numerous state and federal agencies, including the Federal Bureau of Investigation, Environmental Protection Agency (EPA), Department of Justice (DOJ), and TVA's OIG. ECJTF focuses enhanced law enforcement resources against individuals and companies involved in environmental crimes and prosecutes those individuals and companies by applying the most effective federal and state criminal and civil statutes. In part because of an ECJTF criminal investigation, a Fortune 500 chemical company located in Tennessee settled an administrative enforcement action for alleged violations of the Resource+ Conservation and Recovery Act (RCRA). The Consent Agreement and Consent Order (CACO) required the company to pay a civil penalty of $2.75 million to the U.S. Treasury. Federal and state regulations required the company to measure the composition and monitor the hourly flow rate of hazardous waste delivered to seven boilers that burn a combination of hazardous waste and coal to generate energy. The Administrative Complaint, which accompanied the CACO, alleged the company failed to accurately monitor the amount of hazardous waste burned in seven boilers over a period of time. Further, the company failed to notify the Tennessee Department of Environment and Conservation of the noncompliance until a year later. A major penalty was pursued because of the extended period of noncompliance and the company's five-month delay in notification.

Auditing Initiative

TVA has established a safety program designed to help the agency conduct all of its programs and operations in a manner that protects the safety and health of its employees. TVA's safety program must meet applicable regulations issued by the Occupational Safety and Health Administration (OSHA) as required by Executive Order. They conducted a review of one aspect of the safety program, the handling of material safety data sheets (OMSDS). MSDS contain critical information regarding the handling of chemicals in the event of an accident. Specifically, they reviewed the internal controls associated with MSDSs to ensure that TVA maintains and updates MSDSs and allows employee access to MSDSs, as required by OSHA regulations. They found the internal controls were not functioning properly in the areas of written hazard communications programs and MSDS accessibility. Management has agreed to take corrective action.

Training, qualifications, and application procedures are similar to those found under the Department of Agriculture. For further information, contact:

Office of Inspector General
Tennessee Valley Authority
400 W. Summit Hill Drive
Knoxville, Tennessee 37902-1499
Telephone: (865) 632-4120

U.S. INTERNATIONAL TRADE COMMISSION

The U.S. International Trade Commission is a quasi-judicial, independent, bipartisan agency established by Congress, with broad investigative powers on matters of trade. The Commission's mission is to develop factual, objective research and information on a wide variety of matters pertaining to international economics and trade development. Commission activities include making recommendations to the President regarding relief for industries that are seriously injured by increasing imports; determining whether U.S. industries are materially injured by imports sold at less than fair value or benefiting from subsidies; taking actions, subject to Presidential disapproval, to prevent unfair trade practices such as patent infringement; advising the President whether imports interfere with agricultural price-support programs; conducting studies on trade and tariff issues; and participating in the development of uniform statistical data on imports, exports, and domestic production and the establishment of an international harmonized commodity code.

OFFICE OF INSPECTOR GENERAL

The Office of Inspector General in the U.S. International Trade Commission was established in 1988 and reports directly to the Chairman of the Commission. The Inspector General is responsible for directing and carrying out audits and investigations relating to programs and operations and for commenting on proposed legislation, regulations and procedures as to their economy, efficiency, and effectiveness.

For further information, visit the U.S. International Trade Commission OIG online at http://www.uistc.gov/oig or contact:

Office of the Inspector General
U.S. International Trade Commission
500 E Street SW, Room 220
Washington, DC 20436
Telephone: (202) 205-2210
E-mail: oig@usitc.gov

U. S. POSTAL SERVICE

The United States Postal Service provides mail processing and delivery services to individuals and businesses within the United States. The Service is committed to serving customers through the development of efficient mail-handling systems and operates its own planning and engineering programs. It is also the responsibility of the Postal Service to protect the mails from loss or theft and to apprehend those who violate Postal laws.

OFFICE OF INSPECTOR GENERAL

The Office of Inspector General (OIG) of the U.S. Postal Service was authorized by law in 1996. The OIG provides independent and objective oversight for the Postal Service, a $67 billion business with more than 900,000 employees nationwide that delivers 668 million pieces of mail daily.

The Inspector General, who is independent of postal management, is appointed by and reports directly to the nine presidentially appointed Governors of the Postal Service.

The OIG conducts independent audits and investigations of U.S. Postal Service programs and operations to help ensure their economy, efficiency, effectiveness, and integrity. The OIG office also prevents fraud, waste, abuse, and mismanagement.

The OIG is continuing an aggressive hiring initiative to staff the organization with highly skilled employees. The OIG has more than 650 employees, of whom 50 percent are women and 47 percent are minorities. The senior staff is composed of 39 percent women and 28 percent minority.

OIG Auditors, Evaluators, and Investigators

Auditors and evaluators review postal operations, conduct systemic audits, protect postal revenue, and ensure the integrity of the financial statements of the Postal Service. Investigators apprehend violators of the law and work closely with prosecutors and other law enforcement agencies. Their work also includes crime prevention. The OIG investigators have full law enforcement authority and are authorized to carry firearms, make arrests, and investigate postal offenses.

Auditors, evaluators, and investigators work together on audits, investigations, and other matters. Combining skills through joint work initiatives provides for increased efficiency and promotes teamwork.

The OIG's culture is defined by the diversity of its employees, who share the organization's core values of teamwork, leadership, creativity, communication, and conceptualization.

Auditing Investigative Initiatives

An audit of the Postal Service's leased fleet of about 8,700 trailers to determine compliance with federal safety standards identified that more than 25 percent of the leased trailers used to transport mail did not meet standards. The OIG also found that the Postal Service could not account for $5 million in leased trailer inventory and did not always secure and protect trailers. In addition, the OIG projected that the Postal Service could reduce costs by more than $17.5 million over a five-year period by properly administering damage claims on leased trailers and improving controls over trailer use. The OIG recommended and Postal Service management agreed to include requirements regarding safety maintenance and liability insurance in contracts, establish procedures to account for trailer inventory, secure and protect trailers, and update policies governing damage claims.

An investigation of a contract with a large telecommunications contractor resulted in a total recovery of $12.2 million to date.

An audit of the removal process of underground storage tanks resulted in the identification of ninety-one sites improperly capitalizing $4.7 million for tank removal and replacement, unnecessarily spending $1.5 million for premature removal of tanks, and unnecessary expenditures of $200,000 for installation of noncompliant tanks.

An investigation of two postal managers resulted in a federal grand jury returning a thirty-six-count indictment charging the pair with committing mail fraud, conspiracy to commit money laundering, and money laundering in connection with contract fraud.

An audit of contracting practices for the procurement of mail transport equipment disclosed that the Postal Service may pay up to $53 million more than if the contracts had been competitively awarded. In addition, OIG auditors found that the Postal Service paid a contractor more than $1.3 million for work that was not properly authorized. As a result, the Postal Service is at risk of being billed an additional $11.2 million by the same contractor for unauthorized work.

An audit of the warranty repair of tractors concluded that the Postal Service had not been reimbursed between $977,598 and $1,879,104 in costs incurred for warranty repair work performed by Vehicle Maintenance Facilities. Further, unless Postal Service management implements a system to obtain reimbursements, the Postal Service may continue to incur unreimbursed warranty repair costs of about $400,000 over the next two years.

An investigation of medical providers who submitted fictitious and fraudulent medical claims resulted in multiple arrests, indictments, and convictions nationwide.

A review of telecommunications identified numerous vulnerabilities in the security of the production servers at the Postal Service's San Mateo Computer Operations Service Center. These vulnerabilities, if exploited, could result in a compromise of the confidentiality, integrity, and availability of agency operations and harm the agency's reputation as a trusted business partner. OIG provided a listing that detailed each case of vulnerability to network administrators so that a national corrective action plan could be devised.

Position availability, qualifications, and application procedures can be found on the OPM Web site at http://www.usajobs.opm.gov. For further information, contact:

Office of Inspector General
U.S. Postal Service
Human Resources
1735 North Lynn Street
Arlington, Virginia 22209-2020
Telephone: (888) OIG-4476 (toll-free)

FEDERAL LAW ENFORCEMENT TRAINING FACILITIES

FBI ACADEMY

MISSION

The mission of the FBI Academy is to lead and inspire, through excellence in training and research, the education and development of the criminal justice community and influence change and forge partnerships that ensure the safety and security of the citizens of the United States and around the world.

HISTORICAL REVIEW

The FBI Academy is located on the U.S. Marine Corps Base at Quantico, Virginia. The facility, which opened in 1972, is situated on 385 wooded acres of land providing the security, privacy, and safe environment necessary to carry out the diverse training and operations functions for which the FBI is responsible. The Drug Enforcement Administration also has their training academy at Quantico, Virginia.

The main training complex has three dormitory buildings, a dining hall, library, a classroom building, a Forensic Science Research and Training Center, a 1,000-seat auditorium, a chapel, administrative offices, a large gymnasium and outside track, and a fully equipped garage. In addition to the main complex, there is a mock city known as Hogan's Alley, which consists of facades replicating a typical small town. The Hogan's Alley facades are primarily used for FBI and DEA new agent training. Located behind the facades are fully functioning classrooms, audiovisual facilities, storage areas, and administrative and maintenance offices. Just beyond Hogan's Alley is a 1.1 mile pursuit/defensive driving training track. The extensive firearms training provided to all FBI/DEA and other law enforcement officers is conducted at the indoor firing range, the eight outdoor firing ranges, four skeet ranges, or the 200-yard rifle range.

The FBI Academy is a security facility and, as such, is not open to the public for tours.

The FBI National Academy

The FBI National Academy (NA) experience and its sister program, Field Police Training, provide a wide range of leadership and specialized training, as well as an opportunity for professional law enforcement officers to share ideas, techniques, and experiences.

The National Academy Program was founded on July 29, 1935, with 23 students in attendance. Since then, the NA program has graduated more than 34,000 qualified students to date. The program has enjoyed a worldwide reputation among international law enforcement, and nearly 3,000 officers representing more than 130 countries have taken advantage of this training program.

With the opening of the FBI Academy in the summer of 1972, National Academy classes were provided on a quarterly basis, consisting of eleven weeks of training for upper- and mid-level law enforcement officers. The curriculum focuses on leadership and management training and consists of courses relating to management science, behavioral science, law, education, forensic science, and health and fitness.

FUNCTIONS AND ACTIVITIES

Behavioral Science Unit

The Behavioral Science Unit is one of the instructional components of the FBI's Training Division at Quantico. Its mission is to develop and provide programs of training, research, and consultation in the behavioral and social sciences for the FBI and law enforcement community that will improve or enhance their administration, operational effectiveness, and understanding of crime. This work includes high-impact research and the presentation of a variety of cutting edge courses on topics such as applied criminal psychology, clinical forensic psychology, community policing and problem-solving strategies, crime analysis, death investigation, gangs and gang behavior, interpersonal violence, law enforcement officers killed and assaulted in the line of duty, research methodology, stress management in law enforcement, and violence in America.

The Behavioral Science Unit conducts specialized and applied training in the above disciplines as they pertain to law enforcement for new agents, FBI in-service training and symposia, as well as the FBI National Academy Program, international police officers, field police schools, and criminal justice-related organizations and conferences consistent with goals and objectives, and available resources.

Field Police Training Unit

The Field Police Training Program serves as the foundation for the FBI's comprehensive training assistance to local, county, and state law enforcement. The goals of this program are to render training assistance regarding investigative, managerial, technical, and administrative aspects of law enforcement. FBI police instructors provide, upon request, education and training programs throughout the United States, thus contributing to the enhanced professionalism in American law enforcement.

International Training Program

The breakup of the former Soviet Union and the move to democracy by all of the countries of Central and Eastern Europe forced profound change, not only in the region, but also throughout the world. These changes are not merely political, but have significant impact on national economies, social structures, and law enforcement. The weakening or elimination of borders and the increased availability of electronic forms of communication and commerce have allowed criminals almost unlimited mobility. These social, political, and economic changes have occurred much faster than law enforcement is able to respond to these new challenges. This is particularly true in some emerging democracies of the world, who have ill-equipped and poorly trained police, little if any money, and inadequate laws that are not effective in allowing the police to attack organized criminal enterprises. If these organized criminal enterprises with roots elsewhere in the world are allowed to grow and migrate beyond their borders, they will inevitably invade the United States.

The mission of the International Training Section is to administer and coordinate all international mission-oriented training for the FBI. Through coordination with other FBI operational divisions, the International Relations Section, Department of Justice Office of International Programs, the Department of State, and affected U.S. embassies overseas, prioritized training is provided in support of the FBI's international investigative responsibilities.

Firearms Training Unit

The primary mission of the Firearms Training Unit is to train new special agents to become safe and competent with issued handguns, shotguns, and carbines through a three-tier training program consisting of:

■ fundamental marksmanship

■ combat/survival shooting

■ judgmental shooting

The Firearms Training Unit also administers comprehensive firearms training programs for agents and law enforcement officers both at the FBI Academy and in the field. These programs are supported through ongoing research and the procurement of weapons, ammunition, and related equipment appropriate for the needs of modern law enforcement. The Firearms Training Unit provides maintenance and inventory for all of the FBI's firearms.

Forensic Science Research and Training Center

The Forensic Science Research and Training Center is a section of the FBI Laboratory Division, which supports the FBI Training Division by providing forensic training to new FBI and DEA agents, the National Academy, FBI in-service students, and personnel from federal, state, and local law enforcement agencies, including crime laboratories. Additionally, it supports the FBI Laboratory with forensic science research and quality assurance functions.

Forensic science training is provided to FBI and DEA new agent classes in a variety of technical areas. Forensic science courses are offered to the FBI National Academy and accredited through the University of Virginia's Division of Continuing Education. The FBI in-service training program offers forensic science courses for FBI special agents and FBI laboratory examiners and technicians. The forensic science training program also includes other federal agencies as well as state and local agencies, providing crime laboratory personnel with hands-on training to enhance their basic skills and procedures and introducing them to new or more advanced techniques used in the examination of physical evidence. All courses offered by the Forensic Science Research and Training Center are on a cost-free basis to duly constituted law enforcement agencies and crime laboratories.

Forensic science research is conducted to develop new and improved methods for the analysis of forensic evidence. The program concentrates in the areas of biochemistry, genetics, chemistry, and physics. The staff collaborates with researchers from academia, private industry, and other government laboratories, as well as state and local forensic laboratories. For example, one of the most notable ongoing research initiatives is DNA analysis technology. This initiative includes research and development of valid and reliable DNA typing methods; training of state, local, and foreign crime laboratory personnel; providing expert testimony in DNA admissibility hearings; development of a system for the comparison of DNA profiles among American crime laboratories; and hosting symposia for the exchange of scientific data on DNA.

Technology Services Unit

The Technology Services Unit (TSU) is an instructional and communications tool for the FBI's Training Division. Located in Hogan's Alley, TSU consists of seven individual services, each with a specific mission. They are:

■ Audiovisual

■ Engineering Technology

■ The FBI Training Network (FBITN)

■ Graphics

■ Information Technology

■ Photography

■ Video

Investigative Training Unit

The Investigative Training Unit instructs every category of student at the FBI Academy, as well as law enforcement personnel throughout the United States and the world. Instruction is provided in all areas of white-collar crime, organized crime/drugs, and other criminal investigative matters.

Law Enforcement Communication Unit

The Law Enforcement Communications Unit has two primary responsibilities: training National Academy students and FBI new agents and publishing the *FBI Law Enforcement Bulletin*.

Within the framework of this mission, unit instructors conduct a wide variety of training. Courses for the NA include classes in interview/interrogation, instructor development, public speaking, media relations, contemporary issues in law enforcement, and effective writing. For new agents, the concentration of training is on interviewing, informant development, and field office communications. Unit personnel also participate in supervisory and management training programs, in-service training for on-board personnel, and field police training programs.

Leadership and Management Science Unit

The Leadership and Management Science Unit's mission is to enhance effective, practical, and creative leadership and management practices, as well as a spirit of cooperation among FBI, municipal, county, state, and internal law enforcement leaders. This is done through the design and administration of programs and development experiences that foster growth and lifelong learning.

There are two primary programs for municipal, county, state, and international executives. One is the National Executive Institute (NEI) for executives of major jurisdictions. The other is the Law Enforcement Executive Development Seminar (LEEDS) for heads of mid-sized and smaller agencies. These programs are designed to develop leaders who have great influence on those charged with maintaining order in a democracy.

Office of Information and Learning Resources

The Office of Information and Learning Resources' mission is to improve organizational productivity by facilitating access to and management of information for students, faculty and staff members of the Training Division, other FBI personnel, and the larger law enforcement community. This mission is accomplished through the provision of library services and the support of academic and administrative computing in the Training Division.

Physical Training Unit

The Physical Training Unit manages the Bureau's Fitness and Defensive Tactics programs. This unit provides training to NA attendees, new agent trainees, in-service personnel, and state and local law enforcement agencies. Courses are taught by nutrition advisers, NA fitness advisers, defensive tactics instructors, and FBI fitness instructors.

New Agents' Training Unit

The New Agents' Training Unit (NATU) coordinates sixteen weeks of instruction at the FBI Academy. New Agent Trainees (NATS) are exposed to three components of curriculum involving the following areas:

- investigative/tactical

- non-investigative

- administrative

The above components total 655 hours of instruction, which are spread over four major concentrations in academics, firearms, physical training/defensive tactics, and practical exercises.

NATS must pass eight academic examinations (with a score of 85 percent or better) in the following disciplines:

- legal (2 exams)

- communications

- ethics

- white collar crime

- drugs/organized crime/violent crime

- forensic evidence techniques

- national security matters

While engaged in the aforementioned training, the NATS are given a case to investigate, which will culminate in the arrest of multiple subjects. The investigation mirrors what they will experience in the field, as it is conducted at Hogan's Alley. The NATS conduct interviews, perform surveillance, and put to use the street survival techniques taught by the instructors at Hogan's Alley.

Graduation from the FBI Academy is determined by the successful completion of the training program and adherence to FBI core values.

Practical Applications Unit

The FBI Academy's Hogan's Alley complex is a realistic, urban, practical problem–training area which was initiated in March 1987. The Practical Applications Unit (PAU) manages and schedules all practical training events, administers practical problem exercises primarily to new agent trainees, and provides safety and survival training to law enforcement officers and FBI agents. In addition, the PAU has two sub-programs, the Law Enforcement Training for Safety and Survival Program (LETSS) and the Tactical Emergency Vehicle Operators Course Program (TEVOC). The LETSS program provides tactical training to law enforcement officers at the FBI Academy and throughout the nation and the world. The TEVOC program instructs new agents and other law enforcement personnel in the area of defensive driving and emergency vehicle operation techniques.

New agents are taught at PAU in the areas of surveillance, arrest procedures, and tactical street survival techniques. The new agents are then taken through real-life training exercises such as a bank robbery, day- and nighttime surveillance, kidnapping, and assault on a federal officer. New agents are also exposed to complaint and armed and dangerous arrest scenarios. Paint gun exercises are also utilized in order to test the new agents' tactical skills. Training at the Hogan's Alley complex is a unique method that allows new agents to apply principles taught in other areas at the FBI Academy, including firearms, academics, physical training, and legal training in order to successfully resolve the practical exercises at PAU. During exercises, students are provided with the tools similar to those in the field, such as bureau vehicles, radios, and electronic surveillance equipment.

During the exercises, a contractor company provides role players to confront trainees and portray various roles in order to create reactions that are more spontaneous and representative of the general population. Supervisory Special Agents within the FBI are assigned as instructors and as evaluators for the new agents.

Public Affairs Unit

The FBI Academy's Public Affairs Office is responsible for all media and public relations for the Training Division. The office provides media and public relations assistance to other FBI divisions represented at the Academy, including the Critical Incident Response Group, Engineering Research Facility, and the Forensic Science Research and Training Center. Events coordinated through the Public Affairs Office include:

- on-location filming/interviews

- dignitary visits

■ briefings

■ public relations–related events.

Computer Training Unit

The Computer Training Unit (CTU) provides investigative computer instruction, training, and curriculum development to FBI and other law enforcement personnel. Primarily, CTU trains new agents and NA students in a variety of computer topics including how to use the computer as an investigative tool, computer fraud, computer crimes (intrusions), search and seizure of computers, as well as how to use the computer as a source of information. Secondarily, through numerous in-service efforts, it trains the regional computer crime squads, Computer Analysis Response Team (CART) personnel, National Infrastructure Protection Center (NIPC) personnel, and technically trained white-collar crime and FCI agents.

For further information, visit the FBI online at http://www.fbi.gov or contact:
The Federal Bureau of Investigation
935 Pennsylvania Avenue, NW
Washington, D.C. 20535
Telephone: (202) 324-3000

FEDERAL LAW ENFORCEMENT TRAINING CENTER (FLETC)

DEPARTMENT OF THE TREASURY

The Federal Law Enforcement Training Center (FLETC) serves as an interagency law enforcement training organization for more than seventy federal agencies with personnel located throughout the United States and its territories. The Center also provides services to state, local, and international law enforcement agencies.

The Center is headquartered at Glynco, Georgia, near the port city of Brunswick, halfway between Savannah, Georgia, and Jacksonville, Florida. In addition to Glynco, the FLETC operates a second training center in Artesia, New Mexico, and supports a temporary center in Charleston, South Carolina. Each of these facilities is designed primarily for residential training operations.

A majority of the Center's participating organizations have transferred portions or all of their law enforcement training operations to Glynco. More than twenty have established training offices at the Center to coordinate the training activities of their personnel and conduct advanced and agency-specific training programs.

Consolidation of law enforcement training permits the federal government to emphasize training excellence and cost-effectiveness. Professional instruction and practical application provide students with the skills and knowledge necessary to meet the demanding challenges of a federal law enforcement career. They learn not only the responsibilities of a law enforcement officer but, through interaction with students from many other agencies, they also become acquainted with the missions and duties of their colleagues. This interaction provides the foundation for a more cooperative federal law enforcement effort.

The Center's parent agency, the Department of the Treasury, supervises its administrative and financial activities.

History of Consolidated Training

Prior to 1970, the quality of training received by Federal law enforcement officers and agents varied greatly among agencies. Standardized training was an unexplored concept. Inadequate facilities and duplication of effort were prevalent as each agency independently trained its own personnel.

Studies conducted in the late 1960's showed an urgent need for high-quality, cost-effective training by a cadre of professional instructors using modern facilities and standardized course content.

Congress responded by authorizing funds for the Consolidated Federal Law Enforcement Training Center (CFLETC). In 1970, the CFLETC was established as a bureau of the Department of the Treasury (Treasury Order #217) and began training operations in temporary facilities in Washington, D.C.

The permanent location of the FLETC was originally planned for the D.C. area. However, numerous delays led Congress to survey surplus Federal installations to determine if one could serve as the permanent site. In May 1975, after extensive reviews, the former Glynco Naval Air Station near Brunswick, Georgia, was selected. The Center relocated to Glynco that summer and began training in September.

Programs

The FLETC offers several basic law enforcement training programs of varying lengths. In addition, the Center supports and conducts numerous advanced and specialized training programs for its participating organizations. Other organizations may also attend these programs on a space-available basis. More than seventy-five government agencies which do not have traditional law enforcement functions regularly utilize the FLETC on this basis.

The FLETC also offers selected specialized training programs for state, local, and international law enforcement personnel through the Office of State and Local Training and the International Programs Division. These offerings are designed to meet training needs not generally available to these agencies and to enhance networking and cooperation throughout the domestic and international law enforcement communities.

Basic Training

The major portion of the Center's training activity is devoted to basic programs for criminal investigators and uniformed police officers who have the authority to carry firearms and make arrests.

The Center's three flagship programs are the Criminal Investigator Training Program (CITP), the Land Management Training Program (LMTP), and the Mixed Basic Police Training Program (MBPTP).

The CITP is designed primarily for incoming criminal investigators employed by any of the FLETC's participating organizations. The LMTP is designed principally for officers of those federal agencies that have a land management mission, such as the National Park Service and U.S. Forest Service. The MBPTP is designed principally for uniformed officers of Federal agencies that have a security or police mission, such as the U.S. Secret Service Uniformed Division and U.S. Capitol Police.

These and the Center's other basic programs provide students with a combination of classroom instruction and hands-on practical exercises. Students must apply their classroom knowledge during exercises that simulate typical situations encountered on the job. To add realism, these exercises often involve contract role players who act as victims, witnesses, or suspects.

Advanced Training

In addition to the basic investigator and uniformed police training programs, the FLETC develops and offers advanced and specialized training in subjects that are common to two or more of its participating organizations.

Examples of some advanced programs include Law Enforcement Photography, Marine Law Enforcement, Archeological Resources Protection, Wildfire Investigation, Criminal Investigations in an Automated Environment, Antiterrorism Management, and Physical Security Management. Also included are instructor programs in firearms training, driver training, physical fitness, nonlethal control, impact weapons, financial forensics techniques, international banking money laundering, and seized computers and evidence recovery.

Agency-Specific Training

Participating organizations can design and conduct basic and advanced programs to meet their particular training requirements. The Center's resources, support services, and staff expertise are available to assist in developing and conducting a wide variety of agency-specific training programs.

More than 100 different agency-specific basic and advanced programs are conducted at the FLETC, including the Alcohol, Tobacco and Firearms New Professional Training (for agents and inspectors); Bureau of Prisons Basic; the Immigration and Naturalization Service Journeyman Immigration Examiner; and the U.S. Customs Service Undercover Operatives School.

State and Local Training

The National Center for State and Local Law Enforcement Training trains personnel from state and local law enforcement agencies in advanced topics designed to develop specialized law enforcement skills. The participants benefit from the federal expertise and specialized training available at FLETC and receive instruction specific to their needs. Additionally, the National Center's program offerings are in subjects not generally available from state and local police academies or colleges and universities.

Examples of these programs include Crisis Management, Fraud and Financial Investigations, Explosives Investigative Techniques, Environmental Crimes, and many others.

International Training

In an effort to help combat global crime and to protect U.S. interests abroad, the FLETC offers a range of training programs to international law enforcement agencies. Administered by the International Programs Division, the training focuses on three main areas: the U.S. Government's Law and Democracy Program; the Antiterrorism Assistance (ATA) Program; and the International Law Enforcement Academy (ILEA) operations in Europe, Asia, Africa, and other regions elsewhere in the world.

DIVISIONS AND OFFICES

Glynco

The Glynco physical plant includes modern traditional facilities such as classrooms, residence halls, recreation areas, administrative and logistical support structures, and a dining hall capable of serving more than 4,000 meals per day. In addition, Glynco has indoor and semi-enclosed multipurpose firearms ranges, a driver training complex, a variety of physical training facilities, and numerous other structures which support the entire training effort.

Among these is a thirty-four-building "neighborhood" practical exercise area, which includes houses equipped with video cameras for recording various kinds of practical exercises.

The classroom buildings house various special purpose areas including a library, interviewing complexes, and criminalistics teaching laboratories for rolling and lifting fingerprints and identifying narcotics. A computer resource learning center is available to help students complete required courses that are available on interactive computer disks and to explore several hundred pieces of public domain software during off-duty hours.

In a joint venture with the U.S. Customs Service, the FLETC has established a distributed learning capability. The Distributed Learning Studio is a fully equipped, interactive television studio, which affords the FLETC and its participating organizations the capability to broadcast training to field units throughout the United States and overseas.

Behavioral Science Division

Basic training students are introduced to a foundation for law enforcement decision making that is both ethically and culturally sound. They learn the fundamentals of both verbal and nonverbal communication. Students learn to understand the principal barriers to communication and the means to prevent and resolve conflict. They learn techniques of interviewing that help ensure successful communication with victims, witnesses, and suspects. Students have the opportunity in laboratories and practical exercises to practice the principles learned in the classroom through interaction with contract role players. These exercises take place in specially designed interview suites and are often videotaped to aid in critiques designed to further enhance students' skills.

Division advanced program offerings include Law Enforcement Advanced Interviewing Training Program, Law Enforcement Instructor Training Program, Law Enforcement Field Instructor Training Program, and the Distributed Learning Instructor Training Program.

Driver and Marine Division

The Driver and Marine Division at Glynco is made up of four distinct branches. These branches include the Tactical Training Branch (TTB), the Technical Skills and Concepts Branch (TSCB), the Driver and Marine Support Branch (DMSB), and the Marine Training Branch (MTB).

The TTB and the TSCB are responsible for conducting basic instruction in vehicle dynamics involving highway response, skid control, pursuit, van and bus operations, nonemergency vehicle operation, and vehicular traffic stops. Practical application of these and other driving techniques improve or enhance student performance, confidence, and driving abilities. These branches also conduct advanced training programs.

The DMSB is responsible for providing support for the other three branches. The DMSB is responsible for caring for and maintaining the fleet of nearly 300 vehicles; researching, developing, and providing specialized training vehicles for basic and advanced training; and performing general maintenance on all Marine trailers at the FLETC.

The MTB provides specialized basic and advanced training programs relating to marine law enforcement operations. Instructional topics include navigation, rules of the road, mechanical troubleshooting, pursuing, intercepting, boarding, and searching; the use of weapons on a boat; boating accident investigations; safety and survival; and others. All of this training is conducted on navigable waterways and open ocean near Glynco.

Enforcement Operations Division

Students acquire basic knowledge and skills in various law enforcement operations and are provided contemporary scientific and technological skills to perform those operations as criminal investigators or uniformed police officers. They receive instruction in planning and executing a variety of law enforcement activities, such as working with informants, conducting surveillance, executing search warrants, using technical investigative equipment, proper note taking, preparing law enforcement reports, using operational and patrol skills, and conducting undercover operations.

Advanced programs managed by the Enforcement Operations Division include the Introduction to Criminal Investigations Training Program and Technical Investigative Equipment Training Program.

Enforcement Techniques Division

Basic training students learn and apply techniques that have a forensic science application. They learn the importance of protecting, preserving, documenting, and properly packaging key physical evidence that can be instrumental in criminal cases. Students are also taught the effects of aerosol/chemical irritants on criminal suspects. Both theoretical classroom and hands-on laboratory and practical exercise methodologies are used to provide students with the knowledge and experience to properly and safely perform their jobs.

Basic courses include Drugs of Abuse, Fingerprinting, Crime Scene Investigation, Rape and Death Investigation, Crime Lab, Photography, and others.

Advanced program offerings include Advanced Photography, Archeological Resources Protection, National Wildfire Investigations, and Advanced Video.

Financial Fraud Institute

The FFI develops and delivers training for both basic and advanced programs. The subject matter of the FFI is broadly divided between financial crimes investigations and computer crimes investigations.

Fifteen advanced programs are currently offered by the FFI. Almost 100 iterations of these programs are delivered each year to the Center's participating organizations, state and local departments, and international audiences.

Financial crimes investigations programs include international banking and money laundering, money laundering/asset forfeiture, financial crimes investigations, financial forensics techniques, health-care fraud investigations, and several others.

Computer and technical training programs include Computer Investigations in an Automated Environment, Seized Computer Evidence Recovery Specialist, Microcomputers for Investigators, Telecommunications Fraud, Computer Network Investigations, Case Organization and Presentation, and Internet Investigations Training. Several other programs complete this subject area; others are under development.

Firearms Division

The Glynco Center's firearms training is conducted in both indoor and outdoor facilities. The indoor range complex includes eight 25-yard ranges and one 50-yard range. Glynco has eight indoor/outdoor multipurpose ranges designed to accommodate both static and dynamic live-fire exercises. These ranges offer unique applications for shotgun, handgun, and rifle training; police vehicles are used to create a realistic experience. Dual running-person targets and sophisticated lighting are also used for night-fire exercises. Steel target training can also be accommodated within these fully-baffled ranges.

Firearms training involves classroom lectures supplemented with a variety of laboratory and practical exercises using revolvers, semiautomatic pistols, and shoulder-fired weapons. Students receive training in the safe handling, proficient application, and justifiable use of weapons using a variety of targets, equipment, and officer survival techniques.

FLETC Management Institute

The FMI staff designs, develops, coordinates, and administers training programs for federal law enforcement supervisors and managers. The FMI's goal is to provide customers with practical and usable training and development opportunities that address the management and supervisory competencies of federal law enforcement organizations.

International Programs Division

Over the years, the federal government's role in international law enforcement matters has intensified. As a result, the Center's international training initiatives have also intensified. Under agreement with the Department of State, the Center provides specialized training to international law enforcement in an effort to combat global crime.

Through the International Programs Division at Glynco, training focuses on three main areas:

- the United States Government's Law and Democracy Program

- Antiterrorism Assistance Program

- International Law Enforcement Academies in Hungary, Thailand, Gaborone, and Costa Rica

Legal Division

Basic law enforcement officers and criminal investigators receive instruction in the fundamentals of law, the Constitution, and the Bill of Rights. They become acquainted with legal rules and principles, especially as they relate to investigation, detention, arrest, and search and seizure.

The changing nature of the law necessitates that officers and investigators be well informed on evolving legal issues and principles so they can make proper arrests, gather admissible evidence, and respect the rights of individuals.

Advanced program offerings include the Continuing Legal Education Training Program.

Office of State and Local Training

The National Center for State and Local Law Enforcement Training was established as a component of the FLETC at Glynco in 1982. The National Center is responsible for training personnel from state and local law enforcement agencies in advanced topics designed to develop specialized law enforcement skills. The participants benefit from the federal expertise and specialized training facilities already available at Glynco and receive instruction specific to their needs.

The National Center's program offerings are in subject areas not generally available from state and local police academies or colleges and universities. The training is a cooperative effort that utilizes course developers and instructors from numerous federal agencies, state and local law enforcement jurisdictions, and professional law enforcement organizations. As with the training provided for the federal agencies, the state and local effort emphasizes practical hands-on training exercises which reinforce classroom lectures and materials.

Examples of these programs include Gang Resistance Education and Training (GREAT), Crisis Management, and Environmental Crimes.

To meet the needs of 91 percent of police agencies in the United States–those located outside of large metropolitan areas– a Small Town and Rural (STAR) training series was developed. Numerous tuition-free programs are delivered throughout the United States at police academies and colleges. Most programs use a train-the-trainer format and adult learning methodology. Programs in the series include Hate and Bias Crimes, Domestic Violence, Community Policing, and Rural Crime and Drug Enforcement Tasks Forces.

Physical Techniques Division

The FLETC imparts skills, knowledge, and confidence through the teaching of physical techniques and fitness. This includes training in specific law enforcement related activities, such as nonlethal control techniques (arrest techniques and defensive tactics), impact weapons, trauma management, cardiopulmonary resuscitation, awareness of blood-borne pathogens, water safety and survival, and physical conditioning for both basic and advanced law enforcement personnel.

Glynco's Physical Techniques Complex encompasses more than 3 acres, including staff offices, mat rooms, classrooms, weight rooms, athletic training rooms, gymnasium, racquetball courts, indoor pool, locker rooms, and other facilities devoted to training and recreational activities.

Security Specialties Division

Basic training students are taught courses in officer safety and survival, bombs and explosives, physical security, antiterrorism, weapons of mass destruction, hazardous materials, and a variety of other security-related topics. Classroom lectures, reinforced by laboratory and practical exercises, assure the students meaningful learning experiences. Advanced programs taught and managed by the Security Specialties Division include Physical Security; First Response; Officer Safety and Survival; Seaport Security/Antiterrorism Training Program; and Land Transportation Antiterrorism.

The division makes use of a Physical Security/Antiterrorism Training Complex at Glynco, which incorporates the latest technology in exterior perimeter defenses, including fencing, security lighting, gate entrance systems, antivehicle and antipersonnel intrusion systems, and closed-circuit television.

Artesia

The FLETC's Artesia Center, located midway between Roswell and Carlsbad, New Mexico, provides advanced training for such agencies as the Immigration and Naturalization Service, the U.S. Border Patrol, the Bureau of Prisons, and other participating organizations with large concentrations of personnel in the Western United States. The Artesia Center also supports state and local law enforcement training.

The Bureau of Indian Affairs Indian Police Academy is located in Artesia and conducts basic and advanced training programs there.

Artesia is also home to the Law Enforcement Spanish Training Program (LESTP). This is a ten-day, total immersion program designed for law enforcement officers that covers arrest-related language, street Spanish, interviewing, and grammar.

The Artesia physical plant includes modern, fully equipped, permanent and modular classroom buildings, auditoriums, laboratories, videoconferencing, and Law Enforcement Television

Network reception. A 28,000-square-foot classroom building provides five 52-person and five 26-person classrooms, six breakout rooms, three 2-room interviewing suites, a 24-person courtroom with interview area and holding cell, and three 26-person labs.

The Artesia Center also has a 165-room single- or double-occupancy dormitory and a seventy-six-room single occupancy dormitory. Construction of a new 286-room single occupancy dormitory is expected to be complete by September 2001. Each dormitory complex includes associated student services, such as a laundry, television lounge, and library. All dormitory rooms include cable television and telephones.

Driver and Firearms Training Branch

The Artesia Training Division's Driver and Firearms Training Branch plans, develops, and presents formal basic and advanced training and practical exercises relating to the specialized nature and use of police vehicles and firearms.

Driver training includes highway response, skid-control, nonemergency vehicle operations (NEVO), and vehicle ambush countermeasures.

The firearms complex includes judgment pistol shooting simulators, three 30-point basic marksmanship ranges, a twenty-four-point rifle range that doubles as a steel target range, a drive-and-shoot steel target range, a chemical agent range, a cover and concealment multipurpose range, and a short shotgun range. Two semi-enclosed thirty-point ranges are currently under construction and should be completed in mid-2001.

General and Physical Training Branch

The Artesia Training Division's General and Physical Training Branch plans, develops, and presents formal training and practical exercises relating to physical fitness, officer safety and survival (including water survival), first aid, and arrest techniques. It also provides training in interpersonal relations, including interviewing, handling crisis situations, professional ethics and conduct, oral and written communications, and various law enforcement operational procedures and investigative skills.

The GPT utilizes a complex of eight "raid houses" and rappelling facilities for a variety of operational law enforcement practical exercises, including raids, cell extraction, and building and room clearing.

Physical training is conducted in a 36,000-square-foot complex, complete with mat rooms, gymnasium, weight room, health unit, and office space.

An additional 36,000 square feet of physical training space will soon be completed. The facility will provide expanded uniform issue, additional weight rooms, larger student and staff locker/shower rooms, additional mat rooms, larger health services facilities, and more instructor office space.

Staff and Support

As an interagency training organization, FLETC has assembled the finest professionals from diverse backgrounds to serve on its faculty and staff. Approximately one-half of the instructor staff members are permanent FLETC employees. The remainder are federal officers and investigators on short-term assignment from their parent organizations. This mix of permanent and detailed instructors provides a balance of experience and fresh insight from the field.

The operation of the FLETC is facilitated by a Planning and Resources Directorate, which includes the Budget, Environmental and Safety, Facilities Management, Finance, Human Resources, Information Systems, Procurement, Property Management, and Strategic Planning and Evaluation Divisions, and other individual agency administrative staffs.

In addition, the Office of Training Support (OTS), within the Training Directorate, provides key operational support through the Research and Evaluation, Training Analysis and Coordination, and Student Services Divisions. The OTS also administers the Center's Distributed Learning Program.

The Student Services Division oversees a wide range of contractor-provided services at the Center, including dormitory and off-Center lodging management, food service, role players and transportation. This Division also has oversight of the Critical Incident Stress Management, Health Services, and Technology Support branches.

The Research and Evaluation Division provides key evaluative, research, and program development support to all training activities at the Center. The RED applies Instructional Systems Design (ISD) concepts to identify program improvements, assist instructors in developing learning objectives and test items, and participate in course and program development. RED is responsible for the Automated Testing and Evaluation System, which entails the development, maintenance, scoring, and analysis of all written tests; collection and analysis of feedback regarding training programs and administrative support; and evaluation of the effectiveness of programs in preparing graduates to perform their law enforcement duties. The RED also provides ISD and program evaluation training to FLETC instructors.

For further information, visit the Federal Law Enforcement Training Center online at www.ustreas.gov/fletc or contact:

Federal Law Enforcement Training Center
Public Affairs Office
Department of the Treasury
Glynco, Georgia 31524
Telephone: (912) 267-2447

NATIONAL INTERAGENCY CIVIL-MILITARY INSTITUTE

MISSION

The mission of the National Interagency Civil-Military Institute (NICI) is to improve the efficiency and effectiveness of joint civilian-military initiatives through education and training. The Institute supports National Guard efforts to further international cooperation and other programs directed by the Chief of the National Guard Bureau.

FUNCTIONS AND ACTIVITIES

To fulfill its mission, NICI:

- directly supports the National Drug control Strategy and the Federal Response Plan

- trains middle- and upper-level managers from the military, law enforcement agencies, emergency management and public safety organizations, as well as community leaders

- provides research and information services such as lessons learned from previous operations. These lessons help make future operations more effective by sharing information about mistakes to avoid and successful techniques to emulate.

NICI specializes in providing ideal training environments. Classes are conducted at Camp San Luis Obispo, California, and other sites across the nation. The Institute is located on the scenic California Central Coast, equidistant from Los Angeles and San Francisco, but NICI courses have been conducted nationwide and internationally. NICI is funded by the Department of Defense through the National Guard Bureau.

NICI Specialized Training Support

In addition to core course offerings, NICI tailors its courses to an organization's requirements. The Institute has provided customized training support for the Drug Enforcement Administration, the Regional Information Sharing Systems, the California Bureau of Narcotic Enforcement, the Bureau of Land Management, community coalitions, and California Narcotics Officers Association. The Institute has conducted Military Support to Civil Authorities programs simultaneously translated into numerous languages for the National Guard Bureau's State Partnership Program.

NICI has harnessed the latest in educational technologies and utilizes interactive two-way audio/video telecommunications systems including VTC and satellite transmissions. Not only does this allow for instructional broadcast to remote sites, but it also allows NICI to receive broadcasts from nationally and internationally recognized instructors who would otherwise not be available to instruct in California. NICI's computer-enhanced classroom provides an ideal setting for software exercises, which simulate emergencies that require student input and provide immediate feedback.

NICI is an interagency program with two advisory boards: counterdrug (supply and demand reduction) and all hazards emergency management / WMD consequence management. The advisory board members advise the NICI director on curriculum, institute operations, and other timely issues. Board members are representatives from key federal, state, and local organization, including state emergency services, sheriffs and police, professional associations, the drug prevention community, and the States' Adjutants General.

NICI offers tuition-free courses that are P.O.S.T.-certified in most states and eligible for college credits.

For more information on current course offerings, visit the NICI Web site at www.nici.org or contact:

National Interagency Civil-Military Institute
P.O. Box 4209
San Luis Obispo, California 93403-4209
Telephone: (800) 906-8839 (toll-free)
(800) 926-5637 (toll-free)

PART FIVE

Civil Service Career Information Resources

HOW TO FIND A GOVERNMENT JOB

Very often finding a job is a matter of luck. However, we'd like to take some of the luck out of it and make it more directive. Below are a variety of sources you can contact in your search for employment. Keep in mind that as a State Trooper, Highway Patrol Officer, or State Traffic Officer, you will be working for the state. That's where the jobs are.

STATE EMPLOYMENT

Almost every state has its own Web site. In order to access the state systems via the Internet, there's a very simple way to find each state, although it may take some searching once you're on line.

To find the state Internet site, enter the following: www.state.___.us. In the blank, enter the two-letter code for that state. For Arizona, for example, you would enter www.state.az.us. For Wisconsin, enter www.state.wi.us. Here's a list of the latest URLs for the state sites. Be aware, however, that they change from time-to-time.

Alabama: www.state.al.us
Alaska: www.state.ak.us
Arizona: www.state.az.us
Arkansas: www.state.ar.us
California: www.state.ca.us
Colorado: www.state.co.us
Connecticut: www.state.ct.us
Delaware: www.state.de.us
District of Columbia: www.washingtondc.gov
Florida: www.state.fl.us
Georgia: www:state.ga.us
Hawaii: www.state.hi.us
Idaho: www.state.id.us
Illinois: www.state.il.us
Indiana: www.state.in.us
Iowa: www.state.ia.us
Kansas: www.state.ks.us
Kentucky: www.state.ky.us
Louisiana: www.state.la.us
Maine: www.state.me.us
Maryland: www.state.md.us
Massachusetts: www.state.ma.us
Michigan: www. state.mi.us
Minnesota: www.state.mn.us
Mississippi: www.state.ms.us
Missouri: www.state.mo.us

Montana: www.state.mt.gov
Nebraska: www.state.ne.us
Nevada: www.state.nv.us
New Hampshire: www.state.nh.us
New Jersey: www.state.nj.us
New Mexico: www.state.nm.us
New York: www.state.ny.us
North Carolina: www.state.nc.us
North Dakota: www.state.nd.us
Ohio: www.state.oh.us
Oklahoma: www.state.ok.us
Oregon: www.state.or.us
Pennsylvania: www.state.pa.us
Rhode Island: www.state.ri.us
South Carolina: www.state.sc.us
South Dakota: www.state.sd.us
Tennessee: www.state.tn.us
Texas: www.state.tx.us
Utah.: www.state.ut.us
Vermont: www.state.vt.us
Virginia: www.state.va.us
Washington: www.wa.gov
West Virginia: www.state.wv.us
Wisconsin: www.state.wi.us
Wyoming: www.state.wy.us

If that state also has a Job Bank, you can find that the same way. This time you would enter www.abj.org/___, and enter the state's two-letter code in the blank space.

There are, however, specific State Trooper Web sites. Here's a complete list of them, current as of this edition.

Alabama	www.dps.state.al.us
Alaska	www.dps.state.ak.us
Arizona	www.dps.state.az.us
Arkansas	www.state.ar/asp/asp.html
California	www.chp.ca.gov/index.html
Colorado	www.state.co.us/gov-dir/cdps/csp.htm
Connecticut	www.state.ct.us/dps/csp.htm
Delaware	www.state.de.us/dsp
Florida	www.fhp.state.fl.us/
Georgia	www.ganet.org/dps/index.html
Hawaii	www.hawaii.gov/icsd/psd/psd.html
Idaho	www.isp.state.id.us
Illinois	www.state.il.us/isp/index
Indiana	www.ai.org/isp/index
Iowa	www.state.ia.us/government/dps/isp/
Kansas	www.ink.org/public/khp
Kentucky	www.state.ky.us/agencies/ksp/ksphome.htm
Louisiana	www.lsp.org
Massachusetts	www.state.ma.us/msp/massachu.htm
Maryland	www.inform.umd.edu/ums+state/md_resources/mdsp/index.htm/
Maine	www.janus.state.me.us/dps/msp/homepage.htm
Michigan	www.msp.state.mi.us
Minnesota	www.dps.state.mn.us/patrol/index.htm
Missouri	www.mshp.state.mo.us/hp32p001.nsf
Mississippi	www.dps.state.ms.us/

Montana	www.doj.state.mt.us/mhp/index.htm
North Carolina	www.shp.state.nc.us/
North Dakota	www.state.nd.us/ndhp
Nebraska	www.nebraska-state-patrol.org
New Hampshire	www.state.nh.us/nhsp/index.html
New Jersey	www.state.nj.us/lps/njsp/index.html
New Mexico	www.nmsp.com
Nevada	www.state.nv.us/dmv_ps/nhphome.htm
New York	www.troopers.state.ny.us
Ohio	www.state.oh.us/ohiostatepatrol/
Oklahoma	www.dps.state.ok.us/
Oregon	www.osp.state.or.us/
Pennsylvania	www.state.pa.us/pa_exec/state_police/
Rhode Island	www.risp.state.ri.us/
South Carolina	www.schp.org
South Dakota	www.state.sd.us/state/executive/dcr/hp/page1sdh.htm
Tennessee	www.state.tn.us/safety/
Texas	www.txdps.state.tx.us/
Utah	www.uhp.state.ut.us/
Virginia	www.state.va.us/vsp/vsp.html
Vermont	www.dps.state.vt.us/vsp/index.html
Washington	www.wa.gov/wsp
Wisconsin	www.dot.state.wi.us/dsp/
West Virginia	www.wvstatepolice.com
Wyoming	www.wydotweb.state.wy.us/docs/patrol/patrol.html

If you're interested in more personal information, there is an excellent site that provides links to everything from Academies to Forensics to Mounted Police and SWAT Troops. It can be found at www.StateTroopersDirectory.com/troops.htm. The site also features individual personal Trooper pages, tributes to fallen officers, and so on.

You can also use some of the popular search vehicles, such as Yahoo.com, Ask.com, Altavista.com, and so on, to locate other job-related sites. Use search terms such as *jobs*, *employment*, *labor*, *business*, and *help-wanted* as well as *trooper*, *patrol officer*, and so on. Add that to the specific city or state, and you'll be surprised at the number of suggested sites you'll get. You might enter into the search box something like *Miami+trooper*. The plus sign (+) indicates that you want both Miami and jobs to be in the same suggested sites.

HOW TO GET A GOVERNMENT JOB

Now that you know where to look for a job, it's important to understand the procedure. The procedure you must follow to get a government job varies little from job to job and from one level of government to another. There are variations in details, of course, but certain steps are common to all.

Once you have found a *Notice of Examination* (it may be called an Announcement), read it very carefully. If you can get a copy for yourself—all the better. If not, take lots of time to take notes. Make sure you write down all of the details. The Notice of Examination gives a brief job description. It tells the title of the job and describes some of the job duties and responsibilities. On the basis of the job description, you decide whether or not you want to try for this job. If the job appeals to you, you must concentrate on:

▪ **Education and experience requirements.** If you cannot meet these requirements, do not bother to apply. Government service is very popular; many people apply. The government has more than enough applicants from which to choose. It will not waive requirements for you.

■ **Age requirements.** Discrimination on the basis of age is illegal, but a number of jobs demand so much sustained physical effort that they require retirement at an early age. For these positions there is an entry age limit. If you are already beyond that age, do not apply. If you are still too young, inquire about the time lag until hiring. It may be that you will reach the minimum age by the time the position is to be filled.

■ **Citizenship requirements.** Many jobs are open to all people who are eligible to work in the United States, but all law enforcement jobs and most federal jobs are limited to citizens. If you are well along the way toward citizenship and expect to be naturalized soon, inquire as to your exact status with respect to the job.

■ **Residency requirements.** If there is a residency requirement, you must live within the prescribed limits or be willing to move. If you are not willing to live in the area, do not waste time applying.

■ **What forms must be filed.** The announcement of the position for which you are applying will specify the form of application requested. For most federal jobs, you may submit either the Optional Application for Federal Employment (OF 612) or a resume that fulfills the requirements set forth in the pamphlet, "Applying for a Federal Job (OF 510)." For other than federal jobs, the Notice of Examination may tell you where you must go or write to get the necessary form or forms. Be sure you secure them all. The application might be a simple form asking nothing more than name, address, citizenship, and social security number, or it may be a complex Experience Paper. An Experience Paper, as its title implies, asks a great deal about education, job training, job experience, and life experience. Typically, the Experience Paper permits no identification by name, sex, or race; the only identifying mark is your social security number. The purpose of this procedure is to avoid permitting bias of any sort to enter into the weighting of responses. The Experience Paper generally follows a short form of application that does include a name. When the rating process is completed, the forms are coordinated by means of the social security number

■ **Filing dates, place, and fee.** There is great variation in this area. For some positions, you can file your application at any time. Others have a first day and last day for filing. If you file too early or too late, your application will not be considered. Sometimes it is sufficient to have your application postmarked by the last day for filing. More often, your application must be received by the last date. If you are mailing your application, allow five full business days for it to get there on time. Place of filing is stated right on the notice. Get the address right! Most applications may be filed by mail, but occasionally in-person filing is specified. Follow directions. Federal and postal positions require no filing fee. Most other government jobs do charge a fee for processing your application. The fee is not always the same. Be sure to check this out. If the Notice specifies "money order only," purchase a money order. Be sure the money order is made out properly. If you send or present a personal check, your application will be rejected without consideration. Of course, you would never mail cash; but if the announcement specifies "money order only," you cannot submit cash, even in person.

■ **How to qualify.** This portion of the Notice of Examination tells you the basis on which the candidates are chosen. Some examination scores consist of a totaling up of weighted education and experience factors. This type of examination, called "an unassembled exam" because you do not come to one place to take the exam, is based upon your responses on the application and supplementary forms. Obviously these must be very complete for you to get full credit for all you have learned and accomplished. The notice may tell you of a qualifying exam, which is an exam that you must pass in addition to scoring high on an unassembled written or performance test, or the notice may tell you of a competitive exam—written, performance, or both. The competitive exam may be described in very general terms or may be described in detail. It is even possible that a few sample questions will be attached. If the date of the exam has been set, that date will appear on the notice. Write it down.

When you have the application forms in hand, photocopy them. Fill out the photocopies first. That way, you can correct mistakes, change the order of information, or add or delete information. You can work at fitting what you have to say into the space allowed. Do not exaggerate, but be sure to give yourself credit for responsibilities you've taken on, for cost-saving ideas you've given your prior employer, and for any other accomplishments. Be clear and thorough in telling what you have learned and what you can do.

When you are satisfied with your draft, copy over the application onto the form(s). Be sure to include any backup material that is requested; by the same token, do not send more "evidence" than is truly needed to support your claims of qualification. Your application must be complete according to the requirements of the announcement, but it must not be overwhelming. You want to command hiring attention by exactly conforming to the requirements.

Check over all forms for neatness and completeness. Sign wherever indicated. Attach the fee, if required. Then mail or personally file the application on time.

WARNING! If you are currently employed, do not give your notice now. Stay at your present job. If you are job hunting, continue your search. The time lag between application for a government job and actual employment is always many months; it may even be a year or two. You cannot afford to sit back and wait for the job.

If the Notice of Examination told you that there is a competitive exam and told you about subjects of the examination, you can begin to study now. If not, just continue working and await notice of next steps.

When the civil service commission or personnel office to which you submitted your application receives it, the office will date, stamp, log, and open your file. The office may acknowledge receipt with more forms, with sample exam questions, or with a simple receipt slip. Or, you may hear nothing at all for months.

Eventually you will receive a testing date or an interview appointment. Write it on your calendar in red so that you don't let the dates slip by. Write the address to which you are to report in the same place. If you receive an admission ticket for an exam, be sure to put it in a safe place; but keep it in sight so that you will not forget to take it with you to the exam. With an exam date, you should also receive information about the exam. Tine may be short. If you have not already done so, begin to study and prepare right away.

If the next step is an exam, that exam might be either a written exam or a performance exam. The type of exam depends on the nature of the job. The applicant for a locksmith's position might be asked to cut some complicated keys and to repair a broken lock; the track maintainer hopeful might have to replace ties or reset switches. The applicant for a position as a clerk-stenographer might have to take dictation and a typing test as well as a multiple-choice test of general clerical abilities. Applicants for most jobs take only a written test. The written test is most frequently a multiple-choice test, one in which the test-taker chooses the best of four or five answer choices and marks its number on a separate answer sheet. Multiple-choice tests are machine scored. Machine scoring insures accuracy and objectivity. No one can misinterpret your answers. Machine scoring also allows many applicants to be rated at the same time. It speeds up the process, but if you are waiting to hear about your job you may doubt this fact.

Occasionally, the written test consists of an essay portion along with the multiple-choice section or even of essays alone. Essays usually appear at levels above initial entry level, where there are fewer applicants and fewer papers to score. On an essay, the examiners are looking for indications that you can organize your thoughts and can express them effectively in writing.

If you are called for an exam, arrive promptly and dress appropriately. Neatness is always appropriate; however, you do not need to "dress up" for a performance exam or for a written exam. If you will do manual work for your performance exam, wear clean work clothes. For a written exam, neat and casual clothing is fine.

THE INTERVIEW

If there is no exam and you are called directly to an interview, what you wear is more important. Take special care to look businesslike and professional. You must not appear to be too casual, and you must certainly not look sloppy. Overdressing is also inappropriate. A neat dress or skirted suit is fine for women; men should wear a shirt and tie with a suit or slacks and a jacket. In addition, pay attention to your grooming.

Interviews take up an interviewer's time. If you are called for an interview, you are under serious consideration. There may still be competition for the job, someone else may be more suited than you, but you are qualified and your skills and background have appealed to someone in the hiring office. The interview may be aimed at getting information about:

■ **Your knowledge.** The interviewer wants to know what you know about the area in which you will work. For instance, if you will be doing data entry in a budget office, what do you know about the budget process? Are you at all interested in this area of financial planning? You may also be asked questions probing your knowledge of the agency for which you are interviewing. Do you care enough to have educated yourself about the functions and role of the agency, whether it's child welfare, pollution control, or international trade?

■ **Your judgment.** You may be faced with hypothetical situations, job-related or in interpersonal relations, and be asked, "What would you do if . . . ?" questions. Think carefully before answering. You must be decisive but diplomatic. There are no "right answers." The interviewer is aware that you are being put on the spot. How well you can handle this type of question is an indication of your flexibility and maturity

■ **Your personality.** You will have to be trained and supervised. You will have to work with others. What is your attitude? How will you fit in? The interviewer will be trying to make judgments in these areas on the basis of general conversation with you and from your responses to specific lines of questioning. Be pleasant, polite, and open with your answers, but do not volunteer a great deal of extra information. Stick to the subjects introduced by the interviewer. Answer fully, but resist the temptation to ramble on.

■ **Your attitude towards work conditions.** These are practical concerns: If the job will require frequent travel for extended periods, how do you feel about it? What is your family's attitude? If you will be very unhappy about the travel, you may leave the job and your training will have been a waste of the taxpayers' money. The interviewer also wants to know how you will react to overtime or irregular shifts.

Remember, working for the government is working for the people. Government revenues come from taxes. The hiring officers have a responsibility to put the right people into the right jobs so as to spend the taxpayers' money most effectively. And, as a government employee, you have a responsibility to give the people (including yourself) their money's worth.

Other steps along the hiring route may be a medical examination, physical performance testing, and psychological interviewing. If there is a written test, these steps do not occur until the written test is are scored and ranked. Steps that require the time of one examiner with one applicant are taken only when there is reasonable expectation of hiring.

THE MEDICAL EXAMINATION

The state police officer's route must be covered at all times. This means that the assigned officer must show up. Otherwise, the scheduling officer must find a substitute and must rearrange the work tours of many other officers. The candidate with a history of frequent illness or one with a chronic ailment that may periodically crop up and interfere with attendance is not an acceptable candidate. Likewise, the applicant with an underlying physical condition that presents no problems in everyday life but that might be aggravated under the stressful activity of a police officer must be rejected.

Every candidate under consideration must undergo a thorough medical examination. This examination always occurs after the applicant has passed the written exam and often before the test of physical fitness or physical performance. The reason many police examining boards conduct the medical examination before the physical test is so that candidates whose health might be jeopardized by the strenuous activity of the physical test are screened out ahead of time. The police department does not want its applicants collapsing on the floor of the physical testing arena. In the interest of cost-efficiency, however, you may be asked to take the physical performance test before your medical examination. Since applicants who cannot qualify on the physical performance test need not undergo the more expensive medical examination, the department saves money. If you are to take the physical performance test before taking your medical examination, you will probably be asked to bring a certificate of fitness in order to participate in the physical exam, which has been signed by your own doctor. Then, after you have qualified on the physical performance test, the police physician will conduct the departmental examination. Both the physical performance test and the medical exam are administered to one applicant at a time, but the medical exam needs a physician while the physical performance exam can be administered by a police department employee with a stopwatch. Disqualification on the basis of either the physical performance test or the medical exam stops the screening process and eliminates the candidate from further consideration.

The medical exam will resemble an army physical more than a visit to your personal physician. You will start by filling out a lengthy questionnaire relating to your medical history. This questionnaire will be used by the physician to single out special health areas for consideration. It may also be used by the personnel interviewer when you approach the final step of the screening process.

Do not lie on the medical questionnaire. Your medical history is a matter of record at school, in your service dossier, and in the hospital or clinic files. If you lie, you will be found out. If the medical condition does not disqualify you, the fact of your untruthfulness will. On the other hand, there is no need to tell more than is asked. You do not need to expand upon your aches and pains. You needn't make an illness or injury more dramatic than it was. Stick to the facts and do not raise any questions. If you have any current concerns, the police department's examining officer is not the person to ask.

Your medical examination almost certainly will include height and weight measurement, chest x-ray, eye test, hearing test, blood tests, urinalysis, cardiogram, blood pressure, and actual visual and physical examination by the doctor. If you have any doubts as to how you will fare with any of these examinations, you might want to consult your personal physician ahead of time. You may be able to correct a borderline situation before you appear for the exam.

Most police departments provide candidates with height-weight standards and with lists of medical requirements before their scheduled medical examinations. If you receive these, look them over carefully. If they present any problems to you, see your doctor. Your worry may be misplaced, or it may be real. Possibly you will have to change your career goals. Or, likely, you can correct the situation, pass the medical exam, and go on to serve on the police force.

Read over the medical specifications very carefully before you visit your personal physician. Some state police departments require nearly perfect uncorrected vision. Others permit glasses and/or contact lenses. Some departments welcome applicants who have had their vision surgically corrected. Others specify that applicants who have undergone Radial Keratotomy, Epikeratoplasty, or Ortho Keratology are not acceptable. If your own status cannot satisfy their requirements, you may have to move to another state or consider a city, town, or county force that has different requirements.

Not all state police departments have the same standards for medical conditions. Some will accept conditions that are absolutely disqualifying in others. The height-weight charts and the list of medical requirements on the following pages are illustrative. They are typical of those of many police departments. They should serve you as a general guide at this time. If your own medical position is way out of line, you may need to reconsider or embark on a major health reform campaign right away. Once you get your own department's official set of guidelines, follow those standards rather than the ones printed here.

HEIGHT AND WEIGHT FOR FEMALES

ACCEPTABLE: WEIGHT IN POUNDS ACCORDING TO FRAME

Height (in bare feet)		Small Frame	Medium Frame	Large Frame
Feet	**Inches**			
4	10	92–98	96–107	104–119
4	11	94–101	98–110	106–122
5	0	96–104	101–113	109–125
5	1	99–107	104–116	112–128
5	2	102–110	107–119	115–131
5	3	105–113	110–122	118–134
5	4	108–116	113–126	121–138
5	5	111–119	116–130	125–142
5	6	114–123	120–135	129–146
5	7	118–127	124–139	133–150
5	8	122–131	128–143	137–154
5	9	126–135	132–147	141–158
5	10	130–140	136–151	145–163
5	11	134–144	140–155	149–168
6	0	138–148	144–159	153–173
6	1	142–152	148–163	157–177

NOTE: Although the above table commences at a specified height, no minimum height requirement has been prescribed. This table of height and weight is adhered to in all instances except where the Civil Service examining physician certifies that weight in excess of that shown in the table (up to a maximum of twenty pounds) is lean body mass and not fat. Decision as to frame size of candidate is made by the examining physician. The following tests will be part of the medical examination:

- Vision

- Hearing

- Serology

- Urinalysis

- Chest X-Ray

- Blood Pressure

- Electrocardiogram

HEIGHT AND WEIGHT FOR MALES

ACCEPTABLE WEIGHT IN POUNDS ACCORDING TO FRAME

Height (in bare feet)		Small Frame	Medium Frame	Large Frame
Feet	Inches			
5	3	115–123	121–133	129–144
5	4	118–126	124–136	132–148
5	5	121–129	127–139	135–152
5	6	124–133	130–143	138–156
5	7	128–137	134–147	142–161
5	8	132–141	138–152	147–166
5	9	136–145	142–156	151–170
5	10	140–150	146–160	155–174
5	11	144–154	150–165	159–179
6	0	148–158	154–170	164–184
6	1	152–162	158–175	168–189
6	2	156–167	162–180	175–194
6	3	160–171	167–185	178–199
6	4	164–175	172–190	182–204
6	5	168–179	176–194	186–209
6	6	172–183	180–198	190–214

NOTE: Although the above table commences at a specified height, no minimum height requirement has been prescribed. This table of height and weight is adhered to in all instances except where the Civil Service examining physician certifies that weight in excess of that shown in the table (up to a maximum of twenty pounds) is lean body mass and not fat. Decision as to frame size of candidates is made by the examining physician.

The following tests will be part of the medical examination:

- Vision

- Hearing

- Serology

- Urinalysis

- Chest X-Ray

- Blood Pressure

- Electrocardiogram

Candidates are required to meet the physical and medical requirements stated below at the time of the medical examination, at the time of appointment, and at appropriate intervals thereafter.

1. **Weight.** Candidates should have weight commensurate to frame. Weight should not interfere with candidate's ability to perform the duties of the position of Police Officer.

2. **Vision.** Candidates must have binocular visual acuity not less than 20/20 with or without correction; if correction is required, binocular visual acuity not less than 20/40 without correction. Binocular peripheral vision should not be less than 150 degrees.

3. **Color Vision.** Candidates must be able to distinguish individual basic colors against a favorable background.

4. **Hearing.** Candidates must be able to pass an audiometric test of hearing acuity in each ear. A binaural hearing loss of greater than 15 percent in the frequency ranges of 500, 1000, 2000 Hz would be considered disqualifying. Hearing appliances should correct the deficiency so the binaural hearing loss in the combined frequency level of 500, 1000, 2000 Hz is not greater than 15 percent.

5. **Heart.** Candidates must be free of functionally limited heart disease and must have functional cardiac classification of no greater than Class 1. This determination is to be made clinically or by cardiac stress test.

6. **Lungs.** The respiratory system must be free of chronic disabling conditions that would interfere with the candidate's performance of required duties.

7. **Diabetes.** Candidates who are diabetic must not require insulin injections or oral hypoglycemic agents for control.

8. **Neurological Health.** Candidates must be free of neurological disorders that may affect job performance. Candidates with epilepsy or seizure disorders must provide evidence of one-year seizure-free history without drug control.

9. **Musculoskeletal Health.** Candidates must be free of musculosketetal defects, deformities, or disorders that may affect job performance. Functional use of the arms, hands, legs, feet, and back must be demonstrable at the examination. Candidates will be asked to demonstrate physical fitness through tests of strength, agility, flexibility, and endurance.

10. **Hernia.** Candidates must be free of abdominal and inguinal hernia that would interfere with job performance.

11. **Blood/Vascular Health.** Candidates must be free of blood or vascular disorders that would interfere with the performance of duties. Candidates with uncontrolled high blood pressure will be disqualified unless it is remediable.

12. **Mental Health.** Candidates must be free of mental illness, serious emotional disturbances or nervous disorders, alcoholism, and drug dependence or abuse.

13. **General Medical Statement.** Candidates must be free of any medical and/or nervous condition that would jeopardize the safety and health of others. Candidates with communicable diseases will be disqualified unless they are remediable.

FORMULATION OF MEDICAL REQUIREMENTS FROM ANOTHER STATE POLICE DEPARTMENT

The duties of these positions involve physical exertion under rigorous environmental conditions; irregular and protracted hours of work; patrol duties on foot, in motor vehicles, and in aircraft; and participation in physical training. Applicants must be in sound physical condition and of good muscular development.

Vision

- Binocular vision is required and must test 20/40 (Snellen) without corrective lenses,

- Uncorrected vision must test at least 20/70 in each eye, although some agencies limit this to 20/50,

- Vision in each eye must be corrected to 20/20 (again, some agencies permit vision to be corrected to 20/30, using soft contact lenses),

- Near vision, corrected or uncorrected, must be sufficient to read Jaeger Type 2 at 14 inches, and

- Ability to distinguish basic colors by pseudoisochromatic plate test (missing no more than four plates) is required, as is normal peripheral vision.

Hearing

■ Without using a hearing aid, the applicant must be able to hear the whispered voice at 15 feet with each ear; or

■ Using an audiometer for measurement, there should be no loss of 30 or more decibels in each ear at the 500, 1000, and 2000 levels.

Speech

■ Diseases or conditions resulting in indistinct speech are disqualifying.

Respiratory System

■ Any chronic disease or condition affecting the respiratory system that would impair the full performance of duties of the position is disqualifying; e.g., conditions that result in reduced pulmonary function, shortness or breath, or painful respiration.

Cardiovascular System

The following conditions are disqualifying:

■ Organic heart disease (compensated or not),

■ Hypertension with repeated readings that exceed 150 systolic and 90 diastolic without medication, and

■ Symptomatic peripheral vascular disease and severe varicose veins.

Gastrointestinal System

■ Chronic symptomatic diseases or conditions of the gastrointestinal tract are disqualifying.

■ Conditions requiring special diets or medications are disqualifying.

Endocrine System

■ Any history of a systemic metabolic disease, such as diabetes or gout, is disqualifying.

Genitourinary Disorders

■ Chronic symptomatic diseases or conditions of the genitourinary tract are disqualifying.

Hernias

■ Inguinal and femoral hernias with or without the use of a truss are disqualifying. Other hernias are disqualifying if they interfere with performance of the duties of the position.

Nervous System

■ Applicants must possess emotional and mental stability with no history of a basic personality disorder.

■ Applicants with a history of epilepsy or convulsive disorder must have been seizure-free for the past two years without medication.

■ Any neurological disorder with resulting decreased neurological or muscular function is disqualifying.

MISCELLANEOUS

Though not mentioned specifically above, any other disease or condition that interferes with the full performance of duties is also grounds for medical rejection. Before entrance on duty, all applicants must undergo a pre-employment medical examination and be medically suitable to perform the full duties of the position efficiently and without hazard to themselves and others. Failure to meet any one of the required medical qualifications will be disqualifying for appointment. These standards are considered minimum standards and will not be waived in any case. Applicants found to have a correctable condition may be restored to any existing list of eligibles for further consideration for appointment when the disqualifying condition has been satisfactorily corrected or eliminated.

PHYSICAL PERFORMANCE TESTS

The physical performance requirements for all police officers are very similar. All police officers must be able to jump in an instant, must be able to move very quickly, must be strong, must have the stamina to maintain speed and strength for a long time, and must be able to continue physically stressful activity at a high level while withstanding discomfort and pain. The ideal police officer is "Superman." The actual police officer does well to approach those qualities.

While police departments have similar physical performance requirements, they tend to measure fitness in many different ways. Three different police officer physical fitness tests follow. Read them through and note the variations. Try each out to the extent that you can without the actual testing course. See how you do. You may need to get yourself into a regular body-building routine some time before you are called for examination. Strength and fitness cannot be it developed overnight. You will need to work yourself up to par over a long period. Set up a program and get started right away. You will not be called for a physical fitness test until after you have passed the written examination and until there is some possibility that your place on the list will soon be reached. The hiring process moves along slowly, but it does move. You have time, but not that much time. Start now.

A TYPICAL QUALIFYING PHYSICAL FITNESS TEST FOR POLICE OFFICER

Instructions for Candidates

These subtests are electronically timed by your stepping on the start mat and the finish mat.

Stair Climb/Restrain: (One Trial)
(Maximum Time Allowed: 2 Minutes)

In this subtest, you will be expected to run up 3 flights of stairs, down 1 flight, push and pull a box 5 times, and run 5 feet to the finish line.

- On the signal GO, step on the start mat, run up the stairs on your right, and continue up to the landing on the third floor.

- Both feet must be placed on the landing.

- Run quickly down one flight of stairs and into the lobby.

- Grab the box and pull it towards you until the front of the box reaches the tape on the floor.

- Now push it back to its starting position.

- Repeat 4 more times as the examiner announces the count.

- After the last trip, turn RIGHT and step on the finish mat.

Dummy Drag: (Two Trials)
(Maximum Time Allowed: 1 Minute)

In this subtest, you will be expected to drag a dummy 30 feet.

- Step on the start mat.

- Grab the dummy under the shoulders.

- Holding the dummy in this position, move backwards around the traffic cone set 15 feet away and return.

- Place the dummy EXACTLY as you found it in the starting position.

- Step on the finish mat.

Wall Climb/Obstacle Run: (Two Trials)
(Maximum Time Allowed: 1 Minute)

In this subtest, you will be expected to go over the 5-foot wall and continue through the obstacle run.

- Step on the start mat.

- Run to the wall and go over. You are NOT allowed to use the support bars.

- Follow the tape on the floor around the cones.

- If you miss a cone or go around it the wrong way, you must go back and go around the cone CORRECTLY.

- If you knock a cone over, you must STOP and set it up before you continue.

- Step on the finish mat.

ANOTHER PHYSICAL FITNESS TEST

Medical evidence to allow participation in the physical fitness test may be required, and the Department of Personnel reserves the right to exclude from the physical test any eligibles who, upon examination of such evidence, are apparently medically unfit. Eligibles will take the physical fitness test at their own risk of injury, although efforts will be made to safeguard them.

Candidates must complete the entire course consisting of seven events in not more than *65 seconds*.

Candidates who do not successfully complete events 3, 5, and 6 will fail the test.

Description of Events

1. Run up approximately 40 steps.

2. Run approximately 40 yards, following a designated path, including at least four 90-degree turns, to a sandbag.

3. Push the sandbag, weighing approximately 100 pounds, forward a distance of approximately 5 yards and then back to its original position. (Failure to meet all of the conditions for this event will result in failure of the test as a whole.)

4. Run approximately 10 yards to a dummy, weighing approximately 110 pounds, which is hanging with its lowest point approximately 3 feet above the floor.

5. Raise the dummy so as to lift the attached ring off the metal pipe. Allow the dummy to slide onto the floor or place it on the floor. *You must not drop it or throw it down.* (Failure to meet all of the conditions for this event will result in failure of the test as a whole.)

6. Step up approximately 18 inches and walk across a 12-foot beam by placing one foot in front of the other until you reach the other end. (You must be in control at all times, and falling off the beam will result in failure of the test as a whole.)

7. Run approximately 10 yards to the finish line.

Candidates who fail the test on their first trial will be allowed a second trial on the same date after a rest period.

Candidates who do not successfully complete all the events in their proper sequence will fail the test.

ONE MORE PHYSICAL FITNESS TEST, VERY DIFFERENT IN STYLE

The candidates who qualify on the medical examination will be required to pass the qualifying physical fitness test. A total score of twenty is required for passing this test; the scores attained on the five individual tests are added together to obtain your final score.

Test I: Trunk Flexion Test (Three Chances)

Candidates will assume a sitting position on the floor with the legs extended at right angles to a line drawn on the floor. The heels should touch the near edge of the line and be 5 inches apart. The candidate should slowly reach with both hands as far forward as possible on a yardstick that is placed between the legs with the 15-inch mark resting on the near edge of the heel line. The score is the most distant point (in inches) reached on the yardstick with fingertips.

Rating	Trunk Flexion (Inches)	Points
Excellent	22 and over	6
Good	20–21	5
Average	14–19	4
Fair	12–13	3
Poor	10–11	2
Very Poor	9 and under	1

Test II: Hand Grip Strength Test (Three Chances)

The candidate places the dynamometer (hand grip tester) at the side and, without touching the body with any part of the arm, hand, or the dynamometer, should grip the dynamometer as hard as possible in one quick movement. The best of the three tries will be recorded.

Rating	Hand Grip in Kg.	Points
Excellent	65 and above	6
Good	57–64	5
Average	45–56	4
Fair	37–44	3
Poor	30–36	2
Very Poor	29 and under	1

Test III: Standing Broad Jump (Three Chances)

Candidates will be permitted three chances in consecutive order, and the longest distance will be credited. Candidates will be required to jump from a standing position, both feet together. Distance of jump will be recorded from starting point to back of heels. It is each candidate's responsibility to have a nonskid surface on the soles of his or her sneakers.

Rating	Distance	Points
Excellent	7'10" or better	6
Good	7'0" to 7'9"	5
Average	6'1" to 6'11"	4
Fair	5'6" to 6'0"	3
Poor	5'0" to 5'5"	2
Very Poor	Less than 5' 1	1

Test IV: One-Minute Sit-Up Test

The candidate will start by lying on the back with the knees bent so that the heels are about 18 inches away from the buttocks. An examiner will hold the ankles to give support. The candidate will then perform as many correct sit-ups (elbows alternately touching the opposite knee) as possible within a 1-minute period. The candidate should return to the starting position (back to floor) between sit-ups.

Rating	Sit-Ups in 1 Minute	Points
Excellent	35	6
Good	30–34	5
Average	20–29	4
Fair	15–19	3
Poor	10–14	2
Very Poor	9 and under	1

Test V: Three-Minute Step Test

The candidate will step for 3 minutes on a 1-inch bench at a rate of twenty-four steps per minute. The time will be maintained by a metronome. Immediately after the 3 minutes of stepping, the subject will sit down and relax without talking. A 60-second heart rate count is taken starting 5 seconds after the completion of stepping.

Rating	Pulse	Points
Excellent	75–84	6
Good	85–94	5
Average	95–119	4
Fair	120–129	3
Poor	130–139	2
Very Poor	Over 140	1

SLIDING SCALE STANDARDS

The Americans with Disabilities Act requires that age not be a consideration in hiring except where youth, or maturity, is a bona fide qualification for performance of the job. The federal government has established 37 as the highest age at which persons can and may effectively enter certain federal law enforcement positions. In order to establish an age-based hiring limit, each jurisdiction must justify the age it has chosen. At this time, not all guidelines are clear. Each jurisdiction makes its own interpretation of the requirements of the Americans with Disabilities Act, and its interpretation remains in effect until challenged and overturned by a court of law. Some states have chosen to take the Act at face value and have done away with upper age limits altogether.

When states, or jurisdictions within those states, discard upper age limits, they open themselves to new complications. According to the U.S. Justice Department, physical fitness standards that are the same for everyone violate the Americans with Disabilities Act. In response to this determination, many states have relaxed the physical fitness requirements for state police officers. The following is a recently announced Physical Fitness Screening Test that takes into consideration both age and sex.

PHYSICAL FITNESS SCREENING TEST

Candidate will go from Stations I through IV in order. Each station is pass/fail. Candidate must pass each station in order to proceed to the next station. Candidate will be allowed up to 3 minutes' rest between stations. Once a station is started, it must be completed according to protocol. See the chart below:

Station I:

Sit-up—Candidate lies flat on the back, knees bent, heels flat on the floor, fingers interlaced behind the head. Monitor holds the feet down firmly. In the up position, candidate should touch elbows to knees and return with shoulder blades touching floor. To pass this component, candidate must complete the requisite number of correct sit-ups in one minute.

Station II:

Flex—Candidate removes shoes and places feet squarely against box with feet no wider than 8 inches apart. Toes are pointed directly toward ceiling, knees remain extended throughout test. With hands placed one on top of the other, candidate leans forward without lunging or bobbing and reaches as far down the yardstick as possible. The hands must stay together and the stretch must be held for one second. Three attempts are allowed with the best of three recorded to the nearest $\frac{1}{4}$ inch to determine whether the candidate passed/failed.

Station III:

Bench—Monitor loads weights to $\frac{1}{2}$ of candidate-required weight. Candidate is permitted to "press" this weight once. Monitor increases weight to $\frac{2}{3}$ of candidate-required weight. Candidate is permitted to "press" this weight once. The required test weight is then loaded. The candidate has up to four (4) attempts to "press" required (maximum) weight. In order to pass, buttocks must remain on the bench. Candidate will be allowed up to 2 minutes' rest between each "press." (Universal Bench Press Equipment)

Station IV:

1.5-Mile Run—Candidate must be successful on Stations I, II and III in order to participate in Station IV. It will be administered on a track. Candidate will be informed of his/her lap time during the test.

SCORING CHART

| AGE/SEX | | TEST | | |
MALE	SIT-UP	FLEX	BENCH	1.5 MI RUN
20–29	38	16.5	99	12.51
30–39	35	15.5	88	13.36
40–49	29	14.3	80	14.29
50–59	24	13.3	71	15.26
60+	19	12.5	66	16.43
FEMALE				
20–29	32	19.3	59	15.26
30–39	25	18.3	53	15.57
40–49	20	17.3	50	16.58
50–59	14	16.8	44	17.54
60+	6	15.5	43	18.44

THE BACKGROUND CHECK

The police officer is in a position of public trust. He or she must be deserving of that trust. The police department must feel very certain that the police officer will not use his or her position for personal gain, will not use it to harass individuals or groups that he or she dislikes, will not be easily corrupted, and will not take advantage of privileged knowledge. It is for this reason that the background check is such an important part of the police selection process. The background check is a time-consuming process. Therefore, the police personnel office will not initiate the background check until an applicant appears to be qualified in nearly every way; that is, the background check occurs after the written test, physical performance test, and full medical examination.

The standard predictor of future behavior is past behavior. The police department must find out how you have behaved in the past. It will do this by first having you fill out a questionnaire. As with the medical questionnaire, there is no point in lying or cheating. You will be found out and will be disqualified. State the facts clearly. Explain fully and factually.

If you have a totally clean record and face no problems in your personal or family life, then you need have no concern about the background check. Fill in the blanks. List references, and inform those people whose names you have given, so that they are not upset when they are contacted by the police.

Most people have something in their backgrounds that can spark more inquiry. The problem may be financial: If you are strapped for money, the police department may fear that you might be corruptible. The problem may be marital: The police department may worry that you will be distracted. The problem may be one of frequent job changes: The police department questions your stability and the value of investing in your training. The problem may be one of poor credit: Are you responsible and reliable? Or the problem may be one of a brush with the law, minor or major. Most minor infractions can be explained at an interview; reassure the interviewer that these were youthful indiscretions unlikely to recur. Arrests for felonies, and, worse still, convictions, present greater obstacles. It may be wise to consult an attorney who specializes in expunging criminal records to see what can be done to clear your name. Some offenses are absolutely disqualifying. You may as well know ahead of time and take all possible steps to make yourself employable by the police department.

A felony record needs the service of an attorney. So might multiple misdemeanor convictions. You can help yourself in many other situations. If you have a poor credit rating, pay up and have your rating upgraded. If you are behind on alimony payments, catch up. If you have an unanswered summons, go to court and answer it. Pay your parking tickets. Even if these past problems turn up in the background check, your positive attitude in clearing them up will be in your favor.

Be sure that you are able to document any claims you make with reference to diplomas, degrees, and honors. You may have to produce these at an interview. Likewise, be certain that you understand the nature and gravity of the problems in your background. Be prepared to admit that you misbehaved and to reassure the examiners that you have matured into a responsible citizen.

THE PSYCHOLOGICAL EVALUATION

THE PURPOSE OF THE PSYCHOLOGICAL EVALUATION

Some states subject all police officer candidates to a psychological evaluation before appointment; others, because of the expense involved, limit psychological evaluations to those cases where there are signs that one might be necessary. However, in all cases the sole purpose of a psychological evaluation is to determine the candidate's mental fitness for performing the specific duties of a police officer. The evaluation is not concerned with other aspects of mental well-being. In fact, because of this exclusive focus on police work, a candidate might be judged psychologically unfit to be a police officer even if he or she is perfectly suited for other types of employment.

What makes police work so different from other occupations? Soon after orientation and the usual training at the police academy, the police officer begins functioning more or less independently. Although the officer functions under supervision, that supervision is present only periodically, and although the officer should be guided by the department's rules of procedure, many times the officer will be thrust into situations where immediate action is required to save lives or protect property. For example, the officer who encounters a pregnant woman about to give birth must take decisive action at once. In such situations, there is no time to consult the rules of procedure. The officer must do whatever is necessary right away.

Another crucial difference is that the police officer carries a gun as part of the job. Prudent use of this weapon requires not only conformity to the rules of procedure but also a good sense of police judgment. The officer who must decide in an emergency whether to use that gun must have a very high degree of psychological stability.

Psychological evaluations of police officer candidates are usually conducted by a psychologist or psychiatrist who is trained to detect signs of deficiencies that could interfere with the proper performance of police work. The job is twofold: to look for signs of potential trouble and to evaluate the sincerity of the candidate. For example, consider the possible responses when the psychologist asks, "Why do you want to become a police officer?" A proper response would be: "I want a career in public service, and I feel that effective law enforcement will make for a better society for my children and eventually for my grandchildren." There is nothing wrong with this response. The only thing to be judged is the sincerity of the candidate. Now look at the following response to the same question: "I have always liked uniforms. They bring respect and admiration, and they permit you to perform your duties without interference." Something is wrong here. Or consider this response: "I hate criminals. They take advantage of the weak and elderly. They are cowards, and I want to do everything I can to eliminate them." This intense hatred may indicate the need for further investigation of this candidate's psychological stability.

TYPICAL EVALUATION QUESTIONS

The questions that you will be asked will, for the most part, be quite predictable. The majority of them will be based on your responses to application forms and other papers that you have been required to file. The psychologist will ask you to amplify or to explain the personal data that you listed on those papers. Sometimes you will be asked to describe your feelings about events that happened to you. Also, as a way of encouraging you to talk, you may be asked more open-ended questions about your personal likes, dislikes, or emotions.

You may also be asked your opinion about what you might do in a hypothetical police work situation, but such questions are unlikely to form the bulk of the evaluation. In this case, the psychologist is not testing your knowledge of police procedures but only your ability to make reasoned judgments and to avoid rash behavior. Because most of the questions you will be asked are predictable, it is relatively easy to prepare answers for them. Begin your preparation by looking over the application forms that you filled out and any other papers that you were required to file. You should be able to pick out the points that a psychologist will want to clarify or explain.

Typical questions you might encounter include the following:

- Why did you choose your area of concentration in school?

- What particularly interests you about that subject?

- Why did you transfer from school x to school y?

- How did you get the job with _____?

- Which of the duties described in your second job did you like best? Which least? Why?

- What did you do during the nine months between your second and third jobs?

- Explain the circumstances of your leaving a particular job.

- Please clarify: armed forces service, arrest record, hospitalization record, etc., as applicable.

Other questions are much like those asked at a routine job interview. They can be anticipated and prepared for as well.

- Why do you want to leave the kind of work you are doing now?

- Why do you want to be a state trooper?

- How does your family feel about your becoming a state police officer?

- What do you do in your leisure time?

- Do you have a hobby? What is it? What do you particularly like about your hobby?

- What is your favorite sport? Would you rather play or watch?

- How do you react to criticism? If you think the criticism is reasonable? If you consider the criticism unwarranted?

- What is your pet peeve?

- What are your greatest strengths? Weaknesses?

- What could make you lose your temper?

- Of what accomplishment in your life are you most proud?

- What act do you regret?

- If you could start over, what would you do differently?

- What traits do you value in a coworker? In a friend?

- What makes you think you would make a good state police officer?

Still other questions may be more specific to police work. You should have prepared answers to:

- How much sleep do you need?

- Are you afraid of heights?

- What is your attitude toward working irregular hours?

- Do you prefer working alone or on a team?

- Are you afraid of dying?

- What would you do with the rest of your life if your legs were crippled in an injury?

- How do you deal with panic? Your own? That of others?

- What is your attitude toward smoking? Drinking? Playboy magazine? Gambling?

- What is your favorite TV program? How do you feel about watching the news? Sports? Classical drama? Rock music? Opera? Game shows?

Now make a list of your own. The variety of evaluation questions is endless but most can be answered with ease. Preparation makes the whole process much more pleasant and less frightening.

There is one question that strikes terror into the heart of nearly every candidate for police officer or any other job. This question is likely to be the first and, unless you are prepared for it, may well throw you off guard. The question is "Tell me about yourself." For this question you should have a prepared script (in your head, not in your hand). Think well ahead of time about what you want to tell. What could the psychologist be interested in? This question is not seeking information about your birth weight nor about your food preferences. The psychologist wants you to tell about yourself with relation to your interest in and qualifications for police work. Think of how to describe yourself with this goal in mind. What information puts you into a good light with reference to the work for which you are applying? Organize your presentation. Then analyze what you plan to say. What is a psychologist likely to pick up on? To what questions will your answer lead? You must prepare to answer these questions to which you have opened yourself.

Toward the end of the evaluation, the psychologist will most likely ask if you have any questions. You undoubtedly will have had some before hand and should have come prepared to ask them. If all of your questions have been answered in the course of the evaluation, you may tell this to the psychologist. If not, or if the evaluation has raised new questions in your mind, by all means ask them. The evaluation should serve for your benefit; it is not just to serve the purposes of the Police Department.

The invitation of your questions tends to be the signal that the evaluation is nearly over. The psychologist is satisfied that he or she has gathered enough information. The time allotted to you is up. Be alert for the cues. Do not spoil the good impression you have made by trying to prolong the evaluation.

SHOULD YOU REVEAL PERSONAL OPINIONS AND FEELINGS?

The psychologist does not expect candidates to be devoid of personal feelings. After all, everyone has likes and dislikes. However, the mature, psychologically stable person is able to keep those feelings from interfering with the performance of job duties. The police office will encounter a very wide variety of people on the job. Some the officer may find personally likable; others may be unlikable, even downright unpleasant. However, whatever the officer's true feelings about the persons encountered, he or she must serve those individuals in an effective manner or serious repercussions—even loss of life—may result. This type of behavior takes mental maturity and stability, qualities every officer must possess. It is these qualities that the psychologist is looking for at the evaluation, not an absence of personal feelings. The successful candidate does not have to like everyone he or she meets. What is important is the ability to control personal feelings in order to function effectively.

Sometimes during an evaluation a candidate will express "extreme" views on certain subjects. Unlike typical opinions or feelings, these may indeed be cause for disqualification. An obvious example is a display of unreasonable dislike for people from a particular ethnic or religious background. To the psychologist, this is a sure sign of trouble. The candidate who says, "People from ethnic group X are always the ones who commit the violent crimes," will never be appointed a state police officer.

SHOULD YOU VOLUNTEER INFORMATION?

One very important point to remember at the evaluation is to limit your responses to what is asked. An evaluation session of this type is one of the very few opportunities most people have to reveal their true inner selves to others. The psychologist knows this and will often encourage the person being evaluated to talk freely and openly about personal matters and opinions. An unthinking candidate may use this opportunity to bring up matters that ordinarily he or she would never discuss. The talkative candidate might even know that he or she is getting in too deep but may be unable to refrain from continuing. The psychologist will encourage this type of individual to talk at length in order to reveal personal matters that will indicate the level of the candidate's psychological stability.

One device that psychologists use to make candidates keep talking is to assume a facial expression that indicates further explanation is expected. It is very important not to respond to this suggestion! If you do, you are likely to say things that can only be harmful to you. Try to be satisfied with your original response and have the maturity to stand by it no matter what expression you see on the psychologist's face. Display a sense of self-assurance that convinces the psychologist that you are satisfied with your answers.

HOW TO EXPLAIN PROBLEM INCIDENTS IN YOUR PAST

One concern of many police officer candidates is how to handle questions about problem incidents in their past. More than a few candidates have at some time—usually in their youth—gotten into trouble in some incident involving property damage or even personal injury to others. Such incidents almost always come to light during the candidate's background check, often through school, court, or military records. If you have such an incident in your past and are questioned about it by the psychologist, the wisest course is to accept full responsibility for it and to attribute it to your youthful immaturity at the time. Claiming that the record is false or giving excuses for your bad behavior is not likely to be regarded favorably. The psychologist is much more apt to respond positively if you accept responsibility and, just as importantly, if you attribute any such incident to an immature outlook that you have now outgrown. One mistake of this type will not necessarily disqualify you if you can convince the psychologist that you have become a fully responsible adult and will never do anything of the kind again.

"PENCIL-AND-PAPER" EVALUATIONS

As part of the psychological evaluation, some jurisdictions use standardized personality tests that you answer by marking a sheet of paper. These tests may contain a hundred or more questions. Your responses help the psychologist determine your specific personality traits. Your answer to any one question by itself usually means very little, but your answers to a group of questions, taken together, will have significance to the psychologist. Your wisest course when taking one of these written personality tests is to give honest, truthful answers. Any attempt to make yourself appear different from the way you really are is not likely to be successful.

KEEP A POSITIVE ATTITUDE

One final word of advice: It is important to approach all psychological evaluations with a positive attitude. Think of the evaluation not as an ordeal that you must endure but rather as an opportunity to prove that you are qualified to become a police officer. In truth, the psychologist will be looking for traits that qualify you, not ones that disqualify you. And if disqualifying evidence exists, it is the psychologist's responsibility to consider every factor before making a negative recommendation. So go into the evaluation with confidence and be prepared to "sell" yourself to the psychologist. You will be given every chance to prove your worth.

EVALUATION CHECKLIST

Here are some valuable points to remember as you prepare for the psychological evaluation.

1. Get a good night's sleep the night before the evaluation.

2. Do not take any medication beforehand to calm yourself. You may be tested for drugs before the evaluation.

3. Dress neatly and conservatively.

4. Be polite to the psychologist or psychiatrist.

5. Respond to all questions honestly and forthrightly.

6. Use as few words as possible to communicate your thoughts. When you have finished answering a question, do not let the psychologist's behavior lead you to think that you have not said enough.

7. Admit responsibility for any youthful indiscretions and attribute them to your immaturity at the time of the incident.

8. Do not permit any deep-seated prejudices to assert themselves. If you can control them during the evaluation, you will be able to control them while performing the duties of a police officer.

9. Most important, be yourself. You're bound to do better than if you pretend to be someone you're not.

APPEALS

A police officer candidate who is marked "not qualified" on the psychological evaluation will be afforded an opportunity to appeal. In most jurisdictions, a notice of disqualification will include information on appeal procedures and on any time limitations.

Because the official disqualification is made by a psychologist or psychiatrist, the best way for the candidate to appeal is to engage another psychologist or psychiatrist to testify on the candidate's behalf. To start preparing the appeal, the candidate should obtain the official notice of the examination, the medical standards on which the evaluation was based, and a document telling the precise reason for the disqualification. If these items are not furnished by the examining agency, the candidate should petition for them at once. If necessary, the candidate should be prepared to resort to the procedures specified in the Freedom of Information Act in order to find out the exact reasons for rejection. This information is crucial to preparing a proper appeal. Any psychological testimony on the candidate's behalf must respond to the reasons given for disqualification. It is not enough for a psychologist to simply assert that the candidate is generally mentally stable. The psychologist must show that the candidate is, in fact, psychologically competent to perform the specific duties of a state police officer.

If you are disqualified as a result of the psychological evaluation, you should certainly consider filing an appeal. Often this kind of show of determination has influenced a hiring jurisdiction to take a chance on a "borderline" candidate. You will find many psychologists and psychiatrists who specialize in helping rejected police officer candidates.

Reading all the applications and weeding out the unqualified ones takes time. Weighing education and experience factors takes time. Administering and scoring of exams takes time. Interviews, medical exams, and physical performance tests take time. Verifying references takes time. And, finally, the vacancies must occur, and the government agency must have the funds to fill the vacancies.

All of this clarifies why you must not leave a job or a job search at any step along the way. Wait until you are offered your government job before you cut other ties. But when you finally do get that job, you will have a good income, many benefits, and job security.